In the name of God, the Compassionate, the Merciful

Sayyid Quṭb

❧

IN THE SHADE OF
THE QUR'ĀN

Fī Ẓilāl al-Qur'ān

VOLUME X

❧

SŪRAHS 12–15

Yūsuf – Al-Ḥijr

❧

Translated and Edited by
Adil Salahi

❧

THE ISLAMIC FOUNDATION
AND
ISLAMONLINE.NET

Published by

THE ISLAMIC FOUNDATION,

Markfield Conference Centre,
Ratby Lane, Markfield, Leicestershire LE67 9SY, United Kingdom
Tel: (01530) 244944, Fax: (01530) 244946
E-mail: i.foundation@islamic-foundation.org.uk
Website: www.islamic-foundation.org.uk

Quran House, PO Box 30611, Nairobi, Kenya

PMB 3193, Kano, Nigeria

ISLAMONLINE.NET,
PO Box 22212, Doha, Qatar
E-mail: webmaster@islam-online.net
Website: www.islamonline.net

British Library Cataloguing-in-Publication Data
Qutb, Sayyid, 1903–1966
   In the shade of the Qur'an: Fi zilal al-Qur'an,
   Vol. 10: Surahs 12–15: Yusuf – al-Hijr
   1. Koran – Commentaries
   I.   Title   II. Salahi, M.A.   III. Islamic Foundation
   IV. Fi zilal al-Qur'an
   297.1'229

ISBN 0 86037 389 4
ISBN 0 86037 394 0 pbk

Typeset by: N.A.Qaddoura
Cover design by: Imtiaze A. Manjra

Printed and bound in Great Britain by
Antony Rowe Ltd, Chippenham, Wiltshire

Contents

Transliteration Table

Consonants. Arabic

initial: unexpressed medial and final:

ء	'	د	d	ض	ḍ	ك	k
ب	b	ذ	dh	ط	ṭ	ل	l
ت	t	ر	r	ظ	ẓ	م	m
ث	th	ز	z	ع	'	ن	n
ج	j	س	s	غ	gh	هـ	h
ح	ḥ	ش	sh	ف	f	و	w
خ	kh	ص	ṣ	ق	q	ي	y

Vowels, diphthongs, etc.

short: ◌َ a   ◌ِ i   ◌ُ u

long: ◌َا ā   ◌ِي ī   ◌ُو ū

diphthongs: ◌َوْ aw

                ◌َىْ ay

Islamic Advocacy Through Qur'ānic Interpretation

Introduction by Adil Salahi

In the Shade of the Qur'ān is an exposition of the meaning of the Qur'ān written by an author who was held in high regard within literary circles. He had written a widely acclaimed work on literary criticism, a number of literary titles including a novel, a large collection of poetry, and a few books on Islam and modern social and political problems. The author's style is both lucid and powerful. His understanding of the Qur'ān is profound. His approach is that of a believer who knows that when God addresses His message to human beings, it is one that they can easily grasp and act upon. In Sayyid Quṭb's view, the Qur'ān presents a simple and direct message to people, which is consistent and free of ambiguity, yet which is expressed in the most refined literary style known to us.

The Arabs, who were the first community addressed by the Qur'ān, possessed a special talent which enabled them to appreciate literary discourse. There were an exceptional number of poets among them, even though most could neither read nor write. Whether they responded positively or negatively to the Islamic message, they were unanimous in admiring the special merits of the Qur'ān. Throughout Islamic history, numerous volumes have been written about the Qur'ān, describing its exceptional literary excellence, and its unique features that employ a concise style relying on economy of words to express broad meanings in a clear and precise way. This continues to be the case up to the present day. Doubtless, it will continue into the future. Thus, *In the Shade of the Qur'ān* is a recent addition to a long tradition of Qur'ānic studies that seek to bring the Qur'ān and its message closer to people's minds.

However, *In the Shade of the Qur'ān* is not, strictly speaking, an academic commentary on the final divine revelations to mankind. Commentaries normally resort to explaining the meanings of individual words, sentences and verses. Other studies comment on, or set out to explain, the general theme of a particular passage or *sūrah*. Such studies provide, no doubt, a very useful service. But Sayyid Quṭb would not have undertaken his task if he meant only to provide another explanation of the meanings of the Qur'ān. He had in mind a more important task.

By nature, Sayyid Quṭb was a very sensitive person who respected others' feelings. It is the sensitivity of the poet who is completely committed to his community aiming to make his work an expression of its hopes and aspirations. His regular articles in different magazines in the 1940s demonstrated a very keen sense of awareness of the problems faced by the Egyptian people, and a consistent call for reform. His early, non-literary works addressed social and economic problems of vital importance. All his writings at the time reflect a keen awareness of the many aspects of social injustice that plagued Egyptian society. Later, when he committed himself to work for Islamic revival, he was one of the many thousands that were the immediate target of political injustice. He felt that only freedom could correct these ills, but, to him, true freedom could only be achieved under Islam. No other system has the guarantees necessary to ensure true freedom, for the individual and for society.

One day in prison he looked up to see a fellow member of the Muslim Brotherhood being driven away, but trying to wave to him. It was a momentary picture, with a hand stretched out waving and a man being pushed away so that he could not extend a greeting at a distance. Sayyid Quṭb recorded his feelings in a long poem that became a rallying anthem for Islamic advocates as they faced persecution. The poem opens as follows:

> My brother! You are free behind your prison walls;
> You are free despite the fetters on your hands;
> If you keep alive your bond with God.

To his perceptive mind, the gulf between the miserable present of the Muslims throughout the world and their glorious past could not be wider. Yet that glorious past started with the Qur'ān first addressing the Arabs, a nation divided into countless warring tribes and clans, and moulding them into "the best community ever raised for mankind." The transformation the Arabs underwent was colossal by any standards. And it was produced only by the Qur'ān, revealed to the Prophet and delivered to them by him. Yet the Qur'ān was being read throughout the Arab and Muslim world, day and night, in mosques, on the radio, by individuals and by reciters with melodious voices who made an art of Qur'ānic recitation. Nevertheless, contemporary Muslims continued to be backward, weak, trodden on by their enemies, with no end in sight to their dire situation. To him, the cause of this persistent weakness was their wrong approach to the Qur'ān.

Sayyid Quṭb realized that making an academic study of how the Qur'ān produced those early generations of Muslims so as to make them the guiding light for all humanity might be an interesting exercise, but of itself would not be enough to change the fortunes of contemporary Muslims. What the Muslims needed to break with their miserable situation was to interact with the Qur'ān in the same way as the first Muslim generation did when they received it from the Prophet. Only such committed interaction, with a willingness to modify individual and social attitudes, concepts and practices and to bring them in line with the Qur'ān, could bring about the desired reform. Such reform is not introduced by legislation through government or parliament. It is brought about through the implementation of Islamic teachings and principles. He often repeated that admiring the beauty of the Qur'ānic text, or the values stressed by Islam, is meaningless unless such values and principles are put into practice. This is a two-fold responsibility: every Muslim individual is accountable before God for implementing whatever applies to him or her, and the community is collectively accountable for bringing its society in line with Islam.

Awareness of both responsibilities and acting on them were the main features of the first Muslim generation of the Prophet's Companions, and also of the subsequent Muslim generations. It is through these features that Islamic civilization came into existence, to provide the model described by God as "the best community ever raised for mankind."

What Sayyid Quṭb aimed at was to make *In the Shade of the Qur'ān* a medium through which Muslims could understand the Qur'ān in the same way as those early generations understood it. Thus, *In the Shade of the Qur'ān* is primarily a book that illustrates the message of Islam through explaining the Qur'ān.

Some critics have discounted *In the Shade of the Qur'ān* as a commentary on the Qur'ān, or a book of *Tafsīr*, pointing out that *Tafsīr* has certain rules and methodology which the book does not observe. But this is just hair-splitting, because if the prime concern of *Tafsīr*, or Qur'ānic commentary, is to explain the meanings of the text, then *In the Shade of the Qur'ān* provides this with a high degree of excellence. It presents the meaning of the Qur'ān to a wide readership who would otherwise find it difficult to deal with classical commentaries. However, the work goes beyond this to add the vital dimension of showing how relevant the Qur'ān is today in the life of humanity in general and Muslims in particular. Thus, it represents an important exercise of Islamic advocacy, by virtue of its ability to make the Qur'ān easier to understand.

An important feature of *In the Shade of the Qur'ān* is that it steers away from controversy. When it comes to presenting different legal views on any particular text, the author makes it clear that he is not interested in a comparative study of such views and the evidence supporting each. Where differences have no legal aspect, but merely relate to the meaning of a particular sentence or verse, he tries to accommodate such differences. Only where he feels a particular view is better supported by evidence and gives a clearer interpretation of the text does he make his preference clear, outlining its basis.

To appreciate this feature of *In the Shade of the Qur'ān* we need only to refer to any one of the classical commentaries which outline different views and list numerous explanations advanced by earlier scholars. We realize then that Sayyid Quṭb's method spares the reader much confusion and presents a clear vision for understanding the Qur'ān. What helped him in this regard was his superior literary talent, coupled with an approach to the Qur'ān that was free of preconceived ideas and unrestricted by narrow methodologies.

In doing so, Sayyid Quṭb placed himself in the same position of the Arab who listened to the Prophet for the first time, recognizing the quality of the Qur'ān, realizing that it could not have been composed by a human being and accepting it. He then reflected on the meaning of the Qur'ānic revelations and interacted with them, formulating a complete and coherent concept of faith, life and man. Given his personal qualities, education and talent, Sayyid Quṭb was in a uniquely suitable position for such an undertaking. He then set about his task with dedication and devotion, realizing as he progressed that the more he gave the Qur'ān of his thought and feeling, the clearer its message became and the more it opened up to him. Hence he repeatedly states, with emphasis, that the Qur'ān does not reveal its treasures except to those who adopt an interactive approach to it, willing to make it their constitution and source of guidance. When they are committed to its implementation, they begin to appreciate its blessings. They then realize how the quality of their lives changes so as to lift them to a summit they could not have dreamt of, in the same way as the Arabs who accepted the Prophet's address achieved their unique standard of excellence.

His method of work helped him much in his task. When he embarked on writing a volume of *In the Shade of the Qur'ān*, Sayyid Quṭb read the relevant Qur'ānic text carefully several times, reflecting on its meanings, without referring to any books of commentary or *Fiqh* that may be relevant to it. This process normally took a month. When he was satisfied that he had fully understood the message of the Qur'ānic text he was dealing with, he began to write his thoughts, explaining the meaning and the message of that part of the Qur'ān. He worked on his first draft with total commitment, trying to finish it in as few sessions as possible. He preferred to so complete a *surah* in one session, if that were at all possible. On completing this first draft, he would read what was written on it by the leading commentators of different periods. He would also refer to books of *Fiqh* in order to check any rulings relevant to any verses he was dealing with. He then revised his earlier draft in the light of his new readings, amending and editing it as necessary. This method gave him the best of two approaches: the natural one of a discerning reader and the scholarly one based on research of earlier works. Hence, he was able to score great success in achieving his aim of making *In the Shade of the Qur'ān* a book of Islamic advocacy through interpreting the Qur'ān.

A discerning reader of *In the Shade of the Qur'ān* does not merely develop a better understanding of God's book. He also understands the secret of the success of the Qur'ān in producing a long line of committed advocates of Islam throughout history, ready to serve its cause regardless of the sacrifices they are called on to make. It also becomes clear to him that a proactive approach to the Qur'ān by even a small number of followers will inevitably achieve success in bringing into existence a Muslim community committed to its implementation and conducting its life on the basis of its values and principles. Hence Sayyid Qutb and his monumental work, *In the Shade of the Qur'ān*, have come under attack from narrow-minded Muslims who reject any deviation from traditional methods of commentary, which is not surprising. More importantly, they have been subjected to unscrupulous attacks by different quarters who think of Islam as a menace threatening their privileges and interests and view with immense gloom any serious attempt to bring about a proper Islamic revival. That *In the Shade of the Qur'ān* should be attacked by both groups is testimony to its success.

London   **Adil Salahi**
Ṣafar 1425
March 2004

SŪRAH 12

Yūsuf

(Joseph)

Prologue

This *sūrah* is a Makkan revelation, and it follows *Sūrah* 11, Hūd, in the chronological order of revelation. This means that it belonged to the critical period we mentioned in the Prologues to *Sūrah*s 10 and 11, Jonah and Hūd, respectively. This is the intervening period between what is known as the year of sorrow, when the Prophet lost his uncle Abū Ṭālib and his wife Khadījah, both of whom gave him unfailing support, and the time when the new Muslims of Madinah, the *Anṣār*, gave the Prophet their first and second pledges of loyalty and support at 'Aqabah. These pledges brought in new support and heralded a far-reaching change in the fortunes of the Islamic message and the Muslim community, beginning with the migration of the Prophet and his Companions to Madinah.

The whole *sūrah* was revealed in Makkah, contrary to what is mentioned in some copies of the Qur'ān, stating that verses 1–3 and 7 were Madinan revelations. The first three verses read as follows: "Alif. Lām. Rā. *These are the verses of the Book that clearly shows [the truth]. We have revealed it as a discourse in Arabic so that you may understand. In revealing this Qur'ān We relate to you the best of narratives. Before it you were among those who are unaware [of revelation]."* These verses serve as a logical prelude to what immediately follows, namely Joseph's

1

story: "*Joseph said to his father: 'Father, I saw in a dream eleven stars, as well as the sun and the moon; I saw them prostrate themselves before me.'*" (Verse 4) Then the events of the story begin to unfold, right up to its conclusion. Hence, the reference to Qur'ānic narratives in the opening verse is a perfect prelude to the story.

Moreover, the message of the first three verses belongs fully to the Makkan Qur'ān, emphasizing that it is a revelation from on high, in Arabic, refuting the idolaters' accusation that a non-Arab taught it to the Prophet. They state that prior to receiving this revelation, the Prophet was totally unaware of its message and the subjects it addressed.

Furthermore, this introduction to the *sūrah* fits perfectly with the comments the *sūrah* provides on the story towards the end: "*That is an account which We have now revealed to you, speaking of things that have been beyond your perception. You were not present when they [i.e. Joseph's brothers] resolved upon their plans and completed their schemes.*" (Verse 102) We see how the prelude to the story dovetails with its concluding comments, indicating that the entire *sūrah*, prelude, narrative and comments, were all revealed at the same time.

As for verse 7, it is an integral part of the progressing narrative. For it to have been added later, in Madinah, is inconsistent with the whole. For one thing, verse 8 includes a pronoun that refers to Joseph's brothers mentioned in verse 7, which means that verse 8 could not be properly understood unless it were preceded by verse 7. The two verses together read: "*Surely in Joseph and his brothers there are signs for those who inquire. (Verse 7) They said [to one another]: 'Truly, Joseph and his brother are dearer to our father than we, even though we are many. Surely our father is in manifest error.'*" (Verse 8) All this clearly indicates that the two verses were revealed together as part of the unfolding narrative.

Trials in Plenty

The *sūrah* is a single, complete unit with a clear Makkan character reflected in its subject matter, message and ambience. It reflects the nature of the critical period in which it was revealed. The Prophet was enduring a time when he felt lonely and alienated from his social surroundings, and his followers felt the strains of isolation. With the revelation of this *sūrah*, God tells His noble Messenger, Muḥammad, the story of a noble brother, one Joseph ibn Jacob ibn Isaac ibn Abraham, (peace be upon them all). Joseph too had to endure a series of tests and trials: first, his brothers schemed to get rid of him, then he was thrown into the well where he found himself in fear of his life. This was followed by his becoming a slave sold like an inanimate object, having no say in the matter and losing all the care and love of his parents. He then faced temptation and seduction, followed by the wicked scheming of his master's wife and her fellow women. He then had to endure long imprisonment after having lived comfortably in a palace. A change of fortunes then sees him in a position of power where he had full control of people's basic food requirements and their lives. He subsequently faces a trial of a totally different nature when he meets his brothers whose plot against him started this whole scenario. Throughout, however, Joseph remained a steadfast believer, using these trials to propagate the divine message. He emerged triumphant at the end, reunited with his parents and family, witnessing the realization of his early dream in perfect relief: *"Joseph said to his father: 'Father, I saw in a dream eleven stars, as well as the sun and the moon; I saw them prostrate themselves before me.'"* (Verse 4)

At this point, all Joseph's thoughts and concerns are focused on turning to God, his Lord, with pure devotion and dedication, giving little importance to worldly considerations: *"When they all presented themselves before Joseph, he drew his parents to himself, saying: 'Enter Egypt in peace, if it so pleases God.' And he raised his parents to the highest place of honour, and they fell down on their knees, prostrating themselves before him. He said: 'Father, this is the real meaning of my dream of long ago. My Lord has made it come true. He has been gracious to me, releasing me from prison, and bringing you all from the desert after Satan had sown discord between me and my brothers. My Lord is gracious in whatever way He wishes. He is All-Knowing, truly Wise.' 'My Lord, You have given me power and imparted to me some understanding of the real meaning of statements. Originator of the heavens and the earth! You are my guardian in this world and in the life to come. Let me die as one who has surrendered himself to You, and admit me among the righteous.'"* (Verses 99–101) This was his ultimate request at the moment when he was in a position of power and affluence, reunited with his family. All he wanted was that God should let him die in a state of complete self-surrender to Him and to admit him among the righteous. To him, this was the crowning jewel after a long series of trials, endurance and then triumph.

A Hint of Future Prospects

It is no wonder that this *surah*, and the account and comments it gives, was revealed to the Prophet during that particularly difficult time in Makkah, giving him and his followers solace, comfort and reassurance. Indeed the way I think about the *surah* gives me the feeling that it carries a subtle hint that the Muslims will be made to leave Makkah to settle somewhere else, where they will enjoy power and achieve victory. It is true that the migration appeared to be enforced by the long persecution endured by the Muslim community. But so was the case with Joseph who was taken away from his parents to endure a long series of trials and tribulations: *"Thus We established Joseph in the land, and We imparted to him some understanding of the real meaning of statements. God always prevails in whatever be His purpose; though most people may not know it."* (Verse 21) This is stated in relation to the moment when Joseph first arrived in Egypt as a young lad being sold as a slave to the Chief Minister.

These thoughts that press on my mind now give me a special appreciation of the ending of the *surah* with its final comments on the story. I can only refer to what I feel, though putting such feelings into words is difficult. So the best I can do is to refer to the final verses themselves: *"Even before your time, We only sent [as messengers] men to whom We gave Our revelations, choosing them from among their people. Have they not travelled the land and seen what was the end of those [unbelievers] who lived before them? Better indeed is the life to come for those who remain God-fearing. Will you not, then, use your reason? When at length [Our] messengers lost all hope and thought that they were denied, Our help came to them, saving those whom We willed [to be saved]. Never can Our [mighty] punishment be averted from people who are guilty. Indeed their stories give a lesson to those who are endowed with understanding. This [revelation] could not possibly be an invented discourse. It is a confirmation of earlier revelations, an explanation of all things, as well as guidance and mercy for people who believe."* (Verses 109–111)

4

These verses suggest that the laws God has set in operation in human life take a certain course when God's messengers lose all hope, as did Joseph in his long series of trials. The course indicates a departure against one's will that then leads to the desired release. Such hints and inspiration are felt by believers who go through a similar period of trial and hardship as they begin to look forward to a forthcoming release, even though it seems distant.

The *sūrah* is unique in that it relates Joseph's story in full. Other stories related elsewhere in the Qur'ān are always split into episodes, given in different *sūrahs* so that each episode serves the purpose and theme of the *sūrah* in which it is narrated. When a historical account is given fully in one *sūrah*, as in the case of the stories of Prophets Hūd, Ṣāliḥ, Lot and Shuʿayb, these stories are sketched in summarized form. Joseph's story, by contrast, is told in full, with complete details, in one *sūrah*, which is unique in the Qur'ān.

This unique approach suits this particular story. The story starts with relating Joseph's dream and ends with its realization. To give a partial account here, comprising one or a few episodes, and completing it in another *sūrah* would have been unsuitable. Besides, this approach fulfils all artistic aspects while, at the same time, serves the purpose for which the story is included in the Qur'ān.

Artistic Narrative

As narrated in this *sūrah*, Joseph's story provides the perfect example of the Islamic method of story-telling while enhancing its psychological and educational effects that aim to reinforce faith and strengthen trust in its line of action. Although the Qur'ān maintains the same theme and method of presentation, Joseph's story stands out as a perfect example of its artistic features.

Joseph, the main protagonist, is shown interacting with all aspects of life across a wide variety of situations. His trials, greatly varied in nature and effect, are all fully portrayed with natural human reactions in each case. Joseph, a perfect model of God's humble servant, emerges from all these trials pure, untarnished, fully dedicated, addressing to God a heartfelt prayer that expresses his devotion.

Other characters in the story are presented with varying degrees of exposure, space and focus. The story in this way reveals profound insight into the human psyche, presenting a variety of situations, feelings, reactions and interactions. One such case is that of Jacob, a loving father full of sorrow and a reassured prophet who has been granted special knowledge. Another is that of Joseph's brothers motivated by envy, jealousy and personal grudges into devising a wicked scheme, which weighs heavily on them and leaves them weak and confused. One of them, however, emerges with a different personality that asserts itself in the various stages of the story. A third case is that of the Chief Minister's wife: driven by sexual desire, unashamedly explicit in her expression, and reflecting the situation in the palaces of Egypt during a period of *jāhiliyyah*. She is clearly delineated so as to give us an insight into her personal character and how she is influenced by her environment. We also have an example of aristocratic women in Egypt at the time. Their gossip about the Chief Minister's wife and her slave boy, (note, see my comments in later chapters about this term of reference), their attempts to seduce Joseph, and the threat he receives from his mistress in front of them all give us a clear picture of the Egyptian social environment. We also see a sample of the plots that are continually hatched in the upper echelons of society. This is clearly shown in Joseph's imprisonment. Furthermore, the Chief Minister reflects the attitude of his ruling class in dealing with crimes of honour. The King appears briefly, then moves into the background as does the Chief Minister. All these characters present a multitude of human feelings, attitudes and behaviour that accurately reflect human nature as a whole.

Artistic presentation in the story remains remarkably faithful, realistic and accurate. It does not ignore a single human reality, without creating the sort of squalor of carnal motives and wickedness certain Western circles call 'realism'. Different types of human weakness, including the inability to resist a strong sexual urge, are portrayed showing a perfectly accurate picture of human nature without overlooking a single aspect of it. Nevertheless, the story maintains the highest standard of propriety with clear realism.

Realism and Consistency

Take the case of Joseph's brothers: petty grudges grow in their hearts, reaching great proportions so as to make them lose sight of the enormity of their ghastly crime. They then come up with a 'moral justification' to quieten their consciences. This justification reflects the reality of their religious environment, since they are the children of the Prophet Ya'qūb ibn Isḥāq ibn Ibrāhīm (peace be upon them all). Their environment leaves its clear impressions on their way of thinking, feelings and traditions. They know that they need some sort of justification so as to reduce the ghastliness of their crime:

> Surely in Joseph and his brothers there are signs for those who inquire. They said [to one another]: 'Truly, Joseph and his brother are dearer to our father than we, even though we are many. Surely our father is in manifest error. Kill Joseph, or cast him away in some faraway land, so that you have your father's attention turned to you alone. After that you will [repent and] be righteous people.' One of them said: 'Do not kill Joseph, but rather – if you must do something – cast him into the dark depth of this well. Some caravan may pick him up.' [Thereupon] they said [to their father]: 'Father, why do you not trust us with Joseph, when we are indeed his well-wishers? Send him with us tomorrow, that he may enjoy himself and play. We will certainly take good care of him.' He answered: 'It certainly grieves me that you should take him with you; and I dread that the wolf may eat him when you are heedless of him.' They said: 'If the wolf were to eat him when we are so many, then we should surely be lost.' And when they went away with him, they resolved to cast him into the depth of the well. We revealed [this] to him: 'You will tell them of this their deed at a time when they shall not know you.' At nightfall they came to their father weeping, and said: 'Father, we went off racing and left Joseph behind with our belongings, and the wolf devoured him. But you will not believe us even though we are saying the truth.' And they produced his shirt stained with false blood. He said: 'No, but your minds have tempted you to evil. Sweet patience! It is to God alone that I turn for support in this misfortune that you have described.' (Verses 7–18)

We subsequently see them reflecting the same characteristics on every occasion, just as we see one of them always adopting a different stance. Later on, to comply with Joseph's demand, they take his brother to him, not knowing Joseph's true identity but aware only that he is the Chief Minister of Egypt. They only want to buy their supply of grain from him during that period of drought. God, however, allows Joseph to retain his brother under the pretext of finding the King's measure in his luggage. The other brothers had no idea how this had come about, but their old grudges against Joseph immediately surface: "*They said: 'If he has stolen – well, a brother of his had stolen previously.' Joseph kept his secret to himself and revealed nothing to them, saying [within himself]: 'You are in a far worse position, and God knows best what you are speaking of.'*" (Verse 77)

Their old grudges manifest themselves again when they tell their father, now an old and sorrowful man, about the second calamity. They realize how this second event will renew all his grief for Joseph. Again, their old grudges against their lost brother are seen at full strength. They pay little heed to their father's old age and his sense of bereavement: "*He then turned away from them and said: 'Oh, woe is me for Joseph!' His eyes became white with grief, and he was burdened with silent sorrow. They said: 'By God, you will continue to remember Joseph until you wither away or until you are dead.'*" (Verses 84–85)

The same may be said about their remarks when Joseph sent his shirt to his father after having identified himself to them. When they saw their father detecting Joseph's aura, they were upset as this indicated the profound relationship that still existed between father and absent son. They were quick to remonstrate with their father and reproach him: "*As the caravan set out, their father said [to the people around him]: 'I feel the breath of Joseph, though you will not believe me.' They replied: 'By God! You are still lost in your old illusions.'*" (Verses 94–95)

Realism and Propriety

The Chief Minister's wife is another character that reflects consistency in all situations. We see her first in the grip of desire, heeding nothing as she tries to satisfy her uncontrolled lust. She is restrained neither by feminine shyness, self respect, social position nor by a potential family scandal. She is quick to employ all her female guile and craftiness in order to show herself free of blame and at the same time protect her loved one, at whom she deliberately levelled a false accusation. Her aim here is that he should be given a mild sentence that spares his life. Again her guile helps her to answer other women's accusations, utilizing their similar weakness against sexual desire. When her own lack of control is exposed, she owns up to her determination to get what she wants, declaring this to the other women who share with her the same lust that sees nothing wrong in satisfying carnal desires.

Although the story paints this type of woman realistically and faithfully, showing the moment of uncontrolled desire at its most urgent, the Qur'ānic account, which provides the best example of Islamic artistry, maintains a very clean line throughout. Even in the description of a woman exposing her physical and mental nakedness, the Qur'ān steers away from the squalor of explicit eroticism which characterizes what is called realism in literary works of contemporary societies that pay little regard to religious values.

The man from Egypt who bought him said to his wife: 'Be kind to him. He may well be of use to us, or we may adopt him as our son.' Thus We established Joseph in the land, and We imparted to him some understanding of the real meaning of statements. God always prevails in whatever be His purpose; though most people may not know it. And when he attained his full manhood, We bestowed on him wisdom and knowledge. Thus do We reward those who do good. She in whose house he was living tried to seduce him. She bolted the doors and said, 'Come.' He said: 'God protect me. Goodly has my master made my stay here. Those who do wrong come to no good.' She truly desired him, and he desired her. [He would have succumbed] had he not seen a clear sign from his Lord. Thus We averted from him evil and indecency. He was truly one of Our faithful servants. And they both rushed to the door. She tore his shirt from behind. And at the door they met her husband. She said: 'What ought to be the punishment of someone who had evil designs on your wife other than that he should be thrown in prison or some grievous punishment.' [Joseph] said: 'It was she who sought to seduce me.' One of her own household testified: 'If his shirt has been torn from the front, then she is speaking the truth and he is lying. But if it has been torn from behind, then she is lying, and he is speaking the truth.' When [her husband] saw that Joseph's shirt was torn from behind, he said to her: 'This is indeed [an instance] of the guile of you, women. Your guile is awesome indeed!' 'Joseph, let this pass! And you, woman, ask forgiveness for your sin. You have been seriously at fault.' In the city, women were saying: 'The Chief Minister's wife is trying to seduce her slave boy, as she is passionately in love with him. We see that she is clearly going astray.' When she heard of their malicious talk, she sent for them, and prepared for them a sumptuous repast, and handed each one of them a knife and said [to Joseph]: 'Come out and present yourself to them.' When they saw him, they were amazed at him, and they cut their hands, exclaiming: 'God preserve us! This is no mortal man! This is none other than a noble angel.' Said she: 'This is he on whose account you have been blaming me! Indeed I have tried to seduce him, but he guarded his chastity. Now, however, if he does not do what I bid him, he shall certainly be thrown in prison, and shall indeed be humiliated.' [Joseph] said: 'My Lord, I would sooner be put in prison than comply with what they are inviting me to do. Unless You turn away their guile from me, I may yield to them and lapse into folly.' His Lord answered his prayer and warded off their guile from him. It is He alone who hears all and knows all. (Verses 21–34)

We meet her again after Joseph had been a prisoner for years as a result of her and the other women's scheming. It was only when the King experienced his dream that Joseph's former fellow prisoner remembered that Joseph was the only one who could unravel a true interpretation of dreams. When the King ordered that he should be brought to him, Joseph refused until the King had investigated his case to determine his innocence. The King thus called the Chief Minister's wife and the other women. As she responds, we see her again as a woman in love, even though time, aging and events have left their mark on her. But we also realize that faith, which she had observed with Joseph, found its way into her heart. *"The King said: 'Bring this man before me.' But when the [King's] envoy came to him, Joseph said: 'Go back to your lord and ask him about the women who cut their hands.*

My Lord has full knowledge of their guile.' The King asked [the women]: 'What was the matter with you when you tried to seduce Joseph?' The women said: 'God save us! We did not perceive the least evil on his part.' The Chief Minister's wife said: 'Now has the truth come to light. It was I who tried to seduce him. He has indeed told the truth. From this he will know that I did not betray him behind his back, and that God does not bless with His guidance the schemes of those who betray their trust. And yet, I am not trying to claim to be free of sin. Indeed man's soul does incite him to evil, except for those upon whom God has bestowed His mercy. My Lord is Much-Forgiving, Merciful.'" (Verses 50–53)

Joseph, a goodly type of man, is painted faithfully. The Qur'ān does not alter the slightest feature of his character. Having been brought up in a prophet's home as very religious, he is shown as a young man facing the trial of temptation. Indeed, his real character combines his natural human tendencies with his religious upbringing. When the woman tempted him openly, he almost responded to her, but the other influence saved him from falling into her trap. He felt his own weakness as he faced the women's guile coupled with the pull of his environment and the social milieu. But he remained steadfast. There is no distortion of his character. He is faithfully painted.

Then we have the very special character of the Chief Minister, who has to balance the dignity of his position with the weakness of pride. With him, social pretences and covering up what is unbecoming are essential characteristics: *"When [her husband] saw that Joseph's shirt was torn from behind, he said to her: 'This is indeed [an instance] of the guile of you, women. Your guile is awesome indeed!' 'Joseph, let this pass! And you, woman, ask forgiveness for your sin. You have been seriously at fault.'"* (Verses 28–29)

We also see the women in that society: their gossip about the Chief Minister's wife and her slave boy whom she tries to seduce; their disapproval of her conduct based on jealousy rather than the error involved; their infatuation with Joseph; their feminine cognition of the reason behind the conduct of the woman at the centre of their gossip; her awareness of this recognition prompting her to complete confession feeling completely safe to do so; their collective attempt to seduce Joseph despite their immediate recognition of his purity: *"When they saw him, they were amazed at him, and they cut their hands, exclaiming: 'God*

preserve us! This is no mortal man! This is none other than a noble angel.'"
(Verse 31) We understand all this from Joseph's prayer: *"He said: 'My
Lord, I would sooner be put in prison than comply with what they are
inviting me to do. Unless You turn away their guile from me, I may yield
to them and lapse into folly.'"* (Verse 33) It was no longer his mistress that
was after him, but the whole array of upper class women.

The whole social environment is clearly seen in the way Joseph's
fate is determined even though his innocence is fully established. In
this way, the decision was taken to suppress the social scandal, even
though a wholly innocent person was made a scapegoat: *"Yet for all
the evidence they had seen, they felt it right to put him in jail for a
time."* (Verse 35)

The Development of Joseph's Character

If we follow Joseph across the whole story, we find his character
shining throughout, reflecting its essential characteristics in every
environment he finds himself in. He is a God-fearing young man
brought up in a prophet's home where he acquired his faith. At no
point do we see him losing sight of any of these elements. In the dark
hours when he is unjustly thrown into prison, he continues to advocate
his faith gently but firmly, aware of his environment and knowing
how to approach people in such an environment. He realizes that he
must always reflect the superiority of his faith by his conduct which
maintains high moral standards and values:

*Two young men went to prison with him. One of them said: 'I saw
myself [in a dream] pressing wine.' The other said: 'And I saw myself
[in a dream] carrying bread on my head, and birds were eating of
it.' 'Tell us the meaning of these dreams, for we can see that you are
a man of virtue.' [Joseph] answered: 'Your food which is provided
for you will not have come to you before I have informed you of the
real meaning of [your dreams]. That is part of the knowledge which
my Lord has imparted to me. I have left the faith of people who do
not believe in God, and who deny the truth of the life to come. I
follow the faith of my forefathers, Abraham, Isaac and Jacob. It is
not for us to associate any partners with God. This is part of God's*

grace which He has bestowed on us and on all mankind, but most people do not give thanks. My two prison companions! Which is better: [to believe] in diverse lords, or to believe in God, the One who holds sway over all that exists? Those you worship instead of Him are nothing but names you and your fathers have invented, and for which God has given no sanction from on high. All judgement rests with God alone. He has ordained that you should worship none but Him. This is the true faith, but most people do not know it. My two prison companions! One of you will give his lord wine to drink. The other will be crucified, and the birds will eat from his head. The matter on which you have sought to be enlightened has thus been decided.' (Verses 36–41)

Nevertheless, he is a man with normal human weaknesses. He is eager that the King be informed of his case, hoping that the King would uncover the plot that ended with him being unjustly imprisoned. But God wanted to teach him to place his hopes in Him alone. *"And [Joseph] said to the one whom he believed would be released: 'Remember me in the presence of your lord.' But Satan caused him to forget to mention Joseph to his lord, and so he remained in prison for several years."* (Verse 42)

We see the same personality again after the lapse of several years. During which time Joseph has gone through the divine educative process and has placed his full trust in God, reassured about his future and fate. The King has his dream and his nobles and religious leaders cannot find a suitable interpretation for it. At this point, the released former prisoner remembers Joseph and obtains his interpretation of the King's dream. The King orders that Joseph be brought to him. But Joseph is reassured, confident of his position. He refuses to leave prison until his case is properly investigated and he is acquitted:

And the King said: 'I saw [in a dream] seven fat cows being devoured by seven emaciated ones, and seven green ears of wheat next to seven others dry and withered. Tell me the meaning of my vision, my nobles, if you are able to interpret dreams.' They replied: 'This is but a medley of dreams, and we have no deep knowledge of the real meaning of dreams.' At that point, the man who had been released from prison

13

suddenly remembered [Joseph] after all that time and said: 'I will tell you the real meaning of this dream, so give me leave to go.'

'Joseph, man of truth, tell us of the seven fat cows being devoured by seven emaciated ones, and seven green ears of wheat next to seven others dry and withered, so that I may return to the people [of the court], and that they would come to know.' He replied: 'You shall sow for seven consecutive years, but let the grain you harvest remain in its ear, except for the little which you may eat. Then after that there will come seven hard years which will devour all that you have laid up for them, except a little of what you have kept in store. Then after that there will come a year of abundant rain, in which the people will be able to press [oil and wine]. The King said: 'Bring this man before me.' But when the [King's] envoy came to him, Joseph said: 'Go back to your lord and ask him about the women who cut their hands. My Lord has full knowledge of their guile.' The King asked [the women]: 'What was the matter with you when you tried to seduce Joseph?' The women said: 'God save us! We did not perceive the least evil on his part.' The Chief Minister's wife said: 'Now has the truth come to light. It was I who tried to seduce him. He has indeed told the truth.' From this he will know that I did not betray him behind his back, and that God does not bless with His guidance the schemes of those who betray their trust. And yet, I am not trying to claim to be free of sin. Indeed man's soul does incite him to evil, except for those upon whom God has bestowed His mercy. My Lord is Much-Forgiving, Merciful. And the King said: 'Bring him before me. I will choose him for my own.' And when he had spoken to him, the King said: 'You shall henceforth be in a position of high standing with us, invested with all trust.' Joseph replied: 'Give me charge of the store-houses of the land. I am able to look after them with wisdom.' (Verses 43–55)

Here we see that Joseph has matured. He is fully aware of what goes on around him. He is calm, confident, reassured. From this point onward, he is the central character in the story, while the King, the Chief Minister, the women and the whole set up move out of stage. The *sūrah* prepares us for this change with a couple of verses: "*Thus did We establish Joseph in the land, free to do what he willed. We bestow Our mercy on whom We will, and We never fail to give their reward to those who do good. But as for those who believe in God and keep away from evil, the reward of the life to come is much better indeed."* (Verses 56–57) From this point onward, Joseph faces new types of trial, unlike those he had hitherto faced. In all these, he loses nothing of his calmness or reassurance.

First we see Joseph encountering his brothers for the first time after their crime against him. Now however he is far superior to them and in a stronger position. Yet his actions reflect his self control: *"Joseph's brothers arrived and presented themselves before him. He immediately knew them, but they did not recognize him. And when he had given them their provisions, he said: 'Bring me that brother of yours from your father's side. Do you not see that I give just measure and that I am the best of hosts? But if you do not bring him, you shall never again receive from me a single measure [of provisions], nor shall you come near me.' They said: 'We shall endeavour to persuade his father to let him come. We will make sure to do so.' Joseph said to his servants: 'Place their merchandise in their camel-packs, so that they may discover it when they return to their people. Perchance they will come back.'"* (Verses 58–62)

We meet Joseph again carrying out a plan sanctioned by God to detain his brother. With this we see a mature and wise person, one who is full of confidence and self control:

> *And when they presented themselves before Joseph, he drew his brother to himself, and said: 'I am your brother. Do not grieve over their past deeds.' And when he had given them their provisions, he placed the [King's] drinking-cup in his brother's camel-pack. Then an announcer called out: 'You people of the caravan! You are surely thieves.' Turning back towards them, they said: 'What is it that you have lost?' 'We have lost the King's goblet," they answered. 'Whoever brings it shall have a camel-load [of grain as a reward]. I pledge my word for it.' They said: 'By God, you know that we have not come to commit any evil deed in this land, and that we are no thieves.' [The Egyptians] said: 'But what shall be the punishment for this deed, if you are proved to be lying?' They replied: 'He in whose camel-pack it is found shall be enslaved in punishment for it. Thus do we*

punish the wrongdoers.' Thereupon, [Joseph] began to search their bags before the bag of his brother, and then took out the drinking-cup from his brother's bag. Thus did We contrive for Joseph. He had no right under the King's law to detain his brother, had God not so willed. We do exalt [in knowledge] whom We will, but above everyone who is endowed with knowledge there is One who knows all. [Joseph's brothers] said: 'If he has stolen – well, a brother of his had stolen previously.' Joseph kept his secret to himself and revealed nothing to them, saying [within himself]: 'You are in a far worse position, and God knows best what you are speaking of.' They said: 'Chief Minister, this boy has a father who is very old. Take one of us instead of him. We see that you are indeed a generous man.' He answered: 'God forbid that we should take any other than the man with whom we found our property; for then we would be wrongdoers.' (Verses 69–79)

Once more we see Joseph when the trial had taken its toll on Jacob and God has willed that the trials that engulfed him and his household should now come to an end. Joseph is now longing to be reunited with his parents, and he feels sympathetic towards his brothers who appear before him suffering hardship. He gently remonstrates with them as he identifies himself to them, and follows this with total forgiveness stated at the most opportune moment. All circumstances lead to such forgiveness which is the only attitude to be expected from Joseph, the God-fearing, mature, kind and reassured person.

When they presented themselves before [Joseph] again, they said: 'Exalted one! Hardship has befallen us and our people, and so we have brought but little merchandise. Give us our full measure [of grains], and be charitable to us. Indeed God rewards those who are charitable.' He said: 'Do you know what you did to Joseph and his brother, when you were still unaware?' They said: 'Why – is it indeed you who are Joseph?' He replied: 'I am Joseph, and this is my brother. God has indeed been gracious to us. If one remains God-fearing and patient in adversity, God will not fail to reward those who do good.' They said: 'By God! Most certainly has God raised you high above us, and we were indeed sinners.' He replied: 'None shall reproach you today. May God forgive you. He is indeed the Most Merciful of those who show mercy. Now go and take this shirt of mine and lay it over my father's face, and he will recover his sight. Then come back to me with all your family.' (Verses 88–93)

We finally see him at the climax, when the reunion takes place, Joseph is at the height of his power, his dream has come true and all his aspirations have been fulfilled. At this moment, he steps aside to be alone addressing a prayer of complete devotion and full humility. His position of power means nothing to him at that moment: *"My Lord, You have given me power and imparted to me some understanding of the real meaning of statements. Originator of the heavens and the earth! You are my guardian in this world and in the life to come. Let me die as one who has surrendered himself to You, and admit me among the righteous."* (Verse 101)

Joseph's character reflects his integrity, consistency and the environment in which he was raised.

The Bereaved Father

Another character is Jacob, the loving kindly father and confident prophet who experiences a combination of apprehension and hope when his son tells him of his dream. He recognizes that the dream heralds a very promising future, but he fears at the same time that Satan might prompt his other children to take some undesirable action. We see him here reflecting on all aspects of his character: *"Joseph said to his father: 'Father, I saw in a dream eleven stars, as well as the sun and the moon; I saw them prostrate themselves before me.' 'My son,' he replied, 'do not relate your dream to your brothers, lest they plot some evil against you. Satan is indeed man's open enemy. Even thus will your Lord make you His chosen one, and will impart to you some understanding of the real meaning of statements. He will perfect His favour to you and to the House of Jacob, as He perfected it to your forefathers, Abraham and Isaac. Your Lord is certainly All-Knowing, Wise.'"* (Verses 4–6)

We then meet him again as his sons try to persuade him to let them take Joseph with them, followed by them giving him the shocking news of Joseph's disappearance:

17

[Thereupon] they said [to their father]: 'Father, why do you not trust us with Joseph, when we are indeed his well-wishers? Send him with us tomorrow, that he may enjoy himself and play. We will certainly take good care of him.' He answered: 'It certainly grieves me that you should take him with you; and I dread that the wolf may eat him when you are heedless of him.' They said: 'If the wolf were to eat him when we are so many, then we should surely be lost.' And when they went away with him, they resolved to cast him into the depths of the well. We revealed [this] to him: 'You will tell them of this their deed at a time when they shall not know you.' At nightfall they came to their father weeping, and said: 'Father, we went off racing and left Joseph behind with our belongings, and the wolf devoured him. But you will not believe us even though we are saying the truth.' And they produced his shirt stained with false blood. He said: 'No, but your minds have tempted you to evil. Sweet patience! It is to God alone that I turn for support in this misfortune that you have described.' (Verses 11–18)

Again we meet him, in all his humanity, when his sons are trying once more to persuade him to part company with another son, Joseph's full brother, now the focus of all his love and kindness. For them, they must get Jacob's consent that the brother travel with them, because the Egyptian Chief Minister, whose identity is unknown to them, requires his presence in order to give them their full measure of grain.

When they returned to their father, they said: 'Father, any [further] grain is henceforth denied us. Therefore, send our brother with us so that we may obtain our full measure [of grain]. We will take good care of him.' He replied: 'Am I to trust you with him in the same way as I trusted you with his brother in the past? But God is the best of guardians; and of all those who show mercy He is the Most Merciful.' When they opened their camel-packs, they discovered that their merchandise had been returned to them. 'Father,' they said, 'what more could we desire? Here is our merchandise: it has been returned to us. We will buy provisions for our people, and we will take good care of our brother. We will receive an extra camel-load: that should be an easy load.' He said: 'I will not send him with you until you give me a solemn pledge before God that you will indeed bring him back to me, unless the worst befalls you.' When they had given him their solemn pledge, [Jacob] said: 'God is witness to all that we say.' And he added: 'My sons, do not enter [the city] by one gate, but enter by different gates. In no way can I be of help to you against God. Judgement rests with none but God. In Him have I placed my trust, and in Him alone let all those who trust place their trust.' And when they entered as their father had bidden them, it did not profit them in the least against God. It was but a wish in Jacob's soul which he had thus fulfilled. He was endowed with knowledge which We had given him. But most people do not know it. (Verses 63–68)

We meet him again after his second calamity, to see him once more as a bereaved father and a reassured prophet. Joseph carried out his plan sanctioned by God to detain his brother. But another of Jacob's sons, who stands out as one with a special character that distinguishes his attitude at different junctures in the story, decides to stay behind as well. He cannot face his father after having given him a solemn pledge that he could not now honour. Therefore, he decides to stay until his father gives him permission to do otherwise, or until God has judged in his case:

When they despaired of [moving] him, they withdrew to begin earnest consultations among themselves. The eldest of them said: 'Do you not recall that your father took from you a pledge in God's name, and that previously you were at fault with respect to Joseph? I shall not depart from this land until my father gives me leave or God judges for me. He is certainly the best of judges.' Go back to your father and say: 'Father, your son has stolen. We testify only to that which we know. We cannot guard against the unforeseen. You may ask the [people of the] town where we were, and the caravan with which we travelled. We are certainly telling the truth.' He said: 'No, but your minds have tempted you to evil. Sweet patience! God may well bring them all back to me. He is All-Knowing, Wise.' He then turned away from them and said: 'Oh, woe is me for Joseph!' His eyes became white with grief, and he was burdened with silent sorrow. They said: 'By God, you will continue to remember Joseph until you wither away or until you are dead.' He said: 'It is only to

19

God that I complain and express my grief. For I know of God what you do not know. My sons, go and seek news of Joseph and his brother; and do not despair of God's mercy; for none but unbelievers can ever despair of God's mercy.' (Verses 80–87)

In the last episode of his long trial we see Jacob, the old man, demonstrating the same characteristics, holding Joseph's shirt and recognizing his son's odour. He is being reproached by his sons, but his trust in his Lord is never in doubt. *"As the caravan set out, their father said [to the people around him]: 'I feel the breath of Joseph, though you will not believe me.' They replied: 'By God! You are still lost in your old illusions.' But when the bearer of good news arrived [with Joseph's shirt], he laid it over his face; and he regained his sight. He said: 'Did I not say to you that I know from God something that you do not know?' [His sons] said: 'Father, pray to God to forgive us our sins, for we were sinners indeed.' He said: 'I shall pray to God to forgive you. He is certainly Much-Forgiving, Most Merciful.'"* (Verses 94–98)

The Carnal and the Sublime

The Qur'ānic approach of faithfully painting reality while maintaining the values of purity and propriety is not limited to the sketching of human characteristics. It is also clearly seen in the faithful narration of events, showing them as they took place, accurately outlining their circumstances, background, time and place. Every movement, feeling, reaction and indeed every word is given at the appropriate time. All this is similarly true of the characters painted.

Even sexual feelings and attitudes are given their full space, within the limits of the clean approach that suits man. We see no falsification, distortion or suppression of the human reality, its scope or integrity. However, giving these moments their proper space in relation to the rest of events does not mean focusing on them as if they were the total reality of humans and the pivotal element in their life. This is contrary to the un-Islamic or *jāhiliyyah* approach which wants us to believe that only such focus produces realist art.

Jāhiliyyah deforms man under the pretext of artistic realism. It zooms in on sex as if it were the entire object of human life, making of it a deep swamp surrounded by tempting but evil flowers. It is not faithfulness to reality that makes *jāhiliyyah* adopt this approach to sex. It is done because the Zionist Protocols encourage it. These Protocols want to see man stripped of all values except the animal and carnal, so that the Zionists are not seen as the only people who shed all non-material values. They want humanity to fall into the quagmire of sex, directing all its potentials to it. This is the surest way to destroy humanity and make it prostrate before the approaching Zionist Kingdom. They make art their means to bring about all this evil. In addition, they try hard to propagate new doctrines, exploiting them in such a way that serves the same purpose, while they maintain that such doctrines are 'scientific'. Examples of these are Darwinism, Freudianism, Marxism and Scientific Socialism. All these share in common the purpose of serving evil Zionist designs.

Historical Dimension

The story does not only relate events and draw characters. It goes beyond this to point out the period in history when these events took place, and describes its general features. Thus the stage acquires an international historical dimension. We will briefly refer to some of these.

Egypt was not ruled at the time by pharaohs of Egyptian descent. It was instead under the rule of a nomadic people who had learnt something about the divine faith from Abraham, Ishmael, Isaac and Jacob who lived nearby. We deduce this from the fact that the ruler of Egypt at the time is given in the Qur'ān the title of King, while the ruler of Egypt in the story of Moses is given the well-known Egyptian title, Pharaoh. This distinction determines the time when Joseph was in Egypt, namely between the 13th and 17th dynasties, which belonged to the nomads whom the Egyptian people called the Hyksos. This was said to be a derogatory appellation which referred to pigs or pig farmers. Their rule in Egypt lasted about one and a half centuries.

Joseph was sent as a Messenger of God during this period. He started his advocacy of islam, in its broader sense, which means the religion of absolute monotheism, whilst in prison. We see him there making it clear that it was the faith of his ancestors, Abraham, Isaac and Jacob, and giving an accurate outline of what it meant: "*I have left the faith of people who do not believe in God, and who deny the truth of the life to come. I follow the faith of my forefathers, Abraham, Isaac and Jacob. It is not for us to associate any partners with God. This is part of God's grace which He has bestowed on us and on all mankind, but most people do not give thanks. My two prison companions! Which is better: [to believe] in diverse lords, or to believe in God, the One who holds sway over all that exists? Those you worship instead of Him are nothing but names you and your fathers have invented, and for which God has given no sanction from on high. All judgement rests with God alone. He has ordained that you should worship none but Him. This is the true faith, but most people do not know it."* (Verses 37–40)

This is a very clear and comprehensive picture of islam, as preached by all God's messengers. It outlines the essential beliefs, including belief in God, the Day of Judgement, God's oneness without entertaining any thought of associating partners with Him, a clear understanding of God's attributes, the One, the Overpowering. It also involves a declaration that none other than God has any power, which entails that the deities given control over people have no such status. All power and authority belongs to God alone who has commanded that all worship be addressed to none other than Him. To exercise power, authority and lordship is to demand worship from people, which is contrary to God's order that all worship be dedicated to Him. It defines worship as being subject to authority, rule and lordship, while the true faith is to acknowledge that all worship and rule are God's own. In this sense, the two are synonymous: *"All judgement rests with God alone. He has ordained that you should worship none but Him. This is the true faith."* (Verse 40) This is the clearest, most comprehensive, accurate and perfect description of Islam.

It is also clear that when Joseph held the reins of power in Egypt, he continued to advocate the divine faith. There is no doubt that this faith spread in Egypt by his efforts, particularly because he did not merely hold power but also controlled people's food provisions. It must also have spread into neighbouring areas, as they sent some of their people to Egypt to buy grains which had been stored there through Joseph's wise policies. As the story describes, Joseph's brothers came from the land of Canaan with caravans that brought provisions from Egypt. This shows that the drought affected the whole area at that time.

Early in the story there are hints at some vague influence of the divine faith which the Hyksos were aware of. The first reference occurs in quoting what the women said when they were surprised by Joseph's appearance: "*When they saw him, they were amazed at him, and they cut their hands, exclaiming: 'God preserve us! This is no mortal man! This is none other than a noble angel.'*" (Verse 31) A similar indication is seen in the Chief Minister's counsel to his wife: "*Joseph, let this pass! And you, woman, ask forgiveness for your sin. You have been seriously at fault.*" (Verse 29) Further reference is made later by the Chief Minister's wife who clearly appears to have believed in Joseph's religion and declared her submission to God: "*The Chief Minister's wife said: 'Now has the truth come to light. It was I who tried to seduce him. He has indeed told the truth.' From this he will know that I did not betray him behind his back, and that God does not bless with His guidance the schemes of those who betray their trust. And yet, I am not trying to claim to be free of sin. Indeed man's soul does incite him to evil, except for those upon whom God has bestowed His mercy. My Lord is Much-Forgiving, Merciful.*" (Verses 51–53)

Since the monotheistic faith was known in Egypt before Joseph assumed power, it must have subsequently spread during his reign and in subsequent Hyksos dynasties. When the Pharaohs of Egypt regained power with the 18th dynasty, they began to suppress the monotheistic faith and its adherents, particularly Jacob's descendants, in order to reinstate the idolatry that gave the Pharaohs their authority.

This explains a major cause behind the persecution of the Children of Israel. Israel's, i.e. Jacob's, sons settled in Egypt and ruled it during the Hyksos period. When the Egyptians expelled the Hyksos, they persecuted their allies, the Children of Israel. But the conflict between the two faiths is in fact the prime reason for such persecution, because the spread of the monotheistic faith destroys the very basis of Pharaohs' rule, since it stands firmly against all tyranny.

There is a reference to this elsewhere in the Qur'ān, when it relates the argument of a believer from Pharaoh's household as he defended Moses, trying hard to persuade Pharaoh and his people to leave Moses alone. Pharaoh felt that his very rule was threatened by the monotheistic faith Moses preached:

A believing man of Pharaoh's family, who had concealed his faith, exclaimed: 'Would you slay a man merely because he says, "My Lord is God" – seeing that he has brought you all evidence of this truth from your Lord? Now if he be a liar, his lie will fall back on him; but if he is speaking the truth, a part at least of what he warns you is bound to befall you. God would not grace with His guidance one who is a lying transgressor. My people! Yours is the dominion today, and you have the upper hand in the land. But who will rescue us from God's punishment, should it befall us?'

Said Pharaoh: 'I but point out to you that which I see myself; and I would never make you follow any path but that of rectitude.'

The man who had attained to faith said: 'My people! I fear for you the like of what had befallen those others who were leagued together [against God's truth], the like of what happened to Noah's people, the 'Ād, the Thamūd and those who came after them. God never wishes any injustice for His servants. And, my people, I fear for you that day when people will cry out to one another, when you will turn your backs and flee, having none to defend you against God. For he whom God lets go astray can never find any guide. In times gone by, Joseph had come to you with all evidence of the truth; but you never ceased to throw doubt on all that he brought you; and when he died you said: "No messenger will God send after him." Thus God lets go astray a transgressor who is lost in doubt; those who call in question God's revelations, with no authority vouchsafed to them. Exceedingly abhorrent is [their conduct] in the sight of God and of the believers. Thus God sets a seal on every arrogant, self-exalting heart.' (40: 28–35)

Thus we see that the true conflict was between the monotheistic faith which acknowledges Godhead and lordship as belonging to God alone and the idolatrous faith that gave the Pharaohs the basis of their power.

Perhaps the distorted version of monotheism associated with Akhenaton was a confused version of the lingering influence of the divine faith advocated by Joseph (peace be upon him) in Egypt. This could be seen more so if historical reports to the effect that Akhenaton's mother was Asian, and not of Pharaohnic descent.

The story is not confined to Egypt. It accurately reflects the historical period, with the related dreams and predictions spread across a wider area. We see this clearly reflected first in Joseph's dream and its fulfilment at the end, as also in the dreams of the two prisoners, and then the King's dream. All these dreams receive due attention from those who experience or hear them, which is an indication of the prevalent culture at the time.

Artistic elements in the story are varied and plenty. It is rich with the human element, reflected in the feelings and movements described. The narrative clearly highlights all these. Moreover, the Qur'ānic mode of expression is always inspiring, using varying rhythms to suit the particular atmosphere of every situation.

A father's love is clearly seen in varying degrees. We see it in Jacob's love of Joseph, his brother and also in his love for the rest of his sons. His love is also reflected in the way he reacts to events involving Joseph, from the beginning of the story up to its last line.

We also see envy and jealousy between brothers born to different mothers, according to how they see their father's love expressed. The way these feelings surface also varies, with some of the brothers entertaining murder while others, aghast at the thought of such a crime, advise instead that a much less impacting scheme should be sufficient.

Another prominent trait is that of plotting and scheming. Joseph's brothers plot to get rid of him, while the Chief Minister's wife's plots target Joseph, her husband and the women who gossip against her.

Desire and sex are described, as also the different responses to these. Here we see an unrestrained drive as well as self control. Appeal and fancy on the one side and chastity and restraint on the other. Other feelings and emotions are expressed such as regret, forgiveness and delight at the reunion of long lost family members. The *sūrah* also paints some aspects of the upper class of the then *jāhiliyyah* society: at home, in prison, at the market-place and in government offices in Egypt. Other aspects of the Hebrew society are also drawn, with emphasis on dreams and prophecies.

The story begins with the dream related by Joseph to his father who tells him that he will have a great role to play, but urging him to withhold his dream from his brothers so that their jealousy does not motivate them to scheme against him. The story then proceeds as though it is a realization of the dream, fulfilling Jacob's warnings. When the dream is finally fulfilled the story is ended, unlike what the writers of the Old Testament did. It thus has an artistic closure making it serve its religious purpose fully.

A clear plot adds to the artistic aspect of the story. The fulfilment of the dream is withheld to the end, even though it unfolds little by little. At the end, the plot is explained most naturally.

The story is divided into sections, each relating a number of episodes and scenes, leaving gaps between them to be filled in by the reader. In this way, it increases the story's appeal and entertainment.

We may finally say that the story shows the way for future literary works that benefit from fine artistic features and remain faithful to reality, without indulging in any vulgarity that is unbecoming to human art.

Moral Lessons

For the Islamic movement, the story provides clear lessons, some of which are particularly relevant to certain stages of its progress, while others answer clear permanent needs. In addition, certain facts are established through the story and within the *sūrah* as a whole, particularly in its final comments. We will briefly refer to some of these.

We have already mentioned that the revelation of this *sūrah* and the story it narrates were particularly suited to the critical period the Islamic message went through in Makkah, and the hardship endured by the Prophet and his few followers. This is manifested through the relation of the trials endured by Joseph, a noble brother of Muḥammad, God's Messenger, and how he had to depart from his land until he was given power elsewhere. This gives us an aspect of the moral of the story which fits in with the needs of the Islamic message at that particular time. We thus have an insight into the action-oriented nature of the Qur'ān, as it explains the nature of the message and gives the Muslim community practical directives with clear and well defined objectives.

In our analysis of the story, we have also referred to the clear, detailed and accurate picture of the divine faith, Islam, drawn by Joseph (peace be upon him). This picture merits long reflection. It begins by establishing the unity of the faith based on full submission to God and preached by all God's messengers. We see that the basic elements of this faith are incorporated in full in every message. They are all based on perfect monotheism, emphasizing God's oneness and His Lordship of mankind, who must submit themselves completely to Him alone. This faith, in all its messages, also establishes the essential belief in the life to come. This is contrary to what is known as the study of Comparative Religion which alleges that humanity began to believe in the One God and in the hereafter only at a very late stage in human history, after having gone through different forms of idolatry and dualism. It also alleges that progress in the field of religion mirrors human progress in science and industry. Thus, Comparative Religion implies that all religions were the product of man, like science and industry.

The *sūrah* also affirms the nature of the divine faith advocated by all God's messengers. It is not confined to the oneness of Godhead, but it also includes the oneness of Lordship. All judgement in all human affairs belongs to God alone, as a result of the divine order that only God may be worshipped. The Qur'ānic statement gives a very precise definition of worship. Judgement belongs to God and people must submit to His judgement. This is indeed the true faith, and not any other form or set of beliefs. No form of worship is valid when people submit to anyone other than God even in a single matter of the whole life spectrum. To believe that God is One means, necessarily, that the Lord is One, and in practice this means that all judgement belongs to Him, and all worship is dedicated to Him alone. The two are synonymous. The sort of worship that classifies people as Muslims or non-Muslims means submission to God and implementing His judgement, to the exclusion of anything else. This definitive Qur'ānic statement should end all argument on this issue.

Another impression that the story radiates shows pure and dedicated faith that fills the hearts of two of the noble and chosen servants of God, Jacob and Joseph. We have already spoken about Joseph's final attitude as he turns to his Lord in all humility, discarding all worldly things and addressing Him in total devotion: "*My Lord, You have given me power and imparted to me some understanding of the real meaning of statements. Originator of the heavens and the earth! You are my guardian in this world and in the life to come. Let me die as one who has surrendered himself to You, and admit me among the righteous.*" (Verse 101)

27

But this final attitude is not the only one sketched in the story. Indeed throughout his life Joseph remains close to his Lord, responding to Him and doing His bidding. When he is the target of seduction, being made very tempting offers, he says: "*God protect me. Goodly has my master made my stay here. Those who do wrong come to no good.*" (Verse 23) And when he fears that he may weaken before the temptation, he prays: "*My Lord, I would sooner be put in prison than comply with what they are inviting me to do. Unless You turn away their guile from me, I may yield to them and lapse into folly.*" (Verse 33)

Similarly, when he identifies himself to his brothers, he does not forget to acknowledge God's grace and express his gratitude for it: "*They said: 'Why – is it indeed you who are Joseph?' He replied: 'I am Joseph, and this is my brother. God has indeed been gracious to us. If one remains God-fearing and patient in adversity, God will not fail to reward those who do good.'*" (Verse 90)

All these attitudes go beyond answering the particular needs of the Islamic message in its early period in Makkah. They answer its needs in all situations at all times.

With Jacob the truth of God appears close and profound in every situation and on every occasion. As the trial deepens, this truth becomes still clearer in his heart and more sublime. At the beginning, when Joseph relates his vision, he reminds his son of God and expresses his gratitude to Him: "*Even thus will your Lord make you His chosen one, and will impart to you some understanding of the real meaning of statements. He will perfect His favour to you and to the House of Jacob, as He perfected it to your forefathers, Abraham and Isaac. Your Lord is certainly All-Knowing, Wise.*" (Verse 6) As he is given the first blow with Joseph's disappearance, he appeals to his Lord, saying: "*Your minds have tempted you to evil. Sweet patience! It is to God alone that I turn for support in this misfortune that you have described.*" (Verse 18)

We see him speaking to his sons as a loving father fearing that some misfortune should befall them. He recommends them not to make their entry into the city from the same gate, but to use different gates. However, he clearly states that such a precaution would avail them nothing against God's will. The only judgement that is certain to take effect is God's. Yet his recommendation may answer a need he feels within himself: "*And he added: 'My sons, do not enter [the city] by one gate, but enter by different gates. In no way can I be of help to you against God. Judgement rests with none but God. In Him have I placed my trust, and in Him alone let all those who trust place their trust.'"* (Verse 67)

He suffers another bereavement in his old age, when he had grown weak and sorrowful. But at no time does he ever lose hope that God will turn in His mercy to him: *"He said: 'No, but your minds have tempted you to evil. Sweet patience! God may well bring them all back to me. He is All-Knowing, Wise.'"* (Verse 83)

This truth reaches its most sublime as his sons reproach him for his continued sorrow for Joseph, to the extent that he loses his eyesight through crying. He tells them that he knows God as they do not know Him. Hence, he addresses his complaint to Him only and hopes for nothing other than God's grace: *"He then turned away from them and said: 'Oh, woe is me for Joseph!' His eyes became white with grief, and he was burdened with silent sorrow. They said: 'By God, you will continue to remember Joseph until you wither away or until you are dead.' He said: 'It is only to God that I complain and express my grief. For I know of God what you do not know. My sons, go and seek news of Joseph and his brother; and do not despair of God's mercy; for none but unbelievers can ever despair of God's mercy.'"* (Verses 84–87) He again reminds them of the truth he feels deep in his heart about God of whom he knows what they do not know. *"As the caravan set out, their father said [to the people around him]: 'I feel the breath of Joseph, though you will not believe me.' They replied: 'By God! You are still lost in your old illusions.' But when the bearer of good news arrived [with Joseph's shirt], he laid it over his face; and he regained his sight. He said: 'Did I not say to you that I know from God something that you do not know?'"* (Verses 94–96)

It is a glittering picture of how God's truth fills the hearts of the chosen among God's servants. This picture generates impressions that suit the period of hardship suffered by the Muslim community in Makkah, but it also shows the fundamental truth of faith to everyone who advocates Islam at any future time.

Suitable Comments

The first comment the *sūrah* makes in its final passage that follows the long story shows the absurdity of the Quraysh's denial of the truth of revelation with a statement based on the history related in this *sūrah*. It states that the Prophet was not present when the events of this history took place: "*That is an account which We have now revealed to you, speaking of things that have been beyond your perception. You were not present when they [i.e. Joseph's brothers] resolved upon their plans and completed their schemes.*" (Verse 102) This comment ties up with the introductory one at the beginning of the *sūrah*: "*In revealing this Qur'ān We relate to you the best of narratives. Before it you were among those who are unaware [of revelation].*" (Verse 3)

The introductory statement thus dovetails with the end one to form a picture of the truth. In this way it also counters the objections and denials raised.

This is followed with a comforting message to the Prophet so that he does not give those who deny his message undue importance. It shows how stubbornly they refuse to consider the signs that God has placed all around them in the universe. These signs are sufficient to alert human nature to the truth of faith and make it listen to the divine message and accept the evidence confirming it. They are threatened with God's punishment which could take them unawares: "*Yet however strongly you may desire it, most people will not believe. You ask no recompense from them for it. It is but God's reminder to all mankind. Yet many are the signs in the heavens and the earth which they pass by, paying no heed to them. And most of them do not even believe in God without also associating partners with Him. Do they feel confident that the overwhelming scourge of God's punishment will not fall upon them, or that the Last Hour will not come upon them suddenly, taking them unaware.*" (Verses 103–107) These verses deliver some fundamental truths about people who do not believe in the true divine faith. This is particularly noted in the statement: "*And most of them do not even believe in God without also associating partners with Him.*" (Verse 106) This is a true description of many people who have not formulated a true concept of God's oneness, allowing faith to be confused with unfaith.

At this point, the *sūrah*, with strong rhythm and decisive clarity, calls on the Prophet to define his way, showing it to be clearly distinguished from all others: "*Say: 'This is my way. I call [all mankind] to God on the basis of sure knowledge, I and all those who follow me.*

Limitless is God in His glory. I am not one of those who associate partners with Him.'" (Verse 108)

The *sūrah* concludes with another telling comment, explaining the value of giving historical accounts in the Qur'ān for the Prophet and the small band of believers who follow him. The comment also provides solace and reassurance to the believers, together with a promise of better things to come. The unbelievers who persist with their unbelief are also given reminders and warnings. A further assurance is given to both believers and unbelievers of the truth of revelation to the Prophet who only tells the truth. It reasserts the truth of his message: *"Even before your time, We only sent [as messengers] men to whom We gave Our revelations, choosing them from among their people. Have they not travelled the land and seen what was the end of those [unbelievers] who lived before them? Better indeed is the life to come for those who remain God-fearing. Will you not, then, use your reason? When at length [Our] messengers lost all hope and thought that they were denied, Our help came to them, saving those whom We willed [to be saved]. Never can Our [mighty] punishment be averted from people who are guilty. Indeed their stories give a lesson to those who are endowed with understanding. This [revelation] could not possibly be an invented discourse. It is a confirmation of earlier revelations, an explanation of all things, as well as guidance and mercy for people who believe."* (Verses 109–111)

Effective Harmony

It is useful at the end of this Prologue to the *sūrah* relating Joseph's story to highlight some aspects of the fine harmony that runs throughout the *sūrah*, citing some of its finer examples.

• This *sūrah* follows the same pattern of the Qur'ān when certain words and expressions are often repeated to contribute to the general atmosphere and character of the *sūrah*. For example, here knowledge is mentioned very frequently, while ignorance is mentioned on several occasions:

Even thus will your Lord make you His chosen one, and will impart to you some understanding of the real meaning of statements. He will perfect His favour to you and to the House of Jacob, as He perfected it to your forefathers, Abraham and Isaac. Your Lord is certainly All-Knowing, Wise. (Verse 6)

Thus We established Joseph in the land, and We imparted to him some understanding of the real meaning of statements. God always prevails in whatever be His purpose; though most people may not know it. (Verse 21)

And when he attained his full manhood, We bestowed on him wisdom and knowledge. Thus do We reward those who do good. (Verse 22)

His Lord answered his prayer and warded off their guile from him. It is He alone who hears all and knows all. (Verse 34)

[Joseph] answered: 'Your food which is provided for you will not have come to you before I have informed you of the real meaning of [your dreams]. That is part of the knowledge which my Lord has imparted to me. I have left the faith of people who do not believe in God, and who deny the truth of the life to come.' (Verse 37)

They replied: 'This is but a medley of dreams, and we have no deep knowledge of the real meaning of dreams. (Verse 44)

Joseph, man of truth, tell us of the seven fat cows being devoured by seven emaciated ones, and seven green ears of wheat next to seven others dry and withered, so that I may return to the people [of the court], and that they would come to know.' (Verse 46)

The King said: 'Bring this man before me.' But when the [King's] envoy came to him, Joseph said: 'Go back to your lord and ask him about the women who cut their hands. My Lord has full knowledge of their guile.' (Verse 50)

From this he will know that I did not betray him behind his back, and that God does not bless with His guidance the schemes of those who betray their trust. (Verse 52)

Joseph replied: 'Give me charge of the store-houses of the land. I am able to look after them with wisdom.' (Verse 55)

He was endowed with knowledge which We had given him. But most people do not know it. (Verse 68)

They said: 'By God, you know that we have not come to commit any evil deed in this land, and that we are no thieves.' (Verse 73)

You are in a far worse position, and God knows best what you are speaking of. (Verse 77)

When they despaired of [moving] him, they withdrew to begin earnest consultations among themselves. The eldest of them said: 'Do you not recall that your father took from you a pledge in God's name?' (Verse 80)

We testify only to that which we know. (Verse 81)

God may well bring them all back to me. He is All-Knowing, Wise. (Verse 83)

He said: 'It is only to God that I complain and express my grief. For I know of God what you do not know.' (Verse 86)

He said: 'Do you know what you did to Joseph and his brother, when you were still unaware?' (Verse 89)

He said: 'Did I not say to you that I know from God something that you do not know?' (Verse 96)

My Lord, You have given me power and imparted to me some understanding of the real meaning of statements. (Verse 101)

This is certainly a clear example of how harmony is maintained in this glorious book.

- The *sūrah* also explains some of the attributes of Godhead, notably judgement. This occurs once quoting Joseph in the sense of people being subject to God and willingly obeying Him. It occurs again quoting Jacob in the sense of people's involuntary submission to God's will. The two aspects thus are mutually complementary in defining the concept of judgement and Godhead. There is no chance that this could have been mere coincidence.

  Joseph first states within the context of refuting the claims of Egypt's rulers that they were deities, explaining that this runs against the concept of God's oneness: *"My two prison companions! Which is better: [to believe] in diverse lords, or to believe in God, the One who holds sway over all that exists? Those you worship instead of Him are nothing but names you and your fathers have invented, and for which God has given no sanction from on high. All judgement rests with God alone. He has ordained that you should worship none but Him. This is the true faith."* (Verses 39–40)

Within the context of God's will and that it will always be done with no force able to stop it, Jacob says: *"My sons, do not enter [the city] by one gate, but enter by different gates. In no way can I be of help to you against God. Judgement rests with none but God. In Him have I placed my trust, and in Him alone let all those who trust place their trust."* (Verse 67)

The complementarity in the significance of judgement means that faith is not set on the right footing unless submission to God's will in matters of judgement is equated with submission to His will in matters of fate. Both are aspects of faith. Voluntary submission is as much part of faith as submission to what is determined by God's will, giving man no say in it.

- We see another fine example when Joseph, wise, sagacious and astute as he is, chooses the most suitable of God's attributes when he speaks of a situation that reflects God's gracious handling of all affairs: *"And he raised his parents to the highest place of honour, and they fell down on their knees, prostrating themselves before him. He said: 'Father, this is the real meaning of my dream of long ago. My Lord has made it come true. He has been gracious to me, releasing me from prison, and bringing you all from the desert after Satan had sown discord between me and my brothers. My Lord is gracious in whatever way He wishes. He is All-Knowing, truly Wise.'"* (Verse 100)

- As we mentioned earlier, harmony is shown in the complementarity of the story's introduction, the immediate comment after it has been told in full, and the final long comments that follow. All these confirm the same issues given at the beginning and at the end.

I

A Favourite Child Is Lost

Yūsuf (Joseph)

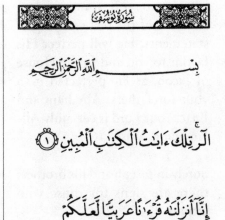

In the Name of God, the Merciful, the Beneficent

Alif. Lām. Rā. These are the verses of the Book that clearly shows [the truth]. (1)

We have revealed it as a discourse in Arabic so that you may understand. (2)

In revealing this Qur'ān We relate to you the best of narratives. Before it you were among those who are unaware [of revelation]. (3)

Joseph said to his father: 'Father, I saw in a dream eleven stars, as well as the sun and the moon; I saw them prostrate themselves before me.' (4)

35

'My son,' he replied, 'do not relate your dream to your brothers, lest they plot some evil against you. Satan is indeed man's open enemy. (5)

قَالَ يَٰبُنَىَّ لَا تَقْصُصْ رُؤْيَاكَ عَلَىٰ إِخْوَتِكَ فَيَكِيدُواْ لَكَ كَيْدًا إِنَّ ٱلشَّيْطَٰنَ لِلْإِنسَٰنِ عَدُوٌّ مُّبِينٌ ۝

Even thus will your Lord make you His chosen one, and will impart to you some understanding of the real meaning of statements. He will perfect His favour to you and to the House of Jacob, as He perfected it to your forefathers, Abraham and Isaac. Your Lord is certainly All-Knowing, Wise.' (6)

وَكَذَٰلِكَ يَجْتَبِيكَ رَبُّكَ وَيُعَلِّمُكَ مِن تَأْوِيلِ ٱلْأَحَادِيثِ وَيُتِمُّ نِعْمَتَهُ عَلَيْكَ وَعَلَىٰٓ ءَالِ يَعْقُوبَ كَمَآ أَتَمَّهَا عَلَىٰٓ أَبَوَيْكَ مِن قَبْلُ إِبْرَٰهِيمَ وَإِسْحَٰقَ إِنَّ رَبَّكَ عَلِيمٌ حَكِيمٌ ۝

Surely in Joseph and his brothers there are signs for those who inquire. (7)

لَّقَدْ كَانَ فِى يُوسُفَ وَإِخْوَتِهِ ءَايَٰتٌ لِّلسَّآئِلِينَ ۝

They said [to one another]: 'Truly, Joseph and his brother are dearer to our father than we, even though we are many. Surely our father is in manifest error. (8)

إِذْ قَالُواْ لَيُوسُفُ وَأَخُوهُ أَحَبُّ إِلَىٰٓ أَبِينَا مِنَّا وَنَحْنُ عُصْبَةٌ إِنَّ أَبَانَا لَفِى ضَلَٰلٍ مُّبِينٍ ۝

Kill Joseph, or cast him away in some faraway land, so that you have your father's attention turned to you alone. After that you will [repent and] be righteous people.' (9)

ٱقْتُلُواْ يُوسُفَ أَوِ ٱطْرَحُوهُ أَرْضًا يَخْلُ لَكُمْ وَجْهُ أَبِيكُمْ وَتَكُونُواْ مِنۢ بَعْدِهِ قَوْمًا صَٰلِحِينَ ۝

One of them said: 'Do not kill Joseph, but rather – if you must do something – cast him into the dark depths of this well. Some caravan may pick him up.' (10)

قَالَ قَآئِلٌ مِّنْهُمْ لَا تَقْتُلُواْ يُوسُفَ وَأَلْقُوهُ فِي غَيَبَتِ ٱلْجُبِّ يَلْتَقِطْهُ بَعْضُ ٱلسَّيَّارَةِ إِن كُنتُمْ فَٰعِلِينَ ۝

[Thereupon] they said [to their father]: 'Father, why do you not trust us with Joseph, when we are indeed his well-wishers? (11)

قَالُواْ يَٰٓأَبَانَا مَا لَكَ لَا تَأْمَنَّا عَلَىٰ يُوسُفَ وَإِنَّا لَهُۥ لَنَٰصِحُونَ ۝

Send him with us tomorrow, that he may enjoy himself and play. We will certainly take good care of him.' (12)

أَرْسِلْهُ مَعَنَا غَدًا يَرْتَعْ وَيَلْعَبْ وَإِنَّا لَهُۥ لَحَٰفِظُونَ ۝

He answered: 'It certainly grieves me that you should take him with you; and I dread that the wolf may eat him when you are heedless of him.' (13)

قَالَ إِنِّى لَيَحْزُنُنِىٓ أَن تَذْهَبُواْ بِهِۦ وَأَخَافُ أَن يَأْكُلَهُ ٱلذِّئْبُ وَأَنتُمْ عَنْهُ غَٰفِلُونَ ۝

They said: 'If the wolf were to eat him when we are so many, then we should surely be lost.' (14)

قَالُواْ لَئِنْ أَكَلَهُ ٱلذِّئْبُ وَنَحْنُ عُصْبَةٌ إِنَّآ إِذًا لَّخَٰسِرُونَ ۝

And when they went away with him, they resolved to cast him into the depth of the well. We revealed [this] to him: 'You will tell them of this their deed at a time when they shall not know you.' (15)

فَلَمَّا ذَهَبُواْ بِهِۦ وَأَجْمَعُوٓاْ أَن يَجْعَلُوهُ فِي غَيَٰبَتِ ٱلْجُبِّ وَأَوْحَيْنَآ إِلَيْهِ لَتُنَبِّئَنَّهُم بِأَمْرِهِمْ هَٰذَا وَهُمْ لَا يَشْعُرُونَ ۝

At nightfall they came to their father weeping, (16)

وَجَآءُوٓ أَبَاهُمۡ عِشَآءٗ يَبۡكُونَ ١٦

and said: 'Father, we went off racing and left Joseph behind with our belongings, and the wolf devoured him. But you will not believe us even though we are saying the truth.' (17)

قَالُواْ يَـٰٓأَبَانَآ إِنَّا ذَهَبۡنَا نَسۡتَبِقُ وَتَرَكۡنَا يُوسُفَ عِندَ مَتَـٰعِنَا فَأَكَلَهُ ٱلذِّئۡبُۖ وَمَآ أَنتَ بِمُؤۡمِنٖ لَّنَا وَلَوۡ كُنَّا صَـٰدِقِينَ ١٧

And they produced his shirt stained with false blood. He said: 'No, but your minds have tempted you to evil. Sweet patience! It is to God alone that I turn for support in this misfortune that you have described.' (18)

وَجَآءُو عَلَىٰ قَمِيصِهِۦ بِدَمٖ كَذِبٖۚ قَالَ بَلۡ سَوَّلَتۡ لَكُمۡ أَنفُسُكُمۡ أَمۡرٗاۖ فَصَبۡرٞ جَمِيلٞۖ وَٱللَّهُ ٱلۡمُسۡتَعَانُ عَلَىٰ مَا تَصِفُونَ ١٨

And there came a caravan; and they sent their water-drawer, and he let down his bucket into the well – [and when he saw Joseph] he cried: 'What good luck. Here is a boy!' They concealed him with a view to selling him; but God had full knowledge of what they were doing. (19)

وَجَآءَتۡ سَيَّارَةٞ فَأَرۡسَلُواْ وَارِدَهُمۡ فَأَدۡلَىٰ دَلۡوَهُۥۖ قَالَ يَـٰبُشۡرَىٰ هَـٰذَا غُلَـٰمٞۚ وَأَسَرُّوهُ بِضَـٰعَةٗۚ وَٱللَّهُ عَلِيمُۢ بِمَا يَعۡمَلُونَ ١٩

And they sold him for a paltry price, a few silver coins. Thus low did they value him. (20)

وَشَرَوۡهُ بِثَمَنِۢ بَخۡسٖ دَرَٰهِمَ مَعۡدُودَةٖ وَكَانُواْ فِيهِ مِنَ ٱلزَّـٰهِدِينَ ٢٠

The Opening of an Excellent Narrative

This passage serves as an introduction to the *sūrah* and relates the first episode of the story, comprising six scenes. It begins with Joseph's dream and recounts the details of his brothers' conspiracy against him, until he arrives in Egypt.

> Alif. Lām. Rā. *These are the verses of the Book that clearly shows [the truth]. We have revealed it as a discourse in Arabic so that you may understand. In revealing this Qur'ān We relate to you the best of narratives. Before it you were among those who are unaware [of revelation].* (Verses 1–3)

This is yet another *sūrah* which begins with three separate letters, '*Alif. Lām. Rā.*' These and similar letters of the alphabet, which are well known to people and always used by them, are the same that spell out the revealed verses the composition of which is well beyond human ability. They make up the book that shows the truth clearly, i.e. the Qur'ān. God has revealed it in the Arabic tongue which uses these well-known letters, '*so that you may understand.*' (Verse 2) You will realize that the One who makes out of ordinary words a book of surpassing excellence like the Qur'ān cannot be a human being. Hence, it stands to reason that the Qur'ān must be revelation. Human intellect is thus called upon to reflect on this fact and its inevitable implications.

Since a very large part of this *sūrah* is a story, the narrative aspect of this book has been singled out for special mention: '*In revealing this Qur'ān We relate to you the best of narratives.*' (Verse 3) This narrative is part of the Qur'ān We have revealed to you, and it is an excellent story. What were you prior to receiving divine revelations? '*Before it you were among those who are unaware [of revelation].*' (Verse 3) You were an unlettered person like the majority of your people who do not even reflect on such subjects as the Qur'ān discusses.

This is merely an introduction to the story. The curtains are then lifted to reveal the first scene of the first episode. We see Joseph, a young boy, relating his dream to his father: "*Joseph said to his father: 'Father, I saw in a dream eleven stars, as well as the sun and the moon; I saw them prostrate themselves before me.' 'My son,' he replied, 'do not relate your dream to your brothers, lest they plot some evil against you.*

39

Satan is indeed man's open enemy. Even thus will your Lord make you His chosen one, and will impart to you some understanding of the real meaning of statements. He will perfect His favour to you and to the House of Jacob, as He perfected it to your forefathers, Abraham and Isaac. Your Lord is certainly All-Knowing, Wise.' (Verses 4–6)

Joseph was a young boy, but the vision he related to his father was not of the type which boys and young people normally see in their dreams. The most that a boy like him would experience in a dream would be to see those stars and the sun and moon on his lap or close by, with him reaching out his hands to touch them. But Joseph saw them prostrating themselves to him, which means that they took the shape of intelligent creatures who bowed in respect to someone of superior status. The *sūrah* recounts very clearly what he said to his father: *"Joseph said to his father: 'Father, I saw in a dream eleven stars, as well as the sun and the moon.'"* (Verse 4) Then the verb 'saw' is repeated again for greater effect: *"I saw them prostrate themselves before me."* (Verse 4)

Endowed with wisdom and great insight, his father, Jacob, realizes that the dream is a pointer to something great that would happen to his young son. Neither he nor the *sūrah* spells it out at this stage. In fact its early indications begin to appear in the third episode, but it is not revealed completely until the end of the story when everything is made clear. He advises him not to relate his vision to his brothers, lest they should get an inkling of what it indicates for their young half brother. For that could open the way to Satan who would try to arouse their jealousy and instigate some evil scheming against him: *"'My son,' he replied, 'do not relate your dream to your brothers, lest they plot some evil against you.'"* (Verse 5) He then provides the grounds for his fear: *'Satan is indeed man's open enemy.'* (Verse 5) He plays off one person against another, trying to make evil appear pleasant.

Jacob, Isaac's son and Abraham's grandson, feels that his young son will have some distinguished role to play, and he hopes that this will be in the realm of religion and divine guidance. He is right to do so as he himself is a prophet and he knows that his grandfather, Abraham, received God's blessings which were also bestowed on the believers in his household. He thus expects that Joseph may be the one whom God will choose from among his children to receive His blessings and continue the blessed chain among Abraham's descendants: "*Even thus will your Lord make you His chosen one, and will impart to you some understanding of the real meaning of statements. He will perfect His favour to you and to the House of Jacob, as He perfected it to your forefathers, Abraham and Isaac. Your Lord is certainly All-Knowing, Wise.*' (Verse 6)

It is only natural that Jacob should feel that Joseph's dream indicates that he may be God's choice to receive His perfect blessings, just as these were bestowed on his forefathers, Abraham and Isaac. What captures our attention here is his statement: "*And [He] will impart to you some understanding of the real meaning of statements.*" (Verse 6) The Arabic word, *ta'wīl*, rendered here as 'understanding' means literally 'knowledge of the outcome.' So, to what does the word 'statements' refer? Does Jacob mean that God will choose Joseph, teach and provide him with penetrating insight so that he knows the outcome of a statement or an event by knowing its beginning? For that is an inspiration God grants to those who have true knowledge. The comment at the end of this verse is most appropriate: "*Your Lord is certainly All-Knowing, Wise.*" (Verse 6) Or does Jacob merely refer here to dreams and visions, as actually happened to Joseph? Both are possible and both fit in well with the general atmosphere in the lives of Joseph and his father Jacob.

Interpretation of Dreams

Here we need to refer to dreams and visions which are part of the subject matter of this *sūrah*.

We must inevitably believe that some dreams prophesy something that will happen in the near or distant future. Two reasons may be identified here: the first is that Joseph's, his two fellow prisoners' and the King of Egypt's dreams all came true. Secondly, in our own lives we find that some dreams come true and this is frequent enough to make it impossible to deny the relationship.

So what is the nature of dreams then? The school of analytical psychology considers them as the subconscious expression of suppressed desires. This accounts for some dreams, but not all of them. Freud himself, despite his grossly unscientific and arbitrary approach, acknowledges that there are prophetic dreams. So what is the nature of this type of dream?

First of all we have to say that whether we know their nature or not does not affect the fact that there are such dreams and that some of them are true. We are here only trying to understand certain aspects of man's nature, and some of the laws God has set in operation in the universe.

Our concept of these dreams is as follows: time and place constitute barriers which prevent man from seeing what we call the past, the future or the whole of the present. The past and future are screened by a time factor, while the present that is not in our immediate vicinity is screened by a place factor. A sense which we do not know about in man's make-up may at times become alert or may at times have extra strength and go beyond the time factor to see vaguely what lies beyond it. This is not true knowledge, but rather a form of discerning, similar to what happens to some people while awake and to others while asleep, when they are able to go beyond the barriers of either time or place, or indeed both. We do not in fact know anything about the true nature of time, nor is the nature of place or matter known to us fully: "*You have been given but scanty knowledge.*" (17: 85) Anyway, Joseph has seen his dream, and we will consider its interpretation later.

The First Thread in a Sinister Plot

Next, we find ourselves looking at Joseph's brothers discussing some sort of plot. This begins with a clear indication that what follows is particularly important.

"*Surely in Joseph and his brothers there are signs for those who inquire.*" (Verse 7) Anyone who looks for signs, indications and clues will find plenty in the story of Joseph and his brothers. This opening is sufficient to alert our attention and interest. Hence, it is similar to the raising of the curtains to allow events to take place.

Did Joseph tell his dream to his brothers as mentioned in the Old Testament? The sequence of the narrative here implies that he did not. They speak of their father's favouritism of Joseph and his full brother. Had they known of his dream, they would have mentioned it, because it would have been an added reason for their grudge against him. What Jacob feared would happen, should Joseph relate his dream to his brothers, did eventually happen but for different reasons, namely because of Joseph being his favourite. It had to happen anyway, because it was simply an episode in the great line of events which led Joseph to his appointed destination. All his life circumstances, his family position, and the fact that he was born to an elderly father led to his position of special favour. The youngest children, as Joseph and his brother were, are normally the dearest, particularly when the father is elderly.

"*They said [to one another]: 'Truly, Joseph and his brother are dearer to our father than we, even though we are many.'*" (Verse 8) As a group we are able to protect our family and ensure its position. "*Surely our father is in manifest error.*" (Verse 8) He bestows his greatest love and favours on two young children, ignoring what we accomplish.

Their rage at this situation soon reaches its flash point, and they are no longer able to evaluate matters properly. Unimportant factors are seen by them to be of great significance, while important ones are given little attention. Sons of a prophet as they are – although they themselves are not prophets – they think lightly of murder, even when the victim is their own little, defenceless brother. That their father appears to love him more than he loves them is blown out of all proportion so that it seems equal to murder, the greatest crime on earth after that of associating partners with God. "*Kill Joseph, or cast him away in some faraway land.*" (Verse 9) The two alternatives are not dissimilar in their effect. To cast a little child off in a faraway land where he has no one to look after him will most probably lead to his death. And why do they want to do this? "*So that you have your father's attention turned to you alone.*" (Verse 9) Joseph would no longer be his preoccupation. It is as if they feel that when their father no longer sees Joseph his mind and heart will be free and his love and attention will be turned to them. But what about the crime itself? It is only an offence and repentance is sure to erase it. They would then be able to wipe away its consequences. "*After that you will [repent and] be righteous people.*" (Verse 9)

Thus Satan weaves his schemes, making people accept what is unacceptable, when they have lost control and no longer see matters in the proper perspective. When their jealousy reaches boiling point, Satan puts forward his suggestion: "*Kill.*" He wraps his wicked suggestion around an appealing prospect, viz., that repentance will mend the offence. But repentance is not like that. Repentance is remorse and regret for an error which someone commits blindly, when he does not remember God and the consequences of his offence. Repentance is never of the ready rehearsed type prepared before the crime to reduce the sense of guilt. This does not constitute repentance. It is part of the justification of the crime, to make it appear less heinous.

One of the brothers, however, felt a shudder at the atrocity they were contemplating. He put forward a suggestion which would rid them of Joseph without killing him or abandoning him in the middle of nowhere. Thus they would have all their father's attention. He proposed that they should cast him into a well on the caravan route. It was very likely that a caravan would find him and take him to a faraway land. "*One of them said: 'Do not kill Joseph, but rather – if you must do something – cast him into the dark depths of this well. Some caravan may pick him up.'*" (Verse 10) The phrase, '*if you must do something,*' gives the impression of doubt, as if he is raising doubt in their minds about harming Joseph. This expression of reservation aims to weaken the resolve of the other party. But Joseph's brothers bore a deep grudge and they had to do something about their situation. They had no intention of going back on what they had decided. This is clearly apparent in the next scene.

Deceiving an Elderly Father

Now we see them with their father trying to persuade him to let them take Joseph with them the following day. They are intent on deceiving their father and carrying out their wicked scheme against Joseph. "*[Thereupon] they said [to their father]: 'Father, why do you not trust us with Joseph, when we are indeed his well-wishers. Send him with us tomorrow, that he may enjoy himself and play. We will certainly take good care of him.' He answered: 'It certainly grieves me that you should take him with you; and I dread that the wolf may eat him when you are heedless of him.' They said: 'If the wolf were to eat him when we are so many, then we should surely be lost.'*" (Verses 11–14) Here we see through fine words and expressions how much effort they exerted in trying to win over their father's heart.

As they begin, they address him by virtue of their relationship, "*Father!*" Then they follow this with a question that suggests tacit remonstration: "*Why do you not trust us with Joseph?*" (Verse 11) This invites Jacob's denial, so that he admits what is opposite and allows Joseph to go with them. Jacob had thus far prevented Joseph from going with his brothers to the pasture land and open areas they frequented because he loved him so dearly and feared that at his young age he might not withstand the tiring journey and the hard weather. It was not because he suspected any foul play. Hence, by suggesting that their father did not trust them, the brothers sought his denial of the same. In this way, his resolve to keep Joseph at home was weakened. It was a foul trick with a foul aim in mind.

"*Father, why do you not trust us with Joseph, when we are indeed his well-wishers?*" (Verse 11) They are emphasizing here that their hearts are full of good intentions towards their brother. However, a schemer often betrays himself. The stress they placed on wishing their brother well almost betrayed the ill feelings they harboured against him. "*Send him with us tomorrow, that he may enjoy himself and play. We will certainly take good care of him.*" (Verse 12) Once again they emphasized their awareness of their responsibility to guard and protect Joseph. They also painted a pleasant picture of what awaited Joseph of play and pleasure to persuade their father to send him with them.

In reply to their remonstrations, Jacob indirectly denied that he did not trust them with their brother. He justified keeping Joseph with him by saying that he would miss him even if he were absent for a day or so, and he would worry about Joseph being attacked by wolves: "*He answered: 'It certainly grieves me that you should take him with you; and I dread that the wolf may eat him when you are heedless of him.'*" (Verse 13) In effect, he said he always wanted Joseph beside him. This must have intensified the brothers' grudge even further. How could it be that their father missed him even when he went out to play for a few hours!

"*I dread that the wolf may eat him when you are heedless of him.*" (Verse 13) They must have found in his words the excuse they were looking for, for they immediately reassure Jacob that they will take good care of Joseph. "*They said: 'If the wolf were to eat him when we are so many, then we should surely be lost.'*" (Verse 14) If a wolf should beat us when we are so many and so strong, then we are good for nothing. We lose everything.

Thus the protective father gives way to the strong persuasion and impassioned assurances of his sons. It was against his better judgement that he should let them take Joseph, but he was clearly embarrassed. Thus, God's will came to pass and the events of the story unfolded.

Fast-Changing Fortunes

Then we see them on their way, Joseph with them, and they intent on putting their wicked plot into effect. God Almighty inspires the young boy, reassuring him that it is only a trial that is certain to come to an end. He will survive and he will remind his brothers of their plot against him on a day when they will not know him to be Joseph. "*And when they went away with him, they resolved to cast him into the depths of the well. We revealed [this] to him: 'You will tell them of this their deed at a time when they shall not know you.'*" (Verse 15)

Their resolve, then, was to cast him into the dark depths of a well to remove him altogether from their family life. At this point when Joseph fears for his life, when there's no one to help him and ten adult and powerful brothers against him, a mere young child, reassurance comes to him through inspiration that he will be saved and will live until such a time as he reminds them of their crime. At that point in the future, they will not know that he is their brother whom they had thrown into the well.

We leave Joseph now to face his ordeal, undoubtedly reassured by God's inspiration, to look at his brothers facing their saddened father after committing their crime: "*At nightfall they came to their father weeping, and said: 'Father, we went off racing and left Joseph behind with our belongings, and the wolf devoured him. But you will not believe us even though we are saying the truth.' And they produced his shirt stained with false blood. He said: 'No, but your minds have tempted you to evil. Sweet patience! It is to God alone that I turn for support in this misfortune that you have described.'*" (Verses 16–18)

46

Their blindness meant their plot was imperfect. Had they taken a calmer approach, they would not have harmed Joseph the first time their father permitted them to take him with them. But they were impatient, fearing that they might not have another chance. We also see an aspect of their impatience in their choice of excuse, accusing the wolf. Their father warned them against this possibility only the night before, and they made the whole episode sound outrageous. It was just not plausible that they abandoned Joseph to the risk their father specifically warned them against. The same impatience is seen in the way they stained Joseph's shirt with blood, without bothering to make it look real. The action was hasty, betraying their lies, so much so that the blood itself is described as lies, or false.

They did all this and then *"At nightfall they came to their father weeping, and said: 'Father, we went off racing and left Joseph behind with our belongings, and the wolf devoured him.'"* (Verses 16–17) As they said this, they seemed to realize it was all too thin. A liar often betrays himself. Hence they followed their false statement with this remark: *"But you will not believe us even though we are saying the truth."* (Verse 17) You have your doubts and you do not trust us, so you will not believe us even when we say the truth.

With such strong indications, and with something in his heart telling him otherwise, Jacob felt that Joseph had not been eaten by a wolf, and that his brothers had ditched him somewhere. He realized that their story was concocted and what they described was plainly false. He faced them with this, saying that their minds had made something ghastly appear acceptable to them and urged them to commit it. He declared that he would be patient under this adversity. He would neither panic nor complain. He would seek only God's support against their fabricated lies: *"He said: 'No, but your minds have tempted you to evil. Sweet patience! It is to God alone that I turn for support in this misfortune that you have described.'"* (Verse 18)

Now we quickly return to Joseph in the well to see the last scene of this first episode: *"And there came a caravan; and they sent their water-drawer, and he let down his bucket into the well – [and when he saw Joseph] he cried: 'What good luck. Here is a boy!' They concealed him with a view to selling him; but God had full knowledge of what they*

47

were doing. And they sold him for a paltry price, a few silver coins. Thus low did they value him." (Verses 19–20)

The well was by the side of the caravan route, and caravans always take water wherever they can find it, whether in wells or in pits where rain water gathers.

"*There came a caravan.*" The term used here to refer to the caravan is *sayyārah*, which derives from long travel. "*They sent their water-drawer*," i.e. the person assigned the task of finding water for the caravan because he is experienced in such a vital matter. He does the normal thing, letting down his bucket into the well, to make sure that it is not dry, or to fill the bucket. The *sūrah* does not mention any details of Joseph's reaction when he saw the bucket being lowered and his quick movement to attach himself to it, so as to keep it a surprise to reader and listener alike.

When the water-drawer sees Joseph, he lets out a cry: "*What good luck. Here is a boy!*" Once again, all that follows is deleted: what was said, what action was taken, and how pleased Joseph was when he was pulled out of the well. Instead, the *sūrah* speaks immediately of his situation with the caravan: "*They concealed him with a view to selling him.*" (Verse 19) This means that they considered him secret merchandise and thereby something they could sell.

They realized that he was not a slave, which accounts for why they hid him. Then, they sold him on the cheap: "*And they sold him for a paltry price, a few silver coins.*" (Verse 20) That was their currency at the time. People only counted coins however when the price was low, and weighed them when the price was high. Here the *sūrah* speaks of counting the coins to indicate how cheaply they sold him.

"*Thus low did they value him.*" (Verse 20) They wanted rid of him quickly so that they did not have to account for enslaving and selling a free child.

Thus the first trial in the life of this noble prophet is over.

2

Facing Up to Trial

The man from Egypt who bought him said to his wife: 'Be kind to him. He may well be of use to us, or we may adopt him as our son.' Thus We established Joseph in the land, and We imparted to him some understanding of the real meaning of statements. God always prevails in whatever be His purpose; though most people may not know it. (21)

وَقَالَ ٱلَّذِى ٱشْتَرَىٰهُ مِن مِّصْرَ لِٱمْرَأَتِهِ أَكْرِمِى مَثْوَىٰهُ عَسَىٰ أَن يَنفَعَنَآ أَوْ نَتَّخِذَهُۥ وَلَدًا وَكَذَٰلِكَ مَكَّنَّا لِيُوسُفَ فِى ٱلْأَرْضِ وَلِنُعَلِّمَهُۥ مِن تَأْوِيلِ ٱلْأَحَادِيثِ وَٱللَّهُ غَالِبٌ عَلَىٰٓ أَمْرِهِۦ وَلَٰكِنَّ أَكْثَرَ ٱلنَّاسِ لَا يَعْلَمُونَ ٢١

And when he attained his full manhood, We bestowed on him wisdom and knowledge. Thus do We reward those who do good. (22)

وَلَمَّا بَلَغَ أَشُدَّهُۥٓ ءَاتَيْنَٰهُ حُكْمًا وَعِلْمًا وَكَذَٰلِكَ نَجْزِى ٱلْمُحْسِنِينَ ٢٢

She in whose house he was living tried to seduce him. She bolted the doors and said, 'Come.' He said: 'God protect me. Goodly has my master made my stay here. Those who do wrong come to no good.' (23)

وَرَٰوَدَتْهُ ٱلَّتِى هُوَ فِى بَيْتِهَا عَن نَّفْسِهِۦ وَغَلَّقَتِ ٱلْأَبْوَٰبَ وَقَالَتْ هَيْتَ لَكَ قَالَ مَعَاذَ ٱللَّهِ إِنَّهُۥ رَبِّىٓ أَحْسَنَ مَثْوَاىَ إِنَّهُۥ لَا يُفْلِحُ ٱلظَّٰلِمُونَ ٢٣

49

She truly desired him, and he desired her. [He would have succumbed] had he not seen a clear sign from his Lord. Thus We averted from him evil and indecency. He was truly one of Our faithful servants. (24)

وَلَقَدْ هَمَّتْ بِهِ ۖ وَهَمَّ بِهَا لَوْلَا أَن رَّءَا بُرْهَانَ رَبِّهِ ۚ كَذَٰلِكَ لِنَصْرِفَ عَنْهُ ٱلسُّوٓءَ وَٱلْفَحْشَآءَ ۚ إِنَّهُۥ مِنْ عِبَادِنَا ٱلْمُخْلَصِينَ ﴿٢٤﴾

And they both rushed to the door. She tore his shirt from behind. And at the door they met her husband. She said: 'What ought to be the punishment of someone who had evil designs on your wife other than that he should be thrown in prison or some grievous punishment.' (25)

وَٱسْتَبَقَا ٱلْبَابَ وَقَدَّتْ قَمِيصَهُۥ مِن دُبُرٍ وَأَلْفَيَا سَيِّدَهَا لَدَا ٱلْبَابِ ۚ قَالَتْ مَا جَزَآءُ مَنْ أَرَادَ بِأَهْلِكَ سُوٓءًا إِلَّآ أَن يُسْجَنَ أَوْ عَذَابٌ أَلِيمٌ ﴿٢٥﴾

[Joseph] said: 'It was she who sought to seduce me.' One of her own household testified: 'If his shirt has been torn from the front, then she is speaking the truth and he is lying. (26)

قَالَ هِيَ رَٰوَدَتْنِي عَن نَّفْسِي ۚ وَشَهِدَ شَاهِدٌ مِّنْ أَهْلِهَآ إِن كَانَ قَمِيصُهُۥ قُدَّ مِن قُبُلٍ فَصَدَقَتْ وَهُوَ مِنَ ٱلْكَٰذِبِينَ ﴿٢٦﴾

But if it has been torn from behind, then she is lying, and he is speaking the truth.' (27)

وَإِن كَانَ قَمِيصُهُۥ قُدَّ مِن دُبُرٍ فَكَذَبَتْ وَهُوَ مِنَ ٱلصَّٰدِقِينَ ﴿٢٧﴾

When [her husband] saw that Joseph's shirt was torn from behind, he said to her: 'This is indeed [an instance] of the guile of you, women. Your guile is awesome indeed!' (28)

فَلَمَّا رَءَا قَمِيصَهُۥ قُدَّ مِن دُبُرٍ قَالَ إِنَّهُۥ مِن كَيْدِكُنَّ ۖ إِنَّ كَيْدَكُنَّ عَظِيمٌ ﴿٢٨﴾

50

'Joseph, let this pass! And you, woman, ask forgiveness for your sin. You have been seriously at fault.' (29)

يُوسُفُ أَعۡرِضۡ عَنۡ هَٰذَا وَٱسۡتَغۡفِرِى لِذَنۢبِكِ إِنَّكِ كُنتِ مِنَ ٱلۡخَاطِـِٔينَ ٢٩

In the city, women were saying: 'The Chief Minister's wife is trying to seduce her slave lad, as she is passionately in love with him. We see that she is clearly going astray.' (30)

وَقَالَ نِسۡوَةٌ فِى ٱلۡمَدِينَةِ ٱمۡرَأَتُ ٱلۡعَزِيزِ تُرَٰوِدُ فَتَىٰهَا عَن نَّفۡسِهِۦ قَدۡ شَغَفَهَا حُبًّا إِنَّا لَنَرَىٰهَا فِى ضَلَٰلٍ مُّبِينٍ ٣٠

When she heard of their malicious talk, she sent for them, and prepared for them a sumptuous repast, and handed each one of them a knife and said [to Joseph]: 'Come out and present yourself to them.' When they saw him, they were amazed at him, and they cut their hands, exclaiming: 'God preserve us! This is no mortal man! This is none other than a noble angel.' (31)

فَلَمَّا سَمِعَتۡ بِمَكۡرِهِنَّ أَرۡسَلَتۡ إِلَيۡهِنَّ وَأَعۡتَدَتۡ لَهُنَّ مُتَّكَـًٔا وَءَاتَتۡ كُلَّ وَٰحِدَةٍ مِّنۡهُنَّ سِكِّينًا وَقَالَتِ ٱخۡرُجۡ عَلَيۡهِنَّ فَلَمَّا رَأَيۡنَهُۥ أَكۡبَرۡنَهُۥ وَقَطَّعۡنَ أَيۡدِيَهُنَّ وَقُلۡنَ حَٰشَ لِلَّهِ مَا هَٰذَا بَشَرًا إِنۡ هَٰذَآ إِلَّا مَلَكٌ كَرِيمٌ ٣١

Said she: 'This is he on whose account you have been blaming me! Indeed I have tried to seduce him, but he guarded his chastity. Now, however, if he does not do what I bid him, he shall certainly be thrown in prison, and shall indeed be humiliated.' (32)

قَالَتۡ فَذَٰلِكُنَّ ٱلَّذِى لُمۡتُنَّنِى فِيهِ وَلَقَدۡ رَٰوَدتُّهُۥ عَن نَّفۡسِهِۦ فَٱسۡتَعۡصَمَ وَلَئِن لَّمۡ يَفۡعَلۡ مَآ ءَامُرُهُۥ لَيُسۡجَنَنَّ وَلَيَكُونًا مِّنَ ٱلصَّٰغِرِينَ ٣٢

[Joseph] said: 'My Lord, I would sooner be put in prison than comply with what they are inviting me to do. Unless You turn away their guile from me, I may yield to them and lapse into folly.' (33)

قَالَ رَبِّ ٱلسِّجْنُ أَحَبُّ إِلَيَّ مِمَّا يَدْعُونَنِي إِلَيْهِ وَإِلَّا تَصْرِفْ عَنِّي كَيْدَهُنَّ أَصْبُ إِلَيْهِنَّ وَأَكُن مِّنَ ٱلْجَٰهِلِينَ ۝

His Lord answered his prayer and warded off their guile from him. It is He alone who hears all and knows all. (34)

فَٱسْتَجَابَ لَهُۥ رَبُّهُۥ فَصَرَفَ عَنْهُ كَيْدَهُنَّ إِنَّهُۥ هُوَ ٱلسَّمِيعُ ٱلْعَلِيمُ ۝

Overview

This passage relates the second episode of Joseph's story, after he had reached Egypt where he was sold as a slave. However, the man who bought him felt that the boy was a good person. Such feelings may be sensed from a person's looks, particularly if they are coupled with good manners. Hence the man recommends his wife to take good care of the boy. Here begins the first thread in how his dream comes true.

But another trial of a totally different type was awaiting Joseph when he reached his prime. Prior to this, he would have been given wisdom and knowledge which would help him confront the forthcoming trial, one which only those on whom God bestows His grace can stand up to and resist. It was a trial of seduction in palaces where the aristocratic environment is often characterized by loose morality. Joseph emerged unscathed from it in his moral and religious values.

Settling in Egypt

The man from Egypt who bought him said to his wife: 'Be kind to him. He may well be of use to us, or we may adopt him as our son.'

Thus We established Joseph in the land, and We imparted to him some understanding of the real meaning of statements. God always prevails in whatever be His purpose; though most people may not know it. (Verse 21)

The *sūrah* does not as yet reveal the identity of the person who bought him. After a long time we learn that he is a person in a very high position, perhaps Egypt's chief minister. But for now we only know that Joseph has reached a safe place, and that his first trial is over, and that bright prospects await him.

"*Be kind to him.*" (Verse 21) This is how most translators of the Qur'ān render the first statement said by the man who bought Joseph. Literally the man says: "Be generous in his place of abode." Although this is meant to be an instruction to treat him kindly, the expression signifies greater kindness to be contrasted with his stay in the well and all the fears that were associated with that experience.

But the man goes further and tells his wife of what he hopes for the boy's future: "*He may well be of use to us, or we may adopt him as our son.*" (Verse 21) Perhaps they did not have any children, as some reports suggest. Hence, the man started thinking that should the boy prove himself to be up to his master's expectations, with regard to intelligence, character and good looks, he might adopt him as his own.

At this point in the narrative, the *sūrah* pauses a little to state that all this was God's arrangement. It was through His design that Joseph was established in the land. This began with him occupying a firm position in the man's heart and in his home. The *sūrah* then says that Joseph would continue along the same road, and that God would give him the faculty to interpret statements properly and accurately. It comments on the early steps in consolidating Joseph's position by saying that God's will shall always be done. Nothing can impede or stop it. He is in full control of everything in the universe. "*Thus We established Joseph in the land, and We imparted to him some understanding of the real meaning of statements. God always prevails in whatever be His purpose.*" (Verse 21)

Here we see Joseph caught between what his brothers wanted to do to him and what God wanted for him. Since God prevails in whatever His purpose may be, His will was done. Joseph's brothers could not

53

achieve their purpose: "*God always prevails in whatever be His purpose, though most people may not know it.*" (Verse 21) Most people do not know that God's law always operates, and that His will is always done.

The *sūrah* goes on to state that what God willed for Joseph came to pass. This is a reference to what the *sūrah* stated: "*We imparted to him some understanding of the real meaning of statements.*" (Verse 21) Furthermore, when Joseph attained adulthood, more was given to him: "*And when he attained his full manhood, We bestowed on him wisdom and knowledge. Thus do We reward those who do good.*" (Verse 22) He was given a good sense to judge matters well, and also knowledge of the meaning of statements or the interpretation of dreams, or what is more general, such as knowledge of life and its different circumstances. The statement here is very general, admitting broad interpretation. That was Joseph's reward for having done well in both belief and behaviour: "*Thus do We reward those who do good.*" (Verse 22)

A Trial of Temptation

At this point Joseph experiences the second trial in his life. It is much more severe and profound than the first one. It comes when he has been given wisdom and knowledge as a gesture of God's grace. Hence, he faces it squarely, and he is saved from it as a reward for doing good. This trial takes the form of temptation, and the *sūrah* paints a very charged picture of the whole encounter, when Joseph was vulnerable to great risks.

> *She in whose house he was living tried to seduce him. She bolted the doors and said, 'Come.' He said: 'God protect me. Goodly has my master made my stay here. Those who do wrong come to no good.' She truly desired him, and he desired her. [He would have succumbed] had he not seen a clear sign from his Lord. Thus We averted from him evil and indecency. He was truly one of Our faithful servants. And they both rushed to the door. She tore his shirt from behind. And at the door they met her husband. She said: 'What ought to be the punishment of someone who had evil designs on your wife other than that he should be thrown in prison or some grievous punishment.' [Joseph] said: 'It was she who sought*

to seduce me.' One of her own household testified: 'If his shirt has been torn from the front, then she is speaking the truth and he is lying. But if it has been torn from behind, then she is lying, and he is speaking the truth.' When [her husband] saw that Joseph's shirt was torn from behind, he said to her: 'This is indeed [an instance] of the guile of you, women. Your guile is awesome indeed!' 'Joseph, let this pass! And you, woman, ask forgiveness for your sin. You have been seriously at fault.' (Verses 23–29)

The *sūrah* does not mention the ages of Joseph and the woman at the time. So let us consider the matter and estimate their respective ages.

Joseph was in early adolescence at the time the caravan picked him up and sold him in Egypt. He must have been around 14, or maybe less, but certainly no more than that. He was at an age when the Arabic term, *ghulām,* may be applied to him. After that he would be described as a youth, then as a man. At that time, the woman was already married, and apparently neither she nor her husband had had any children. This is implied by her husband's words, "*We may adopt him as a son*". (Verse 21) The thought of adoption does not normally occur unless the one who entertains it is childless, and has practically given up hope of having a child. This means that she must have been married for quite a long time, which was sufficient for them to realize that they would not have a child. Moreover, the man who was Egypt's chief minister must have been at least 40 years of age, and she, his wife, around 30.

Furthermore, we expect that at the time of this event, she must have been at least 40, and Joseph probably 25 or near to that. We imagine that this was her age because her behaviour during the event and subsequently shows that she was a woman of intelligence, self-possessed but bold, scheming and infatuated at the same time. Further evidence to support this is found in the words of those women who talked about her, saying: "*The Chief Minister's wife is trying to seduce her slave lad.*" (Verse 30) Although the Arabic word, *fatā,* rendered here as '*slave lad*' stresses the sense of his slavery, it would not have been said unless Joseph's age supported it. This is more likely, weighing up all the evidence in the text.

We have discussed all this in order to arrive at the conclusion that Joseph's trial was not merely about resisting temptation. His real trial was that he spent all his adolescent years in this palace, with this woman who was between 30 and 40 years of age, with all that goes on in palaces and in an environment which may be best described by the husband's attitude when he saw his wife with Joseph. All that he had to say was: "*Joseph, let this pass! And you, woman, ask forgiveness for your sin. You have been seriously at fault.*" (Verse 29)

It is a social environment in which women speak ill of the chief minister's wife, and her reply is to invite them to a sumptuous banquet during which she orders Joseph to walk in front of them. They, in turn, are all infatuated with him, and make their feelings public. She then admits to what she had done: "*Indeed I have tried to seduce him, but he guarded his chastity. Now, however, if he does not do what I bid him, he shall certainly be thrown in prison, and shall indeed be humiliated.*" (Verse 32)

A social environment which allows these attitudes is a special one. It is that of affluent aristocracy. Joseph was a slave lad who spent his adolescent years in such an environment. That is indeed the long trial which he endured. He resisted its influences, temptations, frivolity and wicked designs. His age and that of the woman under whose roof he had lived for such a long period are significant in estimating the pressure he was under, the gravity of his trial and his long resistance. As for this particular incident, it would not have been particularly difficult for Joseph to resist, had it come suddenly, without long preparation. It would have been made easier by the fact that he was the target of temptation, not the seeker. For a man may find a woman who throws herself at him not very appealing.

Let us now examine the text as it describes the situation: "*She in whose house he was living tried to seduce him. She bolted the doors and said, 'Come.'*" (Verse 23) This time it was a bold attempt at seduction, with an open invitation to go the full course. The bolting of the doors only comes at the last moment. The woman was already at the point when desire is at its strongest. Hence, she calls out to him, 'Come'. This bold, crude invitation is never the first one made by a woman. Indeed, it is of the ultimate type which may never be used unless the woman is forced to resort to it. The young man was living in her house and his growth, strength and development were all there for her to see, just as her own femininity was at its optimum. There must, therefore, have been earlier attempts at gentle persuasion before she resorted to this crude and sudden invitation.

"*He said: 'God protect me. Goodly has my master made my stay here. Those who do wrong come to no good.'*" (Verse 23) First he appeals to God to protect him against doing such a grave and sinful act: "*God protect me!*" (Verse 23) He then refers to God's grace when He saved him from the well and placed him in a home where he was secure and treated kindly: "*Goodly has my master made my stay here.*" (Verse 23) He then expounds a clear principle: "*Those who do wrong come to no good.*" (Verse 23) The 'wrong' intended here is the one which she wants him to do, but it represents a trespass over what God has forbidden.

The *sūrah* makes it absolutely clear that Joseph's reply to the open attempt at seduction was a straightforward refusal, coupled with remembrance of the grace God had bestowed on him, as well as remembrance of the limits which no one should violate. There was no initial compliance when she invited him openly after bolting the doors and speaking in crude terms of what she wanted him to do. This last point is given in the *sūrah* in a much milder form which hints at what actually took place. This is what we understand from the unusual Arabic expression which we have rendered here as, '*Come*'.

False Accusation and Irrefutable Testimony

"*She truly desired him, and he desired her. [He would have succumbed] had he not seen a clear sign from his Lord.*" (Verse 24) All commentators on the Qur'ān, past and present alike, have focused their attention on this last incident. Those who have taken their information from Jewish sources mention numerous legendary reports describing Joseph as one driven by insatiable desire, and God unable to restrain him despite all His evidence. He is said to have seen his father's image on the ceiling, biting his finger. Another such report suggests that he saw several plates of calligraphy, with verses of the Qur'ān, [Yes, the Qur'ān!] denouncing such action, but he continues as though he saw nothing. Then God sent the angel Gabriel, telling him to save Joseph. The angel hit him in the chest. There are many such reports, but they are all clearly groundless and manifestly fabricated.

Most commentators on the Qur'ān say that her desire was physical, whilst his was mental. Then he saw the evidence from his Lord, and he was able to resist temptation.

The late scholar, Rashīd Ridā', rejects this view altogether. He says that she desired to hit him because of his dignified resistance when she was the mistress to be obeyed. On the other hand, he desired to repel her, but he preferred to try to escape. However, she caught up with him and tore his shirt from behind. To interpret the verse as her desire to hit him and his desire to repel the aggression however is merely an attempt to draw Joseph away from responding to temptation at that particular moment. This is an arbitrary interpretation which lacks proper support.

Looking at the text here, and reviewing Joseph's situation, given that he had lived for quite some time in the palace, I feel that the Qur'ānic statement, *"She truly desired him, and he desired her. [He would have succumbed] had he not seen a clear sign from his Lord,"* represents the culmination of a long line of temptation on the one hand, and initial resistance on the other. This is a true description of a goodly human soul, resisting temptation, then weakening a little, then turning to God for support and escaping unscathed. The *sūrah* does not dwell for long on these conflicting emotions, because the Qur'ān does not aim to paint that moment into a panoramic scene that is far larger than what is appropriate to the story, or to human life in general. Hence, the *sūrah* mentions Joseph's resistance at the outset and at the end, with a moment of weakness in between. This then gives us a credible and practical picture.

This interpretation of the text is closer to human nature and to the protection God grants prophets. Joseph was only a human being. It is true that he was chosen by God. That is indeed the reason why his weakness was limited to feelings only, and lasted just for a brief moment. When he saw a sign from his Lord shining in his heart and conscience, he resumed his resistance to all temptation.

"Thus We averted from him evil and indecency. He was truly one of Our faithful servants." (Verse 24) When he came to himself, he wanted to rush away while she went after him, excited, out of control: *"And they both rushed to the door."* (Verse 25) As she tried to pull him away from the door, *"she tore his shirt from behind."* (Verse 25) At this

moment, a totally unexpected surprise awaited them: "*And at the door they met her husband.*" (Verse 25) The mature woman who is in control of the situation emerges here. An answer to the question raised by the husband to the very suspicious scene is readily given. An unhesitating accusation of Joseph being the offender is immediately stated. However, she still loves him and does not want him to collect a very severe punishment, so she suggests a safe one:: "*She said: 'What ought to be the punishment of someone who has evil designs on your wife other than that he should be thrown in prison or some grievous punishment?'*" (Verse 25) But Joseph would not accept this false accusation, so he speaks out in reply: "*It was she who sought to seduce me.*" (Verse 26)

The *surah* states here that someone from her household came forward as a witness to put an end to the dispute. "*One of her own household testified: 'If his shirt has been torn from the front, then she is speaking the truth and he is lying. But if it has been torn from behind, then she is lying, and he is speaking the truth.'*" (Verses 26–27) Where and when did this witness give his testimony? Did he arrive with the husband and witness the event? Or was he called in by her husband for consultation as people sometimes call in a respectable person of the wife's family? This may fit well with the practices of the aristocracy which is often devoid of moral values.

Both alternatives are possible. Neither affects the outcome. His view is described as a testimony because it provides a way for establishing the truth, considering that the woman's word is set against Joseph's. Joseph's shirt was to be examined: if it was torn from the front, then she must have torn it as she tried to repel his assault. On the other hand, if his shirt was torn from behind, then he was trying to move away from her as she chased him towards the door. In this case, she would be the one who was lying while he stated the truth. The first possibility is stated first because it would mean that she was right. After all, she was the mistress and he was the slave. It was only proper that this possibility be given prominence.

"*When [her husband] saw that Joseph's shirt was torn from behind,*" he realized, both logically and practically, that it was the woman who tried to seduce the man, and then made her accusations against him. Here we see a picture of the high class in ignorant, or *jāhiliyyah* society. Although this picture was drawn several thousand years ago, it is still applicable today. There is clear complacency when faced with sex scandals, followed by attempts to suppress them. Such suppression is the overriding concern. Hence, the woman's husband merely says to her: *"This is indeed [an instance] of the guile of you, women. Your guile is awesome indeed!' 'Joseph, let this pass! And you, woman, ask forgiveness for your sin. You have been seriously at fault.'"* (Verses 28–29)

That is all he said: it is a matter of awesome feminine guile. It is an altogether too diplomatic approach to something that would make one's blood boil. The aristocratic lady is addressed in a very gentle way, with the question of seduction attributed to the female sex in general, with an overtone even of approval. No woman is offended when she is told, in comment on her action, that women's guile is awesome! Instead, she takes this as recognition of her full female status, able to match others with her guile.

As for Joseph, whose innocence is thus established, he is told to let the matter drop. He should not give it too much attention, and should not talk about it to others. This is the main point, so that appearances are maintained.

On the other hand, the woman who tried to seduce her slave and whose guilt is established through his torn shirt receives some admonition: *"Seek forgiveness for your sin. You have been seriously at fault."* (Verse 29)

The same sort of low morality is found in aristocratic classes and those close to government in all *jāhiliyyah* societies, with little difference in substance.

Thus the curtains are drawn and the whole incident is brought to a close. All this without using the sort of language usually associated with pornographic descriptions.

A Scandal Must be Hushed

The husband did not take any action to separate his wife and his slave. He simply let matters go on as previously, because this is how palaces deal with such affairs. But palaces are walls with ears, and gossip is always rife. For such scandals always provide interesting conversations: *"In the city, women were saying: 'The Chief Minister's wife is trying to seduce her slave lad, as she is passionately in love with him. We see that she is clearly going astray.*" (Verse 30)

This is the sort of thing women say about such matters in all *jāhiliyyah* societies. For the first time we learn who the woman is, and we learn that the man who bought Joseph was Egypt's Chief Minister. This is announced as the scandal becomes public, with her position graphically described: "*The Chief Minister's wife is trying to seduce her slave lad, as she is passionately in love with him.*" (Verse 30) Hers is a consuming love that takes complete hold. Hence the comment: "*We see that she is clearly going astray.*" (Verse 30) She is supposed to be the role model as she is married to a leading personality in government. Yet she is infatuated with the young man her husband had bought. Or perhaps they were merely commenting on the fact that she had become the centre of a scandal. It is not the offence itself that is reproachable, but of being found out doing it. If it remains concealed, no blame is attached.

Again we see something that happens only amongst the higher classes. We are shown a scene of that bold woman's further engineering: "*When she heard of their malicious talk, she sent for them, and prepared for them a sumptuous repast, and handed each one of them a knife and said [to Joseph]: 'Come out and present yourself to them.' When they saw him, they were amazed at him, and they cut their hands, exclaiming: 'God preserve us! This is no mortal man! This is none other than a noble angel.' Said she: 'This is he on whose account you have been blaming me! Indeed I have tried to seduce him, but he guarded his chastity. Now, however, if he does not do what I bid him, he shall certainly be thrown in prison, and shall indeed be humiliated.'*" (Verses 31–32)

She arranged for a banquet in her own palace, which suggests that the women so invited also belonged to the same milieu. It is women in such a class that are invited to a palace banquet. They are the ones who love such gentle appearances. It seems that as they ate, they reclined on cushions and couches, as was the custom in eastern countries. Hence, she prepared this repast, and gave a knife to each one of her guests. This also suggests that material civilization had attained a high standard in Egypt at the time. Luxurious life was at a high standard. The use of knives with a meal several thousand years ago is indicative of the level of luxury that obtained. But as they were engaged with cutting meat or peeling fruit, the hostess surprised her guests with Joseph's appearance. She instructed him to: "*Come out and present yourself to them.*" (Verse 31) So what was their reaction? "*When they saw him, they were amazed at him.*" They were taken by surprise. "*They cut their hands.*" (Verse 31) In their surprise, they cut their hands. They uttered a word that is normally used to express amazement at God's wonderful creation. "*God preserve us! This is no mortal man! This is none other than a noble angel.*" (Verse 31) These words also indicate that there were traces of the divine faith, based on God's oneness, in their community.

At this point she felt that she had scored her point and gained a victory over the women of her class. They could not stop their surprised admiration of Joseph. Victorious as she felt, she saw no need for modesty in front of these other women. Indeed she could boast that he was under her command. If he resisted her at one point, he could not do so forever. Hence, her statement: "*This is he on whose account you have been blaming me.*" (Verse 32) You can see how handsome and manly he is, so much so that you cannot help admiring him: "*Indeed I have tried to seduce him, but he guarded his chastity.*" (Verse 32)

She goes on to press the point that she was his mistress and that he would have to do as he was told. In that society, a woman in her position could afford to be boastful and arrogant. She could declare publicly in front of other women the sexual urge she felt: "*Now, however, if he does not do what I bid him, he shall certainly be thrown in prison, and shall indeed be humiliated.*" (Verse 32)

What a mixture of temptation, persistence and threat. And this is coupled with a new phase of temptation hidden under a mask of warning.

What could Joseph do when he heard this said openly in a social gathering of women who were undoubtedly revealing their beauty and expressing their admiration of him. What was his attitude on hearing his mistress openly declare her intention to carry on attempting to seduce him? He simply turns to his Lord with this appeal: "*My Lord, I would sooner be put in prison than comply with what they are inviting me to do.*" (Verse 33)

We note here that Joseph did not say, 'what *she* is inviting me to do'. They were all part of the seduction attempt, either by word, look or movement. He felt that the only way for him to evade their tricks was to appeal to his Lord. That would be the only way he would not yield to their temptation. Hence, he declares: *"Unless You turn away their guile from me, I may yield to them and lapse into folly."* (Verse 33) This is a declaration by one who knows his own human weakness. He prays for more of God's care and protection, because that is the best way to resist all temptation.

"His Lord answered his prayer and warded off their guile from him. It is He alone who hears all and knows all." (Verse 34) This might have taken the form of making them despair of him ever yielding to their approaches and persuasion, or might have been in the shape of stronger resistance to their temptation.

"It is He alone who hears all and knows all." (Verse 33) He hears their scheming, and Joseph's prayers. He knows the intention behind the scheming and the purpose of the prayer.

Thus Joseph was able to stand firm through this second trial. He had to rely on God's grace and good care to do so, and through this managed to avoid falling into sin. With this, the second episode in Joseph's story is over.

3

From Prison to Palace

Yet for all the evidence they had seen, they felt it right to put him in jail for a time. (35)

ثُمَّ بَدَا لَهُم مِّنْ بَعْدِ مَا رَأَوُا ٱلْآيَـٰتِ لَيَسْجُنُنَّهُ حَتَّىٰ حِينٍ ﴿٣٥﴾

Two young men went to prison with him. One of them said: 'I saw myself [in a dream] pressing wine.' The other said: 'And I saw myself [in a dream] carrying bread on my head, and birds were eating of it.' 'Tell us the meaning of these dreams, for we can see that you are a man of virtue.' (36)

وَدَخَلَ مَعَهُ ٱلسِّجْنَ فَتَيَانِ قَالَ أَحَدُهُمَا إِنِّي أَرَىٰنِي أَعْصِرُ خَمْرًا وَقَالَ ٱلْآخَرُ إِنِّي أَرَىٰنِي أَحْمِلُ فَوْقَ رَأْسِي خُبْزًا تَأْكُلُ ٱلطَّيْرُ مِنْهُ نَبِّئْنَا بِتَأْوِيلِهِ إِنَّا نَرَىٰكَ مِنَ ٱلْمُحْسِنِينَ ﴿٣٦﴾

[Joseph] answered: 'Your food which is provided for you will not have come to you before I have informed you of the real meaning of [your dreams]. That is part of the knowledge which my Lord has imparted to me. I have left the faith of people who do not believe in God, and who deny the truth of the life to come. (37)

قَالَ لَا يَأْتِيكُمَا طَعَامٌ تُرْزَقَانِهِ إِلَّا نَبَّأْتُكُمَا بِتَأْوِيلِهِ قَبْلَ أَن يَأْتِيَكُمَا ذَٰلِكُمَا مِمَّا عَلَّمَنِي رَبِّي إِنِّي تَرَكْتُ مِلَّةَ قَوْمٍ لَّا يُؤْمِنُونَ بِٱللَّهِ وَهُم بِٱلْآخِرَةِ هُمْ كَـٰفِرُونَ ﴿٣٧﴾

65

I follow the faith of my forefathers, Abraham, Isaac and Jacob. It is not for us to associate any partners with God. This is part of God's grace which He has bestowed on us and on all mankind, but most people do not give thanks. (38)

وَٱتَّبَعْتُ مِلَّةَ ءَابَآءِى إِبْرَٰهِيمَ وَإِسْحَٰقَ وَيَعْقُوبَ مَا كَانَ لَنَآ أَن نُّشْرِكَ بِٱللَّهِ مِن شَىْءٍ ذَٰلِكَ مِن فَضْلِ ٱللَّهِ عَلَيْنَا وَعَلَى ٱلنَّاسِ وَلَٰكِنَّ أَكْثَرَ ٱلنَّاسِ لَا يَشْكُرُونَ ﴿٣٨﴾

My two prison companions! Which is better: [to believe] in diverse lords, or to believe in God, the One who holds sway over all that exists? (39)

يَٰصَٰحِبَىِ ٱلسِّجْنِ ءَأَرْبَابٌ مُّتَفَرِّقُونَ خَيْرٌ أَمِ ٱللَّهُ ٱلْوَٰحِدُ ٱلْقَهَّارُ ﴿٣٩﴾

Those you worship instead of Him are nothing but names you and your fathers have invented, and for which God has given no sanction from on high. All judgement rests with God alone. He has ordained that you should worship none but Him. This is the true faith, but most people do not know it. (40)

مَا تَعْبُدُونَ مِن دُونِهِ إِلَّآ أَسْمَآءً سَمَّيْتُمُوهَآ أَنتُمْ وَءَابَآؤُكُم مَّآ أَنزَلَ ٱللَّهُ بِهَا مِن سُلْطَٰنٍ إِنِ ٱلْحُكْمُ إِلَّا لِلَّهِ أَمَرَ أَلَّا تَعْبُدُوٓا۟ إِلَّآ إِيَّاهُ ذَٰلِكَ ٱلدِّينُ ٱلْقَيِّمُ وَلَٰكِنَّ أَكْثَرَ ٱلنَّاسِ لَا يَعْلَمُونَ ﴿٤٠﴾

My two prison companions! One of you will give his lord wine to drink. The other will be crucified, and the birds will eat from his head. The matter on which you have sought to be enlightened has thus been decided.' (41)

يَٰصَٰحِبَىِ ٱلسِّجْنِ أَمَّآ أَحَدُكُمَا فَيَسْقِى رَبَّهُۥ خَمْرًا وَأَمَّا ٱلْآخَرُ فَيُصْلَبُ فَتَأْكُلُ ٱلطَّيْرُ مِن رَّأْسِهِ قُضِىَ ٱلْأَمْرُ ٱلَّذِى فِيهِ تَسْتَفْتِيَانِ ﴿٤١﴾

And [Joseph] said to the one whom he believed would be released: 'Remember me in the presence of your lord.' But Satan caused him to forget to mention Joseph to his lord, and so he remained in prison for several years. (42)

وَقَالَ لِلَّذِى ظَنَّ أَنَّهُۥ نَاجٍ مِّنْهُمَا ٱذْكُرْنِى عِندَ رَبِّكَ فَأَنسَىٰهُ ٱلشَّيْطَـٰنُ ذِكْرَ رَبِّهِۦ فَلَبِثَ فِى ٱلسِّجْنِ بِضْعَ سِنِينَ ﴿٤٢﴾

And the King said: 'I saw [in a dream] seven fat cows being devoured by seven emaciated ones, and seven green ears of wheat next to seven others dry and withered. Tell me the meaning of my vision, my nobles, if you are able to interpret dreams.' (43)

وَقَالَ ٱلْمَلِكُ إِنِّى أَرَىٰ سَبْعَ بَقَرَٰتٍ سِمَانٍ يَأْكُلُهُنَّ سَبْعٌ عِجَافٌ وَسَبْعَ سُنۢبُلَـٰتٍ خُضْرٍ وَأُخَرَ يَابِسَـٰتٍ يَـٰٓأَيُّهَا ٱلْمَلَأُ أَفْتُونِى فِى رُءْيَـٰىَ إِن كُنتُمْ لِلرُّءْيَا تَعْبُرُونَ ﴿٤٣﴾

They replied: 'This is but a medley of dreams, and we have no deep knowledge of the real meaning of dreams.' (44)

قَالُوٓا۟ أَضْغَـٰثُ أَحْلَـٰمٍ وَمَا نَحْنُ بِتَأْوِيلِ ٱلْأَحْلَـٰمِ بِعَـٰلِمِينَ ﴿٤٤﴾

At that point, the man who had been released from prison suddenly remembered [Joseph] after all that time and said: 'I will tell you the real meaning of this dream, so give me leave to go.' (45)

وَقَالَ ٱلَّذِى نَجَا مِنْهُمَا وَٱدَّكَرَ بَعْدَ أُمَّةٍ أَنَا۠ أُنَبِّئُكُم بِتَأْوِيلِهِۦ فَأَرْسِلُونِ ﴿٤٥﴾

'Joseph, man of truth, tell us of the seven fat cows being devoured by seven emaciated ones, and seven green ears of wheat next to seven others dry and withered, so that I may return to the people [of the court], and that they would come to know.' (46)

يُوسُفُ أَيُّهَا الصِّدِّيقُ أَفْتِنَا فِي سَبْعِ بَقَرَاتٍ سِمَانٍ يَأْكُلُهُنَّ سَبْعٌ عِجَافٌ وَسَبْعِ سُنبُلَاتٍ خُضْرٍ وَأُخَرَ يَابِسَاتٍ لَّعَلِّي أَرْجِعُ إِلَى النَّاسِ لَعَلَّهُمْ يَعْلَمُونَ ﴿٤٦﴾

He replied: 'You shall sow for seven consecutive years, but let the grain you harvest remain in its ear, except for the little which you may eat. (47)

قَالَ تَزْرَعُونَ سَبْعَ سِنِينَ دَأَبًا فَمَا حَصَدتُّمْ فَذَرُوهُ فِي سُنبُلِهِ إِلَّا قَلِيلًا مِّمَّا تَأْكُلُونَ ﴿٤٧﴾

Then after that there will come seven hard years which will devour all that you have laid up for them, except a little of what you have kept in store. (48)

ثُمَّ يَأْتِي مِن بَعْدِ ذَلِكَ سَبْعٌ شِدَادٌ يَأْكُلْنَ مَا قَدَّمْتُمْ لَهُنَّ إِلَّا قَلِيلًا مِّمَّا تُحْصِنُونَ ﴿٤٨﴾

Then after that there will come a year of abundant rain, in which the people will be able to press [oil and wine]. (49)

ثُمَّ يَأْتِي مِن بَعْدِ ذَلِكَ عَامٌ فِيهِ يُغَاثُ النَّاسُ وَفِيهِ يَعْصِرُونَ ﴿٤٩﴾

The King said: 'Bring this man before me.' But when the [King's] envoy came to him, Joseph said: 'Go back to your lord and ask him about the women who cut their hands. My Lord has full knowledge of their guile.' (50)

وَقَالَ الْمَلِكُ ائْتُونِي بِهِ فَلَمَّا جَاءَهُ الرَّسُولُ قَالَ ارْجِعْ إِلَى رَبِّكَ فَسْأَلْهُ مَا بَالُ النِّسْوَةِ اللَّاتِي قَطَّعْنَ أَيْدِيَهُنَّ إِنَّ رَبِّي بِكَيْدِهِنَّ عَلِيمٌ ﴿٥٠﴾

The King asked [the women]: 'What was the matter with you when you tried to seduce Joseph?' The women said: 'God save us! We did not perceive the least evil on his part.' The Chief Minister's wife said: 'Now has the truth come to light. It was I who tried to seduce him. He has indeed told the truth. (51)

قَالَ مَا خَطْبُكُنَّ إِذْ رَٰوَدتُّنَّ يُوسُفَ عَن نَّفْسِهِۦ قُلْنَ حَٰشَ لِلَّهِ مَا عَلِمْنَا عَلَيْهِ مِن سُوٓءٍ قَالَتِ ٱمْرَأَتُ ٱلْعَزِيزِ ٱلْـَٰٔنَ حَصْحَصَ ٱلْحَقُّ أَنَا۠ رَٰوَدتُّهُۥ عَن نَّفْسِهِۦ وَإِنَّهُۥ لَمِنَ ٱلصَّٰدِقِينَ ﴿٥١﴾

From this he will know that I did not betray him behind his back, and that God does not bless with His guidance the schemes of those who betray their trust. (52)

ذَٰلِكَ لِيَعْلَمَ أَنِّى لَمْ أَخُنْهُ بِٱلْغَيْبِ وَأَنَّ ٱللَّهَ لَا يَهْدِى كَيْدَ ٱلْخَآئِنِينَ ﴿٥٢﴾

And yet, I am not trying to claim to be free of sin. Indeed man's soul does incite him to evil, except for those upon whom God has bestowed His mercy. My Lord is Much-Forgiving, Merciful.' (53)

وَمَآ أُبَرِّئُ نَفْسِىٓ إِنَّ ٱلنَّفْسَ لَأَمَّارَةٌۢ بِٱلسُّوٓءِ إِلَّا مَا رَحِمَ رَبِّىٓ إِنَّ رَبِّى غَفُورٌ رَّحِيمٌ ﴿٥٣﴾

And the King said: 'Bring him before me. I will choose him for my own.' And when he had spoken to him, the King said: 'You shall henceforth be in a position of high standing with us, invested with all trust.' (54)

وَقَالَ ٱلْمَلِكُ ٱئْتُونِى بِهِۦٓ أَسْتَخْلِصْهُ لِنَفْسِى فَلَمَّا كَلَّمَهُۥ قَالَ إِنَّكَ ٱلْيَوْمَ لَدَيْنَا مَكِينٌ أَمِينٌ ﴿٥٤﴾

Joseph replied: 'Give me charge of the store-houses of the land. I am able to look after them with wisdom.' (55)

قَالَ ٱجْعَلْنِي عَلَىٰ خَزَآئِنِ ٱلْأَرْضِ إِنِّي حَفِيظٌ عَلِيمٌ ﴿٥٥﴾

Thus did We establish Joseph in the land, free to do what he willed. We bestow Our mercy on whom We will, and We never fail to give their reward to those who do good. (56)

وَكَذَٰلِكَ مَكَّنَّا لِيُوسُفَ فِي ٱلْأَرْضِ يَتَبَوَّأُ مِنْهَا حَيْثُ يَشَآءُ نُصِيبُ بِرَحْمَتِنَا مَن نَّشَآءُ وَلَا نُضِيعُ أَجْرَ ٱلْمُحْسِنِينَ ﴿٥٦﴾

But as for those who believe in God and keep away from evil, the reward of the life to come is much better indeed. (57)

وَلَأَجْرُ ٱلْآخِرَةِ خَيْرٌ لِّلَّذِينَ ءَامَنُوا۟ وَكَانُوا۟ يَتَّقُونَ ﴿٥٧﴾

Overview

This third episode of Joseph's story witnesses yet another trial he has to endure. It is the third and final test of hardship in his life. What comes after this is good fortune which also constitutes a test of his perseverance. The present trial sees him thrown in jail after his innocence has been established. When an innocent person is put in prison, he finds it especially difficult, although he can console himself that he has committed no crime.

During Joseph's trial we see an aspect of the grace God bestows on him as He gives him knowledge which enables him to interpret dreams and visions, and gives him the ability to explain forthcoming events on the basis of indications he may see. Then God's grace is further bestowed on him when he is declared innocent in the presence of the King. His abilities are also recognized, giving him the chance to assume high position, coupled with the King's trust and wide powers.

An Innocent Man Goes to Prison

"Yet for all the evidence they had seen, they felt it right to put him in jail for a time." (Verse 35) Such is the type of action taken in palaces. It is the action typical of the aristocracy, despotic regimes and social conditions reflecting a state of ignorance or *jāhiliyyah*. When all the signs point to Joseph's innocence, the decision is taken to put him in prison. What a travesty of justice. The Chief Minister's wife behaves with no sense of shame, throwing a party and inviting women of her class to show them the young man, Joseph. She then declares in public her infatuation with him. They experience the same feelings and so too try to tempt him. Joseph's only recourse in the face of such tantalizing appeals is to turn to his Lord for protection. His mistress declares, shamelessly, before the other women that he will have to do as he is told or else be thrown in prison where he is sure to be humiliated. His choice is prison, and ultimately this is what occurs.

Despite all this, the decision is made to imprison him. Most probably by this time the woman has despaired of him responding to her attempts. Moreover, it must have become the subject of conversation among the public, and not confined to the aristocracy. It was, therefore, necessary to protect the reputation of high class families. Since the men in these families have been unable to safeguard their own reputation and that of their women, they are certainly able to throw a young man in prison, knowing that he has committed no offence other than not responding to the temptation of an aristocratic woman. After all, it is his resistance of temptation that made her the talk of all classes.

A Platform to Advocate True Faith

"Two young men went to prison with him." (Verse 36) We will presently know that they belonged to the King's private staff.

The *sūrah* does not dwell on what happened to Joseph in prison, and how he was recognized as a man of integrity and kindness, and that he soon won the trust of all those around him. There must also have been quite a few among them who had had the misfortune to work in the palace or for courtiers, yet had incurred the anger of their masters for one reason or another, and, as a result, were now in jail. All this is omitted. For the *sūrah* immediately moves on to portray a scene of Joseph, in prison, speaking to two young men who had found him to be a man of wisdom. They related their dreams to him, requesting that he interpret them.

> *One of them said: 'I saw myself [in a dream] pressing wine.' The other said: 'And I saw myself [in a dream] carrying bread on my head, and birds were eating of it.' 'Tell us the meaning of these dreams, for we can see that you are a man of virtue.'* (Verse 36)

Joseph seizes the opportunity to speak to the prisoners about his faith, which is the true faith. The fact that he is in prison does not exempt him from his duty to preach the true faith and to criticize any situation that assigns lordship to human rulers. For submission to such rulers means that they usurp the rights of lordship and become pharaohs.

Joseph starts at the point which preoccupies his fellow prisoners. He reassures them that he will give them the correct interpretation of their dreams because his Lord has given him special knowledge as a result of his dedication in worshipping Him alone and his associating no partners with Him. In this way Joseph makes it clear that he follows the faith of his forefathers who were similarly dedicated. At the very outset then, he wins their trust, stating that he will rightly interpret their dreams. At the same time he also presents his faith in appealing guise.

> *[Joseph] answered: 'Your food which is provided for you will not have come to you before I have informed you of the real meaning of [your dreams]. That is part of the knowledge which my Lord has imparted to me. I have left the faith of people who do not believe in God, and who deny the truth of the life to come. I follow the faith of my forefathers, Abraham, Isaac and Jacob. It is not for us to associate any partners with God. This is part of God's grace which He has bestowed on us and on all mankind, but most people do not give thanks.'* (Verses 37–38)

The approach Joseph employs is particularly appealing. He is pleasant to listen to, moving from one aspect to the next in a relaxed, easy way. This is characteristic of Joseph throughout the story.

The first part of his statement is emphatic, inspiring confidence that he has divine knowledge whereby he is informed of what is coming and he tells it as he sees it. This indicates that what he knows is a gift given to him by God for his sincere devotion. Moreover, it is fitting with what was fashionable at the time, since prophesying was a common practice. However, his assertion that it is all taught to him by his Lord is made at the most appropriate moment so as to make them more receptive to his call on them to believe in God.

"*I have left the faith of people who do not believe in God, and who deny the truth of the life to come.*" (Verse 37) This refers to the people who raised him in Egypt, in the Chief Minister's home, and to the courtiers and aristocracy who hold sway in society. Needless to say, the two young men whom he was addressing followed the same religion as the rest of their people. Joseph does not, however, confront them with this fact, but rather speaks about people in general so that they are not embarrassed. This demonstrates Joseph's delicacy in approaching the subject and his choice of proper method to introduce his faith.

Joseph's mention of the hereafter at this point confirms, as stated earlier, that belief in the Day of Judgement has always been a fundamental concept of faith, preached by all God's messengers and prophets right from the beginning of human life. It is false to assume, as teachers of comparative religion do, that it is a recent concept in human faith in general. It may have been introduced at a late stage into pagan religions, but it has always been an essential concept of divine messages.

Joseph continues to outline the distinctive characteristics of false beliefs in order to highlight those of the true faith which he and his forefathers have followed. "*I follow the faith of my forefathers, Abraham, Isaac and Jacob. It is not for us to associate any partners with God.*" (Verse 38) It is a faith based on the concept of God's oneness. Indeed it is part of God's grace to mankind that they are guided to believe in His oneness. To enjoy this aspect of God's grace is easy. Mankind have only to decide to accept it and it is theirs, because this belief is ingrained in their nature and in the universe around them. It is also explained in all divine messages. It is only human beings who choose to ignore it and not thank God for it. "*This is part of God's grace which He has bestowed on us and on all mankind, but most people do not give thanks.*" (Verse 38)

A Comparison of Beliefs

Joseph's approach is subtle, taking them carefully step by step before going deep into their hearts to reveal his faith plainly and completely. He couples this with an explanation that the misery they suffer in life is due to the false beliefs which they and their people generally hold. *"My two prison companions! Which is better: [to believe] in diverse lords, or to believe in God, the One who holds sway over all that exists? Those you worship instead of Him are nothing but names you and your fathers have invented, and for which God has given no sanction from on high. All judgement rests with God alone. He has ordained that you should worship none but Him. This is the true faith, but most people do not know it."* (Verses 39–40)

In a few clear, lucid and enlightening words, Joseph outlines the main features of the true faith based on the oneness of God. He shakes violently the whole structure of polytheism and the very concept of associating partners with God.

"My two prison companions! Which is better: [to believe] in diverse lords, or to believe in God, the One who holds sway over all that exists?" (Verse 39) Joseph makes them his companions, drawing them close with his affable approach. This facilitates an easy way into the main subject, namely the essence of faith. He does not call on them directly to adopt it, but instead presents it as a subject for objective discussion: *"Which is better: [to believe] in diverse lords, or to believe in God, the One who holds sway over all that exists?"* The question makes a direct and strong appeal to human nature which recognizes only one deity. How come that several beings are described as gods when the one who deserves to be Lord and to be worshipped and obeyed in all that He orders is the One who has complete sway over all beings. He is the One whose law must be implemented in life. When God is declared to be One and His absolute power in the universe is recognized, then Lordship must be declared to belong to the One Lord whose power over people's lives must also be recognized. It should never happen that people who recognize God as One and Almighty, then accept someone else as having power over them, effectively making him a lord beside God. The Lord must be God who has absolute control over the whole universe. Anyone who does not have such power cannot

be taken as lord and given power over people's lives. If he cannot make the universe submit to his will, he must not be the one to whom people submit.

It is infinitely better that people should submit to God and acknowledge Him as their only Lord than that they submit to diverse, ignorant and powerless lords which they invent for themselves. This description applies to all lords other than God. No misery that has ever been suffered by mankind is greater than that caused by acknowledging a multiplicity of lords to each of whom a section of humanity submits. These earthly lords either usurp God's power and authority directly, or are given such power and authority by ignorant human beings who may be influenced by superstition or legend. It is also true that people can be overpowered or tricked into such submission. These earthly lords cannot rid themselves for a moment of their own selfish desires, or their urge to ensure their own survival and the maintenance of their power and authority. Hence, they seek to destroy all forces and elements that constitute even the slightest threat to their power and authority. They employ all means and mobilize all resources to glorify themselves so that their power continues to be acknowledged by the masses.

God Almighty is in no need of anyone. He does not want anything from His servants other than righteousness and that they work for their own betterment, and to build human life in accordance with the code He has laid down. He then considers all this part of their worship. Even the worship rites He requires them to observe aim at keeping them on the right track, ensuring that they conduct their lives properly. Indeed He is in no need of any of His servants. *"Mankind, it is you who stand in need of God, and God is All Sufficient, Glorious."* (35: 15)

Joseph then takes another step to demonstrate the falsehood of their idolatrous beliefs: *"Those you worship instead of Him are nothing but names you and your fathers have invented, and for which God has given no sanction from on high."* (Verse 40) These lords, whether they be human or non-human, spirits, devils, angels or forces of the universe that operate by God's will are not real lords. Indeed they have nothing of the qualities of lordship. Lordship belongs to God alone, the One who has power over all things, and who creates and controls all. But in all ignorant societies, people invent names and attribute to them

75

qualities and characteristics. The first of these is that of judgement and authority. But God has not given any authority to them, nor has He sanctioned what people invent.

To Whom Judgement Belongs

At this point Joseph makes his final and decisive point, making it clear to his interlocutors where all power and judgement lie, and to whom obedience is owed and how it must be acknowledged. Or, in short, to whom worship should be offered: *"All judgement rests with God alone. He has ordained that you should worship none but Him. This is the true faith, but most people do not know it."* (Verse 40)

Judgement and authority belong to no one other than God. It is He who is the Godhead, with authority to legislate and judge. Indeed, sovereignty, belongs to Him, for sovereignty is one of God's basic attributes. Whoever claims any right to it is indeed disputing God's power, whether the claimant be an individual, a class, a party, an organization, a community or an international organization representing mankind. Anyone who claims this very basic attribute of God's for himself disbelieves in God. His disbelief is in the form of denying a part of faith which is essentially and universally known as a fact.

Usurping the rights of sovereignty which belong to God alone does not come in one form only. For a person to claim the basic characteristic of Godhead, which is sovereignty, he need not be so crude as to say, 'I know no God whom you may worship other than myself,' or, 'I am your Lord, the Most High,' as Pharaoh did. He actually claims these rights disputing God's authority when he starts to derive laws from any source other than God's law, declaring that the source of power and authority belongs to some institution or being other than God. Even when that institution is the whole nation or all humanity, the result is the same. In the Islamic system, the nation selects the ruler, giving him the authority to govern in accordance with God's law. The nation, or the community, is not the source of sovereignty which enacts the law and gives it its power. The source of sovereignty is God. Many are those who confuse the exercise of power and its source. This confusion is found even among

76

Muslim scholars. What we say is that human beings, in their total aggregate, do not have the right of sovereignty. They only implement what God has legislated. What He has not legislated has no legitimacy. It does not carry God's sanction.

Joseph (peace be upon him) justifies his statement that all sovereignty belongs to God alone by saying: "*All judgement rests with God alone. He has ordained that you should worship none but Him.*" (Verse 40) We cannot understand this justification as the Arabs did at the time of the revelation of the Qur'ān unless we understand the meaning of 'worship' which can only be offered to God.

The meaning of the verb, '*abada*, or 'to worship' in Arabic is 'to submit or surrender'. In the early days of Islam it never meant, in Islamic terminology, only 'to offer worship rituals'. In fact none of the worship rituals was as yet imposed as a duty. So the statement was rather understood in the manner it was meant linguistically, and this later became its Islamic meaning. What it meant then was submission to God alone, and obeying His orders and commands, whether they related to worship rituals, moral directives or legal provisions. To submit to God in all these was the essence of worship which must be addressed to God alone. It could never be addressed to any of His creatures.

When we understand the meaning of worship in this light, we understand why Joseph stated that worship can only be addressed to God as his justification for saying that all judgement and sovereignty belong to Him alone. Submission to God will not become a reality if judgement and sovereignty belong to someone else. This applies to matters where God's will is done by the laws of nature which God has set in operation in the universe, and to matters where human beings have a choice with regard to their actions and practices. True submission to God applies in both areas.

Once more we say that to dispute God's right of sovereignty takes the disputant out of the religion of Islam altogether. This is a basic rule of Islam that is essentially known to all. This is because disputing God's right and authority means a rejection of worshipping Him alone. It is essentially an act of associating partners with God, which means that those who dispute God's rights of sovereignty are not Muslims at all. The same applies to those who approve their claims and obey them without rejecting, even mentally, their action of usurping God's right and authority. The claimant and those who obey him are the same in the Islamic view.

Joseph (peace be upon him) states that the true faith is that which assigns all judgement to God alone in implementation of His being the only one to be worshipped. "*This is the true faith.*" (Verse 40) This is a statement of limitation. No faith can be true unless it gives all sovereignty to God and makes this a practical implementation of worshipping Him alone.

"*But most people do not know it.*" (Verse 40) The fact that they do not know does not make them followers of the true faith. A person who does not know something cannot believe in it or implement it. If people do not know the essence of faith, it is illogical to say that they follow it. Their ignorance is not an excuse for describing them as Muslims. Rather, their ignorance bars them from that characteristic in the first place. To believe in something presupposes knowing it. That is a basic, logical fact.

In a few clear words Joseph (peace be upon him) outlines his faith completely, showing all its constituent elements and shaking to the core the foundations of disbelief, polytheism and tyranny.

Tyranny cannot take place in any land without its claiming the most essential quality of Godhead, namely His lordship over people's lives. This is the right to make people submit to its laws and orders, and implement its ideology. Even if it does not say so in words, it actually practises it. Tyranny does not exist unless the true faith has been removed from people's thoughts and lives. For only when people firmly believe that all sovereignty and judgement belong to God alone, because worship belongs to Him, is there no room left for tyranny in their lives.

At this point Joseph has completed his task of preaching God's faith to them, having attached it initially to the matter which preoccupied them. He therefore reverts to that point and interprets their dreams for them, so that their trust in what he says is strengthened, and they are more amenable to what he preaches: "*My two prison companions! One of you will give his lord wine to drink. The other will be crucified, and the birds will eat from his head.*" (Verse 41) He does not point out directly who will be released and who will meet the depressing end as he does not want to confront anyone with bad news. He stresses that he is certain of the knowledge imparted to him by God: "*The matter on which you have sought to be enlightened has thus been decided.*" (Verse 41) It will only be as God has decreed. There is no escape from it.

Joseph was an innocent prisoner, jailed on the strength of false accusations, without any proper investigation of his case. It may be that the incident of the Chief Minister's wife and the other women was portrayed to the King in a way that totally misrepresented the facts, as often happens in such cases. It was only natural then that Joseph wanted his case to be put to the King in the hope that he would order that it be looked into properly. Hence, Joseph "*said to the one whom he believed would be released: 'Remember me in the presence of your lord.'*" (Verse 42) He actually asked him to mention his case and situation to the King and to tell him of the truth he had seen in him. He describes him as his lord because he was the ruler to whom he submitted. The term 'lord' here means 'master, ruler, a person of acknowledged authority and a legislator'. This re-emphasizes the meaning of lordship in Islamic terminology.

At this point, the *sūrah* leaves out mentioning that the two prisoners' dreams came true in exactly the manner Joseph described. There is a gap here, as well as an implication that it is sufficient for us to know that all this took place. The prisoner whom Joseph felt would be released was actually released, but he did not act on what Joseph requested. He forgot all the lessons that Joseph had taught him. He forgot to remember his true Lord as he was distracted by the demands of life in the palace after he returned there. Indeed, he forgot all about Joseph: "*But Satan caused him to forget to mention Joseph to his lord, and so he remained in prison for several years.*" (Verse 42)

The pronoun '*he*' in the last clause refers to Joseph. God wanted to teach him a lesson so that he would sever all ties in favour of his tie with God Himself. Hence, He did not make the achievement of what he wanted dependent on any human being or on anything relating to a human being. This is an aspect of the honour God gave Joseph. God's true servants should be totally dedicated to Him. They must leave all decisions concerning their lives to God alone. When human weakness initially makes this impossible, He bestows on them His grace and makes them unable to adopt a different attitude so that they know its blessing. They are then able to accept it out of love and obedience to God. He then gives them more of His blessings and grace.

The King's Dream

Now we move into the court with the King asking his courtiers and priests to interpret a disturbing dream he had had: "*And the King said: 'I saw [in a dream] seven fat cows being devoured by seven emaciated ones, and seven green ears of wheat next to seven others dry and withered. Tell me the meaning of my vision, my nobles, if you are able to interpret dreams.' They replied: 'This is but a medley of dreams, and we have no deep knowledge of the real meaning of dreams.'*" (Verses 43–44)

None could offer a plausible interpretation of the King's dream. Or they might have felt that it signalled something unpleasant and hence did not wish to put it to the King. This is often the attitude of courtiers and advisors who prefer to deliver to their masters only that which is pleasant. Hence they said that it is all '*but a medley of dreams.*' They described it as disturbed visions that did not constitute a proper dream. They followed this by saying, "*We have no deep knowledge of the real meaning of dreams,*" i.e. when they are so blurred and confused.

So far we have mentioned three dream incidents: the first was Joseph's, the second was those of the two young men in prison and now we have the King's dream. Each time interpretation was requested. That so much emphasis was placed on dreams tells us something about the atmosphere that prevailed in Egypt and elsewhere.

At this point, Joseph's prison companion who was released remembered him and how he accurately interpreted his own dream and that of his fellow prisoner. "*At that point, the man who had been released from prison suddenly remembered [Joseph] after all that time and said: 'I will tell you the real meaning of this dream, so give me leave to go.'*" (Verse 45)

The King's Dream Interpreted

He requests leave to go and see the man who was certain to give a true interpretation of the dream no one else dared interpret. The curtains drop here, and when they are raised again we are in the prison looking at Joseph and his former companion asking him to interpret the King's dream: "'*Joseph, man of truth, tell us of the seven fat cows being devoured by seven emaciated ones, and seven green ears of wheat next to seven others dry and withered, so that I may return to the people [of the court], and that they would come to know.'*" (Verse 46)

The man, who is the drink master of the King, calls Joseph a '*man of truth*,' which is testimony that Joseph always tells the truth according to the man's own experience with him. "*Tell us of the seven fat cows...*" Here the man quotes the King's own words in relating the dream. Since he was asking for an interpretation of the dream, he had to quote the description accurately. The *sūrah* uses the same words again to indicate the accuracy of the reporting, and to enable the interpretation to immediately follow the statement.

However, what Joseph gives is not a passive interpretation of the dream. Instead it is coupled with advice on how best to cope with the consequences of what is going to happen. "*He replied: 'You shall sow for seven consecutive years.'*" (Verse 47) These are seven years without a gap when there is a rich harvest. Hence they are depicted in the dream as seven fat cows. "*But let the grain you harvest remain in its ear,*" (Verse 47) because that would protect the crop against insects and atmospheric effects that may cause it to decay. "*Except for the little which you may eat.*" (Verse 47) What you need for eating you may take out of its ear. The rest must be stored for the following seven years of poor harvest which are depicted in the dream as seven emaciated cows.

"*Then after that there will come seven hard years,*" (Verse 48) when the land produces little or nothing. Hence these hard years "*will devour all that you have laid up for them except a little of what you have kept in store.*" (Verse 48) It is as if these years are the ones which do the devouring themselves. Their lack of harvest is described here as hunger. And they will eat all except a little which is kept from them.

"*Then after that there will come a year of abundant rain, in which the people will be able to press [oil and wine].*" (Verse 49) This brings to an end the hard years without harvest. They are followed by a year of abundance when people will have plenty of water and a plentiful harvest. Their vineyards will yield richly and they will be able to press their wine. They will have plenty of sesame and olives which they will then press into oil.

We note here that this plentiful year is not symbolized in the King's dream. Joseph mentions it, however, on the basis of the knowledge given to him by God. He gives the happy news of the approach of this year to the man who will transmit it to the King and the people. They will be happier that the seven hard years will be followed by a year of rich harvest.

Court Summons

At this point the *sūrah* again moves to the next scene, leaving a gap between the one just ending and the one about to begin. What happens during this gap is left for us to imagine. The curtains are then once again raised in the King's palace. The *sūrah* leaves out what the man tells of the interpretation of the King's dream, and what he says about Joseph, his imprisonment and its cause, and his present situation. What we have instead is the effect of all this, embodied in the King's expressed desire to see him and his order that he should be brought before him.

"*The King said: 'Bring this man before me.'*" (Verse 50) Again the *sūrah* leaves out the details of carrying out the King's order. We simply find Joseph replying to the King's emissary. He has spent so long in prison that he is in no hurry to leave until his case has been properly investigated. He wants the truth to be clearly known and his innocence to be declared to all people. All the false accusations hurled at him must be known for what they were: mere lies. He has been looked after by his Lord, and the way he has been brought up gives him reassurance and peace of mind. He is in no hurry until the truth is known.

The impact of the care God has taken of Joseph in bringing him up is clearly seen in the difference between his present attitude and his earlier one. Formerly, he had asked his prison companion to remember him to his master. Now he wants his innocence to be established first. Hence he says to the King's emissary: "*Go back to your lord and ask him about the women who cut their hands.*" (Verse 50) The gulf between these two situations is great indeed.

Joseph refused to go to the King until the latter had investigated his case. He specifically mentions the women who cut their hands so that the circumstances leading to this, and what happened later will all be revealed. Moreover, he wanted all this to be done before leaving prison, so that the whole truth be known and without him having to question the women himself. He could afford to do this because he was absolutely certain of his own innocence, reassured that the truth would not be suppressed.

The Qur'ān quotes Joseph using the term, *Rabb*, or Lord, in its full meaning with regard to himself and to the King's messenger. The King is the messenger's lord, because he is his master whom he obeys, while God is Joseph's Lord whom Joseph obeys and submits to.

The messenger went back to the King and reported Joseph's reply. The King called in the women and interrogated them. The *sūrah* leaves this out, allowing us to know its conclusion: "*The King asked [the women]: 'What was the matter with you when you tried to seduce Joseph?'*" (Verse 51)

Justice Must Be Seen to Be Done

The Qur'ānic text uses a term much stronger than that expressed by the phrase, 'What was the matter with you.' It is much more like 'what calamity came over you.' It appears that the King asked for full information about the matter before he called them in. This the King did so that he would be appraised of the circumstances before he spoke to them. When they are brought before him, his question points an accusing finger, saying that something really serious must have happened: "*What was the matter with you when you tried to seduce Joseph?*" (Verse 51)

The King's very question tells us something about what happened on that day at the Chief Minister's house. We gather something of what the women said to Joseph, or hinted at, trying to tempt him into seduction.

When faced with such an accusation in the presence of the King, the women felt that they could no longer deny the facts: "*The women said: 'God save us! We did not perceive the least evil on his part.'*" (Verse 51) That is the truth that could not be denied, even by them. Joseph was so innocent that no one could realistically accuse him of any misdeed.

At this point, the woman who loved Joseph and could not rid herself of such love, despite her despair of him ever succumbing to her guile, comes forward to confess all in a very frank statement: "*The Chief Minister's wife said: 'Now has the truth come to light. It was I who tried to seduce him. He has indeed told the truth.'*" (Verse 51) It is a full confession admitting her guilt and his commitment to telling the truth.

She goes even further to reveal that she still has a soft spot for him, hoping that she will gain his respect after all that time. There is a further hint that his faith had found its way into her heart and that she believed in it: "*From this he will know that I did not betray him behind his back, and that God does not bless with His guidance the schemes of those who betray their trust.*"[1] (Verse 52)

Her confession and what comes after is described here in highly charged but refined words which tell us much about the feelings behind it. "*It was I who tried to seduce him. He has indeed told the truth.*" (Verse 51) This is a full testimony of his innocence and his having always said the truth. The woman does not mind what happens to her as a result of her confession. Was it then only the truth that she knew which prompted her to deliver that full confession in the presence of the King and nobles of the state?

The text of the *sūrah* implies a different motive. It suggests she was keen to win the respect of a man who is full of faith, and who paid no attention to her physical beauty. She now wanted that he respect her for her faith and honesty in giving a true account of his personality in his absence: "*From this he will know that I did not betray him behind his back.*" (Verse 52) She carries on with a moral statement of the type Joseph loves and appreciates: "*God does not bless with His guidance the schemes of those who betray their trust.*" (Verse 52)

---

1. In translating this verse and the one that follows we have conformed to the author's interpretation which attributes them as statements made by the Chief Minister's wife. This is certainly a valid interpretation. However, many scholars express the view that these two verses quote a statement made by Joseph, declaring his innocence of any betrayal of his master's trust, acknowledging his human susceptibilities and stating some of the principles of his divine faith. – Editor's note.

She even goes a step further to express her new virtuous feelings: "*And yet, I am not trying to claim to be free of sin. Indeed man's soul does incite him to evil, except for those upon whom God has bestowed His mercy. My Lord is Much-Forgiving, Merciful.*" (Verse 53) She was a woman in love. She was several years his senior. Her hopes depended largely on a word from him or a feeling of pleasure that she might feel he entertained.

Thus the human element in the story becomes apparently clear. The story is not told as a work of art and literature, but it is given as a lesson which believers may learn. It tackles the question of faith and its advocacy. The artistic style of the *sūrah* gives a colourful and vivid account of feelings and reactions as it tells of events in an environment where varied influences and circumstances play parts that produce a harmonious effect on the main characters.

Joseph's imprisonment is over. His life now takes a different course, where the trial is one of ease and comfort, not hardship.

A Great Turn in Joseph's Fortunes

And the King said: 'Bring him before me. I will choose him for my own.' And when he had spoken to him, the King said: 'You shall henceforth be in a position of high standing with us, invested with all trust.' Joseph replied: 'Give me charge of the store-houses of the land. I am able to look after them with wisdom.' Thus did We establish Joseph in the land, free to do what he willed. We bestow Our mercy on whom We will, and We never fail to give their reward to those who do good. But as for those who believe in God and keep away from evil, the reward of the life to come is much better indeed. (Verses 54–57)

The King established Joseph's innocence. He also learnt how adept Joseph was in the interpretation of dreams, and how wise he was when he requested an investigation of the women's behaviour. The King also learnt that Joseph was a man of dignity. He did not rush to leave the prison and meet the King of Egypt. He took the stand of an honourable man who had been wrongfully imprisoned. He wanted to prove the falsehood of the accusation even before his release. He wanted to re-establish his integrity and the truth of his faith before seeking any position of favour with the King.

His dignified attitude as a man of integrity and wisdom earned him the King's love and respect. Hence, the King ordered: "*Bring him before me. I will choose him for my own.*" (Verse 54) He does not want him brought before him so that he can release him, or just to know this learned interpreter of dreams, or to grant him audience and tell him that he is pleased with him. He wants him brought to him so that he can choose him for his own and make him a trusted advisor and even a friend.

There are those who are accused of no crime and have full freedom, who shed their dignity at the feet of rulers. They put a leash around their own necks, eagerly seeking a glimpse of satisfaction or a word of praise which keeps them as servants, not trusted advisors. I wish to God that such people would read the Qur'ān and Joseph's story so that they would know that dignity and honour bring much more profit, even material profit, than can ever be gained through humiliating themselves before rulers and tyrants.

"*The King said: 'Bring him before me. I will choose him for my own.'*" (Verse 54) The text of the *sūrah* leaves out the details of how the King's new order was carried out. Instead, we find ourselves looking at the scene of Joseph and the King: "*And when he had spoken to him, the King said: 'You shall henceforth be in a position of high standing with us, invested with all trust.'*" (Verse 54) When the King speaks to him, he is certain that the impression he has had of him is a true one. Hence he assures him that he has a position with the King himself. He is no longer a Hebrew slave, but a man of high standing. He is no longer the accused, but one who is invested with trust. Such a position of trust and security are also with the King himself. So, what does Joseph say in response?

He does not prostrate himself before the King in a gesture of gratitude as do courtiers who strive to win a tyrant's pleasure. He does not say to him may you live long and I always be your obedient servant, as those who vie for a tyrant's favour do. He only asks to be entrusted with the task he feels himself to be the best to discharge in the forthcoming period of hardship and of which he has warned the King by interpreting his dream for him. He feels that if he is entrusted with this task he will save the country from ruin and save many lives. He recognized that the situation needed his expert planning, efficiency, honesty and integrity. Hence he said to the King: "*Give me charge of the store-houses of the land. I am able to look after them with wisdom.*" (Verse 55)

The anticipated years of crisis, preceded by seven years of bumper harvests, required good management, with strict control over agriculture, managing the surplus harvest and ensuring its sound storage so that it did not decay. Joseph mentions the two qualities he possesses which he thinks the task requires: "*I am able to look after them with wisdom.*" (Verse 55) It should be noted that Joseph did not ask a personal favour from the King. This was not the time to make personal gain. Instead, he asked for that which would help the country and its people. He requests a position of very difficult responsibilities which people would rather steer away from, because it could easily cost them their careers or their lives. Hunger encourages lawlessness. A hungry multitude could easily tear apart those in power at a moment of confusion and trouble.

Soliciting a High Position

Nonetheless Joseph's request appears to violate two principles of the Islamic code. The first is a request of position, which is not allowed in Islam, as the Prophet says: "We do not give a position [of government] to anyone who asks for it." [Related by al-Bukhārī and Muslim.] The second is praising oneself, which runs contrary to the Qur'ānic instruction: "*Do not pretend to purity.*" (53: 32) However, such rules were established by the Islamic system laid down at the time of the Prophet Muḥammad (peace be upon him). Hence they did not apply during Joseph's time. Besides, this is only a matter of organization and administration, and such matters are not necessarily the same in all messages sent by God, and they do not apply equally to all communities that accept divine guidance.

Valid as this defence of Joseph's request is, we do not wish to rely on it. The matter is far too serious to rest on such an argument. In fact it is based on different considerations which need to be properly outlined so that we can fully understand the method of deduction and construction on the basis of established statements in the Qur'ān and

Ḥadīth. We will be able then to appreciate the dynamic nature of Islamic jurisprudence, which is totally different from the stale situation which appears to have remained with scholars upheld over generations of inactivity.

Islamic jurisprudence was not born in a vacuum, nor can it function in one. It was born when an Islamic community came into existence. It thus began to answer the needs of that community to ensure that its life was in line with Islamic principles and values. The Islamic community was not the product of Islamic jurisprudence; in fact it is the other way round: the legal code came into being so that it might fulfil the needs of the Islamic community as it began to live and function. Both facts are of great importance, for they provide us with insight into the dynamic nature of Islamic jurisprudence and its provisions.

If we were to take statements and rulings deduced from them without reference to these two facts, or to the circumstances prevailing at the time of the revelation of the statement or the deduction of the rulings, and without understanding the social environment when they were deduced and the needs they tried to meet, we would betray a lack of understanding of the nature of Islam and its jurisprudence. A dynamic jurisprudence is essentially different from an academic legal theory, although the two may be based on the same original statements. Dynamic jurisprudence takes into consideration the practical situation which prevailed at the time of the revelation of the texts and the time when the rulings were deduced and formulated. It considers the practical situation to be inseparable from the statements and rulings. If we separate the two, we place ourselves in an unbalanced situation.

This means that there is no single ruling which may be viewed in isolation of the social environment and circumstances that prevailed at the time when it was deduced. Let us cite here the example relevant to our discussion, namely, recommending oneself for public office. The rule we have is that this is forbidden, on account of the Qur'ānic statement, *"Do not pretend to purity,"* and the *ḥadīth* which states: "We do not give a position [of government] to anyone who asks for it."

This rule was formulated in an Islamic community so that it could be implemented by that community, because it serves its purposes and fits with its historical requirements and general nature. It is an Islamic rule for an Islamic community. It is not a theoretical rule for an idealistic situation. Hence, it produces its beneficial effects only when it is implemented in a community that is Islamic in origin, make-up and commitment. Any community that does not meet these criteria is merely a vacuum, in as much as this rule is concerned. It is not a fitting environment for its implementation. This applies to all provisions of the Islamic legal code, but we are speaking in detail here only about this particular rule because it is the one related to the text of the *sūrah* we are discussing.

We need now to understand why people in Islamic society must not speak about their own good qualities, and why they must not nominate themselves for positions of government. Why are they not allowed to organize an election campaign so that they can be voted into parliament, or to a leadership position? The answer is that in Islamic society people do not need any of this in order to show their suitability for such positions. Moreover, such positions in society are really a heavy burden which does not tempt anyone to seek them, except for reward from God should one be able to discharge heavy responsibilities properly, for the general interest of the community. This means that positions of government are only sought by people who have some purpose of their own which they wish to accomplish by holding office. Such people must not be given such positions. But this fact cannot be properly understood until we have understood the true nature of the Muslim community and its make-up.

The Birth of a Muslim Community

Movement is the constituent element of Islamic society, and this is what gives birth to it. Initially, the faith comes from its divine source, conveyed by God's Messenger in word and deed. In later generations, it is represented by advocates of the divine faith. Some people will respond to this advocacy, and they are met with resistance, and subjected to persecution by tyrannical regimes implementing different forms of *jāhiliyyah*. Some may succumb to persecution and turn away from the faith and its advocating movement, while others remain steadfast. Some of the latter may become martyrs, and others continue the struggle until God has judged between them and their opponents. This latter group will be granted victory by God, who makes them a means of fulfilling His will. He fulfils His promise to them of victory and power, so that they can establish the rule of divine faith. The victory is not theirs as a personal gain or reward. It is a victory of their message, so that they establish God's Lordship of mankind.

This group of people do not limit their faith to a certain piece of land, or to a certain race, nation, colour, language or similarly hollow tie. Their mission is to liberate mankind, the world over, from submission to anyone other than God, and to elevate mankind far above the level of subservience to tyrants, regardless of their type of tyranny.

As this movement goes on, people's qualities become apparent, and their respective positions are identified on the basis of standards and values that are firmly rooted in this faith and acceptable to all the community. These are values such as dedication to the cause, sacrifice, piety, a high standard of morals, efficiency and ability. All these values are judged by practice, as they become apparent through action and movement. Thus the community comes to recognize those who have them. Such people do not need to make any pretension to excellence, nor do they need to seek a position of government or be elected to parliament on the basis of their own campaigns.

In such a Muslim community, the social make-up is based on the distinction achieved through movement and action to implement the values of faith. That is what happened in the first Muslim community, when distinction was achieved by the early group of the *Muhājirīn* and the *Anṣār*, by the army in the Battle of Badr, by those who gave the Prophet the pledge to fight till death before the signing of the Treaty of Al-Ḥudaybiyah, and by the ones who fought in different battles for Islam before the victory that regained Makkah for Islam. In subsequent generations, distinction was achieved through dedication to the cause of Islam. In such a community people do not begrudge others their dues, and they do not deny them their positions of honour, even though human weakness may overcome some people who covet personal gains. This means that people do not need to extol their own virtues and seek power for themselves.

Suitability and Responsibility

Some people may suggest that this quality belongs uniquely to the first Muslim community on the basis of its historical circumstances. They forget, however, that a true Islamic society will have no other foundation or method of existence. It will not come about unless a movement advocates a return to Islam and helps people abandon the *jāhiliyyah* into which they have sunk. That is the starting point. It will inevitably be followed by a period of hardship and trial, just like the first time. Some of its members will succumb to pressure, while others will remain steadfast. There will be martyrs among them while those who survive will be determined to continue the struggle. They will hate sinking back into *jāhiliyyah* as much as they hate being thrown into fire. They keep up the struggle until God has judged between them and their opponents, and gives them victory as He did with the first Muslim community. This means the birth of a new Islamic system in some part of God's land. At this point, the movement will have travelled from the point of beginning to the point of establishing an Islamic society, and in the meantime it will have sorted out its advocates into different grades based on faith and the standards and values they put into effect. These will not need to nominate themselves for positions of power, because their community, which fought the campaign of *jihād* with them, will have recognized their abilities and recommended them.

Some may argue that this only applies in the initial period. That it does not extend to the next period when Islamic society is well established and well settled. This notion betrays a complete lack of awareness of the nature of Islam. This faith of Islam will never stop its movement, because its goal is to liberate all mankind throughout the whole world from submission to tyrannical power. This means that the movement will continue and distinction in the movement will remain the criterion for recognizing those who have talent, ability and dedication. It will not stop unless there is a deviation from Islam. The rule that prohibits self-promotion for positions of government will remain operative within its environment, just as when it was first put into effect.

It may also be said that when the community gets larger, people will not know each other and those who have abilities and talents will need to stand up and speak about themselves, seeking position and authority. Again such an argument is fallacious, influenced by the present-day set up. In a Muslim community, the people of every neighbourhood will know one another well, because that is intrinsic to the Muslim community and its qualities. Hence, every locality will know those of them who have talent and ability, and they evaluate these by Islamic standards. It will not be difficult for them to choose those who are dedicated and hard working for the sake of the community to represent them in local councils or in parliament. As for positions of government, the ruler, who is chosen by the whole community on the recommendation of community leaders or parliament, will fill them with people from among those who have already been identified on the basis of their dedication and ability. As we have said, the movement will continue in Islamic society and *jihād* will continue for the rest of time.

A Maze of Our Own Making

Those who think or write about the Islamic system and its structure today place themselves in a maze, because they try to implement the Islamic system and its rules and values in their present social set-up. Compared with the Islamic system, such a set-up is like a vacuum which provides no room for the implementation of any Islamic rules. There is a fundamental difference in the very make-up of the two types of society. In the Islamic system, people and groups are distinguished through what they do in the process of establishing the Islamic faith in practice and in the struggle against the values and systems of *jāhiliyyah*. It is their perseverance which enables them to endure pressure, persecution and other hardships that continue until the establishment of an Islamic society in the land. Other societies belong to *jāhiliyyah*, and they are stagnating, upholding principles and values that have nothing to do with Islam. As such, they are like a vacuum that cannot support the functioning of Islamic principles and values.

Those writers and researchers look for a solution which enables them to advocate the Islamic system and its institutions, and to operate its values and laws. The first thing to trouble them is how the members of the Consultative Council are to be selected if they cannot put their names forward or speak about their own qualities. How are the right people to be known in communities such as we have today where people do not know each other's virtues and are not judged by the right standards of honesty, efficiency and integrity? They are also troubled by the method of choosing a head of state. Is he to be chosen by public referendum, or by the Consultative Council? If he is the one who nominates the members of the Consultative Council, how are these to select him in future? Will they not feel indebted to him and wish to return his favour? Besides, if they are the ones to select or elect him, will they not have leverage over him, when he is overall leader? When nominating them, will he not choose only those who are loyal to him? Such questions are endless.

The starting point in this maze is the assumption that our society today is a Muslim one, and that we only need to have the rules and laws ready to implement them, changing nothing of society's set-up, values and moral principles. When we start at this point, we are in a vacuum, and as we move on further into this vacuum, we will soon feel dizzy as if we are moving through an endless maze.

The present society in which we live is not an Islamic one, and it will not be the one in which the Islamic system and its rules and values will be implemented. They are impossible to implement in such a society because, by nature, they neither start nor operate in a vacuum. Islamic society is composed of individuals and groups that strive and struggle in order to bring it about, facing all the pressures to which they may be subjected by the state of ignorance, or *jāhiliyyah*, that prevails in other societies. The status and qualities of these individuals come to be recognized during the struggle. Thus the Islamic society is a newborn society that moves along its set course, aiming to liberate mankind, throughout the world from submission to any authority other than God.

Countless other issues are raised along with that of choosing the leader and selecting the Consultative Council. These are all tackled by writers who try to fit Islam to the present society with all its principles, moral values, and various concepts. They preoccupy themselves with questions such as banks and insurance companies and the usurious basis of their work, family planning and similar matters. In all these, they either respond to questions which people put to them, or they try to look at their status in an Islamic society. But they all begin at the point that leads them into the maze, assuming that fundamental Islamic principles will be implemented in the current social structures that have their un-Islamic basis. They think that when this is done, these societies become Islamic. This is both ludicrous and sad at the same time.

It was not Islamic jurisprudence, with all its codes and rules, that gave birth to Islamic society. It was the other way round. Islamic society faced up to *jāhiliyyah* and in the process gave birth to Islamic legal codes which were derived from the basic principles of Islam. The reverse can never take place. Islamic laws are not formulated on paper, but in the practical life of the Muslim community. Hence, it is absolutely essential that a Muslim community first comes into existence to provide the environment where Islamic law takes its roots and begins to be implemented.

In such a situation matters are totally different. There may be a need in such a society for banks, insurance companies, a family planning policy, or there may be no need for one or more of these. We cannot predict in advance what that society may or may not need in order to tailor laws to meet these needs. Moreover, the laws we have neither fit nor satisfy the needs of non-Islamic societies, because Islam does not accept these societies in the first place. It does not concern itself with their needs which arise from their own systems, nor does it trouble itself with finding solutions for them.

It is the divine faith that provides the social basis, and it is the responsibility of human beings to adjust their lives to fit it. Such adjustment can only come about through an active movement that aims to establish the basic principle of God's oneness and His Lordship over mankind, and also to liberate humanity from submission to tyranny. All this comes about through the implementation of God's law in their lives. Inevitably, such a movement will face resistance and persecution. The cycle will also continue with some believers weakening and reverting to *jāhiliyyah*, while others remain steadfast, losing some of their numbers as martyrs while the others persevere until God gives them victory. At this point Islamic society comes into existence, with its advocates having distinguished themselves with its colours and values. Their lives will then have different needs, and the methods to satisfy those needs will also be different from those available in non-Islamic societies. Deduction and construction of rules will begin to meet the needs of that society, and the legal code that is born then is one that lives in a practical environment that has definite needs.

Suppose that an Islamic society comes into existence. It collects *zakāt* and distributes it to its rightful beneficiaries; its people deal with each other on the basis of mutual compassion and a close, caring relationship within each local community, and within the whole of society. Moreover, people have no room for extravagance and arrogant rivalry in worldly riches, but instead uphold all Islamic values. How are we to tell today whether such a society will ever need insurance companies when it has all these values that ensure common social security? If it needs insurance companies, how are we to know whether the present ones, which operate in un-Islamic society and meet its needs, will fit the insurance needs of such an Islamic society? Similarly, how are we to tell whether an Islamic society that goes through a continuous struggle for God's cause, i.e. *jihād*, will ever need to put in place a family planning policy? If we cannot predict the needs of our society when it is based on Islam, because of the great gulf between its values, concerns and aims and those of other societies, why should we waste our time and effort in trying to adapt and modify existing rules in order to fit them to the needs of that society when it comes into existence?

As we have explained, the basic flaw is in taking the present set-up as the starting point and thinking that an exercise of simple self adjustment will bring back the divine faith into practical existence. It is time for the advocates of Islam to think well of their faith and to place it far above a position of mere service to non-Islamic societies and their needs. They have to tell people that they must first declare their acceptance of Islam and willingness to submit to its rule, or in other words, declare their submission to God alone. This means that they are willing to implement Islam fully in their lives, removing all tyranny and acknowledging only God's Lordship over the whole universe and in human life. When people, or a community of people, respond positively, an Islamic society begins to take root. It then provides the social environment for a practical Islamic code to be born and to prosper, as it provides for meeting the needs of that society in accordance with divine faith. Unless such a society comes into existence, busying ourselves with deducing rules and laws to implement now is an exercise in self-delusion which plants seeds in the air. No Islamic code will be formulated in a vacuum just as no plant will ever grow from seeds planted in the air.

Between Theory and Practice

Intellectual research in Islamic jurisprudence may be comfortable, because it involves no risks, but it is not part of Islamic advocacy. In fact it is not a part of Islamic strategy. Those who want to steer away from risk will be better off occupying themselves with literature, art or commerce. Academic study of Islamic jurisprudence on the lines described is in my personal view – and God knows best – a waste of effort and reward. The divine faith does not accept a position of subservience to *jāhiliyyah* which rebels against its rule and which, at times, ridicules it by requesting Islamic solutions for its own problems when it refuses to submit to God and the Islamic faith.

The method of birth of Islamic society is the same, and it follows the same stages. A transformation from *jāhiliyyah* to Islam will never be an easy task, and it will never start with codifying Islamic principles in preparedness for Islamic society whenever it may come into existence. Nor are these codes the ingredient that non-Islamic societies require in order to become Islamic. The difficulty in such a transformation is not due to Islamic laws being inadequate to meet the sophisticated needs of advanced and civilized societies. That is all self-deception. What prevents such societies from becoming Islamic is tyranny that refuses to acknowledge that all sovereignty belongs to God alone. Hence they refuse to acknowledge God's Lordship over human life and over the whole world. Thus they take themselves out of Islam altogether. That is a part of Islam that is essentially known to all. Moreover, when the masses submit to tyranny, they make the tyrants lords beside God, and they obey them. Thus the masses take themselves away from believing in the oneness of God to polytheism, because acknowledging Lordship as belonging to any beings other than God is to place such beings in the same position as God. That is how *jāhiliyyah* is established as a human system. It is founded on misconceptions as much as it is founded on material power.

The codification of Islamic law, then, cannot encounter *jāhiliyyah* with adequate means. What is adequate in encountering it is a movement which calls on society to return to Islam, and which fights *jāhiliyyah* with all its structure. The normal course will then start, and God will eventually judge between the advocates of Islam and their opponents on the basis of complete and pure justice. Only at that point does the role of Islamic law start, when its rules and provisions have a natural environment in which to be implemented. They are then able to meet the needs of the newly born Islamic society, according to the nature, circumstances and extent of these needs. We cannot predict these and what they will be like. To occupy ourselves now with formulating these is not the sort of serious preoccupation that fits with the nature of the Islamic faith.

This does not mean that the laws that the Qur'ān and the *Sunnah* mention are not applicable today. It only means that the society in which they are meant to operate is not yet in existence. Hence, their full application waits until that society becomes a reality. However, they must be implemented by every Muslim individual wherever he or she may be living while they work for the establishment of Islamic society.

To understand the nature of the birth of Islamic society according to the method already explained is the starting point in the real work to re-establish Islam in a real society after it has ceased to exist. It was because of the adoption of man-made laws in preference to God's law over the last two centuries that Islamic society ceased to exist, despite the presence of mosques and minarets, prayers and supplication. All this gives us a false feeling that Islamic society is still alive, when it has rather been uprooted altogether. When Islamic society came into existence the first time, no mosques or worship rituals were available. It was born when people were called upon to believe in God and to worship Him alone, and they responded to that call. Their worship of Him did not take the form of rituals like prayer, because these had not yet been made obligatory. It was represented in their submission to Him alone. When these people acquired material power on earth, legislation was given to them. When they had to meet the practical needs of their life, they were able to deduce codes and legal provisions, in addition to what the Qur'ān and the *Sunnah* legislate. That is the proper and only way.

I wish there was an easy way to transform people generally at the first call made to them to accept Islam and explain its laws to them. But this is wishful thinking. People do not abandon *jāhiliyyah* or change their submission to tyranny in order to adopt Islam and worship God alone except through the hard and arduous route along which the Islamic message advocates itself. It always starts with an individual, followed by a vanguard group. Then the conflict with non-Islamic society begins, bringing in its wake all sorts of trials and hardships. When the conflict is resolved and God grants victory to the Islamic message and its advocates, Islam is established and people enter into God's faith in groups. That faith involves a complete way of life, which is the only way acceptable to God: "*He who seeks a religion other than self-surrender to God, it will not be accepted from him.*" (3: 85)

The above explanation may give us an insight into Joseph's attitude. He was not living in a society that had submitted all its affairs to God's law, thereby prohibiting seeking office or requesting a government position. He felt that the circumstances offered him a chance to be in a position of authority, not a position of subservience in *jāhiliyyah* society. Things turned out as he wished. He was then able to promote his faith in Egypt, while the Chief Minister and the King had their authority substantially curtailed.

High Position and Freedom for Joseph

Having elaborated the point about Joseph's request to be in charge of the Kingdom's store houses, and the issue of seeking government posts in Islamic society, we pick up the thread of the story again. When we consider the text of the *sūrah* we find that it does not mention the King's agreement to Joseph's request. It is as if the request itself implied the King's approval. This is an even higher honour given to Joseph, and it shows his high standing with the King. He only needed to state his request for it to be answered. This is confirmed by the following verses: *"Thus did We establish Joseph in the land, free to do what he willed. We bestow Our mercy on whom We will, and We never fail to give their reward to those who do good. But as for those who believe in God and keep away from evil, the reward of the life to come is much better indeed."* (Verses 56–57)

Thus the proof of Joseph's innocence in the way that it was done, and the King's admiration that he has already won, and the granting of his request, all helped to establish Joseph in the land, giving him a firm and distinguished position.

"Thus did We establish Joseph in the land, free to do what he willed." (Verse 56) He was free to take up the house he wanted, at the place of his choice, and to occupy the position he wished. That freedom contrasts fully with the well in which he was thrown by his brothers and the prison sentence he had to endure, with all the fears and restrictions of both situations. *"We bestow Our mercy on whom We will."* (Verse 56) We replace hardship with ease, fear with security, fetters with freedom, and humiliation with a high position of honour. *"We never fail to give their reward to those who do good."* (Verse 56) Those who demonstrate a strong, unshakeable faith and reliance on God and who deal with other people in fairness and kindness will not fail to have their reward in this life.

"But as for those who believe in God and keep away from evil, the reward of the life to come is much better indeed." (Verse 57) This is not reduced by the fact that such people receive their reward in this life. Yet it is infinitely better than this present reward. Its conditions are that a person should believe and do righteous deeds, steering away from what God has forbidden whether in public or private. Thus has God replaced Joseph's trials with his new position of power, and also with the promise of better things to come in the life to come. All this reward is for faith, righteousness and perseverance in the face of difficulty.

4

Brothers' Reunion

Joseph's brothers arrived and presented themselves before him. He immediately knew them, but they did not recognize him. (58)

وَجَاءَ إِخْوَةُ يُوسُفَ فَدَخَلُواْ عَلَيْهِ فَعَرَفَهُمْ وَهُمْ لَهُ مُنكِرُونَ ﴿٥٨﴾

And when he had given them their provisions, he said: 'Bring me that brother of yours from your father's side. Do you not see that I give just measure and that I am the best of hosts? (59)

وَلَمَّا جَهَّزَهُم بِجَهَازِهِمْ قَالَ ٱئْتُونِي بِأَخٍ لَّكُم مِّنْ أَبِيكُمْ أَلَا تَرَوْنَ أَنِّي أُوفِي ٱلْكَيْلَ وَأَنَاْ خَيْرُ ٱلْمُنزِلِينَ ﴿٥٩﴾

But if you do not bring him, you shall never again receive from me a single measure [of provisions], nor shall you come near me.' (60)

فَإِن لَّمْ تَأْتُونِي بِهِ فَلَا كَيْلَ لَكُمْ عِندِي وَلَا تَقْرَبُونِ ﴿٦٠﴾

They said: 'We shall endeavour to persuade his father to let him come. We will make sure to do so.' (61)

قَالُواْ سَنُرَٰوِدُ عَنْهُ أَبَاهُ وَإِنَّا لَفَاعِلُونَ ﴿٦١﴾

Joseph said to his servants: 'Place their merchandise in their camel-packs, so that they may discover it when they return to their people. Perchance they will come back.' (62)

وَقَالَ لِفِتْيَٰنِهِ ٱجْعَلُواْ بِضَٰعَتَهُمْ فِى رِحَالِهِمْ لَعَلَّهُمْ يَعْرِفُونَهَآ إِذَا ٱنقَلَبُوٓاْ إِلَىٰٓ أَهْلِهِمْ لَعَلَّهُمْ يَرْجِعُونَ ۝

When they returned to their father, they said: 'Father, any [further] grain is henceforth denied us. Therefore, send our brother with us so that we may obtain our full measure [of grain]. We will take good care of him.' (63)

فَلَمَّا رَجَعُوٓاْ إِلَىٰٓ أَبِيهِمْ قَالُواْ يَٰٓأَبَانَا مُنِعَ مِنَّا ٱلْكَيْلُ فَأَرْسِلْ مَعَنَآ أَخَانَا نَكْتَلْ وَإِنَّا لَهُۥ لَحَٰفِظُونَ ۝

He replied: 'Am I to trust you with him in the same way as I trusted you with his brother in the past? But God is the best of guardians; and of all those who show mercy He is the Most Merciful.' (64)

قَالَ هَلْ ءَامَنُكُمْ عَلَيْهِ إِلَّا كَمَآ أَمِنتُكُمْ عَلَىٰٓ أَخِيهِ مِن قَبْلُ فَٱللَّهُ خَيْرٌ حَٰفِظًا وَهُوَ أَرْحَمُ ٱلرَّٰحِمِينَ ۝

When they opened their camel-packs, they discovered that their merchandise had been returned to them. 'Father,' they said, 'what more could we desire? Here is our merchandise: it has been returned to us. We will buy provisions for our people, and we will take good care of our brother. We will receive an extra camel-load: that should be an easy load.' (65)

وَلَمَّا فَتَحُواْ مَتَٰعَهُمْ وَجَدُواْ بِضَٰعَتَهُمْ رُدَّتْ إِلَيْهِمْ قَالُواْ يَٰٓأَبَانَا مَا نَبْغِى هَٰذِهِۦ بِضَٰعَتُنَا رُدَّتْ إِلَيْنَا وَنَمِيرُ أَهْلَنَا وَنَحْفَظُ أَخَانَا وَنَزْدَادُ كَيْلَ بَعِيرٍ ذَٰلِكَ كَيْلٌ يَسِيرٌ ۝

102

He said: 'I will not send him with you until you give me a solemn pledge before God that you will indeed bring him back to me, unless the worst befalls you.' When they had given him their solemn pledge, [Jacob] said: 'God is witness to all that we say.' (66)

قَالَ لَنْ أُرْسِلَهُ مَعَكُمْ حَتَّىٰ تُؤْتُونِ مَوْثِقًا مِّنَ ٱللَّهِ لَتَأْتُنَّنِي بِهِ إِلَّا أَن يُحَاطَ بِكُمْ فَلَمَّا ءَاتَوْهُ مَوْثِقَهُمْ قَالَ ٱللَّهُ عَلَىٰ مَا نَقُولُ وَكِيلٌ ۝

And he added: 'My sons, do not enter [the city] by one gate, but enter by different gates. In no way can I be of help to you against God. Judgement rests with none but God. In Him have I placed my trust, and in Him alone let all those who trust place their trust.' (67)

وَقَالَ يَٰبَنِيَّ لَا تَدْخُلُوا مِنۢ بَابٍ وَٰحِدٍ وَٱدْخُلُوا مِنْ أَبْوَٰبٍ مُّتَفَرِّقَةٍ وَمَآ أُغْنِي عَنكُم مِّنَ ٱللَّهِ مِن شَىْءٍ إِنِ ٱلْحُكْمُ إِلَّا لِلَّهِ عَلَيْهِ تَوَكَّلْتُ وَعَلَيْهِ فَلْيَتَوَكَّلِ ٱلْمُتَوَكِّلُونَ ۝

And when they entered as their father had bidden them, it did not profit them in the least against God. It was but a wish in Jacob's soul which he had thus fulfilled. He was endowed with knowledge which We had given him. But most people do not know it. (68)

وَلَمَّا دَخَلُوا مِنْ حَيْثُ أَمَرَهُمْ أَبُوهُم مَّا كَانَ يُغْنِي عَنْهُم مِّنَ ٱللَّهِ مِن شَىْءٍ إِلَّا حَاجَةً فِى نَفْسِ يَعْقُوبَ قَضَىٰهَا وَإِنَّهُ لَذُو عِلْمٍ لِّمَا عَلَّمْنَٰهُ وَلَٰكِنَّ أَكْثَرَ ٱلنَّاسِ لَا يَعْلَمُونَ ۝

And when they presented themselves before Joseph, he drew his brother to himself, and said: 'I am your brother. Do not grieve over their past deeds.' (69)

وَلَمَّا دَخَلُوا عَلَىٰ يُوسُفَ ءَاوَىٰٓ إِلَيْهِ أَخَاهُ قَالَ إِنِّي أَنَا۠ أَخُوكَ فَلَا تَبْتَئِسْ بِمَا كَانُوا يَعْمَلُونَ ۝

And when he had given them their provisions, he placed the [King's] drinking-cup in his brother's camel-pack. Then an announcer called out: 'You people of the caravan! You are surely thieves.' (70)

فَلَمَّا جَهَّزَهُم بِجَهَازِهِمْ جَعَلَ ٱلسِّقَايَةَ فِي رَحْلِ أَخِيهِ ثُمَّ أَذَّنَ مُؤَذِّنٌ أَيَّتُهَا ٱلْعِيرُ إِنَّكُمْ لَسَارِقُونَ ۝

Turning back towards them, they said: 'What is it that you have lost?' (71)

قَالُوا وَأَقْبَلُوا عَلَيْهِم مَّاذَا تَفْقِدُونَ ۝

'We have lost the King's goblet,' they answered. 'Whoever brings it shall have a camel-load [of grain as a reward]. I pledge my word for it.' (72)

قَالُوا نَفْقِدُ صُوَاعَ ٱلْمَلِكِ وَلِمَن جَآءَ بِهِ حِمْلُ بَعِيرٍ وَأَنَا بِهِ زَعِيمٌ ۝

They said: 'By God, you know that we have not come to commit any evil deed in this land, and that we are no thieves.' (73)

قَالُوا تَٱللَّهِ لَقَدْ عَلِمْتُم مَّا جِئْنَا لِنُفْسِدَ فِي ٱلْأَرْضِ وَمَا كُنَّا سَارِقِينَ ۝

[The Egyptians] said: 'But what shall be the punishment for this deed, if you are proved to be lying?' (74)

قَالُوا فَمَا جَزَٰٓؤُهُۥ إِن كُنتُمْ كَٰذِبِينَ ۝

They replied: 'He in whose camel-pack it is found shall be enslaved in punishment for it. Thus do we punish the wrong-doers.' (75)

قَالُوا جَزَٰٓؤُهُۥ مَن وُجِدَ فِي رَحْلِهِۦ فَهُوَ جَزَٰٓؤُهُۥ كَذَٰلِكَ نَجْزِى ٱلظَّٰلِمِينَ ۝

Thereupon, [Joseph] began to search their bags before the bag of his brother, and then took out the drinking-cup from his brother's bag. Thus did We contrive for Joseph. He had no right under the King's law to detain his brother, had God not so willed. We do exalt [in knowledge] whom We will, but above everyone who is endowed with knowledge there is One who knows all. (76)

فَبَدَأَ بِأَوْعِيَتِهِمْ قَبْلَ وِعَاءِ أَخِيهِ ثُمَّ اسْتَخْرَجَهَا مِن وِعَاءِ أَخِيهِ كَذَٰلِكَ كِدْنَا لِيُوسُفَ مَا كَانَ لِيَأْخُذَ أَخَاهُ فِي دِينِ الْمَلِكِ إِلَّا أَن يَشَاءَ اللَّهُ نَرْفَعُ دَرَجَٰتٍ مَّن نَّشَاءُ وَفَوْقَ كُلِّ ذِى عِلْمٍ عَلِيمٌ ۝

[Joseph's brothers] said: 'If he has stolen – well, a brother of his had stolen previously.' Joseph kept his secret to himself and revealed nothing to them, saying [within himself]: 'You are in a far worse position, and God knows best what you are speaking of.' (77)

قَالُوا إِن يَسْرِقْ فَقَدْ سَرَقَ أَخٌ لَّهُ مِن قَبْلُ فَأَسَرَّهَا يُوسُفُ فِي نَفْسِهِ وَلَمْ يُبْدِهَا لَهُمْ قَالَ أَنتُمْ شَرٌّ مَّكَانًا وَاللَّهُ أَعْلَمُ بِمَا تَصِفُونَ ۝

They said: 'Chief Minister, this lad has a father who is very old. Take one of us instead of him. We see that you are indeed a generous man.' (78)

قَالُوا يَٰأَيُّهَا الْعَزِيزُ إِنَّ لَهُ أَبًا شَيْخًا كَبِيرًا فَخُذْ أَحَدَنَا مَكَانَهُ إِنَّا نَرَاكَ مِنَ الْمُحْسِنِينَ ۝

He answered: 'God forbid that we should take any other than the man with whom we found our property; for then we would be wrongdoers.' (79)

قَالَ مَعَاذَ اللَّهِ أَن نَّأْخُذَ إِلَّا مَن وَجَدْنَا مَتَٰعَنَا عِندَهُ إِنَّا إِذًا لَّظَٰلِمُونَ ۝

An Encounter with Lost Brothers

Years went by, but the *sūrah* leaves out what happened during them. It does not speak about the years of rich harvest, and how the people went about making the best use of them in their agriculture. Nor does it speak about how Joseph managed the system, and how he stocked the unused harvest. All these seem to be implied in Joseph's own statement when he requested his appointment: "*I am able to look after them with wisdom.*" (Verse 55) Nor does the *sūrah* mention the arrival of the hard years with poor harvest, or how the people received them, or how they practically lost their livelihood during them. It all seems to be implied in the interpretation of the King's dream, when Joseph said of these years: "*Then after that there will come seven hard years which will devour all that you have laid up for them, except a little of what you have kept in store.*" (Verse 48)

The *sūrah* does not mention the King or any of his ministers or advisors at any future event. It thus gives us the impression that all matters of importance were left in Joseph's hands. It was he who managed the whole crisis. Joseph is the one given all the limelight, and the *sūrah* makes effective use of this historical fact.

As for the effects of the years of scarcity, the *sūrah* draws attention to this by referring to Joseph's brothers as those that came from the desert, in a faraway land, to look for food in Egypt. This gives us an idea of how widespread the famine was. We realize the sort of policy Egypt adopted under Joseph's direction. It is clear that neighbouring lands looked to Egypt for help, as it became the storehouse for the whole region. At the same time, Joseph's story and his dealings with his brothers move along in a way that fulfils a religious purpose.

Poor harvests caused famine in the Kanaanite land and its surrounding areas. Joseph's brothers, as numerous others, went to Egypt after it became known that it had plenty of supplies after having stored its surplus and managed it wisely. We see them here presenting themselves to Joseph, not knowing him for their brother. He immediately recognizes them because they have not changed much. They could not, in their wildest dreams, imagine that he was their brother. Far removed is the young Hebrew boy whom they cast in the well over 20 years previously from the man in whose presence they now find themselves, the Chief Minister of Egypt in his court and among his assistants and guardsmen.

Joseph did not reveal his identity to them, as he felt they should first learn a few lessons: "*He immediately knew them, but they did not recognize him.*" (Verse 58) But the way the story runs suggests that he accommodated them in comfortable quarters, then he prepared their first lesson: "*When he had given them their provisions, he said: 'Bring me that brother of yours from your father's side. But if you do not bring him, you shall never again receive from me a single measure [of provisions], nor shall you come near me.' They said: 'We shall endeavour to persuade his father to let him come. We will make sure to do so.' Joseph said to his servants: 'Place their merchandise in their camel-packs, so that they may discover it when they return to their people. Perchance they will come back.'*" (Verses 59–62)

We understand from this that he managed to win their confidence so that they told him their situation in detail, mentioning that they had a young half brother whom they did not bring with them because their father loved him so dearly that he could not part with him. Hence when he gave them what they needed and they were ready to depart, he told them that he wanted to see their brother: "*He said: 'Bring me that brother of yours from your father's side.'*" (Verse 59) He justified his request by reminding them that he gives just measure to all who come to buy. He also reminds them that he is very hospitable to all who come. There was nothing to fear if their brother came with them. Indeed he would receive the kind treatment for which Joseph was well known: "*Do you not see that I give just measure and that I am the best of hosts? But if you do not bring him, you shall never again receive from me a single measure [of provisions], nor shall you come near me.*" (Verses 59–60)

As they were aware of their father's attachment to their younger brother, particularly after Joseph's loss, they explained to him that the matter was not so easy. Their father was sure to object, but they, nevertheless, would try to persuade him. They confirm their resolve to ensure that he would come with them on their next trip: "*They said: We shall endeavour to persuade his father to let him come. We will make sure to do so.*" (Verse 61) Use of the term 'endeavour' in this context describes that the matter would involve much effort on their part.

Joseph, for his part, ordered his men to put back in their packs the merchandise they had brought with them. This might have been some wheat and cattle feed, or might have been a mixture of money and some desert produce or animal hide and hair. All such items were used in commercial exchanges in market places. Joseph, however, wanted all their original merchandise returned so that they might find it when they have arrived home: "*Joseph said to his servants: 'Place their merchandise in their camel-packs, so that they may discover it when they return to their people. Perchance they will come back.'*" (Verse 62)

The Brothers Travel Again

The *sūrah* takes us immediately to the land of Kanaan, where the brothers are talking to their father. The *sūrah* says nothing whatsoever about the return journey, and whether anything of importance happened. Here the brothers are telling their father the most important point that they learnt at the end of their trip: "*When they returned to their father, they said: 'Father, any [further] grain is henceforth denied us. Therefore, send our brother with us so that we may obtain our full measure [of grain]. We will take good care of him.'*" (Verse 63) They wanted their father to know this urgently, because they say this even before they open their luggage. They tell him that the Chief Minister of Egypt has decided not to give them any further provisions unless they take their younger brother with them. Hence they request their father to let him go with them so that they can buy such provisions. They promise to take good care of him.

This promise must have awakened old memories in Jacob's mind. It is an exact repeat of their promise to take good care of Joseph. Hence, he speaks of his sorrows that the new promise has revived: "*He replied: 'Am I to trust you with him in the same way as I trusted you with his brother in the past?'*" (Verse 64) He is in effect telling them he will have nothing to do with their promises. He has no need of the care they may take of his younger son. Should he need any guardianship for him, he will seek it elsewhere: "*But God is the best of guardians; and of all those who show mercy He is the Most Merciful.*" (Verse 64)

Once they had rested after their long journey, they opened their camel-packs in order to store the crops they had bought, but they find instead the merchandise they had taken with them to exchange for crops. Joseph has not given them any wheat or such like, but instead returned their merchandise. So, their first report was that they have been prevented from buying crops, then on opening their camel-packs they found their merchandise. All this was intentional, as Joseph wanted them to return quickly with their brother. That was part of the lesson he wanted them to learn.

In this return of their merchandise, they had additional leverage to persuade Jacob to send their brother with them. Furthermore, it showed they had no ill intention. *"When they opened their camel-packs, they discovered that their merchandise had been returned to them. 'Father,' they said, 'what more could we desire? Here is our merchandise: it has been returned to us.'"* (Verse 65) They increase the pressure on Jacob by speaking of the vital interest of his household to obtain food: *"We will buy provisions for our people."* (Verse 65) They then re-emphasize their resolve to make sure that their brother will come to no harm: *"And we will take good care of our brother."* (Verse 65) They tempt him with the extra load which they would be able to get easily if their brother travels with them: *"We will receive an extra camel-load: that should be an easy load."* (Verse 65)

It appears from their saying, *"We will receive an extra camel-load,"* that Joseph (peace be upon him) used to give each person a full camel-load only. He would not just give any buyer all the crops he wanted. This was wise in the years of hardship, because it ensured that there was enough food for all.

Jacob finally relents, but makes a strict condition for allowing his youngest son to go with them: *"He said: 'I will not send him with you until you give me a solemn pledge before God that you will indeed bring him back to me, unless the worst befalls you.'"* (Verse 66) He wants them to make a solemn, binding oath that they will bring their young brother back, unless they are faced with a situation that is not of their own making and which they have no means of overcoming. This situation is expressed by the proviso, *"unless the worst befalls you."* There is no other exception to release them from their pledge, which they readily give: *"When they had given him their solemn pledge, [Jacob] said: 'God is witness to all that we say.'"* (Verse 66) This acts as additional emphasis to remind them always of their pledge.

When that was settled, Jacob warns them of the dangers they may face in their new trip: *"And he added: 'My sons, do not enter [the city] by one gate, but enter by different gates. In no way can I be of help to you against God. Judgement rests with none but God. In Him have I placed my trust, and in Him alone let all those who trust place their trust.'"* (Verse 67)

We pause a little here to consider Jacob's statement: *"Judgement rests with none but God."* It is clear from the text that he is referring to fate which is God's inevitable judgement from which there is no escape. That is God's will which will be done no matter what people do to prevent it. Hence his statement is an expression of his belief in God's will, whether it brings benefit or harm. God's will is done and people have no choice but to submit to it. But beside this type of God's judgement, there is His judgement which people apply willingly, by choice. This is the sum of His orders which require them to do certain things and refrain from others. This also belongs to God. The only difference between the two is that people may willingly implement the latter or indeed choose not to implement it at all. Whichever course they choose will have certain consequences which will affect both their present and future lives. People are not true Muslims unless they choose God's judgement and implement it willingly as a matter of their own choosing.

Looking for Unnecessary Details

The party moves along and Jacob's children carry out their father's instructions: *And when they entered as their father had bidden them, it did not profit them in the least against God. It was but a wish in Jacob's soul which he had thus fulfilled. He was endowed with knowledge which We had given him. But most people do not know it."* (Verse 68) What was the purpose of Jacob's instruction? Why does he want them to enter the city from different gates?

Reports and commentaries provide different explanations for which there is no need. In fact these explanations are against what the Qur'ānic text wants to impart. Had the Qur'ān wanted to enlighten us about the reason for these instructions, it would have stated it, but it does not mention anything other than saying, *"It was but a wish in Jacob's soul which he had thus fulfilled."* (Verse 68) Commentators should likewise stop at this juncture in order to retain the atmosphere the Qur'ān wants to impart. That atmosphere suggests that Jacob feared something for his children, which he felt could be prevented by their entering the city from different gates. At the same time he realizes that he could not avail them anything against God's will. All judgement belongs to God, and all trust must be placed in Him. It was only in an intuitive sense he gave his children this instruction. God had taught him, and he had learnt, that God's will is certain to be done: "*But most people do not know it.*" (Verse 68)

What Jacob feared for his children might have been an evil eye, or the King's jealousy, should he see their number and strength, or perhaps he feared highwaymen. Knowledge of that which he feared does not give us anything of substance to add to the subject of the *sūrah*. It only provides a way for commentators to deviate from the highly effective treatment of the subject in the Qur'ān. On our part, we will leave out the reason for Jacob's instructions and the whole trip with whatever events it might have witnessed, because the *sūrah* does not mention any of these. We will look at the next scene when Joseph's brothers have arrived in Egypt.

A Theft is Announced

"*And when they presented themselves before Joseph, he drew his brother to himself, and said: 'I am your brother. Do not grieve over their past deeds.'*" (Verse 69) We note how the *sūrah* does not keep us in suspense but tells us very quickly that Joseph took his brother aside for a private talk telling him that he was his own brother. He also tells him not to bother himself with what his brothers did to him. The *sūrah* tells us straightaway about that, although naturally it must have happened sometime after their arrival, when Joseph has had a chance to speak to his brother in private. Nevertheless, this was the first thought in Joseph's mind when his brothers entered his place and when he saw his full brother after such a long time. Hence, the *sūrah* mentions it as the first action because it is the first thought. This is one of the finer aspects of the style of this remarkable book.

The *sūrah* then leaves out any details of the hospitality Joseph may have offered his brothers. It simply moves straight to the last scene when the brothers are about to depart. We are made aware of Joseph's plan to keep his brother with him so that his half brothers learn some necessary lessons, which are also useful to all people and all generations: "*And when he had given them their provisions, he placed the [King's] drinking-cup in his brother's camel-pack. Then an announcer called out: 'You people of the caravan! You are surely thieves.' Turning back towards them, they said: 'What is it that you have lost?' 'We have lost the King's goblet,' they answered. 'Whoever brings it shall have a camel-load [of grain as a reward]. I pledge my word for it.' They said: 'By God, you know that we have not come to commit any evil deed in this land, and that we are no thieves.' [The Egyptians] said: 'But what shall be the punishment for this deed, if you are proved to be lying?' They replied: 'He in whose camel-pack it is found shall be enslaved in punishment for it. Thus do we punish the wrongdoers.' Thereupon, [Joseph] began to search their bags before the bag of his brother, and then took out the drinking-cup from his brother's bag. Thus did We contrive for Joseph. He had no right under the King's law to detain his brother, had God not so willed. We do exalt [in knowledge] whom We will, but above everyone who is endowed with knowledge there is One who knows all. [Joseph's brothers] said: 'If he has stolen – well, a brother of his had stolen previously.' Joseph kept his secret to himself and revealed nothing to them, saying [within himself]: 'You are in a far worse position, and God knows best what you are speaking of.' They said: 'Chief Minister, this lad has a father who is very old. Take one of us instead of him. We see that you are indeed a generous man.' He answered: 'God forbid that we should take any other than the man with whom we found our property; for then we would be wrongdoers.'*" (Verses 70–79)

This is a sensational scene, full of movement, action and surprise. Indeed it is one of the most exciting scenes portraying all sorts of reactions. But it is at the same time a real scene portrayed in a breathtaking manner. Very stealthily Joseph puts the King's goblet in the camel-pack which belonged to his younger brother to fulfil a plan which God has inspired him with, and of which we will learn presently. The King's goblet is normally made of gold. It is said that it was used for drinking, but the bottom part was used to measure the wheat, which was a scarce commodity during the years of drought and the famine they brought.

Then as they are about to depart a loud voice announces publicly: "*You people of the caravan! You are surely thieves.*" (Verse 70) Joseph's brothers, the children of Jacob, son of Isaac, son of Abraham, are alarmed at this announcement accusing them of theft. Hence they turn back to defend themselves, asking first: "*What is it that you have lost?*" (Verse 71) The boys who attend to getting people ready for departure, or the guard, one of whom made the announcement, said: "*We have lost the King's goblet.*" (Verse 72) Then there is a further announcement pledging a reward for anyone who brings it forward voluntarily. The reward is very valuable in the prevailing circumstances: "*Whoever brings it shall have a camel-load [of grain as a reward]. I pledge my word for it.*" (Verse 72)

But Joseph's brothers are certain of their innocence. They have not stolen anything. Indeed they have not come to steal or to commit any violation of common law because such violation poisons relations between communities. Hence they make an oath of their innocence: "*By God, you know that we have not come to commit any evil deed in this land.*" (Verse 73) They plead their innocence reminding the people that their own status, family and appearance speak for their character and that they would never commit such an offence: "*We are no thieves.*" (Verse 73)

Joseph Arrests His Brother

At this point, a challenge was put to them by the guards or staff: "*But what shall be the punishment for this deed, if you are proved to be lying?*" (Verse 74)

Here a part of the design which God has inspired Joseph to employ is revealed. It was customary in Jacob's faith that a thief be taken as a hostage or captive or that he be enslaved in compensation for what he had stolen. Since Joseph's brothers were certain of their innocence, they accepted that their law should be enforced against the one who might be proved to have stolen the goblet. Their reply defined the punishment in their own legal system: "*He in whose camel-pack it is found shall be enslaved in punishment for it. Thus do we punish the wrongdoers.*" (Verse 75) A thief is a wrongdoer and wrongdoers must be treated according to the law.

This conversation took place in front of Joseph who then ordered that their camel-packs be searched. Wise as he was, he started by searching the camel-packs of his half brothers before that of his younger brother's, so that he did not raise any doubt about the matter: "*Thereupon, [Joseph] began to search their bags before the bag of his brother, and then took out the drinking-cup from his brother's bag.*" (Verse 76) The narrative leaves us to imagine the great shock Jacob's sons experienced when they were absolutely certain of their innocence, swearing to it in one voice. It mentions nothing of all this, leaving us instead to contemplate it.

Meanwhile it comments on certain objectives behind the story while Jacob's sons and the onlookers come to themselves: "*Thus did We contrive for Joseph.*" (Verse 76) This means that it was God who devised this careful plan for Joseph. "*He had no right under the King's law to detain his brother.*" (Verse 76) Had he applied the King's law, he would not have been able to detain his brother; he would have only been able to punish the thief for his theft. He only could detain his brother by the fact that his brothers declared their willingness to implement their own faith. This is the scheme God made for Joseph, inspiring him with its working, or it is what God 'contrived' for him. 'Contrivance', or the Arabic word used for it, *kidnā*, refers to a subtle design intended for certain ends, good or bad as may be the case, but it is more often used with bad ends in mind. On the surface, this whole design seemed wicked, as it involved a misfortune happening to his young brother, and an embarrassing situation for his other brothers which they would have to face when they returned to their father. Moreover, it would be a sad event for his father, albeit temporarily. Hence, the *sūrah* calls it a contrivance or a plot, using the whole range of meanings for the word, and referring to its appearance in the first place. This is an aspect of the subtlety of Qur'ānic expression.

"*He had no right under the King's law to detain his brother, had God not so willed.*" (Verse 76) His will takes the course we have seen. The verse refers here to the high position achieved by Joseph: "*We do exalt [in knowledge] whom We will,*" (Verse 76) and to the great knowledge he has been given, while reminding us that God's knowledge is perfect and complete: "*But above everyone who is endowed with knowledge there is One who knows all.*" (Verse 76) This last comment is a fine way of putting things in proper perspective.

We need to pause a little here to reflect on this fine Qur'ānic expression: "*Thus did We contrive for Joseph. He had no right under the King's law to detain his brother.*" (Verse 76) We note first that in the original Arabic text the Qur'ān uses the word *dīn* to refer to the King's law and system. This is the Arabic word for 'religion'. Its usage here defines the exact meaning of *dīn* in this context, which is, as we have just said, 'the King's law and system of government,' which did not punish a thief with slavery. That was the law of Jacob based on his faith. Joseph's brothers accepted the implementation of this law, and Joseph applied it to them when he found the King's drinking cup in his younger brother's camel-pack.

Thus the Qur'ān describes a system of government and law as *dīn*. It is a meaning all people have forgotten in these days of ignorance, including those who call themselves Muslims and those who follow un-Islamic systems, or *jāhiliyyah*. All of them limit the significance of *dīn* to beliefs and worship rituals. They consider anyone who believes in God's oneness and acknowledges the truth conveyed by His Messenger and believes in God's angels, revealed books, messengers, and in the Day of Judgement and the working of God's will, as a follower of the divine faith. They do this even though such a person may submit to, and acknowledge, the sovereignty of different lords besides God. The Qur'ān defines the King's *dīn* as his system of government and legal code. The same applies to God's *dīn*, which means His law.

The significance of the term 'God's *dīn*' has weakened and shrunken in people's perception to the extent that most people today limit it to beliefs and worship rituals. But this was not the case when this *dīn* was conveyed by Adam and Noah through to the days of Muḥammad (peace be upon them all). It has always meant submission to God alone, being committed to His law and rejecting any other legislation. It also signifies that He alone is God in heaven and God on earth, and that He alone is the Lord of all mankind. Thus it combines God's sovereignty, law and authority. The difference between believers and unbelievers is that the first submit to God's law alone, while those who accept the 'King's *dīn*' submit to the King's system and law. Or they may take a mixture of the two, submitting to God in matters of belief and worship and to some other authority in matters of systems

115

and laws. This is a basic concept of the Islamic faith and it is essentially known to all.

Some people try to find excuses for people on the grounds of their lack of understanding of the significance of the term 'God's *dīn*', which prevents them from insisting on, or thinking about, the implementation of God's law. They say that their ignorance means that they cannot be classified as polytheists associating partners with God. For myself, I cannot see how people's ignorance of the truth of this faith puts them within its boundaries. To believe in a certain truth comes only after knowing it. How can people be said to believe in a faith when they do not know its true significance or what it means?

Their ignorance may exempt people from accountability on the Day of Judgement, or it may reduce their punishment, or it may put the blame for their failure on those who did not teach them the true meaning of this faith of Islam when they were fully aware of it. But this is a matter that God will decide as He pleases. Argument about reward and punishment in the hereafter is generally futile. It is of no concern to the advocates of Islam in this life. What concerns us is to say that people's beliefs today are not exactly the same as God's faith which signifies, according to clear Qur'ānic statements, the law and system He has revealed. Whoever submits to these belongs to God's faith, or *dīn*, and whoever submits to the King's system and legal code belongs to the King's *dīn*. There can be no argument over this. Those who are unaware of the true significance of this faith cannot be believers in it, because their ignorance includes its basic meaning. Logically, a person who does not know the basic meaning of a faith cannot be a believer in it.

It is indeed much better that instead of trying to find excuses for such people, we should try to make clear to them what faith, or *dīn* signifies. They will then be in a position to either accept or reject it, fully aware of the implications of their response.

This is indeed better for us and for the people themselves. It is better for us because it relieves us of the responsibility for the erroneous ways which people follow as a result of their ignorance of the true nature and significance of *dīn*, which results from lack of belief in it. Making the significance of their attitude clear to people, showing them that they are indeed following the King's *dīn* rather than God's faith, is also better for them as it may shake them to the extent that they decide to abandon their erroneous ways and follow Islam. That was indeed what God's messengers did, and it is what the advocates of the divine faith should do in all communities and at all times when they confront a state of *jāhiliyyah*.

Unsuccessful Appeal

Turning back to Joseph's brothers whose grudge against Joseph and his brother has been aroused, we find them trying their best to deny having anything to do with theft, while they attach it to the other branch of their father's children: "They said: '*If he has stolen – well, a brother of his had stolen previously.*'" (Verse 77) There are countless reports which try to endorse their statement, quoting various excuses and legends, forgetting that these people had themselves previously lied to their father about Joseph. These attempts forget that they could lie again to Egypt's Chief Minister in order to deny their responsibility for an embarrassing act. They thus try to absolve themselves of anything to do with Joseph and his younger brother. Their action shows that they still harboured a grudge against both Joseph and his brother. Hence they put the blame squarely on these two.

"*Joseph kept his secret to himself and revealed nothing to them.*" (Verse 77) He simply bore their accusation without showing that he was affected by it, knowing that both he and his brother were totally innocent. He only said to them: "*You are in a far worse position.*" (Verse 77) What this means is that their false accusation put them in a far worse position in God's sight than that of the accused. His is a statement of fact, not an insult. "*God knows best what you are speaking of.*" (Verse 77) This he says so as not to enter into any argument about their accusation, which he presumably had nothing to do with.

They, however, now start to feel the embarrassing situation they are in. They remembered the solemn pledge they gave to their father when he made it a condition of his consent to send their brother with them that they would "*indeed bring him back to me*", unless the worst befell them. Hence they appeal to Joseph to let their younger brother return with them, pleading the suffering that his detention would cause to his old father. They offer one of themselves in his place, if he would not free him for the sake of his aged father. They further appeal to his kindness and compassion, saying to him: "*Chief Minister, this lad has a father who is very old. Take one of us instead of him. We see that you are indeed a generous man.*" (Verse 78)

Joseph, however, wanted to teach them a lesson, and he wanted to arouse their interest in the surprise he was preparing for them, and for his father and all who knew him, so that its effect would be appreciated by all. Hence he rejects their offer out of hand: "*God forbid that we should take any other than the man with whom we found our property; for then we would be wrongdoers.*" (Verse 79) He does not say that he would not take an innocent person in place of a thief, because he knew that his brother was no thief. He expresses the situation very precisely and accurately: "*God forbid that we should take any other than the man with whom we found our property.*" That is the whole situation without any addition to make the accusation appear true or false. He further comments, "*for then we would be wrongdoers.*" We have no wish to do anyone any wrong. That concludes the whole episode, and Joseph's brothers knew then that their appeals would not bring any desired result. They retreated to reflect on the situation they now faced.

5

A Child's Dream Comes True

When they despaired of [moving] him, they withdrew to begin earnest consultations among themselves. The eldest of them said: 'Do you not recall that your father took from you a pledge in God's name, and that previously you were at fault with respect to Joseph? I shall not depart from this land until my father gives me leave or God judges for me. He is certainly the best of judges.' (80)

فَلَمَّا ٱسْتَيْـَٔسُوا۟ مِنْهُ خَلَصُوا۟ نَجِيًّا قَالَ كَبِيرُهُمْ أَلَمْ تَعْلَمُوٓا۟ أَنَّ أَبَاكُمْ قَدْ أَخَذَ عَلَيْكُم مَّوْثِقًا مِّنَ ٱللَّهِ وَمِن قَبْلُ مَا فَرَّطتُمْ فِى يُوسُفَ فَلَنْ أَبْرَحَ ٱلْأَرْضَ حَتَّىٰ يَأْذَنَ لِىٓ أَبِىٓ أَوْ يَحْكُمَ ٱللَّهُ لِى وَهُوَ خَيْرُ ٱلْحَٰكِمِينَ ﴿٨٠﴾

Go back to your father and say: 'Father, your son has stolen. We testify only to that which we know. We cannot guard against the unforeseen. (81)

ٱرْجِعُوٓا۟ إِلَىٰٓ أَبِيكُمْ فَقُولُوا۟ يَٰٓأَبَانَآ إِنَّ ٱبْنَكَ سَرَقَ وَمَا شَهِدْنَآ إِلَّا بِمَا عَلِمْنَا وَمَا كُنَّا لِلْغَيْبِ حَٰفِظِينَ ﴿٨١﴾

You may ask the [people of the] town where we were, and the caravan with which we travelled. We are certainly telling the truth.' (82)

وَسْـَٔلِ ٱلْقَرْيَةَ ٱلَّتِى كُنَّا فِيهَا وَٱلْعِيرَ ٱلَّتِىٓ أَقْبَلْنَا فِيهَا وَإِنَّا لَصَٰدِقُونَ ﴿٨٢﴾

119

He said: 'No, but your minds have tempted you to evil. Sweet patience! God may well bring them all back to me. He is All-Knowing, Wise.' (83)

قَالَ بَلْ سَوَّلَتْ لَكُمْ أَنفُسُكُمْ أَمْرًا فَصَبْرٌ جَمِيلٌ عَسَى ٱللَّهُ أَن يَأْتِيَنِي بِهِمْ جَمِيعًا إِنَّهُۥ هُوَ ٱلْعَلِيمُ ٱلْحَكِيمُ ۝

He then turned away from them and said: 'Oh, woe is me for Joseph!' His eyes became white with grief, and he was burdened with silent sorrow. (84)

وَتَوَلَّىٰ عَنْهُمْ وَقَالَ يَـٰٓأَسَفَىٰ عَلَىٰ يُوسُفَ وَٱبْيَضَّتْ عَيْنَاهُ مِنَ ٱلْحُزْنِ فَهُوَ كَظِيمٌ ۝

They said: 'By God, you will continue to remember Joseph until you wither away or until you are dead.' (85)

قَالُوا۟ تَٱللَّهِ تَفْتَؤُا۟ تَذْكُرُ يُوسُفَ حَتَّىٰ تَكُونَ حَرَضًا أَوْ تَكُونَ مِنَ ٱلْهَـٰلِكِينَ ۝

He said: 'It is only to God that I complain and express my grief. For I know of God what you do not know. (86)

قَالَ إِنَّمَآ أَشْكُوا۟ بَثِّى وَحُزْنِىٓ إِلَى ٱللَّهِ وَأَعْلَمُ مِنَ ٱللَّهِ مَا لَا تَعْلَمُونَ ۝

My sons, go and seek news of Joseph and his brother; and do not despair of God's mercy; for none but unbelievers can ever despair of God's mercy.' (87)

يَـٰبَنِىَّ ٱذْهَبُوا۟ فَتَحَسَّسُوا۟ مِن يُوسُفَ وَأَخِيهِ وَلَا تَا۟يْـَٔسُوا۟ مِن رَّوْحِ ٱللَّهِ إِنَّهُۥ لَا يَا۟يْـَٔسُ مِن رَّوْحِ ٱللَّهِ إِلَّا ٱلْقَوْمُ ٱلْكَـٰفِرُونَ ۝

When they presented themselves before [Joseph] again, they said: 'Exalted one! Hardship has befallen us and our people, and so we have brought but little merchandise. Give us our full measure [of grains], and be charitable to us. Indeed God rewards those who are charitable.' (88)

فَلَمَّا دَخَلُوا۟ عَلَيْهِ قَالُوا۟ يَـٰٓأَيُّهَا ٱلْعَزِيزُ مَسَّنَا وَأَهْلَنَا ٱلضُّرُّ وَجِئْنَا بِبِضَـٰعَةٍ مُّزْجَىٰةٍ فَأَوْفِ لَنَا ٱلْكَيْلَ وَتَصَدَّقْ عَلَيْنَآ إِنَّ ٱللَّهَ يَجْزِى ٱلْمُتَصَدِّقِينَ ۝

He said: 'Do you know what you did to Joseph and his brother, when you were still unaware?' (89)

قَالَ هَلْ عَلِمْتُم مَّا فَعَلْتُم بِيُوسُفَ وَأَخِيهِ إِذْ أَنتُمْ جَٰهِلُونَ ﴿٨٩﴾

They said: 'Why – is it indeed you who are Joseph?' He replied: 'I am Joseph, and this is my brother. God has indeed been gracious to us. If one remains God-fearing and patient in adversity, God will not fail to reward those who do good.' (90)

قَالُوٓاْ أَءِنَّكَ لَأَنتَ يُوسُفُ قَالَ أَنَا۠ يُوسُفُ وَهَٰذَآ أَخِى قَدْ مَنَّ ٱللَّهُ عَلَيْنَآ إِنَّهُۥ مَن يَتَّقِ وَيَصْبِرْ فَإِنَّ ٱللَّهَ لَا يُضِيعُ أَجْرَ ٱلْمُحْسِنِينَ ﴿٩٠﴾

They said: 'By God! Most certainly has God raised you high above us, and we were indeed sinners.' (91)

قَالُواْ تَٱللَّهِ لَقَدْ ءَاثَرَكَ ٱللَّهُ عَلَيْنَا وَإِن كُنَّا لَخَٰطِـِٔينَ ﴿٩١﴾

He replied: 'None shall reproach you today. May God forgive you. He is indeed the Most Merciful of those who show mercy. (92)

قَالَ لَا تَثْرِيبَ عَلَيْكُمُ ٱلْيَوْمَ يَغْفِرُ ٱللَّهُ لَكُمْ وَهُوَ أَرْحَمُ ٱلرَّٰحِمِينَ ﴿٩٢﴾

Now go and take this shirt of mine and lay it over my father's face, and he will recover his sight. Then come back to me with all your family.' (93)

ٱذْهَبُواْ بِقَمِيصِى هَٰذَا فَأَلْقُوهُ عَلَىٰ وَجْهِ أَبِى يَأْتِ بَصِيرًا وَأْتُونِى بِأَهْلِكُمْ أَجْمَعِينَ ﴿٩٣﴾

As the caravan set out, their father said [to the people around him]: 'I feel the breath of Joseph, though you will not believe me.' (94)

وَلَمَّا فَصَلَتِ ٱلْعِيرُ قَالَ أَبُوهُمْ إِنِّى لَأَجِدُ رِيحَ يُوسُفَ لَوْلَآ أَن تُفَنِّدُونِ ﴿٩٤﴾

They replied: 'By God! You are still lost in your old illusions.' (95)

قَالُواْ تَٱللَّهِ إِنَّكَ لَفِى ضَلَٰلِكَ ٱلْقَدِيمِ ﴿٩٥﴾

But when the bearer of good news arrived [with Joseph's shirt], he laid it over his face; and he regained his sight. He said: 'Did I not say to you that I know from God something that you do not know?' (96)

فَلَمَّآ أَن جَآءَ ٱلْبَشِيرُ أَلْقَهُ عَلَىٰ وَجْهِهِۦ فَٱرْتَدَّ بَصِيرًا قَالَ أَلَمْ أَقُل لَّكُمْ إِنِّىٓ أَعْلَمُ مِنَ ٱللَّهِ مَا لَا تَعْلَمُونَ ۝

[His sons] said: 'Father, pray to God to forgive us our sins, for we were sinners indeed.' (97)

قَالُوا يَـٰٓأَبَانَا ٱسْتَغْفِرْ لَنَا ذُنُوبَنَآ إِنَّا كُنَّا خَـٰطِـِٔينَ ۝

He said: 'I shall pray to God to forgive you. He is certainly Most Forgiving, Most Merciful.' (98)

قَالَ سَوْفَ أَسْتَغْفِرُ لَكُمْ رَبِّىٓ إِنَّهُۥ هُوَ ٱلْغَفُورُ ٱلرَّحِيمُ ۝

When they all presented themselves before Joseph, he drew his parents to himself, saying: 'Enter Egypt in peace, if it so pleases God.' (99)

فَلَمَّا دَخَلُوا عَلَىٰ يُوسُفَ ءَاوَىٰٓ إِلَيْهِ أَبَوَيْهِ وَقَالَ ٱدْخُلُوا مِصْرَ إِن شَآءَ ٱللَّهُ ءَامِنِينَ ۝

And he raised his parents to the highest place of honour, and they fell down on their knees, prostrating themselves before him. He said: 'Father, this is the real meaning of my dream of long ago. My Lord has made it come true. He has been gracious to me, releasing me from prison, and bringing you all from the desert after Satan had sown discord between me and my brothers. My Lord is gracious in whatever way He wishes. He is All-Knowing, truly Wise.' (100)

وَرَفَعَ أَبَوَيْهِ عَلَى ٱلْعَرْشِ وَخَرُّوا لَهُۥ سُجَّدًا وَقَالَ يَـٰٓأَبَتِ هَـٰذَا تَأْوِيلُ رُءْيَـٰىَ مِن قَبْلُ قَدْ جَعَلَهَا رَبِّى حَقًّا وَقَدْ أَحْسَنَ بِىٓ إِذْ أَخْرَجَنِى مِنَ ٱلسِّجْنِ وَجَآءَ بِكُم مِّنَ ٱلْبَدْوِ مِنۢ بَعْدِ أَن نَّزَغَ ٱلشَّيْطَـٰنُ بَيْنِى وَبَيْنَ إِخْوَتِىٓ إِنَّ رَبِّى لَطِيفٌ لِّمَا يَشَآءُ إِنَّهُۥ هُوَ ٱلْعَلِيمُ ٱلْحَكِيمُ ۝

'My Lord, You have given me power and imparted to me some understanding of the real meaning of statements. Originator of the heavens and the earth! You are my guardian in this world and in the life to come. Let me die as one who has surrendered himself to You, and admit me among the righteous.' (101)

رَبِّ قَدْ ءَاتَيْتَنِي مِنَ ٱلْمُلْكِ وَعَلَّمْتَنِي مِن تَأْوِيلِ ٱلْأَحَادِيثِ فَاطِرَ ٱلسَّمَوَاتِ وَٱلْأَرْضِ أَنتَ وَلِيِّ فِي ٱلدُّنْيَا وَٱلْأَخِرَةِ تَوَفَّنِي مُسْلِمًا وَأَلْحِقْنِي بِٱلصَّالِحِينَ ﴿١٠١﴾

The Crisis Reaches Its Climax

When Joseph's brothers realized that all their attempts to rescue their young brother were in vain, they left Joseph and went away. They sat in council, deeply involved in earnest consultations. We see them exchanging views in a very serious manner. The *surah* does not mention all that they said. It only records the last statement which formed the basis of their next steps: "*When they despaired of [moving] him, they withdrew to begin earnest consultations among themselves. The eldest of them said: 'Do you not recall that your father took from you a pledge in God's name, and that previously you were at fault with respect to Joseph? I shall not depart from this land until my father gives me leave or God judges for me. He is certainly the best of judges.' Go back to your father and say: 'Father, your son has stolen. We testify only to that which we know. We cannot guard against the unforeseen. You may ask the [people of the] town where we were, and the caravan with which we travelled. We are certainly telling the truth.'*" (Verses 80–82)

The eldest reminds them of the pledge they had given and of their carelessness about Joseph and his welfare. He combines the two events as the basis for his own decision which is not to leave Egypt or meet his father until the latter has given him permission to do so, or God has made a judgement to which he would certainly submit.

He asks that the rest go back to their father and tell him in all frankness that his son had stolen something, and was subsequently

123

detained on account of this. That was all that they knew. If their brother was innocent, and if there was something different about the whole situation, it was certainly hidden from them, and they could not be answerable for what God, in His wisdom, chose to conceal from them. They had not expected anything like this to happen. It could never have been foreseen. If their father doubted what they said, and did not believe them, he could ask the people of the capital city of Egypt where they had been, and the people in their caravan. They were not alone on this business. Indeed there were many caravans travelling to and from Egypt, buying its grain in those years of poor harvest.

The *sūrah* leaves out everything about their actual trip. It places them face to face with their grieved father as they tell him their distressing news. We are in fact told only his short reply which expresses his great pain and distress. Yet he does not give in to despair. He still has hope that God will return his two sons, or indeed his three sons, including his eldest who vowed not to leave Egypt until God had judged for him. It is indeed remarkable that hope should continue to fill his distressed heart: *"He said: 'No, but your minds have tempted you to evil. Sweet patience! God may well bring them all back to me. He is All-Knowing, Wise.' He then turned away from them and said: 'Oh, woe is me for Joseph!' His eyes became white with grief, and he was burdened with silent sorrow."* (Verses 83–84)

"No, but your minds have tempted you to evil. Sweet patience!" (Verse 83) These were his very words when he lost Joseph. However, this time he adds an expression of high hope that God will return Joseph and his brother to him, as well as his other son: *"God may well bring them all back to me. He is All-Knowing, Wise."* (Verse 83) He certainly knows the state Jacob was in, and knows what lies beyond events and tests. He lets everything take place at the appropriate time, when His purpose is fulfilled according to His wisdom.

Where did this ray of hope come from filling the old man's heart? It is nothing more than placing all hope in God and trusting completely to His wisdom, feeling His existence and His endless

124

compassion. It is a feeling that fills the hearts of the elite of believers and becomes more true and profound than the reality they see, hear and touch. "*He then turned away from them and said: 'Oh, woe is me for Joseph!' His eyes became white with grief, and he was burdened with silent sorrow.*" (Verse 84)

This is an inspirational portrayal of a bereaved father. He feels that his tragedy is all his own. No one around him shares in his distress or feels his pain. Hence, he moves away to nurture the loss of his beloved son, Joseph, whom he has not forgotten despite the passage of so many years. Indeed time has not reduced his sorrow; it has all been brought back to life by the new calamity involving his youngest son, Joseph's younger brother. This is a moment when his sorrow is shown to be stronger than his patient resignation: "*Oh, woe is me for Joseph!*" (Verse 84)

But he soon suppresses his sorrow and hides his feelings. As his intense grief and sadness are suppressed, his eyes lose their sight: "*His eyes became white with grief, and he was burdened with silent sorrow.*" (Verse 84)

But his sons continue to harbour their grudge, hurt that he still misses Joseph and suffers distress on his account. They do not show him any compassion. Indeed they do not even try to encourage his hopes. Instead they want to extinguish his last ray of hope. They say to him: "*By God, you will continue to remember Joseph until you wither away or until you are dead.*" (Verşe 85)

This is indeed a cruel thing to say. They are reproaching him for remembering Joseph and feeling sadness at his loss. They tell him that if he continues in such a state, his sorrow will soon deprive him of all his strength or he will die in despair. Joseph is certain not to return.

Their father tells them to leave him alone, because he is only pinning his hopes in his Lord. He makes no complaint to anyone. His relationship with his Lord is different from theirs, and he knows of Him what they do not know: "*It is only to God that I complain and express my grief. For I know of God what you do not know.*" (Verse 86) These words describe in a most vivid way the true feelings of a firm believer concerning the truth of the Godhead. That truth itself is also brought up here in sharp relief.

Meeting a Lost Brother

Whilst everyone else despairs at Joseph's return, this has no effect on this pious old man who knows the truth about his Lord, which is a knowledge that is not readily apparent to others. Such knowledge is based on real feeling and an experience of God's ability, kindness, grace and the mercy He bestows on pious servants. His statement, '*I know of God what you do not know*,' expresses this fact as we cannot. It embodies a truth which is only appreciated by those who have had a similar experience. Such people do not succumb to hardship or despair in the face of adversity. In fact adversity only enhances their faith and trust in God's power and mercy. We will not say more than that. We praise God for the grace He has bestowed on us. He knows and sees what is between Him and us.

Jacob then instructs his sons to go back and seek information about their two younger brothers: "*My sons, go and seek news of Joseph and his brother; and do not despair of God's mercy; for none but unbelievers can ever despair of God's mercy.*" (Verse 87) That is the attitude of a person whose heart is keenly aware of the truth of Godhead. "*My sons, go and seek news of Joseph and his brother.*" The Arabic expression for 'seek news', *taḥassasū*, adds connotations of gentleness and patient pursuit, so that they can demonstrate something of their own souls in their efforts to find out what happened to their brothers. They must never despair of God for He may yet turn to them in mercy and kindness. Even the Arabic word *rawḥ*, used here to denote 'mercy', adds connotations of a spirit experiencing release from hardship.

"*None but unbelievers can ever despair of God's mercy.*" (Verse 87) Believers, on the other hand, are always in touch with God, enjoying His grace, unshaken by distress or hardship, even though the circumstances may be exceedingly tough. Indeed a believer finds in his faith and bond with his Lord a blessing that gives him reassurance, even in the most difficult moments and under enormous pressure.

For the third time Joseph's brothers go to Egypt. However, their state this time is different. The famine had affected them badly, their money had been spent, and the merchandise they carried with them to barter for food was of a low quality. Hence, they spoke in a tone that invited sympathy, which was not known in their earlier conversations. Their complaint tells of what the famine had done to them: "*When they presented themselves before [Joseph] again, they said: 'Exalted one! Hardship has befallen us and our people, and so we have brought but little merchandise. Give us our full measure [of grains], and be charitable to us. Indeed God rewards those who are charitable.'*" (Verse 88)

At this point, and with such a passionate appeal that tells of their misfortune, Joseph is no longer able to carry on presenting himself only as the Chief Minister of Egypt, hiding his true relationship to them. The lessons he wished that they should learn have become well known to them. It is now time for the great surprise that they could never have expected. Hence he puts it to them in a careful, easy way, reminding them of the past which they alone had full knowledge of. None was aware of it besides them, except God. He says to them gently: "*Do you know what you did to Joseph and his brother, when you were still unaware?*" (Verse 89)

It was a voice that they might have recalled, with features they might have remembered. Perhaps they did not pay attention because they were talking to the Chief Minister in his place of government. A thought presented itself to them suddenly: "*They said: 'Why – is it indeed you who are Joseph?'*" (Verse 90) Could it be true? Their minds, hearts, eyes and ears could now see traces of little Joseph in the man talking to them. He replied: "*I am Joseph, and this is my brother. God has indeed been gracious to us. If one remains God-fearing and patient in adversity, God will not fail to reward those who do good.*" (Verse 90)

It was a great surprise indeed. Joseph announces it, reminding them in general terms of what they did to him and his brother out of impulsive ignorance. He stops at that, adding only an acknowledgement of God's grace to him and his brother, making it clear that it was all the result of fearing God, being patient in adversity, and divine justice. In their turn, they remember vividly what they did to Joseph. They are deeply ashamed of their deeds, particularly as they stand before him acknowledging his kindness after their cruelty, his compassion after the harm they caused him. Hence they acknowledge the disparity between their two attitudes, saying: "*By God! Most certainly has God raised you high above us, and we were indeed sinners.*" (Verse 91)

127

A Long Awaited Piece of Good News

They also acknowledged what they realized to be aspects of God's grace bestowed on Joseph, giving him high position, and qualities of forbearance, piety and benevolence. Joseph replied to their acknowledgement of guilt with charitable forgiveness that ended the need for them to feel ashamed of themselves. This shows that Joseph came through his trial with affluence and power as successfully as he came through the earlier trials with hardship and imprisonment.

Joseph is very charitable to his brothers. He replies to their statement by waiving all reproach: *"None shall reproach you today. May God forgive you. He is indeed the Most Merciful of those who show mercy."* (Verse 92) He thus shows that the events of the past have left no lingering bitterness in him. He prays to God to forgive his brothers and turns the conversation to matters that need attention, such as his father whose sorrow was unabated, and whose eyes had become white with grief. Joseph wants to speed up the process of giving him the good news and to meet him as soon as possible. Most urgent of all, he wanted to remove his distress and to help him regain his strength and his eyesight. Hence he tells his brothers: *"Now go and take this shirt of mine and lay it over my father's face, and he will recover his sight. Then come back to me with all your family."* (Verse 93)

How did Joseph know that his father would regain his eyesight once he received his lost son's scent? That is part of what God had taught him. Sudden surprise may produce miraculous effects. Besides, why should there not be a miracle when both Joseph and Jacob are prophets whom God had chosen to be His messengers?

From now on, the narrative takes us from one surprise to another, until it concludes with the realization of the young Joseph's dream which he related to his father at the opening of the *sūrah*.

"As the caravan set out, their father said [to the people around him]: 'I feel the breath of Joseph, though you will not believe me.'" (Verse 94) Smelling Joseph's breath! Anything is easier to believe than this. No one could even think Joseph was alive after all those long years, and that his smell would be recognized by someone weakened by old age. Hence he qualifies his statement by saying that they will think he has gone crazy. If they had only credited him with what was

his due, they would have believed that he really felt the smell of his long departed son.

How could Jacob smell Joseph's breath as soon as the caravan departed? And from which place of departure? Some commentators on the Qur'ān say that he sensed the scent from Joseph's shirt right from the point of the caravan's departure from Egypt. But there is no evidence to support this. It is reasonable to say that the Qur'ānic statement refers to the caravan's crossing a certain point in the land of Kanaan, heading towards Jacob's quarters. We do not say this to deny that a miracle could happen to a prophet like Jacob involving a prophet like Joseph. All that we propose is to limit ourselves to the exact meaning of the text, unless it is further explained by an authentic *ḥadīth*. We do not have such a report in this case, and the Qur'ānic statement itself does not support what the commentators say.

Those who were with Jacob did not have the same position with their Lord, and they could not smell Joseph's shirt. Hence they say to him: "*By God! You are still lost in your old illusions.*" (Verse 95) They describe all Jacob's feelings about Joseph's return as mere illusions. To them Joseph had gone the way of no return.

But the great surprise is realized, followed by another surprise: "*But when the bearer of good news arrived [with Joseph's shirt], he laid it over his face; and he regained his sight.*" (Verse 96) The first surprise relates to the shirt, which is evidence of Joseph's existence and that Jacob would soon meet him. The other surprise is that of Jacob recovering his eyesight after he lost it as a result of his enduring grief. At this point Jacob refers to the fact that he has true knowledge imparted to him by God. He mentioned this to them earlier, but they could not understand him. "*He said: 'Did I not say to you that I know from God something that you do not know?'*" (Verse 96)

Jacob's sons said: "*Father, pray to God to forgive us our sins, for we were sinners indeed.*" (Verse 97) We notice here that Jacob still held something in his heart against his sons. He had not yet fully forgiven them. Yet he promises to pray to God to forgive them after he had a chance to recover. His reply suggests that. "*He said: 'I shall pray to God to forgive you. He is certainly Most Forgiving, Most Merciful.'*" (Verse 98) That he promises to pray for their forgiveness at a future point in time comes from a heart that has been hurt.

A Happy Family Reunion

The *sūrah* gives us yet another surprise. Leaving out all details about this last trip, it moves directly to a highly charged final scene. We pick up our commentary with the family approaching its appointed meeting with Joseph its long departed son. "*When they all presented themselves before Joseph, he drew his parents to himself, saying: 'Enter Egypt in peace, if it so pleases God.' And he raised his parents to the highest place of honour, and they fell down on their knees, prostrating themselves before him. He said: 'Father, this is the real meaning of my dream of long ago. My Lord has made it come true. He has been gracious to me, releasing me from prison, and bringing you all from the desert after Satan had sown discord between me and my brothers. My Lord is gracious in whatever way He wishes. He is All-Knowing, truly Wise.'*" (Verses 99–100)

It is certainly a most powerful scene. Long years have passed with all that they carried of despair and lost hope, pain and distress, longing and grief, and also an urgent, silent plea for reunion. Long hard years of a test that is not easy to pass. After all that we have this powerful scene, with its intensity of feeling, pleasure, happiness and emotion. It is a final scene that is closely connected to the opening one in the story. The opening scene is long gone, but the final one is now taking place. Between the two, Joseph remembers God, never allowing himself to forget Him: "*When they all presented themselves before Joseph, he drew his parents to himself, saying: 'Enter Egypt in peace, if it so pleases God.'*" (Verse 99)

He also remembers his earlier dream, realizing that it is now fulfilled as he raises his parents to sit on the couch where he normally sits while his brothers prostrate themselves before him. In his dream he had seen eleven stars as well as the sun and the moon prostrating themselves before him. Hence he sees its fulfilment in the scene that now took place before him: "*And he raised his parents to the highest place of honour, and they fell down on their knees, prostrating themselves before him. He said: 'Father, this is the real meaning of my dream of long ago. My Lord has made it come true.'*" (Verse 100)

He then speaks of the grace God has bestowed on him: "*He has been gracious to me, releasing me from prison, and bringing you all from the desert after Satan had sown discord between me and my brothers."* (Verse 100) He moves on to emphasize that God accomplishes His will as He pleases: *"My Lord is gracious in whatever way He wishes."* (Verse 100) He achieves His purpose with grace, while people are totally unaware of how His designs are accomplished. Joseph follows this by making the same statement his father did when he told him about his dream at the beginning of the *sūrah*: *"He is All-Knowing, truly Wise."* (Verse 100) This brings harmony between the beginning and the end, even in the way thoughts are expressed.

Before the curtains are drawn over this last emotional scene, we find Joseph pulling himself away from the overwhelming pleasure of family reunion, and also from the pleasant security of high position and real authority to glorify his Lord and express his gratitude to Him. All that he prays for at this moment is that he should die as a person who surrenders himself to God and to be grouped with the righteous: *"'My Lord, You have given me power and imparted to me some understanding of the real meaning of statements. Originator of the heavens and the earth! You are my guardian in this world and in the life to come. Let me die as one who has surrendered himself to You, and admit me among the righteous.'"* (Verse 101)

"My Lord, You have given me power." (Verse 101) You have given me all that comes with a position of power: real authority, high standing, great respect and wealth. All these are blessings given in this world. And You have *"imparted to me some understanding of the real meaning of statements."* (Verse 101) This gives me a real understanding of where events lead and how statements and dreams are interpreted. This is a blessing of knowledge. I remember the grace You have bestowed on me and the blessings You have granted me. *"Originator of the heavens and the earth!"* (Verse 101) You have created them all by Your design and will. You remain in full control of them all, and of all creatures that take their abode in them. *"You are my guardian in this world and in the life to come."* (Verse 101) It is You alone who gives real support.

My Lord, all that is Your blessing, and everything testifies to Your power. My Lord, I am not appealing to You to give me power, health or wealth. My appeal is for something that is much more valuable, and much longer lasting: *"Let me die as one who has surrendered himself to You, and admit me among the righteous."* (Verse 101)

This ending removes all notions of power and position, and the happiness of meeting long missed family members. The final scene thus appears to be one in which a true servant of God appeals to Him in all humility, requesting Him to enable him to maintain his faith until He gathers him to Himself, and admits him among His righteous servants. This represents the total and perfect success in all tests and trials.

6

One Message to Mankind

That is an account which We have now revealed to you, speaking of things that have been beyond your perception. You were not present when they [i.e. Joseph's brothers] resolved upon their plans and completed their schemes. (102)

ذَٰلِكَ مِنۡ أَنۢبَآءِ ٱلۡغَيۡبِ نُوحِيهِ إِلَيۡكَۖ وَمَا كُنتَ لَدَيۡهِمۡ إِذۡ أَجۡمَعُوٓاْ أَمۡرَهُمۡ وَهُمۡ يَمۡكُرُونَ ﴿١٠٢﴾

Yet however strongly you may desire it, most people will not believe. (103)

وَمَآ أَكۡثَرُ ٱلنَّاسِ وَلَوۡ حَرَصۡتَ بِمُؤۡمِنِينَ ﴿١٠٣﴾

You ask no recompense from them for it. It is but God's reminder to all mankind. (104)

وَمَا تَسۡـَٔلُهُمۡ عَلَيۡهِ مِنۡ أَجۡرٍۚ إِنۡ هُوَ إِلَّا ذِكۡرٌ لِّلۡعَٰلَمِينَ ﴿١٠٤﴾

Yet many are the signs in the heavens and the earth which they pass by, paying no heed to them. (105)

وَكَأَيِّن مِّنۡ ءَايَةٍ فِي ٱلسَّمَٰوَٰتِ وَٱلۡأَرۡضِ يَمُرُّونَ عَلَيۡهَا وَهُمۡ عَنۡهَا مُعۡرِضُونَ ﴿١٠٥﴾

And most of them do not even believe in God without also associating partners with Him. (106)

وَمَا يُؤۡمِنُ أَكۡثَرُهُم بِٱللَّهِ إِلَّا وَهُم مُّشۡرِكُونَ ﴿١٠٦﴾

Do they feel confident that the overwhelming scourge of God's punishment will not fall upon them, or that the Last Hour will not come upon them suddenly, taking them unaware. (107)

أَفَأَمِنُوٓاْ أَن تَأْتِيَهُمْ غَشِيَةٌ مِّنْ عَذَابِ ٱللَّهِ أَوْ تَأْتِيَهُمُ ٱلسَّاعَةُ بَغْتَةً وَهُمْ لَا يَشْعُرُونَ ﴿١٠٧﴾

Say: 'This is my way. I call [all mankind] to God on the basis of sure knowledge, I and all those who follow me. Limitless is God in His glory. I am not one of those who associate partners with Him.' (108)

قُلْ هَٰذِهِۦ سَبِيلِىٓ أَدْعُوٓاْ إِلَى ٱللَّهِ عَلَىٰ بَصِيرَةٍ أَنَا۠ وَمَنِ ٱتَّبَعَنِى وَسُبْحَٰنَ ٱللَّهِ وَمَآ أَنَا۠ مِنَ ٱلْمُشْرِكِينَ ﴿١٠٨﴾

Even before your time, We only sent [as messengers] men to whom We gave Our revelations, choosing them from among their people. Have they not travelled the land and seen what was the end of those [unbelievers] who lived before them? Better indeed is the life to come for those who remain God-fearing. Will you not, then, use your reason? (109)

وَمَآ أَرْسَلْنَا مِن قَبْلِكَ إِلَّا رِجَالًا نُّوحِىٓ إِلَيْهِم مِّنْ أَهْلِ ٱلْقُرَىٰٓ أَفَلَمْ يَسِيرُواْ فِى ٱلْأَرْضِ فَيَنظُرُواْ كَيْفَ كَانَ عَٰقِبَةُ ٱلَّذِينَ مِن قَبْلِهِمْ وَلَدَارُ ٱلْأَخِرَةِ خَيْرٌ لِّلَّذِينَ ٱتَّقَوْاْ أَفَلَا تَعْقِلُونَ ﴿١٠٩﴾

When at length [Our] messengers lost all hope and thought that they were denied, Our help came to them, saving those whom We willed [to be saved]. Never can Our [mighty] punishment be averted from people who are guilty. (110)

حَتَّىٰٓ إِذَا ٱسْتَيْـَٔسَ ٱلرُّسُلُ وَظَنُّوٓاْ أَنَّهُمْ قَدْ كُذِبُواْ جَآءَهُمْ نَصْرُنَا فَنُجِّىَ مَن نَّشَآءُ وَلَا يُرَدُّ بَأْسُنَا عَنِ ٱلْقَوْمِ ٱلْمُجْرِمِينَ ﴿١١٠﴾

Indeed their stories give a lesson to those who are endowed with understanding. This [revelation] could not possibly be an invented discourse. It is a confirmation of earlier revelations, an explanation of all things, as well as guidance and mercy for people who believe. (111)

لَقَدْ كَانَ فِى قَصَصِهِمْ عِبْرَةٌ لِّأُوْلِى الْأَلْبَبِ مَا كَانَ حَدِيثًا يُفْتَرَىٰ وَلَـٰكِن تَصْدِيقَ الَّذِى بَيْنَ يَدَيْهِ وَتَفْصِيلَ كُلِّ شَىْءٍ وَهُدًى وَرَحْمَةً لِّقَوْمٍ يُؤْمِنُونَ ﴿١١١﴾

Overview

Having narrated Joseph's story in detail, the *sūrah* now begins commenting on it, pointing out some fundamental issues. To clarify these, it touches on certain aspects that are clearly apparent in the expanse of the universe around us, and others that are deep in the human soul, or relevant to former nations and communities, or which belong to the realm that lies beyond the reach of human perception. We will discuss these as they occur in this final passage, pointing out at the outset that they are ordered with a specific objective in mind.

Turning Away from True Faith

Joseph's story was not one that the Arabian people among whom Muḥammad lived all his life used to relate. It includes certain secrets of which neither he nor his people were aware. In fact those secrets were known only to the people who lived through its events and took part in them. These had long gone. At the opening of the *sūrah*, God tells the Prophet Muḥammad (peace be upon him): "*In revealing this Qur'ān We relate to you the best of narratives. Before it you were among those who are unaware [of revelation]."* (Verse 3) Now after the story has been told in full, the comment provided here is closely linked to its opening: "*That is an account which We have now revealed to you, speaking of things that have been beyond your perception. You were not present when they [i.e. Joseph's brothers] resolved upon their plans and completed their schemes."* (Verse 102)

That story, with all its intricate details, belongs to what is beyond your knowledge and perception. It is We who reveal it to you. The fact that it is a revelation from God is clearly seen in the fact that you could not have come to know of it by any other means. In so far as you are concerned, it has been something beyond the reach of your perception. You were not present with Joseph's brothers when they indulged in their consultations to which reference was made in different parts of the *sūrah*. Nor were you with them when they indulged in their scheming against Joseph, and against their father. Nor were you present with them after Joseph had detained his younger brother, when they were involved in earnest discussion, which involved some planning and scheming. This is also a reference to the scheming of the aristocrat women against Joseph, and of the people of the court who imprisoned him. All this scheming was not witnessed by the Prophet. It is a part of the revelation bestowed on him from on high and confirmed yet again in the revelation of this *sūrah*, which also confirms other issues of faith illustrated throughout the narrative.

The truth of revelation, the stories that it contains, the various aspects that move listeners' hearts should be sufficient to make people believe in the truth of the Qur'ān. They have seen the Prophet, known his character and personality, and listened to what he had to say. Yet most of them did not believe. They pass by the various signs that are everywhere in the expanse of the universe, without paying much attention to them or understanding their message. They are just like one who turns his face away so that he does not see what is in front of him. What are they waiting for, when it is a fact that God's punishment may overtake them when they are unaware? "*Yet however strongly you may desire it, most people will not believe. You ask no recompense from them for it. It is but God's reminder to all mankind. Yet many are the signs in the heavens and the earth which they pass by, paying no heed to them. And most of them do not even believe in God without also associating partners with Him. Do they feel confident that the overwhelming scourge of God's punishment will not fall upon them, or that the Last Hour will not come upon them suddenly, taking them unaware.*" (Verses 103–107)

The Prophet was very keen that his people should believe, because he knew that his message contained everything that was good and he loved dearly that they should have that good in full. Moreover, he wanted to spare them the hardship that is bound to engulf unbelievers in this world and the punishment of the hereafter. However, God, who knows human nature and how people think and react, tells him that his desire will not lead the majority of unbelievers to faith. That is because they turn away from the numerous signs that are in the universe around them, staring them in the face. Their attitude takes them away from faith, making them unable to benefit from all these signs.

The Prophet is in no need of their positive response to faith. He does not seek any wages for providing them with guidance. In fact their attitude, turning away from these signs is very singular, considering that they are freely given to them. They are not asked to give anything in return: *"You ask no recompense from them for it. It is but God's reminder to all mankind."* (Verse 104) You are reminding them of God's signs and messages, directing their eyes and minds to them. In fact these signs and messages are available to all mankind. They are not given specially to a particular community, race or tribe. No price is sought in return, so that rich people have an advantage over the poor. No condition is attached to them, so that those who are able to meet it would be favoured. They are a reminder for all mankind. Everyone can benefit from them without difficulty. *"Yet many are the signs in the heavens and the earth which they pass by, paying no heed to them."* (Verse 105)

The signs that point to God's existence, oneness and power are numerous, placed everywhere in the universe. They are held out in the heavens and the earth for all to see. They pass by them morning and evening, day and night. They almost speak to people, inviting them to reflect and contemplate. They are directly in front of all people, addressing their hearts and minds. Yet they prefer not to see them or listen to their messages. They turn a deaf ear and a sealed heart to their profound message.

It is sufficient to contemplate a sunrise or sunset for a moment, or to reflect on the shade and how it gently increases or decreases, or to look at the mighty sea, or gushing fountain. Reflect, if you will, on a growing plant, an emerging bud, a glowing flower and mature harvest. Or look at a bird flying as though it is swimming in the air, a fish swimming in water, worms that travel in the soil, ants going ceaselessly about their work. Contemplate the countless number of species and communities of animals and insects. Only a moment of reflection in the depth of night or the great hassle of day, with the human mind receptive to the message given by life and existence is sufficient to make us shudder with awe and respond positively, recognizing the truth of God's oneness. Alas, most people pass by these signs, paying no heed to them and taking no notice of the message they all impart. Hence, the majority of people do not believe.

The Subtle Corruption of Faith

Yet even the believers among them allow an element of disbelief, in one form or another, to creep into their hearts. True faith requires being constantly alert so that any fleeting thought that Satan tries to sneak into our beliefs, and every worldly value in any action or attitude we take are removed straightaway. To do so is to ensure that we address all our actions to God alone. Pure faith needs a firm decision in the question of who has the supreme influence on people's hearts and actions. This ensures that all submission is to God alone. No one else has any position that requires even partial submission.

"And most of them do not even believe in God without also associating partners with Him." (Verse 106) They associate some earthly value in the way they consider events, matters and people, or give to something other than God's will or power a role in what brings them harm or benefit. Or they may acknowledge an element of submission to a ruler or master who does not confine himself to God's law alone; or they look up to someone other than God for the fulfilment of their hopes; or address their sacrifice in a way that seeks to win people's admiration; or strive to ensure some benefit or dispel harm but their striving is not done purely for God's sake; or they may allow something to creep into their worship which makes it not purely dedicated to God alone. Hence, the Prophet says: *"Shirk,* i.e. associating partners with God, may be more subtle than the creeping of an ant." [Related by Abū Ya'lā on the authority of Ma'qil ibn Yasār.]

The Prophet's statements give several examples of such subtle idolatry. 'Abdullāh ibn 'Umar quotes the Prophet as saying: "Whoever swears by something other than God commits idolatry." [Related by al-Tirmidhī.] 'Abdullāh ibn Mas'ūd reports that the Prophet says: "Charms and talismans are marks of idolatry." [Related by Aḥmad and Abū Dāwūd.] He also says: "Whoever wears a charm associates partners with God." [Related by Aḥmad.] The Prophet also relates a statement attributing it to God in a sacred ḥadīth: "I am the least in need of partners. If anyone does something, associating in it someone else with Me, I will abandon him to that partner."

In another ḥadīth the Prophet is quoted as saying: "When all generations, past, present and future, are gathered before God on the Day which will undoubtedly come, an announcement will be made in the following words: 'Whoever associated a partner with God in any action he did for God's sake should seek its reward from someone other than God. For God is the least in need of partners.'"

Imām Aḥmad relates that the Prophet warned: "What I fear most for you is little shirk." When his Companions asked him to explain what he meant by little shirk, he said: "Hypocrisy. When people come with their deeds on the Day of Judgement, God says to them: 'Go to those whom you used to flatter in your first life and seek your reward from them.'"

Such, then, are the subtle forms of associating partners with God. Hence constant alertness is required in order to remove any trace of it so that our faith is true and pure.

On the other hand, there is the clear and apparent form of associating partners with God, which means submission to a being other than God in any matter of this life. This may be in the form of submission to a law other than God's. This is universally accepted. There is also submission to tradition, which may take the form of festivals and other occasions that people may accept without reference to God's orders. People may submit to norms that violate God's orders, as in the case of dress and clothing which reveals what God has ordered to remain covered. What we are talking about here goes beyond submission to a tradition or social custom which people do in flagrant disregard of God's clear orders. That takes their behaviour from the realm of offences committed to make it a belief and a form of submission. This makes it far more serious indeed. Hence God says: "*And most of them do not even believe in God without also associating partners with*

Him." (Verse 106) This applies then to those Arabs whom the Prophet addressed directly and to other generations and communities throughout human life.

Enlightened Advocacy of Divine Faith

Now the question arises: what are those people waiting for when they continue to turn away and pay no heed to all the signs that are present in the universe pointing to God and His oneness? What are they waiting for after they have turned away from God's revelations, for which they have been asked no recompense? *"Do they feel confident that the overwhelming scourge of God's punishment will not fall upon them, or that the Last Hour will not come upon them suddenly, taking them unaware."* (Verse 107)

This is a powerful touch which is meant to wake them up and shed their negligent attitude, so that they do not suffer its aftermath. The timing of God's punishment is unknown to anyone. It may strike them suddenly, or it may be that the Last Hour is so near, and the Day of Judgement, with all its suffering may come suddenly, taking them unaware. The doors leading to the world beyond are all closed, allowing no eye or ear to penetrate through it. No one knows what the next moment brings. How is it that those who turn away from God's signs feel secure?

The verses of the Qur'ān, which embody God's message, are within their grasp, and the signs God has placed in the universe are also there for all to behold and contemplate. But most people pass by both paying no heed, associating partners with God, either openly or in a subtle way. God's Messenger, however, will follow his own way, joined by those who follow him, maintaining the right path, without any deviation, and allowing nothing to influence their determination to follow it. *"Say: 'This is my way. I call [all mankind] to God on the basis of sure knowledge, I and all those who follow me. Limitless is God in His glory. I am not one of those who associate partners with Him.'"* (Verse 108)

"Say: 'This is my way.'" (Verse 108) It is a straightforward road, without any crookedness or concealed turns. There is no doubt about its being the right path. *"I call [all mankind] to God on the basis of sure knowledge, I and all those who follow me."* (Verse 108) We follow God's

guidance which illuminates our way for us. We follow it with open eyes, knowledge and understanding. There is no groping in the dark or following sudden whims or fancies that lack solid foundation. We attribute to God nothing that does not suit His Lordship of the universe. We abandon those who associate partners with Him and show ourselves to follow a road that is completely distinct from any that is followed by those who associate partners with Him. *"Limitless is God in His glory. I am not one of those who associate partners with Him."* (Verse 108) I do no such thing, neither openly nor subtly. This is my way. Whoever wishes to follow me may do so. As for me, I am going along, regardless of who may wish to follow a different way.

The advocates of the divine cause must make this distinction very clearly. They must declare that they belong to a separate community that is distinct from anyone who does not belong to their faith, follow their way and obey their leadership. It is not sufficient that they should call on people to follow their religion while they themselves continue to be part of un-Islamic society. Such advocacy is of little value and produces little return. It is imperative that they should declare, right at the outset, that they are different from ignorant communities, and that they have their own distinctive community based on the bond of faith, and following Islamic leadership. They must distinguish themselves and their leadership from un-Islamic society and its leadership. If they stay within that society and constitute a part of it, deferring to its leadership, they undermine all the authority of their faith, all the results their message may achieve, and all the attraction that message may have.

This fact does not apply merely to Islamic advocacy among idolaters in pre-Islamic Arabia. It applies every time a state of *jāhiliyyah* prevails. *Jāhiliyyah* in the twentieth century does not differ, in its basic elements or distinctive features, from any other state of ignorance, or *jāhiliyyah*, which the Islamic message has had to face in any period of history.

Those who believe that they may achieve something by being diluted within un-Islamic society, or by presenting the message of Islam in a subtle way through such a society are mistaken. They do not fully understand the nature of the Islamic faith and how it appeals to hearts and minds. The advocates of atheism declare their identity and their goals. Would not the advocates of Islam declare their true identity and make their way clear? Would they not make clear that the route they follow is totally different from that of *jāhiliyyah*?

The Bearers of God's Message

The *sūrah* now refers to the divine law concerning the messages given to prophets who delivered them. It also refers to some of the signs shown in the fate met by some past generations. As a Messenger of God, Muḥammad has many predecessors, and his message is not without precedent. Hence people should consider what happened to earlier communities which did not believe their messengers and rejected the faith. Their fate provides some signs that are clearly visible to all beholders.

"Even before your time, We only sent [as messengers] men to whom We gave Our revelations, choosing them from among their people. Have they not travelled the land and seen what was the end of those [unbelievers] who lived before them? Better indeed is the life to come for those who remain God-fearing. Will you not, then, use your reason?" (Verse 109) Reflection on the fate of former communities is bound to shake even hardened hearts. We can imagine their movements, actions and feelings, and we can paint a picture of them going about their business in these places, going from one location to another, full of hope, fear and aspiration, and looking up to the future, then suddenly they are motionless, with all their faculties and senses completely dead. Their quarters are lifeless, and they have gone. All has come to nothing. A complete void is all that is left. Reflection on these facts is bound to shake even the most hardened and cruel of hearts. Therefore, the Qur'ān takes us by the hand to show us the fate of earlier communities, time after time.

"Even before your time, We only sent [as messengers] men to whom We gave Our revelations, choosing them from among their people." (Verse 109) These messengers were neither angels nor any other species of creature. They were human beings, just like the people of the towns. Like you, they were not even desert people, so that they would be gentler and more compassionate, showing more perseverance in the difficult task of advocating the faith. The Prophet's message, then, follows the same pattern of revelation given to other messengers.

"*Have they not travelled the land and seen what was the end of those [unbelievers] who lived before them?*" (Verse 109) Had they done so, they would have realized that their own fate is bound to be the same as that of those earlier communities who denied their messengers when they conveyed to them God's message. They would have realized that the pattern of God's dealings with earlier communities will apply to them, and that they themselves will soon depart along the same way.

"*Better indeed is the life to come for those who remain God-fearing.*" (Verse 109) It is indeed infinitely better than this present life which is, by nature, a life of short duration. "*Will you not, then, use your reason?*" (Verse 109) You should use your reason to contemplate what happened to communities before you and guard against a similar fate. Reason will tell you to opt for the eternal life in preference to the fleeting comforts of this life.

The *sūrah* then describes the very hard period in the life of God's messengers, which precedes the decisive moment when God's promise is fulfilled and His law inevitably takes effect: "*When at length [Our] messengers lost all hope and thought that they were denied, Our help came to them, saving those whom We willed [to be saved]. Never can Our [mighty] punishment be averted from people who are guilty.*" (Verse 110) This is a frightful scene, describing the great difficulties messengers face: the denials, persistent abuse and arrogant refusal to accept the truth. Days and years pass while they continue to convey God's message but meet with only very limited response. Years follow years while falsehood and evil continue to enjoy power and large followings, while the believers who are few in number, muster little or no power.

These are difficult times when evil swells its power, spreads tyranny and deals harshly and treacherously with advocates of the truth. God's messengers await His promise, but it is not fulfilled in this world. At these moments, disturbing thoughts occur to them: have they been belied? Have their souls deceived them when they hoped for victory in this life? No messenger of God would be in this position unless he had been exposed to a measure of distress, hardship, suffering and stress beyond the ability of any other human being to tolerate. I have never read this verse, or the other one in *Sūrah* 2, without feeling a strong shudder as I try to imagine the horror that would cause a messenger of God to entertain such feelings. The verse in *Sūrah* 2 runs as follows:

"Do you reckon that you will enter paradise while you have not suffered like those [believers] who passed away before you? Affliction and adversity befell them, and so terribly shaken were they that the Messenger and the believers with him would exclaim, 'When will God's help come?' Surely, God's help is close at hand." (2: 214) Every time I read either of these two verses I could imagine this great horror giving rise to such feelings of despair, affliction and distress violently shaking a messenger of God, with his morale getting so low, and the pain in his heart so intolerable.

It is at this point when distress reaches its climax, leaving even the messenger powerless, that support is given in full measure, and victory is decisive: *"Our help came to them, saving those whom We willed [to be saved]. Never can Our [mighty] punishment be averted from people who are guilty."* (Verse 110)

Qur'ānic Stories

Such is the normal line of events when it comes to advocacy of God's message. Hardship and adversity are necessary until all the efforts and energy of its advocates are exhausted. When people so despair of victory, it is given by God. Those who deserve to be saved will be saved from the destruction that engulfs the others who deny the truth and from the tyranny of those who wield worldly power. God's might strikes the evil-doers and they can in no way resist it. Neither their own nor their supporters' power can prevent God's punishment.

This is the normal way because God's support does not come cheap. Had it been so, there would be a lot of frivolity about the advocacy of God's message. There would be no shortage of people claiming to be advocates of the true message, since there would only be a small price to pay before God's support were given. The message of the truth should never be treated with frivolity. It provides a complete way of life and a code to be implemented. Hence, it must be protected against false advocates who are not prepared to pay the price. When the price is high, and the truth emerges clearly against the background of hardship and adversity, true advocates are also distinguished by their steadfastness. They do not abandon their message even though they may feel that they will never see victory in their lifetime.

Advocacy of the divine message is not a short-term investment which must yield returns by a certain deadline, or people move to a different investment seeking better returns. No one who undertakes advocacy of God's message in the hostile environment of un-Islamic society which submits to a power other than God's can think that his task will be an easy one, or that his investment will yield quick returns. He must be clear in his mind that he stands against all tyranny in human life that commands physical and financial power, and which deludes the masses until they do all its bidding, even describing as black what they know to be white. Tyrants even turn the masses against the advocates of God's message, tempting them with the satisfaction of their desires and putting in their minds the notion that God's message and its advocates deprive them of such satisfaction.

Those who want to call on people to follow God's message must realize that the task they undertake is tough and demanding. Not only so, but it is even tougher to join it against the power of *jāhiliyyah*. Hence the oppressed masses will not initially join it. Only those who prefer the truth, even though it requires the sacrifice of comfort, safety and all the pleasures of the world, will rise to it. Such people are always few in number, but God will judge between them and their community on the basis of the truth after they have striven hard. It is only when God has judged for them that the masses will join them. This is when people embrace God's message in large numbers.

In Joseph's story we read about the different types of hardship he faced and his despair of people ever coming to realize the truth about him. The outcome however was very good, just as God had promised. For God's promise will always come true. Joseph's story is but an example of the histories of God's messengers. It provides lessons for those who wish to reflect. It confirms what earlier scriptures emphasized, even though Muhammad had no access to these scriptures. What he preached could not have been a fabricated tale. Lies do not confirm one another. They neither provide guidance nor spread an air of mercy over believers' hearts. *"Indeed their stories give a lesson to those who are endowed with understanding. This [revelation] could not possibly be an invented discourse. It is a confirmation of earlier revelations, an explanation of all things, as well as guidance and mercy for people who believe."* (Verse 111)

Thus the beginning and the end of the *sūrah* are brought in line, just as the beginning and end of the story are perfectly matched. Comments at the opening and end of the *sūrah*, as well as those interspersed in the story relate perfectly to the theme and the way it is expressed. The religious objective of relating it is thus fulfilled, while providing an essential artistic element. This is coupled with the fact that it is a true story relating events that actually took place.

The whole story, from beginning to end, is told in a single *sūrah*, because its nature requires that. It is the gradual fulfilment of a dream, which evolves and takes shape day after day, and stage after stage. Hence, its lessons as well as artistic harmony cannot be clearly seen unless it is followed right through to its conclusion. This is different from relating episodes from the history of other messengers where highlighting a single episode serves a particular purpose. This is frequently done in the Qur'ān, as in the case of the story of the Prophet Solomon and the Queen of Sheba, or the birth of Mary, or that of Jesus, or the floods at the time of Noah. In all these cases, a single episode is related in order to serve a certain objective. Joseph's story, on the other hand, needs to be told altogether in order to draw its moral to the fore. God certainly tells the truth as He says: "*In revealing this Qur'ān We relate to you the best of narratives. Before it you were among those who are unaware [of revelation].*" (Verse 3)

SŪRAH 13

Al-Ra'd

(Thunder)

Prologue

I often feel reluctant to comment on Qur'ānic texts, knowing that my style and resources are inadequate. As with *Sūrah* 6, Cattle, I find myself ill-equipped to explain the present *sūrah*. But what am I to do, realizing as I do that our generation needs to receive the Qur'ān with a detailed explanation of its nature, method, subject matter and aims? Unfortunately people have moved too far from the environment in which the Qur'ān was revealed, and from its purpose and goals. They are little aware of its import and dimensions. Even its terminology does not carry to them its true meanings. People today live in a state similar to that the Qur'ān faced at the time of its revelation, but they do not use the Qur'ān to confront this *jāhiliyyah* as the early Muslims did. Without such action, people cannot begin to formulate a proper understanding of the Qur'ān and its secrets, because such secrets remain a closed book for anyone who sits idle, unwilling to act according to Qur'ānic guidance.

Nevertheless, I am overwhelmed whenever I attempt to comment on the Qur'ān. It is impossible for me to put in words and sentences what I feel when I listen to the Qur'ān or reflect on its text. Hence, I know how wide the gulf is between the feelings the Qur'ān generates within me and what I present to my readers.

I am also profoundly aware of the great gulf that separates our generation from that which directly received the Qur'ān. The Qur'ān addressed them directly, and they felt its rhythm, viewed its images, appreciated its inspiration and recognized its hints, interacting with it and making their response clear. They aimed to fulfil its message in their approach to life and their confrontation with its opponents. Hence, they were able to accomplish what was, by all standards, miraculous in a short time-span. They achieved a total about-turn in their feelings, concepts and life generally, and produced a similar and complete change in the life of their community, in human life generally and in the line human history would take to the end of time.

They drank at the Qur'ānic spring, allowing no intermediary between them and the Qur'ān. Their ears felt its music as it was first spoken, and they appreciated its warmth and inspiration. Hence, they took immediate action to mould their lives and thoughts in accordance with its principles, values and the facts it presented. By contrast, our present generation shapes its life pattern in accordance with this or that philosophical approach, little realizing that the opponents of such approaches are only mortals too, liable to all manner of error.

Furthermore, when we consider what those early Muslims achieved within themselves and in the life around them, which was miraculous by any standard, we try to explain such achievements by reference to our own logic based on standards and values that are fundamentally different from theirs. Hence, we err in identifying their motives and goals and in appreciating the results they achieved. We forget that they were made a different creation by the Qur'ān.

I appeal to my readers not to make the understanding of my book their aim. They should read it to draw nearer to the Qur'ān, then put the book aside and approach the Qur'ān as it is. They cannot do so unless they dedicate themselves to the implementation and fulfilment of its values and principles in their lives, fighting opposition forces under its banner.

This was my first thought as I began to look at this *sūrah*, as if I was reading it for the first time, although I had read and heard it countless times. The Qur'ān, however, gives you as much as you give to it. Each time, it opens up to you with new light, inspiration and rhythm, giving as much as you are prepared to receive. It sounds fresh every time, as though you had never read, heard or dealt with it before.

The present *sūrah* is a remarkable one, maintaining the same rhythm and giving the same ambience from start to finish.[1] Nevertheless, it presents us with a multitude of images, feelings and thoughts that fill our imagination and address our hearts and souls in every possible way. With its brilliant light and endless meanings, it travels with our hearts to wider worlds, times and horizons, keeping us fully aware, understanding everything we see and hear.

What we have here is not words and sentences; rather, a strong, hammering rhythm pervades the entire *sūrah*, permeating its images, meanings, and finer touches.

The main theme of the *sūrah*, like all Makkan revelations,[2] is faith and the main issues which surround it: God's oneness and Lordship, submission to Him in this world and in the life to come, revelation, resurrection and its correlatives. Yet this single issue with its multiple strands is never presented in the same way in any two *sūrahs*, whether revealed in Makkah or Madinah. Every time we find it presented in a new way and new light, generating a different impact and inspiration.

These issues are not presented in the form of an academic argument, based on cold logic. Instead they are presented within a framework, which is the universe and its remarkable phenomena which serve as proofs to be appreciated by open minds. These marvellous phenomena are unending. Indeed, they look new every day, as they continue to reveal their secrets time after time. Even what was revealed earlier seems

---

1. The Qur'ānic musical rhythm uses a variety of elements, including harmony between the place and manner of articulation of individual sounds within a single word, sound harmony in each sentence or clause, the type of long vowels chosen, and the long vowels and the consonants used in the final words of each verse. [I have discussed this at length in my book *Al-Taṣwīr al-Fannī fī al-Qur'ān*.] All the elements of rhythm used in this *sūrah* are consistent throughout, except for the long vowels and consonants in the final words of its verses. We note that the first five verses use words with an '*oon (ūn)*' ending. The rest of the *sūrah* uses a long '*a (ā)*' followed by a plosive, or semi-plosive consonant, such as '*aab (āb), aad (ād), aal (āl), aar (ār)*.'

2. Despite the statement in some copies of the Qur'ān, based on reports indicating that the *sūrah* is a Madinan revelation, we maintain that it was revealed in Makkah. This is clearly indicated by its subject matter, method of approach, general atmosphere and ambience which is clearly noted by anyone who is well familiar with the Qur'ān.

to acquire a new perspective in the light of new discovery. Hence, the issues the *sūrah* tackles remain alive.

The *sūrah* takes the human heart on a grand tour, showing it the universe in a variety of spectacular images: the heavens raised without support; the sun and the moon pursuing their courses for a definite time; the night covered by day; the spread of the earth with its firm mountains and running rivers; gardens, plants and date trees with different shapes, tastes and colours yet growing in adjacent land irrigated with the same water; the lightning generating fear and hope; the thunder glorifying and praising God; the angels standing in awe; the thunderbolt God hurls against whomever He wishes; the clouds heavy with rain that pours over riverbeds; and the foam that disappears into nothing to allow what is of benefit to stay.

The *sūrah* pursues the human heart wherever it tries to go. This pursuit is based on God's absolute knowledge which encompasses every little detail, including what is concealed or moving openly in broad daylight. It is the knowledge that records every fleeting thought occurring to any living thing. At the same time, whatever happens to be beyond the reach of human perception is encompassed by God's knowledge, including what every female conceives and whatever falls short or increases in gestation.

The *sūrah* gives an impression of the nature of God's power that encompasses the entire universe: the hidden and the apparent, large and small, present and removed. The part of the universe that human faculties can imagine is great and awesome indeed.

In addition, the *sūrah* includes some parables that are presented in vivid, moving scenes and images. It also adds a scene of the Day of Judgement, with its happiness for some and suffering for others, and people's reactions to both. There are also brief references to the fate of earlier generations and how they conducted themselves, and were subjected to God's law and its operation.

These are, in brief, the main themes and issues tackled in the *sūrah*. The *sūrah* is also remarkable for its artistry in presenting these issues. The general framework within which these issues are presented is the universe, with its remarkable phenomena and spectacular imagery. But the framework here has a special ambience provided by contrasting natural scenes and phenomena: heaven and earth; sun and moon; night and day; entities and shadows; firm mountains and running rivers; useless scum and penetrating water; adjacent but different pieces of land; clustered and non-clustered date trees, etc.

This element of contrast is carried further so as to include all meanings, actions and fates. Thus, the abstract contrast echoes the physical one to perfect its general atmosphere. Thus we see the clear contrast within God's supreme power as He establishes Himself on the throne making both the sun and the moon subservient; embryos in the womb fall short in gestation with others increasing; the one who speaks in whispers and the one who speaks aloud; the one who moves stealthily in the night and the one who walks in broad daylight; fear and hope regenerated by lightning; the glorification of God in praise by the thunder and in fear by the angels. The true prayer addressed to God is contrasted with the false one addressed to false deities. Similarly we see the contrast between those who know and those who are blind; the people of earlier revelations who are delighted by the Qur'ān and those who deny some parts of it; the annulment and the confirmation in God's records. Everything in the *sūrah*: its meanings, directions and movements utilize the element of contrast to the full.

Another aspect of the remarkable harmony of style is seen in the fact that because the *sūrah* raises a background of natural scenes, referring to heaven and earth, sun and moon, thunder and lightning, thunderbolts and rain, it also mentions what is carried in animal wombs, coupled with a reference to "*by how much the wombs may fall short [in gestation], and by how much they may increase.*" These two aspects are in harmony with the water running in riverbeds and the growth of vegetation. Harmony is a consistent aspect of the Qur'ānic style.

All this provides some explanation as to why I feel inadequate and reluctant to tackle Qur'ānic *sūrahs* with my inadequate style. But once more the need is compelling, because people in our generation do not live with the Qur'ān. I therefore seek God's help and support in this task.

I

A Glance at Wide Horizons

Al-Ra'd (Thunder)

In the Name of God, the Merciful, the Beneficent

Alif. Lām. Mīm. Rā. These are verses of the Book. That which is revealed to you by your Lord is the Truth, yet most people will not believe. (1)

It is God who raised the heavens without any support that you could see, and established Himself on the Throne. And He it is who has made the sun and the moon subservient [to His laws], each pursuing its course for a set term. He ordains all things. He makes plain His revelations so that you may firmly believe that you will certainly be meeting your Lord. (2)

It is He who has spread out the earth and placed upon it firm mountains and rivers, and created on it two sexes of every type of fruit, and caused the night to cover the day. In all these there are signs for people who think. (3)

وَهُوَ ٱلَّذِى مَدَّ ٱلْأَرْضَ وَجَعَلَ فِيهَا رَوَٰسِىَ وَأَنْهَٰرًا وَمِن كُلِّ ٱلثَّمَرَٰتِ جَعَلَ فِيهَا زَوْجَيْنِ ٱثْنَيْنِ يُغْشِى ٱلَّيْلَ ٱلنَّهَارَ إِنَّ فِى ذَٰلِكَ لَءَايَٰتٍ لِقَوْمٍ يَتَفَكَّرُونَ ٣

And there are on earth adjoining tracts of land; and vineyards, and fields of grains and date-palms, growing in clusters or non-clustered. [All] are irrigated by the same water; yet some of them are favoured above others with regard to the food [they provide]. In all this there are signs for people who use their reason. (4)

وَفِى ٱلْأَرْضِ قِطَعٌ مُّتَجَٰوِرَٰتٌ وَجَنَّٰتٌ مِّنْ أَعْنَٰبٍ وَزَرْعٌ وَنَخِيلٌ صِنْوَانٌ وَغَيْرُ صِنْوَانٍ يُسْقَىٰ بِمَاءٍ وَٰحِدٍ وَنُفَضِّلُ بَعْضَهَا عَلَىٰ بَعْضٍ فِى ٱلْأُكُلِ إِنَّ فِى ذَٰلِكَ لَءَايَٰتٍ لِقَوْمٍ يَعْقِلُونَ ٤

But if you are amazed, amazing, too, is their saying: 'What! After we have become dust, shall we be raised [to life] in a new act of creation?' These are the ones who deny their Lord. They are the ones who carry their own shackles around their necks; and they are the ones who are destined for the fire wherein they will abide. (5)

وَإِن تَعْجَبْ فَعَجَبٌ قَوْلُهُمْ أَءِذَا كُنَّا تُرَٰبًا أَءِنَّا لَفِى خَلْقٍ جَدِيدٍ أُوْلَٰئِكَ ٱلَّذِينَ كَفَرُوا۟ بِرَبِّهِمْ وَأُوْلَٰئِكَ ٱلْأَغْلَٰلُ فِى أَعْنَاقِهِمْ وَأُوْلَٰئِكَ أَصْحَٰبُ ٱلنَّارِ هُمْ فِيهَا خَٰلِدُونَ ٥

They ask you to hasten evil rather than good, although exemplary punishments have indeed come to pass before their time. Your Lord always extends forgiveness to people despite their wrongdoing. Your Lord is certainly severe in retribution. (6)

وَيَسْتَعْجِلُونَكَ بِالسَّيِّئَةِ قَبْلَ الْحَسَنَةِ وَقَدْ خَلَتْ مِن قَبْلِهِمُ الْمَثُلَتُ وَإِنَّ رَبَّكَ لَذُو مَغْفِرَةٍ لِّلنَّاسِ عَلَىٰ ظُلْمِهِمْ وَإِنَّ رَبَّكَ لَشَدِيدُ الْعِقَابِ ۝

Yet the unbelievers say: 'Why has no miraculous sign been bestowed on him by his Lord?' But you are only a warner. Every community have [their] guide. (7)

وَيَقُولُ الَّذِينَ كَفَرُوا لَوْلَا أُنزِلَ عَلَيْهِ ءَايَةٌ مِّن رَّبِّهِ إِنَّمَا أَنتَ مُنذِرٌ وَلِكُلِّ قَوْمٍ هَادٍ ۝

God knows what every female bears, and by how much the wombs may fall short [in gestation], and by how much they may increase. With Him everything has its definite measure. (8)

اللَّهُ يَعْلَمُ مَا تَحْمِلُ كُلُّ أُنثَىٰ وَمَا تَغِيضُ الْأَرْحَامُ وَمَا تَزْدَادُ وَكُلُّ شَيْءٍ عِندَهُ بِمِقْدَارٍ ۝

He knows all that lies beyond the reach of human perception and all that anyone may witness. He is the Great One, the Most High. (9)

عَالِمُ الْغَيْبِ وَالشَّهَادَةِ الْكَبِيرُ الْمُتَعَالِ ۝

It is all alike [to Him] whether any of you speaks in secret or aloud, whether he seeks to hide under the cover of the night or walks openly in the light of day. (10)

سَوَاءٌ مِّنكُم مَّنْ أَسَرَّ الْقَوْلَ وَمَن جَهَرَ بِهِ وَمَنْ هُوَ مُسْتَخْفٍ بِاللَّيْلِ وَسَارِبٌ بِالنَّهَارِ ۝

Each has guardian angels before him and behind him, who watch him by God's command. Indeed God does not change a people's conditions unless they first change what is in their hearts. When God wills people to suffer some misfortune, none can avert it. Besides Him, they have none to protect them. (11)

لَهُۥ مُعَقِّبَٰتٌ مِّنۢ بَيۡنِ يَدَيۡهِ وَمِنۡ خَلۡفِهِۦ يَحۡفَظُونَهُۥ مِنۡ أَمۡرِ ٱللَّهِ إِنَّ ٱللَّهَ لَا يُغَيِّرُ مَا بِقَوۡمٍ حَتَّىٰ يُغَيِّرُواْ مَا بِأَنفُسِهِمۡ وَإِذَآ أَرَادَ ٱللَّهُ بِقَوۡمٍ سُوٓءًا فَلَا مَرَدَّ لَهُۥ وَمَا لَهُم مِّن دُونِهِۦ مِن وَالٍ ﴿١١﴾

It is He who displays before you the lightning, giving rise to both fear and hope, and originates the heavy clouds. (12)

هُوَ ٱلَّذِي يُرِيكُمُ ٱلۡبَرۡقَ خَوۡفًا وَطَمَعًا وَيُنشِئُ ٱلسَّحَابَ ٱلثِّقَالَ ﴿١٢﴾

And the thunder extols His limitless glory and praises Him, and so do the angels, in awe of Him. He hurls the thunderbolts to smite with them whom He wills. Yet they stubbornly argue about God. His might is both stern and wise. (13)

وَيُسَبِّحُ ٱلرَّعۡدُ بِحَمۡدِهِۦ وَٱلۡمَلَٰٓئِكَةُ مِنۡ خِيفَتِهِۦ وَيُرۡسِلُ ٱلصَّوَٰعِقَ فَيُصِيبُ بِهَا مَن يَشَآءُ وَهُمۡ يُجَٰدِلُونَ فِي ٱللَّهِ وَهُوَ شَدِيدُ ٱلۡمِحَالِ ﴿١٣﴾

To Him is due the prayer aiming at the Truth. Those whom people invoke beside God cannot respond to them in any way. They are just like a man who stretches his open hands towards water, [hoping] that it will come to his mouth; but it will never reach it. The prayer of those without faith is nothing but wandering in grievous error. (14)

لَهُۥ دَعۡوَةُ ٱلۡحَقِّ وَٱلَّذِينَ يَدۡعُونَ مِن دُونِهِۦ لَا يَسۡتَجِيبُونَ لَهُم بِشَيۡءٍ إِلَّا كَبَٰسِطِ كَفَّيۡهِ إِلَى ٱلۡمَآءِ لِيَبۡلُغَ فَاهُ وَمَا هُوَ بِبَٰلِغِهِۦ وَمَا دُعَآءُ ٱلۡكَٰفِرِينَ إِلَّا فِي ضَلَٰلٍ ﴿١٤﴾

To God prostrate themselves, willingly or unwillingly, all those who are in the heavens and on earth, as do their very shadows, morning and evening. (15)

وَلِلَّهِ يَسْجُدُ مَن فِي ٱلسَّمَوَٰتِ وَٱلْأَرْضِ طَوْعًا وَكَرْهًا وَظِلَٰلُهُم بِٱلْغُدُوِّ وَٱلْأَصَالِ ۩ ﴿١٥﴾

Say: 'Who is the Lord of the heavens and the earth?' Say: '[It is] God.' Say: 'Why, then, do you take for your protectors, instead of Him, others who have no power to cause either benefit or harm even to themselves?' Say: 'Can the blind and the seeing be deemed equal? Or is the depth of darkness equal to light?' Or do they assign to God partners that have created the like of His creation, so that both creations appear to them to be similar? Say: 'God is the Creator of all things. He is the One who has power over all things.' (16)

قُلْ مَن رَّبُّ ٱلسَّمَوَٰتِ وَٱلْأَرْضِ قُلِ ٱللَّهُ قُلْ أَفَٱتَّخَذْتُم مِّن دُونِهِۦ أَوْلِيَآءَ لَا يَمْلِكُونَ لِأَنفُسِهِمْ نَفْعًا وَلَا ضَرًّا قُلْ هَلْ يَسْتَوِى ٱلْأَعْمَىٰ وَٱلْبَصِيرُ أَمْ هَلْ تَسْتَوِى ٱلظُّلُمَٰتُ وَٱلنُّورُ أَمْ جَعَلُواْ لِلَّهِ شُرَكَآءَ خَلَقُواْ كَخَلْقِهِۦ فَتَشَٰبَهَ ٱلْخَلْقُ عَلَيْهِمْ قُلِ ٱللَّهُ خَٰلِقُ كُلِّ شَىْءٍ وَهُوَ ٱلْوَٰحِدُ ٱلْقَهَّٰرُ ﴿١٦﴾

He sends down water from the sky, so that riverbeds flow according to their measure, and the torrent bears a swelling foam. Likewise, from what people smelt in the fire to make ornaments or utensils rises similar foam. Thus does God illustrate truth and falsehood. The scum is cast away, while that which is of benefit to mankind abides on earth. Thus does God set forth His parables. (17)

أَنزَلَ مِنَ ٱلسَّمَآءِ مَآءً فَسَالَتْ أَوْدِيَةٌۢ بِقَدَرِهَا فَٱحْتَمَلَ ٱلسَّيْلُ زَبَدًا رَّابِيًا وَمِمَّا يُوقِدُونَ عَلَيْهِ فِي ٱلنَّارِ ٱبْتِغَآءَ حِلْيَةٍ أَوْ مَتَٰعٍ زَبَدٌ مِّثْلُهُۥ كَذَٰلِكَ يَضْرِبُ ٱللَّهُ ٱلْحَقَّ وَٱلْبَٰطِلَ فَأَمَّا ٱلزَّبَدُ فَيَذْهَبُ جُفَآءً وَأَمَّا مَا يَنفَعُ ٱلنَّاسَ فَيَمْكُثُ فِي ٱلْأَرْضِ كَذَٰلِكَ يَضْرِبُ ٱللَّهُ ٱلْأَمْثَالَ ﴿١٧﴾

For those who respond to their Lord is a rich reward. As for those who do not respond to Him, should they have all that the earth contains, and twice as much, they would gladly offer it for their ransom. Theirs shall be an awful reckoning, and hell shall be their abode, an evil resting-place! (18)

لِلَّذِينَ ٱسْتَجَابُواْ لِرَبِّهِمُ ٱلْحُسْنَىٰ وَٱلَّذِينَ لَمْ يَسْتَجِيبُواْ لَهُۥ لَوْ أَنَّ لَهُم مَّا فِى ٱلْأَرْضِ جَمِيعًا وَمِثْلَهُۥ مَعَهُۥ لَٱفْتَدَوْاْ بِهِۦٓ أُوْلَٰٓئِكَ لَهُمْ سُوٓءُ ٱلْحِسَابِ وَمَأْوَىٰهُمْ جَهَنَّمُ وَبِئْسَ ٱلْمِهَادُ ۝

Overview

The *sūrah* opens with a basic issue of faith, namely the revelation of God's book, the Qur'ān, and the truth it contains. This formulates the foundation over which all the other issues of faith are built, including those of the oneness of God, belief in the hereafter, and the need to do good in this life. All these branch out from the central point of believing that the One who gives all orders is God, and that the Qur'ān is His revelation to the Prophet Muḥammad (peace be upon him).

"Alif. Lām. Mīm. Rā. *These are verses of the Book.*" (Verse 1) This is one way of reading the first statement, but it may also be interpreted as, 'These are signs that prove the truth of this Book.' They are clear evidence that it is a revelation from God. The very fact that it is composed of the same material as these separate letters, *alif, lām, mīm, rā,* is sufficient proof that it comes from God, and is not the work of any creature, human or non-human.

"*That which is revealed to you by your Lord is the Truth.*" (Verse 1) That is the real and pure truth which is never coloured with any falsehood. It admits no doubt. These letters are signs that it is revealed by God, and what comes from God must be undoubtedly true. "*Yet most people will not believe.*" (Verse 1) They neither believe that it is divine revelation, nor do they accept the major issues that result from believing in revelation, such as belief in God's oneness, submission to Him alone, resurrection on the Day of Judgement, and the need to do good in this life.

Scenes of Magnificent Splendour

The *sūrah*'s opening sums up its theme, and points out all the issues that it discusses. It moves on to show some aspects of God's unlimited power and some of the spectacular aspects in the universe which indicate God's wisdom and elaborate planning. They clearly indicate that such wisdom requires that there should be revelation to put the issues clearly to human beings, and resurrection so that people are made to account for their deeds. God's infinite power means that He can resurrect people so that they return to Him, the Creator who has originated them and originated the universe before them.

The superb, divine paintbrush begins to draw some of the great universal images, touching on the heavens and on the earth, and a few aspects of the world we live in and life itself. It then wonders at those who deny resurrection, having looked at these great signs. Such people even hasten the infliction of God's punishment on themselves, demanding, at the same time, that other signs are given to them: "*It is God who raised the heavens without any support that you could see, and established Himself on the Throne. And He it is who has made the sun and the moon subservient [to His laws], each pursuing its course for a set term. He ordains all things. He makes plain His revelations so that you may firmly believe that you will certainly be meeting your Lord.*" (Verse 2)

The heavens, or the skies, whatever they indicate to people in different ages, are there to be seen by all. They provide an infinite expanse which strikes us with awe should we contemplate them for even a short while. They are elevated, 'raised without support', exposed so that we can see them. This is the first spectacle of the universe to raise human consciousness. For man immediately realizes that no one can raise the heavens without support, or even with support, except God. The most that people themselves can raise, with or without support, are simply the buildings that we erect for our purposes. We then speak of the skill, mastery, artistic touches and the perfection that go into raising such buildings, heedless of the heavens above us, raised without support, and the great power and perfection that lies behind their creation. It is impossible for human beings even to imagine such power and perfection.

159

The *sūrah* then moves from this awesome scene to the world that lies beyond the reach of human perception: "*And established Himself on the Throne.*" (Verse 2) If the heavens are high and great, then the Throne is higher and infinitely greater. This is indeed the ultimate height, drawn in the usual manner of the Qur'ān to demonstrate relative dimensions to enable human beings to understand. This is another stroke from the same remarkable paintbrush. It adds a dimension of absolute height next to the heights we see.

The *sūrah* then moves to the concept of making the sun and the moon subservient. The great height that people see, with all its exhilarating beauty and breathtaking greatness, is all subservient to the will of God, the Great, the Almighty.

We would like to pause a little here to reflect on the parallels drawn in this scene. We see a great height in our visible world contrasted to a height in the world beyond. We also find an exaltation that is associated with height, contrasted with the notion of subservience to God's will. We also see the sun and the moon providing contrast in kind and time: one is a star shining during the day and the other a planet showing its beauty at night.

We move on to find that exaltation and subservience are coupled with God's elaborate planning and wisdom: "*He it is who has made the sun and the moon subservient [to His laws], each pursuing its course for a set term.*" (Verse 2) There are definite limits and well-defined laws that apply to the sun and the moon as they move in their annual and daily courses, and as they follow their respective orbits, not moving an inch beyond them. Indeed the sun and the moon continue to pursue their courses to a time limit that has been appointed by God.

"*He ordains all things.*" (Verse 2) All matters are ordained according to elaborate planning which includes the subservience of the sun and the moon. This planning applies to the entire universe with all its celestial bodies that pursue their courses for a definite time. There can be no denial of the greatness of this planning and the great wisdom that lies behind it.

Elaborate and Coherent Scenes

It is part of His planning that "*He makes plain His revelations.*" (Verse 2) The term used in the Qur'ān for 'revelations', *āyāt*, also means 'signs'. Thus He bestows His revelations and places His signs in their perfect order, showing each at the right time and for a definite purpose, *"so that you may firmly believe that you will certainly be meeting your Lord."* (Verse 2) When you see these signs clearly pointing to the truth of creation, indicating also what lies beyond them of great signs in the universe, all created by God, and described plainly and clearly in the Qur'ān, in a way which speaks volumes of God's ability and elaborate planning, you will begin to think that your return to the Creator after this first life is inevitable. It is then that the deeds of human beings will be assessed and their reward determined. That is part of the planning that is absolutely perfect and wise.

This inimitable imagery then moves from the heavens to the earth to depict its wider view: *"It is He who has spread out the earth and placed upon it firm mountains and rivers, and created on it two sexes of every type of fruit, and caused the night to cover the day. In all these there are signs for people who think."* (Verse 3)

The main lines here are the spreading out of the earth so that its expanse comes into view. Whatever its total shape, it is spread out to give the appearance of broadness. This is the first aspect. Then the line of firm mountains is drawn, followed by that of flowing rivers to complete the broad lines of the main view. These are made both parallel and contrasting, for they are complemented with a total picture of what the earth contains and what life in it holds. The first refers to the plants that come out of the earth: *'It is He who... has created on it two sexes of every type of fruit,'* while the other is represented in the phenomena of night and day: *'and caused the night to cover the day.'* (Verse 3)

The first of these scenes includes a fact that has only recently been fathomed by scientific research. That is that all living creatures, and plants among them, have a male and female. It used to be thought that plants have no male sex, but it was recently discovered that one-sex plants carry the male and female organs within the same flower, or the same stem. This fact increases the effect of the scene as it urges us to contemplate the secrets of the universe after considering only its apparent aspects.

The other scene speaks of the succession of night and day, with one overwhelming the other in a never-failing system. This invites us to think more carefully about the laws of nature. The arrival of the night after the departure of the day, and the break of dawn when the night begins to move away are phenomena that we are familiar with. Familiarity may make them less striking, but only a little contemplation is needed for them to appear before us as infinitely marvellous. We only need to feel them as if it were all happening for the first time. Moreover, the very elaborate system that helps all celestial bodies move in their respective orbits, without fail, invites us to think of the power that governs all this and ensures that it continues to function with perfect accuracy. "*In all these there are signs for people who think.*" (Verse 3)

We should pause again here to reflect on the contrasting features in the scene before moving to the next one. There is a contrast for example between the firm mountains that appear well established in their positions, and the flowing rivers; between the male and female in all fruits and trees; between the night and the day; and then between the earth and the sky. These last two scenes complement each other in the overall panoramic view of the universe.

As we move along with the *sūrah*, we see this highly creative paintbrush delivering further detail of the scene of the face of the earth: "*And there are on earth adjoining tracts of land; and vineyards, and fields of grains and date-palms, growing in clusters or non-clustered. [All] are irrigated by the same water; yet some of them are favoured above others with regard to the food [they provide]. In all this there are signs for people who use their reason.*" (Verse 4)

Many of us pass by these scenes not looking carefully at what we see, until our souls go back to their nature and re-establish contact with the universe of which they constitute a part. We stand aside to contemplate it before reuniting with it. "*And there are on earth adjoining tracts of land,*" with different characteristics. Had they been the same, they would have constituted a single piece or tract. But they are 'tracts', some of which are fertile and some which are not; some are rocky and some barren. In each type there are grades and colours. Some are built up, while others have subsided; some are cultivated while others abandoned; some are well-watered and others arid, etc. Yet they are all next to each other.

Then we are given yet further detail: vineyards, fields of grains and palm trees. They represent three different types of plant: the creeping grape tree, and the high, upright date-palm and the ordinary grain plants, shrubs of beans, roses, etc. The picture is one of immense variety and colour.

The date-palms may grow in clusters or stand alone. Some date trees have one stem and others have two or more shooting from a single tree. All these are "*irrigated by the same water*," and have the same soil, but the fruits they give taste differently: "*Yet some of them are favoured above others with regard to the food they provide*." (Verse 4) Who other than the Creator, the wise planner, can do all this? Who of us has not found different tastes in fruits from the same piece of land? Yet how many have looked at this aspect to which the Qur'ān draws our attention? It is with touches like these that the Qur'ān remains ever new, because it enhances our feelings and the way these are influenced by what we see around us. These are too numerous to be fully contemplated within the lifetime of any one person. In fact they are too many for all mankind to fathom. Hence the Qur'ānic comment: "*In all this there are signs for people who use their reason*." (Verse 4)

Once more the *sūrah* draws a contrast between the adjoining tracts of land that differ from one another. The date trees can be single or clustered. Moreover, tastes, plants and fruit are all of a rich variety.

The *sūrah* starts with such panoramic scenes from the vast universe, but then speaks of people who remain uninspired by all these signs around them, visible in every aspect of creation. Their hearts and minds remain oblivious to the fact that behind all these marvels lies the great power of the Creator. This is because their minds are in chains and their hearts bound. They cannot contemplate the vast universal scenes around them: "*But if you are amazed, amazing, too, is their saying: 'What! After we have become dust, shall we be raised [to life] in a new act of creation?' These are the ones who deny their Lord. They are the ones who carry their own shackles around their necks; and they are the ones who are destined for the fire wherein they will abide*." (Verse 5)

It is quite amazing that after all these signs people should wonder: '*What! After we have become dust, shall we be raised to life in a new act of creation?*' (Verse 5) The One who has created the great universe and manages its affairs in meticulous fashion is certainly able to resurrect human beings in a new act of creation. But such people refuse to believe this, lacking faith in their Lord who created them. What holds them back are the chains and shackles that restrain their hearts and minds. Just as they are shackled in this life, so will they be in the life to come. Their punishment will only be completed when they are thrown in the fire of hell where they will abide for a very long time. They have switched off all the faculties God has given to people and honoured them on their account. They have also accepted a low position in this life. This earns them an even lower life in the hereafter, simply because they have lived their first life making no use of their faculties, feelings and emotions.

Wrongdoers, Yet Forgiven

These people wonder that God will bring them back to life after their death, yet it is their being amazed that is indeed amazing. They even ask that their punishment be hastened instead of asking that they be given God's guidance and praying for His grace: "*They ask you to hasten evil rather than good.*" (Verse 6)

Just as they do not look at the universe around them and do not contemplate its multitude of signs, they do not look at the fate of those communities before them. Those communities adopted the same attitude, precipitating God's punishment, and it came fast upon them, making of them a lesson to any future community: "*They ask you to hasten evil rather than good, although exemplary punishments have indeed come to pass before their time.*" (Verse 6) They are unaware even of the fate of their own past generations which carry an effective lesson for those who wish to learn. "*Your Lord always extends forgiveness to people despite their wrongdoing.*" (Verse 6) He bestows His mercy on them even if they commit injustice and wrongdoing, allowing them time to reconsider their position. He allows them a chance to repent so that He will forgive them. But those who persist with their evil and wrongdoing, and remain unwilling to enter the gate of forgiveness, will find that God's punishment is severe indeed. "*Your Lord is certainly severe in retribution.*" (Verse 6)

At this instance, the *sūrah* puts God's forgiveness ahead of His punishment to contrast it with those who pray for punishment rather than God's guidance. This demonstrates the great gulf between the goodness that God wants for them and the evil they seek for themselves.

It speaks volumes of how misguided, blind and abject they are. They certainly deserve the fire.

The *sūrah* then moves on to wonder at these people who are unable to see all the signs in the universe, each of which is a miracle on its own. They ask the Prophet for a miraculous sign. But what will they do with such a sign when the universe around them is full of signs pointing to the Creator. "*Yet the unbelievers say: 'Why has no miraculous sign been bestowed on him by his Lord?' But you are only a warner. Every community have [their] guide.*" (Verse 7) They demand a miracle when miracles are neither of the Prophet's own making nor part of his business. It is God who decides, in His wisdom, whether it is necessary. '*But you are only a warner,*' who invites people to consider and reflect, warning them of the consequence of stubborn refusal to see the facts. This is the same task given to every messenger sent before him. God has sent these messengers to their peoples so that they might guide them to the right path: "*Every community have [their] guide.*" (Verse 7) As for miraculous signs, these are God's own affair.

God's Limitless Knowledge

Now the *sūrah* enters a totally different realm, that of human souls and feelings and other creatures.

> God knows what every female bears, and by how much the wombs may fall short [in gestation], and by how much they may increase. With Him everything has its definite measure. He knows all that lies beyond the reach of human perception and all that anyone may witness. He is the Great One, the Most High. It is all alike [to Him] whether any of you speaks in secret or aloud, whether he seeks to hide under the cover of the night or walks openly in the light of day. Each has guardian angels before him and behind him, who watch him by God's command. Indeed God does not change a people's conditions unless they first change what is in their hearts. When God wills people to suffer some misfortune, none can avert it. Besides Him, they have none to protect them. (Verses 8–11)

We are overwhelmed with the effect of these fine touches in the scene drawn before our eyes and the music that is characteristic of the mode of expression. We are infinitely surprised as we imagine how penetrating God's knowledge is, and to what depth it goes. How He is fully aware of every pregnancy in every womb, the secrets in people's hearts, the stealthy who move under the cover of darkness, those who walk in open daylight, and whatever any creature says in public or private. All of these are known to Him as if each one is followed by a ray of His knowledge, and by protectors who count their thoughts and intentions. The whole scene fills us with awe. So much so that we seek refuge with God, appealing for His protection. A believer knows that God's knowledge encompasses everything, but that total concept does not afford the same breadth of feeling as the details given here in such a beautiful image. كمطابا، ونجاء مند، الا إلى الله

No abstract concept or unqualified true statement comes near to the Qur'ānic description of God's absolute knowledge: "*God knows what every female bears, and by how much the wombs may fall short [in gestation], and by how much they may increase. With Him everything has its definite measure.*" (Verse 8) Our imagination starts to follow every female in this whole universe: every female in rural and urban areas, amongst nomadic tribes and city dwellers, in houses, caves, shanty towns and forests. We then consider that God follows every pregnancy carried in every womb, and knows every drop of blood that moves in or out of all these wombs.

No abstraction or generalization compares to the statement that follows: "*It is all alike [to Him] whether any of you speaks in secret or aloud, whether he seeks to hide under the cover of the night or walks openly in the light of day. Each has guardian angels before him and behind him, who watch him by God's command.*" (Verses 10–11) Here our imagination follows every whisperer and open speaker, as well as everyone who moves about under the cover of darkness or who walks in open daylight anywhere in this great universe. We imagine God's knowledge following every individual from the front and from behind, recording every little detail at any time of the night or day.

The *sūrah*'s opening description of the miraculous features to be found in the open universe are no greater and no more profound than the present verses which examine the deeper secrets of the human soul, or the far reaches of the world beyond the reach of human perception. Both sets of signs are of equal magnificence. Let us now reflect on some of the finer aspects of these verses: "*God knows what every female bears, and by how much the wombs may fall short [in gestation], and by how much they may increase. With Him everything has its definite measure.*" (Verse 8)

When God's knowledge is described as total with regard to increase and decrease in gestation, this is followed by a statement saying that with God everything comes according to a clear and definite measure. So harmony is evident between the term, 'measure', and the notion of increase and decrease or falling short. Furthermore, the two situations of wombs falling short and increasing provide contrast, which is characteristic of the whole of this *sūrah*.

"*He knows all that lies beyond the reach of human perception and all that anyone may witness. He is the Great One, the Most High.*" (Verse 9) The two attributes mentioned here, '*the Great One*' and '*the Most High*', have definite impressions that they impart, but which are so difficult to describe in words. There is nothing created that does not have some shortcoming that keeps it within finite limits. Anything of God's creation, whether action or matter, which people describe as great indeed, begins to shrink once God is mentioned. The same applies to the other attribute, '*the Most High*'. Have I said anything at all? No. Nor has any other commentator on the Qur'ān who has reflected on these two attributes, '*the Great One, the Most High*'.

"*It is all alike [to Him] whether any of you speaks in secret or aloud, whether he seeks to hide under the cover of the night or walks openly in the light of day.*" (Verse 10) The contrast is very clear in this verse. But the arresting point is the use of the Arabic word, *sārib*, which is translated as 'walking openly'. Its implication suggesting almost the opposite impression of its meaning. The shade it casts is akin to stealth or something hiding, while it means 'going or moving in the open'. Motion here is the intended feature as contrasted with using the dark night for cover. This shows that both the fine sound of the word and its shades are the cause of its use, so that the general atmosphere remains undisturbed.

"*Each has guardian angels before him and behind him, who watch him by God's command.*" (Verse 11) The guardians that follow every human being, recording every little detail, including thoughts, feelings and whims are not described or defined in any way here, except in so far as they fulfil this task '*by God's command*'. Hence, further description is pointless. We cannot say who they are, or what they are like, or how they watch, or where they are placed. We do not want to take away any of the awesome effect that the verse generates. The description is meant to give a cryptic impression. Anyone who appreciates fine style would hesitate long before trying to spoil this ambiguity by trying to explain what is better left unexplained.

"*Indeed God does not change a people's conditions unless they first change what is in their hearts.*" (Verse 11) He sends His angels to watch them all the time, monitoring any changes they may introduce within themselves or in their way of living, and determines what He does with them on that basis. He does not change any grace, luxury or position of respect, or indeed any hardship or position of humiliation or weakness, until people have changed their actions, feelings and conditions. The change then fits what they themselves have changed. But God knows what they do or change even before they do it themselves, but the consequences of their action take place after they have done it.

This lays a great responsibility on human beings. It is God's will that makes what He does with them dependent on what they themselves do. His laws operate on the basis of how they tackle these laws through their actions. The statement here is very clear, allowing no other interpretation. But it also signifies the position of honour God grants human beings as He has made them and their actions the means to implement God's will with regard to their own position, status and welfare.

Having established this principle, the *sūrah* highlights God's changing the situation of any particular community for the worse. The gist of the first statement indicates that they have changed for the worse, and as a result God has willed them to suffer misfortune: "*When God wills people to suffer some misfortune, none can avert it. Besides Him, they have none to protect them.*" (Verse 11) The *sūrah* stresses this aspect rather than the opposite because it fits here with those who hasten evil rather than good. When that was mentioned forgiveness was stated first so that people's lack of awareness of the truth was highlighted. Here, only the evil alternative is mentioned so as to serve as a warning. If, by their actions, they deserve God's punishment, then it is inevitable; it will not be averted. No support will rescue them from it.

How Thunder Glorifies God

The *sūrah* now takes us on another round to a different but related stage. Here we see natural scenes and human feelings mixed in a perfect harmony of picture and effect. The whole image casts an atmosphere of awe, apprehension, expectation and appeal. We are on our guard as we watch, and the verses here produce a profound effect on us: "*It is He who displays before you the lightning, giving rise to both fear and hope, and originates the heavy clouds. And the thunder extols His limitless glory and praises Him, and so do the angels, in awe of Him. He hurls the thunderbolts to smite with them whom He wills. Yet they stubbornly argue about God. His might is both stern and wise. To Him is due the prayer aiming at the Truth. Those whom people invoke beside God cannot respond to them in any way. They are just like a man who stretches his open hands towards water, [hoping] that it will come to his mouth; but it will never reach it. The prayer of those without faith is nothing but wandering in grievous error. To God prostrate themselves, willingly or unwillingly, all those who are in the heavens and on earth, as do their very shadows, morning and evening. Say: 'Who is the Lord of the heavens and the earth?' Say: '[It is] God.' Say: 'Why, then, do you take for your protectors, instead of Him, others who have no power to cause either benefit or harm even to themselves?' Say: 'Can the blind and the seeing be deemed equal? Or is the depth of darkness equal to light?' Or do they assign to God partners that have created the like of His creation, so that both creations appear to them to be similar? Say: 'God is the Creator of all things. He is the One who has power over all things.'"* (Verses 12–16)

Lightning, thunder and clouds are well-known phenomena, and so are thunderbolts which occasionally accompany them. They have their clear effect on people, whether they know much about their nature or not. The *sūrah* includes here the scenes of all these phenomena, adding to them others that speak of the angels, shadows, glorification of God, prostration to Him, fear and hope, as well as a true prayer and one that remains unanswered. It also adds another picture of a thirsty person who seeks water, stretches his hands to it, and opens his mouth to receive even a drop. These images are gathered here neither haphazardly nor by coincidence. Each one imparts its effect on the whole scene, adding an air of awe and expectation, fear and hope, a prayer full of expectation and anxiety. These feelings are all brought in to depict God's power, for He alone has power over all forces, and causes benefit and harm to all. They serve to emphasize the fact that He has no partner and to warn against associating any such partners with Him.

"*It is He who displays before you the lightning, giving rise to both fear and hope.*" (Verse 12) This phenomenon which you see with your eyes is initiated by the nature that He has given the universe. It is He who has moulded this nature and given it its characteristics. One aspect of it is lightning which you see in accordance with the natural laws He has set in place. You are filled with fear as a result, because, by nature, it shakes people and has a strong effect on them. The real worry is that it becomes a thunderbolt. It may herald devastating floods. At the same time people hope that it brings benefit, as it may be followed by rain that quickens barren land, and it may cause dry rivers and streams to flow again.

Again it is He who "*originates the heavy clouds.*" (Verse 12) These clouds are heavy with the water they bear. It is God who has devised the laws of nature and set them in operation. In accordance with these laws, clouds form and rain falls. Had He created the universe in a different fashion, there would have been no clouds and no rain. The fact that we know how clouds form and gather, and how rain falls, does not detract from the importance or magnificence of this phenomenon. It works in a universal setting that has been put into place by none other than God, and according to certain laws that control that setting. None other than God has had a part in devising or operating these laws. The universe has not created itself, nor has it devised its own laws.

Thunder is the third aspect of the rainy atmosphere. This loud, explosive and resounding noise is a result of the laws of the universe set into operation by God. Whatever we may say about the nature or causes of thunder, it is a consequence of what God has set in the universe. It is a hymn of praise and glorification of the Power that has devised this whole system. Every fine and perfected product praises its Maker through what it reflects of His fine and perfect creation. However, the immediate and direct meaning of the term, 'glorify', may be the one intended here. This means that the thunder actually '*extols His limitless glory and praises Him.*' (Verse 13) If so, it is part of what God has chosen not to reveal to mankind. People have to accept this and believe in it as it is stated by God. After all, people only know very little about the world around them and even about themselves.

The fact that glorification and praise of God by thunder is mentioned here follows the established pattern which we frequently encounter in the Qur'ān. This imparts qualities and aspects of life to silent cosmic scenes, so that they participate in the action, and their action fits perfectly with the overall scene. The scene drawn here shows living things in a natural setting, and includes angels glorifying God, being in awe of Him, an earnest prayer to God, and also invocation of partners, as well as the person stretching out his hands to the water bidding it to reach his mouth, but it will not. Amidst this picture of prayer and worship, thunder is depicted as a living entity, using its distinctive sound to glorify God and pray to Him.

This image of fear, prayer, heavy clouds, lightning and thunder is completed with the mention of thunderbolts hurled by God to hit whomever He wills. Thunderbolts are also a natural phenomenon. These God hurls at those who have changed their situation for the worse, and when He decides not to give them any more chances, knowing that such chances will not produce any change in them.

A Call Without Response

What is most amazing is that in the midst of this terrifying atmosphere of lightning, thunder and thunderbolts, and in the midst of glorification of God by thunder and by the angels, and the uproar of furious tempests, some human noises are raised to argue about the One who controls all these forces, giving them their natural characteristics which can easily drown all argument: "*Yet they stubbornly argue about God. His might is both stern and wise.*" (Verse 13) Their ineffective voices are thus lost in this great and awesome scene whereby prayer and supplication resound like thunder and thunderbolts. Furthermore, these phenomena confirm the presence of God, about whose existence they argue. They also confirm His oneness, and that to Him alone all praises and glorification should be addressed by even the greatest creature in the universe, and the angels who stand in awe of Him. What effect then could the faint voices of such human beings have in their argument about God, the Almighty, the Wise?

As they argue about God, they attribute partners to Him and appeal to those alleged partners, when the prayer of truth belongs only to Him. Every other prayer is of no use, bringing only hardship to those who utter it: "*To Him is due the prayer aiming at the Truth. Those whom people invoke beside God cannot respond to them in any way. They are just like a man who stretches his open hands towards water, [hoping] that it will come to his mouth; but it will never reach it. The prayer of those without faith is nothing but wandering in grievous error.*" (Verse 14)

The scene here is very much alive, vivid, expressing an eager appeal. It shows that only one prayer is a true prayer, and it is answered. It is the prayer which is addressed to God, expressing trust in Him and dependence on Him, seeking His help, mercy and guidance. All other prayers are false and futile. Do you not see what happens to those who address their prayers to false deities whom they claim to be God's partners? Here is one of them, very thirsty, seeking water and stretching his hands towards it, with an open mouth which sends an earnest prayer, asking for the water to reach his mouth, but it never does in spite of his efforts. The same applies to the prayer of those who disbelieve in God's oneness, and pray to alleged partners: "*The prayer of those without faith is nothing but wandering in grievous error.*" (Verse 14) But in what situation is this thirsty, earnestly appealing person deprived of even a drop of water? It is in an atmosphere charged with lightning, thunder and clouds heavy with rain. No wonder! These, like all other natural phenomena, operate according to God's orders.

At a time when such people associate partners with God, appealing to them for help, we see that everything in the universe submits to God's will, operating in accordance with the laws He has set. Whoever of them believes in God willingly submits to Him in total obedience, and whoever disbelieves submits by force. No one is able to challenge God's will, or to live outside the domain of the laws He has set in operation: "*To God prostrate themselves, willingly or unwillingly, all those who are in the heavens and on earth, as do their very shadows, morning and evening.*" (Verse 15)

Because the general atmosphere here is one of prayer and supplication, the *sūrah* expresses the notion of submission to God's will by the act of prostration, which is the clearest symbol of submission. It says that all creatures in the heavens and the earth prostrate themselves before God, but it adds that their shadows also do the same. They submit in the morning and also at the setting of the day when rays are broken and shadows are at their tallest. Thus the person and the shadow share in the prostration, submission and obedience. That is a fact, because shadows do what the persons themselves do. This fact adds its own connotations to the image painted. In effect, we see a double prostration, of both people and shadows. In fact the whole universe with all creatures and their shadows kneel down in submission before God, either willingly through faith or unwillingly. Yet those who are dumb still ascribe partners to God. How strange!

Unequal Contrasts

At this point the *sūrah* reverts to sarcastic questioning. In the general atmosphere the *sūrah* generates, showing the whole universe and all creatures in it submitting to God's will, voluntarily or by force, the only fitting response to anyone who persists in disbelief is that of ridicule and derision.

> Say: 'Who is the Lord of the heavens and the earth?' Say: '[It is] God.' Say: 'Why, then, do you take for your protectors, instead of Him, others who have no power to cause either benefit or harm even to themselves?' Say: 'Can the blind and the seeing be deemed equal? Or is the depth of darkness equal to light?' Or do they assign to God partners that have created the like of His creation, so that both creations appear to them to be similar? Say: 'God is the Creator of all things. He is the One who has power over all things.' (Verse 16)

An instruction is given to the Prophet to put this question to them: "*Who is the Lord of the heavens and the earth?*" (Verse 16) But the question does not invite an answer, because the *sūrah* has already answered it. It is asked here simply so that they may listen to the answer as it is being said, just as they have already seen it with their eyes. "*Say: [It is] God.*" (Verse 16) Then the Prophet is further instructed to put another question to them: "*Say: 'Why, then, do you take for your protectors, instead of Him, others who have no power to cause either benefit or harm even to themselves?'*" Now the question is put to them by way of a denunciation of their actions, because they have already chosen different protectors.

Yet they are still to be questioned in spite of the fact that the whole matter is as clear as the difference between truth and falsehood, or the blind and the seeing, or light and darkness. This reference to the blind and the seeing is a reference to themselves and to believers, because it is only their blindness that prevents them from seeing the clear truth felt by all creatures in the heavens and the earth. Similarly, the reference to light and darkness is a reference to their situation and that of believers. What prevents them from seeing the manifest truth is the darkness that totally covers them. *"Say: 'Can the blind and the seeing be deemed equal? Or is the depth of darkness equal to light?' Or do they assign to God partners that have created the like of His creation, so that both creations appear to them to be similar? Say: 'God is the Creator of all things. He is the One who has power over all things.'"* (Verse 16)

Is it possible that these partners whom they associate with God have created something similar to God's creation, and as a result they cannot distinguish between God's creation and that of the alleged partners? If this were the case, they would have some justification in acknowledging such partners who have the power to create. After all, creation is an attribute which earns the creator the right to be worshipped. Without such ability to create, there is no justification for worshipping any alleged partner of God.

In fact, they deserve all this bitter ridicule. They see that all things have been created by God, and they realize that their alleged partners have created nothing, and cannot create anything, because they themselves are creatures. Nevertheless the unbelievers worship them and submit to them without justification. This is the lowest depth to which human intellect can sink.

The comment at the end of all this ridicule to which no objection is made is: *"Say: 'God is the Creator of all things. He is the One who has power over all things.'"* (Verse 16) This emphasizes the fact that God is the only Creator as He is the One who controls everything, which is the ultimate degree of authority. Thus the issue of attributing partners to God is preceded at the beginning by the prostration of all who are in the heavens and the earth, as well as their shadows, to God, willingly and unwillingly. It concludes by emphasizing that God has power over everything in the heavens and on earth. Recalling also what is mentioned of lightning, thunder, thunderbolts, glorification and praising of God in fear and in hope, we ask: what heart can stand up to all this unless it is blind, living in the depths of darkness until death overtakes it?

Again there are contrasts in the scene here between fear and hope, sudden lightning and heavy clouds, for the heaviness of the clouds not only refers to the rain they carry but also contrasts with the speed of lightning. The contrasts here are also between the fact that thunder glorifies and praises God while the angels do the same, as also between a true prayer and one that goes in vain. Similarly there is a contrast between the heavens and earth, the prostration of all living things willingly and unwillingly, persons and shadows, morning and evening, the seeing and the blind, darkness and light, the overpowering Creator and alleged partners who create nothing and who can cause themselves neither benefit nor harm. The text of the *sūrah* follows the same pattern with clear accuracy and remarkable harmony.

Truth and Falsehood: an Illustration

The *sūrah* moves on to give an example of truth and falsehood, the prayer that is fulfilled and the one that goes with the wind, of quiet goodness and boasting evil. The example provided depicts an aspect of God's power and His elaborate planning of creation: "*He sends down water from the sky, so that riverbeds flow according to their measure, and the torrent bears a swelling foam. Likewise, from what people smelt in the fire to make ornaments or utensils rises similar foam. Thus does God illustrate truth and falsehood. The scum is cast away, while that which is of benefit to mankind abides on earth. Thus does God set forth His parables.*" (Verse 17)

The pouring down of water from the sky to make riverbeds flow and swell fits with the general atmosphere drawn in the previous picture of heavy clouds, lightning and thunder. It forms a part of the overall scene of the universe which is set as a background for the issues the *sūrah* tackles. It also testifies to the great power of God, the Almighty. The fact that each river flows according to a measure that fits its capacity and needs also testifies to God's elaborate planning that includes everything God creates. That is one of the main themes of the *sūrah*. However, both are only a framework for the parable God sets for people, drawn from their practical environment which they see at all times, but rarely contemplate.

When water pours from the sky causing the riverbeds to flow, it gathers along the way a swelling foam that floats on the surface as scum which at times is so thick that it forms a screen covering the water. This foam continues to rise and swell, but it is no more than scum. The water flows underneath, tranquil and peaceful, but it is the water that brings life and benefit. The same is seen with metals that are melted in order to make jewellery, as with gold and silver, or to make useful tools or utensils, as with iron or lead. The scum may float on top covering the metal itself, but it is merely scum that brings no benefit to anyone. It soon disappears to leave the pure and useful metal in place.

This is what truth and falsehood are like in this life. Falsehood may rise and swell so as to look in full control, but it is no more than foam or scum. It is soon ignored or cast away as it has no substance. The truth remains quiet and tranquil, to the extent that some people may think that it has disappeared, or died or has been lost, but it is the one which stays firm, like the water bringing life, or the pure metal that is full of benefit. "*Thus does God set forth His parables.*" (Verse 17) And thus He determines the eventual outcome of beliefs, advocacy efforts, actions and verbal statements. He is the One who has power over all things, and who determines what happens in the universe and the destiny of all life. He knows what is apparent and what is hidden, truth and falsehood, what remains firm and what vanishes without trace.

Whoever responds to Him will have a fine reward, and whoever turns away will face great suffering. So much so that the latter will want to offer the earth's riches twice over, in order to release himself. But there is no chance of release. There is only an awful reckoning and a fitting abode in hell: "*For those who respond to their Lord is a rich reward. As for those who do not respond to Him, should they have all that the earth contains, and twice as much, they would gladly offer it for their ransom. Theirs shall be an awful reckoning, and hell shall be their abode, an evil resting-place!*" (Verse 18)

Here again the contrast is clear between those who respond to their Lord and those who do not. Between the rich reward and the awful reckoning, hell and its painful abode. This follows the same pattern of the *sūrah* in providing one contrasting image after another.

2

The Nature of Faith and Prophethood

Is, then, he who knows that what has been revealed to you by your Lord is the Truth like one who is blind? Only those who are endowed with understanding keep this in mind: (19)

أَفَمَن يَعْلَمُ أَنَّمَا أُنزِلَ إِلَيْكَ مِن رَّبِّكَ الْحَقُّ كَمَنْ هُوَ أَعْمَىٰ إِنَّمَا يَتَذَكَّرُ أُوْلُوا الْأَلْبَٰبِ ۞

those who are true to their bond with God and never break their covenant; (20)

الَّذِينَ يُوفُونَ بِعَهْدِ اللَّهِ وَلَا يَنقُضُونَ الْمِيثَٰقَ ۞

and who keep together what God has bidden to be joined; who fear their Lord and dread the terrors of the reckoning; (21)

وَالَّذِينَ يَصِلُونَ مَا أَمَرَ اللَّهُ بِهِ أَن يُوصَلَ وَيَخْشَوْنَ رَبَّهُمْ وَيَخَافُونَ سُوٓءَ الْحِسَابِ ۞

who remain patient in adversity seeking the countenance of their Lord, and attend to their prayers, and spend on others, secretly and openly, out of what We provide for them, and who repel evil with good. Such will have the attainment of the [ultimate] abode: (22)

وَالَّذِينَ صَبَرُوا ابْتِغَآءَ وَجْهِ رَبِّهِمْ وَأَقَامُوا الصَّلَوٰةَ وَأَنفَقُوا مِمَّا رَزَقْنَٰهُمْ سِرًّا وَعَلَانِيَةً وَيَدْرَءُونَ بِالْحَسَنَةِ السَّيِّئَةَ أُوْلَٰئِكَ لَهُمْ عُقْبَى الدَّارِ ۞

gardens of perpetual bliss, which they will enter together with the righteous from among their parents, their spouses and their offspring. The angels will come in to them from every gate, (23)

جَنَّٰتُ عَدْنٍ يَدْخُلُونَهَا وَمَن صَلَحَ مِنْ ءَابَآئِهِمْ وَأَزْوَٰجِهِمْ وَذُرِّيَّٰتِهِمْ ۖ وَٱلْمَلَٰٓئِكَةُ يَدْخُلُونَ عَلَيْهِم مِّن كُلِّ بَابٍ ۝

[saying]: 'Peace be upon you, because you have persevered.' Blessed indeed is the attainment of the [ultimate] abode. (24)

سَلَٰمٌ عَلَيْكُم بِمَا صَبَرْتُمْ ۚ فَنِعْمَ عُقْبَى ٱلدَّارِ ۝

As for those who break their bond with God after it has been established, and cut asunder what God has bidden to be joined, and spread corruption on earth, the curse will be laid upon them; and theirs shall be an evil abode. (25)

وَٱلَّذِينَ يَنقُضُونَ عَهْدَ ٱللَّهِ مِنۢ بَعْدِ مِيثَٰقِهِۦ وَيَقْطَعُونَ مَآ أَمَرَ ٱللَّهُ بِهِۦٓ أَن يُوصَلَ وَيُفْسِدُونَ فِى ٱلْأَرْضِ ۙ أُوْلَٰٓئِكَ لَهُمُ ٱللَّعْنَةُ وَلَهُمْ سُوٓءُ ٱلدَّارِ ۝

God grants abundant sustenance, or gives it in scant measure, to whomever He wills. They [i.e. the unbelievers] rejoice in the life of this world, even though, compared to the life to come, the life of this world is nought but a fleeting pleasure. (26)

ٱللَّهُ يَبْسُطُ ٱلرِّزْقَ لِمَن يَشَآءُ وَيَقْدِرُ ۚ وَفَرِحُواْ بِٱلْحَيَوٰةِ ٱلدُّنْيَا وَمَا ٱلْحَيَوٰةُ ٱلدُّنْيَا فِى ٱلْءَاخِرَةِ إِلَّا مَتَٰعٌ ۝

The unbelievers say: 'Why has no miraculous sign been bestowed on him by his Lord?' Say: 'God lets go astray anyone who wills [to go astray] and guides to Himself those who turn to Him; (27)

وَيَقُولُ ٱلَّذِينَ كَفَرُواْ لَوْلَآ أُنزِلَ عَلَيْهِ ءَايَةٌ مِّن رَّبِّهِۦ ۗ قُلْ إِنَّ ٱللَّهَ يُضِلُّ مَن يَشَآءُ وَيَهْدِىٓ إِلَيْهِ مَنْ أَنَابَ ۝

those who believe and whose hearts find comfort in the remembrance of God. It is indeed in the remembrance of God that people's hearts find their comfort. (28)

ٱلَّذِينَ ءَامَنُوا۟ وَتَطْمَئِنُّ قُلُوبُهُم بِذِكْرِ ٱللَّهِ أَلَا بِذِكْرِ ٱللَّهِ تَطْمَئِنُّ ٱلْقُلُوبُ ٢٨

Those who believe and do righteous deeds shall have happiness and a most beautiful final goal.' (29)

ٱلَّذِينَ ءَامَنُوا۟ وَعَمِلُوا۟ ٱلصَّٰلِحَٰتِ طُوبَىٰ لَهُمْ وَحُسْنُ مَـَٔابٍ ٢٩

Thus have We sent you to a community before whom other communities had passed away, so that you might recite to them what We have revealed to you. Yet they deny the Most Gracious. Say: 'He is my Lord. There is no deity other than Him. In Him have I placed my trust, and to Him shall I return.' (30)

كَذَٰلِكَ أَرْسَلْنَٰكَ فِىٓ أُمَّةٍ قَدْ خَلَتْ مِن قَبْلِهَآ أُمَمٌ لِّتَتْلُوَا۟ عَلَيْهِمُ ٱلَّذِىٓ أَوْحَيْنَآ إِلَيْكَ وَهُمْ يَكْفُرُونَ بِٱلرَّحْمَٰنِ قُلْ هُوَ رَبِّى لَآ إِلَٰهَ إِلَّا هُوَ عَلَيْهِ تَوَكَّلْتُ وَإِلَيْهِ مَتَابِ ٣٠

Even if there should be a Qur'ān by which mountains could be moved, or the earth cleft asunder, or the dead made to speak! For certain, God's alone is the command in all things. Have they who believe not come to realize that, had God so willed, He would indeed have guided all mankind? As for the unbelievers, because of their misdeeds,

وَلَوْ أَنَّ قُرْءَانًا سُيِّرَتْ بِهِ ٱلْجِبَالُ أَوْ قُطِّعَتْ بِهِ ٱلْأَرْضُ أَوْ كُلِّمَ بِهِ ٱلْمَوْتَىٰ بَل لِّلَّهِ ٱلْأَمْرُ جَمِيعًا أَفَلَمْ يَا۟يْـَٔسِ ٱلَّذِينَ ءَامَنُوٓا۟ أَن لَّوْ يَشَآءُ ٱللَّهُ لَهَدَى ٱلنَّاسَ جَمِيعًا وَلَا يَزَالُ ٱلَّذِينَ كَفَرُوا۟ تُصِيبُهُم بِمَا صَنَعُوا۟ قَارِعَةٌ أَوْ تَحُلُّ

calamity will always befall them or will fall close to their homes, until God's promise is fulfilled. God never fails to fulfil His promise. (31)

قَرِيبًا مِّن دَارِهِمْ حَتَّىٰ يَأْتِيَ وَعْدُ ٱللَّهِ إِنَّ ٱللَّهَ لَا يُخْلِفُ ٱلْمِيعَادَ ﴿٣١﴾

Before your time, other messengers were derided, but for a while I gave rein to the unbelievers; but then I took them to task, and how terrible was My retribution. (32)

وَلَقَدِ ٱسْتُهْزِئَ بِرُسُلٍ مِّن قَبْلِكَ فَأَمْلَيْتُ لِلَّذِينَ كَفَرُوا ثُمَّ أَخَذْتُهُمْ فَكَيْفَ كَانَ عِقَابِ ﴿٣٢﴾

Is, then, He who stands over every soul [and knows] all that it does [like any other]? Yet they ascribe partners to God. Say: 'Name them. Would you tell Him of anything on earth which He does not know; or are these merely empty words?' Indeed their own cunning devices seem fair to the unbelievers, and they are turned away from the right path. Whoever God lets go astray can never find any guide. (33)

أَفَمَنْ هُوَ قَآئِمٌ عَلَىٰ كُلِّ نَفْسٍ بِمَا كَسَبَتْ وَجَعَلُوا لِلَّهِ شُرَكَآءَ قُلْ سَمُّوهُمْ أَمْ تُنَبِّئُونَهُ بِمَا لَا يَعْلَمُ فِي ٱلْأَرْضِ أَم بِظَٰهِرٍ مِّنَ ٱلْقَوْلِ بَلْ زُيِّنَ لِلَّذِينَ كَفَرُوا مَكْرُهُمْ وَصُدُّوا عَنِ ٱلسَّبِيلِ وَمَن يُضْلِلِ ٱللَّهُ فَمَا لَهُ مِنْ هَادٍ ﴿٣٣﴾

They shall endure suffering in the life of this world, but, truly, their suffering in the life to come will be harder still, and they will have none to shield them from God. (34)

لَهُمْ عَذَابٌ فِي ٱلْحَيَوٰةِ ٱلدُّنْيَا وَلَعَذَابُ ٱلْآخِرَةِ أَشَقُّ وَمَا لَهُم مِّنَ ٱللَّهِ مِن وَاقٍ ﴿٣٤﴾

Such is the paradise which the God-fearing have been promised: through it running waters flow. Its fruits will be everlasting, and so will be its shade. Such will be the destiny of those who fear God, while the destiny of the unbelievers is the fire. (35)

مَّثَلُ ٱلْجَنَّةِ ٱلَّتِي وُعِدَ ٱلْمُتَّقُونَ تَجْرِي مِن تَحْتِهَا ٱلْأَنْهَارُ أُكُلُهَا دَآئِمٌ وَظِلُّهَا تِلْكَ عُقْبَى ٱلَّذِينَ ٱتَّقَوا۟ وَعُقْبَى ٱلْكَٰفِرِينَ ٱلنَّارُ ﴿٣٥﴾

Those to whom We have given revelations rejoice at what has been bestowed on you from on high, but among different factions there are some who deny part of it. Say: 'I have only been bidden to worship God, and not to associate any partners with Him. To Him I pray, and to Him do I return.' (36)

وَٱلَّذِينَ ءَاتَيْنَٰهُمُ ٱلْكِتَٰبَ يَفْرَحُونَ بِمَآ أُنزِلَ إِلَيْكَ وَمِنَ ٱلْأَحْزَابِ مَن يُنكِرُ بَعْضَهُۥ قُلْ إِنَّمَآ أُمِرْتُ أَنْ أَعْبُدَ ٱللَّهَ وَلَآ أُشْرِكَ بِهِۦ إِلَيْهِ أَدْعُوا۟ وَإِلَيْهِ مَـَٔابِ ﴿٣٦﴾

Thus have We revealed it, a code of judgement in the Arabic tongue. If you should follow their desires after all the knowledge you have been given, you shall have none to protect or shield you from God. (37)

وَكَذَٰلِكَ أَنزَلْنَٰهُ حُكْمًا عَرَبِيًّا وَلَئِنِ ٱتَّبَعْتَ أَهْوَآءَهُم بَعْدَ مَا جَآءَكَ مِنَ ٱلْعِلْمِ مَا لَكَ مِنَ ٱللَّهِ مِن وَلِيٍّ وَلَا وَاقٍ ﴿٣٧﴾

We have indeed sent messengers before you and given them wives and offspring. Yet no messenger could produce a miracle except by God's permission. Every age has had its revelation. (38)

وَلَقَدْ أَرْسَلْنَا رُسُلًا مِّن قَبْلِكَ وَجَعَلْنَا لَهُمْ أَزْوَٰجًا وَذُرِّيَّةً وَمَا كَانَ لِرَسُولٍ أَن يَأْتِيَ بِـَٔايَةٍ إِلَّا بِإِذْنِ ٱللَّهِ لِكُلِّ أَجَلٍ كِتَابٌ ﴿٣٨﴾

God annuls or confirms what He pleases. With Him is the source of all revelation. (39)

يَمْحُوا۟ اللَّهُ مَا يَشَآءُ وَيُثْبِتُ وَعِندَهُۥٓ أُمُّ ٱلْكِتَٰبِ ﴿٣٩﴾

Whether We let you see some of what We have promised them, or cause you to die [before its fulfilment], your duty is only to deliver your message: it is for Us to do the reckoning. (40)

وَإِن مَّا نُرِيَنَّكَ بَعْضَ ٱلَّذِى نَعِدُهُمْ أَوْ نَتَوَفَّيَنَّكَ فَإِنَّمَا عَلَيْكَ ٱلْبَلَٰغُ وَعَلَيْنَا ٱلْحِسَابُ ﴿٤٠﴾

Do they not see how We gradually reduce the land from its outlying borders? When God judges, there is no power that could repel His judgement. He is swift in reckoning. (41)

أَوَلَمْ يَرَوْا۟ أَنَّا نَأْتِى ٱلْأَرْضَ نَنقُصُهَا مِنْ أَطْرَافِهَا وَٱللَّهُ يَحْكُمُ لَا مُعَقِّبَ لِحُكْمِهِۦ وَهُوَ سَرِيعُ ٱلْحِسَابِ ﴿٤١﴾

Those who lived before them also schemed, but God is the master of all scheming. He knows what is earned by every soul. The unbelievers will in time come to know who will attain the ultimate abode. (42)

وَقَدْ مَكَرَ ٱلَّذِينَ مِن قَبْلِهِمْ فَلِلَّهِ ٱلْمَكْرُ جَمِيعًا يَعْلَمُ مَا تَكْسِبُ كُلُّ نَفْسٍ وَسَيَعْلَمُ ٱلْكُفَّٰرُ لِمَنْ عُقْبَى ٱلدَّارِ ﴿٤٢﴾

The unbelievers say: 'You are no messenger of God.' Say: 'God is sufficient as a witness between me and you, and so are those who have true knowledge of the Book.' (43)

وَيَقُولُ ٱلَّذِينَ كَفَرُوا۟ لَسْتَ مُرْسَلًا قُلْ كَفَىٰ بِٱللَّهِ شَهِيدًۢا بَيْنِى وَبَيْنَكُمْ وَمَنْ عِندَهُۥ عِلْمُ ٱلْكِتَٰبِ ﴿٤٣﴾

Overview

Great scenes drawn from the vast universe and the world beyond, as well as the depths of the human soul were presented in the first half of the *sūrah*. Now, this second half adds a fine rationality that deals with the great issues of revelation and the divine message, God's oneness, the unbelievers' attributing partners to Him, as well as their demand for miracles and their hastening of God's punishment.

This new phase opens with a demonstration of the natures of belief and denial of the truth. The former is evidence of true knowledge, while the latter is blindness. Another touch delineates the nature of believers and unbelievers, and the distinctive qualities of both. This is followed by a scene of the Day of Judgement and the bliss it brings to the former and suffering to the latter. We then have a description of plentiful and stinted provisions as determined by God. Then follows an image of believing hearts gaining reassurance through remembrance of God. Then we move to a description of the Qur'ān which almost makes mountains move, or the earth split apart, or the dead speak. A further image touches on the calamities that befall unbelievers or which strike a short distance from their quarters. This is followed by a sarcastic remark directed at the unbelievers' false gods. Mention is then made of the doom of past communities so as to rid the earth of them time after time. The closing part contains a stern warning to those who deny the message of the Prophet Muḥammad (peace be upon him), threatening to leave them to their inevitable doom.

All this shows that the strong beat we encountered in the first half of the *sūrah* now prepares us for a close look at the issues raised. Our minds are open to receive these issues and accept the message of the *sūrah*. The two parts are mutually complementary, although each has its special effects, all of which serve one issue and promote the same goal.

Qualities of the Righteous

The first question addressed in this part of the *sūrah* was already raised in the first half. Here, however, it is presented rather differently: "*Is, then, he who knows that what has been revealed to you by your Lord*

183

is the Truth like one who is blind? Only those who are endowed with understanding keep this in mind." (Verse 19)

This verse states clearly that the opposite of a person who knows that the revelation received by the Prophet from his Lord is the truth is not one who does not have that knowledge, but one who is blind. This is a unique way of expressing that which touches hearts and magnifies differences. At the same time it states the truth without any exaggeration, addition or distortion. This is a great, clear and readily apparent fact that remains unnoticed only by he who is blind. People, then, belong to one of two groups: those who keep their eyes open, so they know it, and those who are blind, so they do not. Real blindness is that which shuts minds, intelligence and learning faculties. It is a blindness which switches off the source of spiritual knowledge. *"Only those who are endowed with understanding keep this in mind."* (Verse 19) Those are the ones who have open minds and active faculties of understanding. When those are reminded of the truth, they keep it in mind, and when they are alerted to its indications, they appreciate them.

The *sūrah* outlines a few qualities of those who are endowed with understanding: *"Those who are true to their bond with God and never break their covenant."* (Verse 20) God's bond and covenant are referred to here as being absolute. This includes every bond and covenant made with all people. The greatest bond which provides a basis for all others is faith. The most important covenant which embraces all others is that which binds people to fulfil the requirements of faith.

The bond of faith is both old and new. It is as old as human nature which conforms to the law that governs all existence. Human nature is endowed with a direct understanding that there is a single power which has brought the universe into existence, and that this power belongs to the Creator who is the One to be worshipped. It also includes the covenant made with all human generations before they are born, as we interpret the relevant Qur'ānic verse: *"Your Lord brought forth their offspring from the loins of the children of Adam, and called them to bear witness about themselves. [He said]: 'Am I not your Lord?' They replied: 'Yes, indeed, we bear witness to that.'"* (7: 172) At the same time, it is a new bond, renewed with the messengers whom God has sent to re-establish the faith, remind people of it and provide its details.

They do not initiate the bond of faith, but they outline its requirements of submission to God alone to the exclusion of all others. This bond also requires good action, proper behaviour, and turning always to God alone who is the other party to the old covenant.

On the basis of the bond and covenant with God, all bonds and covenants with human beings are established, whether with God's Messenger or with people, relatives or strangers, individuals or communities. A person who remains true to the first bond will remain true to all bonds because this is a duty. When one fulfils the duties required by the original covenant, one will fulfil all that is required towards other people, because this is a stipulation of the original covenant. Thus, in these few words the *sūrah* outlines the basic rule upon which the whole structure of human life is built.

"*And who keep together what God has bidden to be joined; who fear their Lord and dread the terrors of the reckoning.*" (Verse 21) The first of these qualities is expressed in general terms, referring to everything that should remain united or joined together. Hence it means total obedience, following the established rules and the code God has laid down, without deviation. If the details were provided here about everything that should remain joined, it would be a very long list. There is no need to provide such details here. For it is enough to impress on us the need to remain constant, ready to obey, and maintain our bond with God. The last part of the verse implicitly describes the feelings that accompany such complete obedience: "*who fear their Lord and dread the terrors of the reckoning.*" Conscious of God, they dread the reckoning. But as they are endowed with understanding, they prepare for that reckoning before it is due, so that they will have an easy one.

"*Who remain patient in adversity seeking the countenance of their Lord.*" (Verse 22) Patience takes different forms. One aspect is to persevere, fulfilling the requirements of the covenant, such as by dedicated action, diligent striving or *jihād*, and advocacy of God's message, etc. Another is to be patient in situations of affluence and poverty. However, those who are patient when they have abundance of everything are few and far between. Most people become arrogant in such situations and this may lead them to disbelief in God. A different aspect is to be patient in the face of other people's stupidities that result from ignorance. These are all adverse situations that require

185

patience. True believers show such patience out of love for their Lord, which is implied in the expression that they 'seek His countenance'. Their motive is not to spare themselves the embarrassment of people saying that they are afraid, or to solicit the compliment that they have shown patience, or to gain any advantage or avert any harm. Their only motive is that they love God and seek His reward. Hence they endure any trial to which He subjects them, and accept what God's will dictates and are content that He brings them only what is good for them.

"*And attend to their prayers.*" (Verse 22) This is a requirement of remaining true to God's bond and fulfilling the covenant made with Him, but it is given prominence here because it is the cornerstone of such fulfilment. It is also the practical manifestation of turning to God alone, and the relationship between Him and His servants which allows no room for any intervention by anyone else.

"*And spend on others, secretly and openly, out of what We provide for them.*" (Verse 22) This is also part of keeping together what should be united, and part of the fulfilment of the covenant made with God. It is given special mention because it is a bond between God's servants which unites them in this life on the basis of faith. It purges the giver of stinginess, and purifies the recipient of grudge. It makes life in the Muslim community worthy of human beings who co-operate with, and look after, one another and who are honoured by God. The spending is meant to be in secret and in the open. When it is secret it preserves integrity, and spares people embarrassment. When it is open, it gives a motive to others to do the same, and it demonstrates the implementation of God's law. Both ways carry importance and value in life.

"*And who repel evil with good.*" (Verse 22) What is meant here is that in their daily dealings with others, they reply to the evil done by others by doing what is good. The verse, however, stresses the result, rather than the action leading to it. When an evil action is returned with something good, this has a dampening effect on the evil tendency in others, encouraging them to do good instead, and helping them to resist Satan's promptings. Eventually, it repels the evil action and prevents it. Hence, the verse emphasizes this result and gives it prominence by way of encouraging people to reply to an evil action with a good one.

Moreover, there is a subtle reference here to returning evil with good only when this helps to prevent, rather than encourage evil. When evil is uncompromising, it must be overpowered. To return it with good action only emboldens it, making it more intransigent.

Besides, the prevention of evil by means of good action is feasible mostly in relations between equals. When the dispute is over faith, it is normally the case that arrogant aggressors and spreaders of corruption can only be dealt with by strong, decisive action. Qur'ānic directives then should be considered and implemented on the basis of a rational and objective study of every situation to determine the best course under the circumstances.

"*Such will have the attainment of the [ultimate] abode: gardens of perpetual bliss, which they will enter together with the righteous from among their parents, their spouses and their offspring. The angels will come in to them from every gate, [saying]: 'Peace be upon you, because you have persevered.' Blessed indeed is the attainment of the [ultimate] abode.*" (Verses 22–24) Such people possessing such qualities have a high position in heaven where they have their permanent abode. There they will be reunited with their righteous relatives, including their good parents, spouses, children and grandchildren. Everyone of these is admitted into heaven on the basis of their own good actions, because they deserve this goodly reward from God. But they are also blessed with reunion with the people they loved in the life of this world, which is another aspect of their happiness that enhances what they have in heaven.

In this great atmosphere of happy reunion, the angels take part in their reception and hospitality, constantly moving everywhere: "*The angels will come in to them from every gate.*" (Verse 23) The image given here is very real. It is as if we see the angels and hear them welcoming the believers, saying: "*Peace be upon you, because you have persevered.' Blessed indeed is the attainment of the [ultimate] abode.*" (Verse 24) It is a great sight with people and angels meeting, greeting and honouring one another.

On the other side are the ones who are devoid of mind and insight, which means that they neither reflect on, nor see the truth. They are the opposite of the first group in every respect: "*As for those who break their bond with God after it has been established, and cut asunder what*

God has bidden to be joined, and spread corruption on earth, the curse will be laid upon them; and theirs shall be an evil abode." (Verse 25)

They break the covenant God has made with human nature in the first place and, in consequence, break every subsequent covenant. When the first bond is broken, all later ones established on its basis are also broken. A person who does not honour his commitment to God will never be true to any bond or covenant. Therefore, these people cut asunder whatever should be joined and remain united. This is expressed here in absolute terms so as to cover everything that comes under the same heading. They also spread corruption on earth, which contrasts with the perseverance of the first group, their attending to prayers, charitable spending and repelling evil with good. Indeed spreading corruption on earth is the opposite of all these qualities, because abandoning any of them represents or encourages corruption.

Such people are cast away, with a curse laid upon them, which means that they are rejected and turned away. This contrasts with the honour given to the other group. Moreover, they will have *'an evil abode'*, which is not specified because we know it as contrasting with the abode of the good who are in heaven.

This group are delighted with whatever comfort or pleasure they have in the life of this world, and as such, they do not aspire to the far superior happiness in the life to come. Yet it is God who determines what people have in this life. He gives either abundant or stinted provision, which means that He has the final say in both this present life and in the future life alike. Had such people sought the reward of the hereafter, God would not have deprived them of happiness in this life, when it is He who gives it to them in the first place: *"God grants abundant sustenance, or gives it in scant measure, to whomever He wills. They [i.e. the unbelievers] rejoice in the life of this world, even though, compared to the life to come, the life of this world is nought but a fleeting pleasure."* (Verse 26)

True Heart Comfort

We have already referred to the great difference between a person who knows that what has been bestowed from on high to the Prophet Muḥammad (peace be upon him) is the truth and one who is blind.

Now the *sūrah* speaks about the blind who do not see all the signs God has placed in the universe and who are not satisfied with the Qurʾān as a great sign. Hence they demand another miraculous sign. The *sūrah* mentions something of this earlier and comments by saying that the Prophet is only a warner, for miraculous signs rest with God. Now it mentions their demand anew, outlining the reasons that help one person to follow divine guidance and cause another to remain in error. It also paints a picture of hearts content with alertness of God's presence. Such hearts do not worry or demand miracles in order to believe when they have the Qurʾān available to them. For the Qurʾān can make mountains move and the earth split apart. With the Qurʾān, the dead can be addressed. This is sufficient to tell us about the power and authority of the Qurʾān. The *sūrah* concludes its discussion of those who ask for miracles by explaining to the believers that they hope for nothing. It draws their attention to the examples they see before them and to what, from time to time, befalls those who deny the truth.

> The unbelievers say: 'Why has no miraculous sign been bestowed on him by his Lord?' Say: 'God lets go astray anyone who wills [to go astray] and guides to Himself those who turn to Him; those who believe and whose hearts find comfort in the remembrance of God. It is indeed in the remembrance of God that people's hearts find their comfort. Those who believe and do righteous deeds shall have happiness and a most beautiful final goal. Thus have We sent you to a community before whom other communities had passed away, so that you might recite to them what We have revealed to you. Yet they deny the Most Gracious. Say: 'He is my Lord. There is no deity other than Him. In Him have I placed my trust, and to Him shall I return.' Even if there should be a Qurʾān by which mountains could be moved, or the earth cleft asunder, or the dead made to speak! For certain, God's alone is the command in all things. Have they who believe not come to realize that, had God so willed, He would indeed have guided all mankind? As for the unbelievers, because of their misdeeds, calamity will always befall them or will fall close to their homes, until God's promise is fulfilled. God never fails to fulfil His promise. Before your time,

*other messengers were derided, but for a while I gave rein to the
unbelievers; but then I took them to task, and how terrible was
My retribution."* (Verses 27–32)

The answer to their demand is that miracles are not what lead people
to believe. Faith has its solid foundation within the human soul. There
are causes that lead to it, but these have to originate within the soul:
*"Say: 'God lets go astray anyone who wills [to go astray] and guides to
Himself those who turn to Him.'"* (Verse 27) It is their turning to Him
which makes them worthy of His guidance. It is clearly understood
that those who do not turn to God are those who deserve to be left to
go astray. This is indeed what happens to them. What matters, then, is
one's own heart and its being ready to receive God's guidance. If so, it
seeks it and appeals to God for it. Hearts which do not make any
positive move to seek God's guidance remain far removed from it.

This is followed by an image of believing hearts which enjoy a
congenial atmosphere of reassurance, happiness and peace: *"those who
believe and whose hearts find comfort in the remembrance of God."* (Verse
28) They find comfort in their feeling that their bond with God is a
real one, and that they are close to Him, secure with His support.

They are without worry, and worry is normally only generated when
one is left alone or when one is unsure of one's way. Such people
understand God's wisdom behind man's creation, origin and destiny.
They also find comfort in feeling secure against aggression, harm or
evil, except as God wills for them. This is coupled with a resigned
acceptance of whatever trial God wishes to test them with. They are
reassured that God will always bestow on them His grace, giving them
guidance, abundance and security in this life and in the life to come.

*"It is indeed in the remembrance of God that people's hearts find their
comfort."* (Verse 28) Such comfort is a profound reality in the hearts of
believers who deeply and truly feel the meaning of faith. They have a
bond with God which they recognize. They cannot express the meaning
of such a bond in words.

It touches their hearts, generating a feeling of happiness and
reassurance that they do not stand alone in this universe. Whatever
surrounds them is a friend, because it is all made by God under whose
protection they live.

No one on earth is more miserable than those who are deprived of the blessing of a close relationship with God. Those who, having severed the most essential bond with their Creator, feel that they have no relationship with all around them are bound to suffer great misery. Who can be more wretched than one who does not realize why he has been created, or where he is heading, or why he suffers. Forlorn indeed is the one who goes about his life feeling isolated in an endless desert, having to strive without support, guidance or help.

In life we often experience moments which none can withstand unless we are certain of God's support and protection, regardless of whatever resources of fortitude, perseverance and power may be at our command. There are moments in life that render all that useless. But such moments can be faced easily by those who find their comfort in God: "*It is indeed in the remembrance of God that people's hearts find their comfort.*" (Verse 28)

Those who turn to God are reassured when they remember Him, and find fine welcome when they return to Him. This is the same as the outcome of their turning to Him in this life presenting their good deeds: "*Those who believe and do righteous deeds shall have happiness and a most beautiful final goal.*" (Verse 29) The Arabic term, *ṭūbā*, which is used here for 'happiness' is chosen for its added connotations of greatness. Hence, their happiness is great, unending.

Conversely, those who demand a sign are those who have deprived themselves of the contentment, comfort and happiness of faith. They live in worry, and it is this anxiety that makes them demand miracles and signs. The *sūrah* then tells the Prophet that he is not the first messenger to preach the divine message to his people. This means that they should not find the matter too strange. Before them there were numerous communities and many messengers. If they persist with their rejection of the divine faith, you, the Prophet, should continue to follow your own way, putting your trust in God alone: "*Thus have We sent you to a community before whom other communities had passed away, so that you might recite to them what We have revealed to you. Yet they deny the Most Gracious. Say: 'He is my Lord. There is no deity other than Him. In Him have I placed my trust, and to Him shall I return.'*" (Verse 30)

What is extremely odd is that they refuse to believe in God, the Most Gracious, in the remembrance of whose mercy people find inner comfort and contentedness. God's Messenger is being told that all his task requires is that he read to them what God has revealed to him. This is the purpose for which God has given him this message. If they persist in rejecting it, he has to make it clear to them that he places his trust in God alone, and that he turns to Him, seeking help from no one else.

The task the Prophet is sent to accomplish is to recite this remarkable Qur'ān to them. Had there been a divine writ with which mountains move, or the earth split asunder, or the dead made to speak, this Qur'ān would have had the necessary characteristics to achieve such supernatural phenomena. But this Qur'ān is meant to address the living who are accountable for their deeds. If they will not respond, then the believers may despair of their ever turning to God and submitting to Him. They should leave them alone until God's threat to the unbelievers has come true: *"Even if there should be a Qur'ān by which mountains could be moved, or the earth cleft asunder, or the dead made to speak! For certain, God's alone is the command in all things. Have they who believe not come to realize that, had God so willed, He would indeed have guided all mankind? As for the unbelievers, because of their misdeeds, calamity will always befall them or will fall close to their homes, until God's promise is fulfilled. God never fails to fulfil His promise."* (Verse 31)

The Qur'ān has done with those who received it and moulded themselves according to its teachings much more than moving mountains, cleaving the earth asunder or making the dead speak. In fact the miracles it achieved in and with these souls are much greater and more far-reaching in their effects on human life and indeed on the earth itself. Islam and Muslims have not only changed the course of history so often, but they have also changed all that is on the face of the earth.

The very nature of the Qur'ān, its address and expression, its treatment of its subject matter, the truth it outlines and its effect have overwhelming and penetrating power. This power is felt by everyone who appreciates and understands what is being said. Those who moulded themselves in accordance with its teachings moved what is more deeply entrenched than mountains, which is the history of nations and communities. They cut asunder what is far more solid than the earth, which is inflexible thought and rigid tradition. They were able to send life into what was more lifeless than the dead, which is communities that had been suffering under a long history of despotism. If we look at the change that was brought about in the life of the Arabs, and their complete and far-reaching transformation, with no apparent cause other than the effect of the Qur'ān and its method of remoulding hearts and souls, we realize that it is far greater than moving mountains, splitting the earth apart and sending life into what is dead.

"*God's alone is the command in all things.*" (Verse 31) It is He who chooses what to do and the tools for the situation. If after the revelation of the Qur'ān there remain people who are not touched by it, the believers should give up trying to inspire life into such hearts. They should leave the whole matter to God. Had He so wished, He would have created all people with a single tendency to believe in Him, just as He did with the angels. Alternatively, He would have brought about something that would force them to believe. But He has not willed either scenario, because He has created man to fulfil a particular task, and He – limitless is He in His glory – knows that its fulfilment requires that man is created with both tendencies: "*Have they who believe not come to realize that, had God so willed, He would indeed have guided all mankind?*" (Verse 31) The believers, then, should leave them to God.

However, some disaster may befall them, causing them great harm and killing whoever is doomed to destruction: "*As for the unbelievers, because of their misdeeds, calamity will always befall them or will fall close to their homes.*" (Verse 31) When it does, they are left in fear that a similar one may follow, destroying them altogether. It may touch certain hearts and give them life.

This may continue "*until God's promise is fulfilled.*" (Verse 31) This is a reference to the promise God has given. He has delayed their judgement until that time. "*God never fails to fulfil His promise.*" (Verse 31) It will certainly be fulfilled and they will receive whatever they have been promised.

Examples are many, and the fate of earlier communities should provide a lesson to be acted upon before it is too late. "*Before your time, other messengers were derided, but for a while I gave rein to the unbelievers; but then I took them to task, and how terrible was My retribution."* (Verse 32) This last sentence may be read as a question, but it is rhetorical requiring no answer. For such punishment was the subject of discussion for many generations.

Foul Devices with Fair Appearance

The second point discussed here is that of the partners people associate with God. The issue was also discussed in the first part of the *sūrah*. It is raised here in the form of a sarcastic question which compares such alleged partners with God who deals with every soul and rewards it for what it earns in this life. The scene is concluded with a description of the suffering those who invent this fallacy are certain to endure in this life and the greater suffering they will meet in the hereafter. This contrasts with the security and blessings awaiting the righteous: *"Is, then, He who stands over every soul [and knows] all that it does [like any other]? Yet they ascribe partners to God. Say: 'Name them. Would you tell Him of anything on earth which He does not know; or are these merely empty words?' Indeed their own cunning devices seem fair to the unbelievers, and they are turned away from the right path. Whoever God lets go astray can never find any guide. They shall endure suffering in the life of this world, but, truly, their suffering in the life to come will be harder still, and they will have none to shield them from God. Such is the paradise which the God-fearing have been promised: through it running waters flow. Its fruits will be everlasting, and so will be its shade. Such will be the destiny of those who fear God, while the destiny of the unbelievers is the fire."* (Verses 33–35)

God, limitless is He in His glory, watches all souls, has power over them all in every situation and knows what every one of them does in public or private. The Qur'ān, in its inimitable style, describes this in a very vivid way so that we see all this for ourselves, overwhelmed with awe: *"Is, then, He who stands over every soul [and knows] all that it does [like any other]?"* (Verse 33) Now who is this watcher? It is God Himself! What soul will not feel fear to the bottom of its heart? Yet the description is real. The *sūrah* uses a rather physical image because human beings are more influenced by material than abstract matters.

If the situation is such, how come they associate partners with God? Their attitude appears here peculiarly odd. *"Yet they ascribe partners to*

God." (Verse 33) Yes, indeed! They ascribe partners to God Almighty who deals with every soul according to what it has earned. None and nothing escapes His watchful eye.

"*Say: 'Name them.'*" (Verse 33) They are unrecognizable entities. They may have names, but the *sūrah* treats them like entities with no name.

"*Would you tell Him of anything on earth which He does not know?*" (Verse 33) This is particularly sarcastic. Are you, human beings, aware of something which God does not know? Do you know of earth deities unknown to God? They dare not make such a claim, yet they practically say as much when they claim that such deities exist while God asserts that there are none.

"*Or are these merely empty words?*" which have no real significance? Is the question of God's existence so trivial that people approach it in jest, using words that are uttered without meaning or significance?

All this ridicule comes to an end with a decisive statement that puts the issues involved very clearly: "*Indeed their own cunning devices seem fair to the unbelievers, and they are turned away from the right path. Whoever God lets go astray can never find any guide.*" (Verse 33) The real issue, then, is that these people denied God, ignoring all evidence in support of faith, and choosing not to see God's guidance. Thus God's law operates against them, whilst their own souls persuade them that they are right and that their schemes against the advocates of faith is right and fair.

All this turns them away from the path that leads to the truth. A person who, by the operation of God's law, goes astray because he has chosen error over divine guidance will have none to guide him. God's law operates when the causes for its operation come together.

The natural goal for such blind hearts means their suffering: "*They shall endure suffering in the life of this world.*" (Verse 34) A calamity may befall them during their lifetime, or it may strike close to them causing a great deal of apprehension, anxiety and fear. In fact, hearts that are devoid of the comfort and reassurance generated by faith, and do not recognize the presence of divine wisdom behind every event they face are indeed suffering. However, "*truly, their suffering in the life to come will be harder still.*" (Verse 34) The suffering here is left undefined so that there is no limit to how we imagine it to be. "*They will have none to shield them from God.*" (Verse 34) No one will extend them any protection against whatever punishment God inflicts on them.

On the other side stand those who are God-fearing. The word chosen here to describe them, *al-muttaqūn*, is derived from the same root as *wāq*, i.e. 'protector', and is used here to express the fact that the unbelievers stand without protection against God's punishment. The God-fearing actually protect themselves with their faith and righteousness against all suffering and punishment. In addition the promise given to them to be in heaven is fulfilled: "*Such is the paradise which the God-fearing have been promised: through it running waters flow. Its fruits will be everlasting, and so will be its shade. Such will be the destiny of those who fear God.*" (Verse 35) That is an abode of perfect and complete comfort, where both shade and fruit are everlasting. It is an image that gives hearts comfort and reassurance, and which contrasts with the hardship and suffering of the unbelievers.

But the suffering on one side and the happiness of heaven on the other are the right and proper destiny of both groups: "*Such will be the destiny of those who fear God, while the destiny of the unbelievers is the fire.*" (Verse 35)

A Command to Worship

The main themes of this *sūrah* are those of revelation and God's oneness. Speaking of the two together, the *sūrah* mentions the attitude of the people of earlier revelations towards the Qur'ān and the Prophet, making it clear to the Prophet that the revelations he has received from on high constitute the final judgement on what earlier revelations included. It is indeed the final word which includes whatever God wants to remain applicable of the divine faith preached by all His messengers. It omits what God wants to be omitted, because its purpose, which is known to God, has been served. The Prophet, then, must stick to what God has revealed to Him. He must not follow the desires of those who follow earlier revelations, or those who are generally known as the 'People of the Book', in any matter, whether serious or otherwise. As for those who require him to produce a sign, they should be told that signs are given only when God wills them to be given. The Prophet's task is only to convey his message.

Those to whom We have given revelations rejoice at what has been bestowed on you from on high, but among different factions there are some who deny part of it. Say: 'I have only been bidden to worship God, and not to associate any partners with Him. To Him I pray, and to Him do I return.' Thus have We revealed it, a code of judgement in the Arabic tongue. If you should follow their desires after all the knowledge you have been given, you shall have none to protect or shield you from God. We have indeed sent messengers before you and given them wives and offspring. Yet no messenger could produce a miracle except by God's permission. Every age has had its revelation. God annuls or confirms what He pleases. With Him is the source of all revelation. Whether We let you see some of what We have promised them, or cause you to die [before its fulfilment], your duty is only to deliver your message: it is for Us to do the reckoning. (Verses 36–40)

Those among the people of earlier revelations who are sincere in following their faith will find in the Qur'ān an endorsement of the basic rules of the faith built on God's oneness, an acknowledgement of the truth of the earlier religions and their books, a serious consideration of these faiths coupled with deep respect, and also a sincere perception of the bond which unites all those who believe in God. Hence, they rejoice and believe. This rejoicing is experienced by sincere hearts, for it is the uniting of truth, providing a strengthened belief that all God's revelations are true and are endorsed by the new divine message.

"But among different factions there are some who deny part of it." (Verse 36) The factions referred to here could be found among the people of earlier revelations and also the idolaters. The *sūrah* does not mention which part they deny, because the purpose here is just to state the fact that they challenge the truth of this new revelation by denying parts of it: *"Say: 'I have only been bidden to worship God, and not to associate any partners with Him. To Him I pray, and to Him do I return.'"* (Verse 36) He alone is the One to be worshipped, and in whom we call on people to believe, and to whom we all return.

The Prophet is ordered to declare this approach when he confronts anyone who denies a part of his book, the Qur'ān. He should declare his firm belief in the whole book revealed to him by his Lord, whether the people of earlier revelations rejoice at it or deny parts of it. The reason is that what has been revealed to him is the final arbiter, expressed in Arabic, his language which he knows well. Since the Qur'ān is God's final word on faith, all reference should be made to it only: "*Thus have We revealed it, a code of judgement in the Arabic tongue.*" (Verse 37)

"*If you should follow their desires after all the knowledge you have been given, you shall have none to protect or shield you from God.*" (Verse 37) What has been given to you is the true knowledge. Whatever the different factions say is no more than the expression of their desires which have no basis in true knowledge or established fact. This warning addressed to God's Messenger is the clearest expression of this fact. It is one whereby deviation is not tolerated, not even by the Prophet. Far be it from the Prophet to deviate from it in any way.

Anyone who objects to the fact that God's Messenger is a human being should remember that all past messengers were human beings as well: "*We have indeed sent messengers before you and given them wives and offspring.*" (Verse 38) If the objection has something to do with him not producing a physical miracle, then that is something over which he has no control. It is determined by God: "*Yet no messenger could produce a miracle except by God's permission.*" (Verse 38) He determines this when He wills and according to His wisdom. If there are differences in the details of what is revealed to the Prophet Muḥammad and the revelations given earlier, these differences are due to the fact that every period of time has a suitable book. The Qur'ān is the final one to be revealed by God: "*Every age has had its revelation. God annuls or confirms what He pleases. With Him is the source of all revelation.*" (Verses 38–39) He annuls what has served its purpose and confirms what is of benefit. He has His original decree which contains all that is confirmed or annulled. He is the One who has sent down His revelations and He does with it what He pleases, in accordance with His wisdom. His will is always done.

Whether God inflicts any of His threats upon them during the Prophet's lifetime or causes him to die before that, the fact of the matter remains the same. The nature of the message and the nature of

Godhead remain the same: "*Whether We let you see some of what We have promised them, or cause you to die [before its fulfilment], your duty is only to deliver your message: it is for Us to do the reckoning.*" (Verse 40) This clear and decisive directive illustrates the nature of the message and the role of its advocates. Such advocates are required to fulfil their role, as it may be at every stage. They are not responsible for reaching any goal other than that determined by God. It is not for them to precipitate the attainment of any goal. They should never entertain any thought of failure when they see that their efforts have not attained power in the land. They are merely advocates of a message, and they should never go beyond this advocacy role.

God's might is clearly seen in everything around us. When strong and affluent communities deny God, allow corruption to spread and claim that they make their own affluence, God's hand begins to reduce their power, wealth and general standing. They are confined to a limited stretch of land after having had an extended area of rule and influence. When God determines that such communities shrink in their power and area, His rule is carried out, with no power able to stand in its way: "*Do they not see how We gradually reduce the land from its outlying borders? When God judges, there is no power that could repel His judgement. He is swift in reckoning.*" (Verse 41)

Those unbelievers in Arabia are not stronger or more powerful in their scheming than the communities which lived before them. Yet those were smitten by God who is more powerful and more elaborate in His planning: "*Those who lived before them also schemed, but God is the master of all scheming. He knows what is earned by every soul. The unbelievers will in time come to know who will attain the ultimate abode.*" (Verse 42)

The *sūrah* concludes by mentioning the fact that the unbelievers deny God's message given to the Prophet Muḥammad (peace be upon him). Its opening confirms the truth of his message. Thus the beginning and the end address the same point. God's testimony is called for, and it is certainly sufficient. After all, He has absolute knowledge of this book, or divine writ, and of all other revealed books: "*The unbelievers say: 'You are no messenger of God.' Say: 'God is sufficient as a witness between me and you, and so are those who have true knowledge of the Book.'*" (Verse 43)

Thus ends the *sūrah* which has taken us along a trip to discover the great horizons of the universe and to show us some of the inner aspects of the human soul. It makes profound and lasting impressions on our hearts and minds, leaving the final testimony to God, which is made at both the beginning and the end. It is a testimony to put an end to all arguments.

An Irrefutable Testimony

The *sūrah* draws clear outlines of the Islamic faith, following the Qur'ānic method of explaining its principles. It could be said that we should have dwelt on these aspects of the Islamic faith as they are mentioned in the *sūrah*. However, we have chosen instead not to interrupt the flow of the Qur'ānic theme in this *sūrah*, leaving such discussion to the end.

The opening of the *sūrah* and the issues it discusses, as well as a number of directives it contains point clearly to the fact that it is a Makkan revelation. It certainly was not revealed in Madinah as some reports indicate. In fact it was revealed at a time when the unbelievers' attitude was hardened, manifesting itself in outright rejection of the Islamic message, throwing challenges at the Prophet, demanding that he produce miracles and other signs, and precipitating God's punishment against which he warned them. This required a clear statement which aimed at strengthening the Prophet and his Companions so that they held on to what God had revealed, disregarding all opposition. They were to care little for all the false accusations levelled at them and the challenges put to them. They were to feel themselves as having the upper hand since they were following the truth, able to turn to God alone for support, and declare His oneness as the only Lord of the universe. They were to believe their faith as truth, no matter how vehemently it was denied or rejected by the unbelievers and the idolaters. The *sūrah* also puts some irrefutable evidence supporting this truth to the idolaters, which they could witness in the universe around them, within themselves, as also in the events of human history. All these aspects are grouped together and utilized in such a way as to make a profound address to the human mind.

Here are some of the verses stressing the fact that this revealed book, i.e. the Qurʾān, represents the truth, and that rejecting it altogether, denying its truth, or giving a slow response to its appeal does not change this great fact:

These are verses of the Book. That which is revealed to you by your Lord is the truth, yet most people will not believe. (Verse 1)

They ask you to hasten evil rather than good, although exemplary punishments have indeed come to pass before their time. Your Lord always extends forgiveness to people despite their wrongdoing. Your Lord is certainly severe in retribution. Yet the unbelievers say: 'Why has no miraculous sign been bestowed on him by his Lord?' But you are only a warner. Every community have [their] guide. (Verses 6–7)

To Him is due the prayer aiming at the Truth. Those whom people invoke beside God cannot respond to them in any way. They are just like a man who stretches his open hands towards water, [hoping] that it will come to his mouth; but it will never reach it. The prayer of those without faith is nothing but wandering in grievous error. (Verse 14)

Thus does God illustrate truth and falsehood. The scum is cast away, while that which is of benefit to mankind abides on earth. Thus does God set forth His parables. (Verse 17)

Is, then, he who knows that what has been revealed to you by your Lord is the Truth like one who is blind? Only those who are endowed with understanding keep this in mind. (Verse 19)

The unbelievers say: 'Why has no miraculous sign been bestowed on him by his Lord?' Say: 'God lets go astray anyone who wills [to go astray] and guides to Himself those who turn to Him; those who believe and whose hearts find comfort in the remembrance of God. It is indeed in the remembrance of God that people's hearts find their comfort.' (Verses 27–28)

Thus have We sent you to a community before whom other communities had passed away, so that you might recite to them what We have revealed to you. Yet they deny the Most Gracious.

Say: 'He is my Lord. There is no deity other than Him. In Him have I placed my trust, and to Him shall I return.' (Verse 30)

Such is the paradise which the God-fearing have been promised: through it running waters flow. Its fruits will be everlasting, and so will be its shade. Such will be the destiny of those who fear God, while the destiny of the unbelievers is the fire. (Verse 35)

Whether We let you see some of what We have promised them, or cause you to die [before its fulfilment], your duty is only to deliver your message: it is for Us to do the reckoning. (Verse 40)

The unbelievers say: 'You are no messenger of God.' Say: 'God is sufficient as a witness between me and you, and so are those who have true knowledge of the Book.' (Verse 43)

In all these verses we can clearly discern the nature of the confrontation that the idolaters used to challenge the Prophet and the Qur'ān. We also see in this challenge and the divine directives on how to respond to it the nature of the times when this *sūrah* was revealed.

Declaring the Essentials of Faith

A main feature of the divine instructions to God's Messenger is that he should face all the opposition, challenges, denunciations and difficulties thrown in his face by declaring the truth of his message in full. This means that he must declare in all clarity that there is no deity other than God, the only Lord in the universe, the Almighty who must be worshipped alone without associating any partners with Him. All people will inevitably return to Him for judgement, when they will either be admitted into heaven or thrown in hell. These are the basic truths which the unbelievers denied and challenged the Prophet over. He is further instructed not to follow their desires, or seek compromises with them that require that any part of these truths be concealed, suppressed or delayed. In fact the Prophet is warned that God's punishment will apply to him also if he follows their desires in this respect, after all the clear knowledge that has been given to him.

This main feature clearly shows that the advocates of the Islamic message cannot deviate from the nature of the message and its method of advocacy. They must also declare the basic truths of the Islamic faith without hesitation, suppressing nothing and delaying nothing. The first of these essential truths is that all Godhead and Lordship in the universe belong to God alone. Hence, all submission must be to Him. He is the One to be obeyed in all matters. This truth must be declared, no matter what sort of opposition it meets nor how stiff the unbelievers' resistance is. Even in the face of hardship and persecution, its advocates must declare it complete. It is not for them to decide that part of this truth should be put aside, or temporarily suppressed, because tyrants dislike it or persecute those who advocate it, or turn away from the faith on its account. None of these considerations permit advocates of the Islamic message to change its strategy, starting, for example, with matters of worship or moral values, good manners or spiritual considerations. It may appear that such a course is preferable in order to avoid the wrath of tyrants but that would be a grave mistake. For advocates of the Islamic message must at all times declare God's oneness and Lordship over the whole universe, and that all submission and obedience belong to God alone.

This is the proper way to advocate the Islamic faith, as God wants it to be done. It is the strategy followed by the Prophet Muḥammad (peace be upon him), as he was instructed by God. No advocate of Islam can abandon this strategy, or change its method of action. After all, the Islamic faith is God's message and He looks after it. He provides sufficient support for its advocates, and He is always able to protect them against tyrants.

The Qur'ānic method of calling people to Islam brings together the Qur'ān, God's book which we recite, and the open book of the universe. The whole universe, with all the evidence it provides of God's power and elaborate planning, is a source of inspiration for mankind. Combined with these two books is the record of human history which also contains countless proofs of God's power and planning. Human beings are shown all these, as the address is made to their minds, hearts and feelings all at the same time.

This *surah* contains numerous examples from the pages of the book of the universe as it addresses the whole human entity. Here are just some of them:

Alif. Lām. Mīm. Rā. These are verses of the Book. That which is revealed to you by your Lord is the truth, yet most people will not believe. It is God who raised the heavens without any support that you could see, and established Himself on the Throne. And He it is who has made the sun and the moon subservient [to His laws], each pursuing its course for a set term. He ordains all things. He makes plain His revelations so that you may firmly believe that you will certainly be meeting your Lord. It is He who has spread out the earth and placed upon it firm mountains and rivers, and created on it two sexes of every type of fruit, and caused the night to cover the day. In all these there are signs for people who think. And there are on earth adjoining tracts of land; and vineyards, and fields of grains and date-palms, growing in clusters or non-clustered. [All] are irrigated by the same water; yet some of them are favoured above others with regard to the food [they provide]. In all this there are signs for people who use their reason. (Verses 1–4)

The *sūrah* includes all these scenes so that the whole universe becomes a witness giving proof of God's power of creation, origination, and design, according to an elaborate plan. It then wonders at people who see all this evidence but who nonetheless find it difficult to believe in resurrection and a new creation. They deny God's revelations because what He reveals states very clearly this truth which should be felt to be so close at hand, considering God's limitless power which produced these marvellous scenes of creation.

But if you are amazed, amazing, too, is their saying: 'What! After we have become dust, shall we be raised [to life] in a new act of creation?' These are the ones who deny their Lord. They are the ones who carry their own shackles around their necks; and they are the ones who are destined for the fire wherein they will abide. (Verse 5)

It is He who displays before you the lightning, giving rise to both fear and hope, and originates the heavy clouds. And the thunder extols His limitless glory and praises Him, and so do the angels, in awe of Him. He hurls the thunderbolts to smite with them whom He wills. (Verses 12–13)

This scene of universal phenomena enhances the feeling of amazement at people who continue to argue about God, associating partners with Him when they can see the results of His power and Lordship, as well as the submission of the universe to Him. All this proves that He controls all matters in the universe. No one else has similar power to create, plan or control:

> *Yet they stubbornly argue about God. His might is both stern and wise. To Him is due the prayer aiming at the Truth. Those whom people invoke beside God cannot respond to them in any way. They are just like a man who stretches his open hands towards water, [hoping] that it will come to his mouth; but it will never reach it. The prayer of those without faith is nothing but wandering in grievous error. To God prostrate themselves, willingly or unwillingly, all those who are in the heavens and on earth, as do their very shadows, morning and evening. Say: 'Who is the Lord of the heavens and the earth?' Say: '[It is] God.' Say: 'Why, then, do you take for your protectors, instead of Him, others who have no power to cause either benefit or harm even to themselves?' Say: 'Can the blind and the seeing be deemed equal? Or is the depth of darkness equal to light?' Or do they assign to God partners that have created the like of His creation, so that both creations appear to them to be similar? Say: 'God is the Creator of all things. He is the One who has power over all things.'* (Verses 13–16)

An Appeal to Human Feelings

The whole universe is thus turned into a great exhibition proving God's power and pointing out what should motivate people to accept the faith. It addresses human nature with profound logic, and addresses the whole human being with all its faculties of perception and understanding. This is all done in perfect harmony.

To the great book of the universe is added a few pages of human history, together with the visible effects of God's power, control of the universe and His elaborate planning of human life:

> *They ask you to hasten evil rather than good, although exemplary punishments have indeed come to pass before their time.* (Verse 6)

God knows what every female bears, and by how much the wombs may fall short [in gestation], and by how much they may increase. With Him everything has its definite measure. He knows all that lies beyond the reach of human perception and all that anyone may witness. He is the Great One, the Most High. It is all alike [to Him] whether any of you speaks in secret or aloud, whether he seeks to hide under the cover of the night or walks openly in the light of day. Each has guardian angels before him and behind him, who watch him by God's command. Indeed God does not change a people's conditions unless they first change what is in their hearts. When God wills people to suffer some misfortune, none can avert it. Besides Him, they have none to protect them. (Verses 8–11)

God grants abundant sustenance, or gives it in scant measure, to whomever He wills. They [i.e. the unbelievers] rejoice in the life of this world, even though, compared to the life to come, the life of this world is nought but a fleeting pleasure. (Verse 26)

As for the unbelievers, because of their misdeeds, calamity will always befall them or will fall close to their homes, until God's promise is fulfilled. God never fails to fulfil His promise. Before your time, other messengers were derided, but for a while I gave rein to the unbelievers; but then I took them to task, and how terrible was My retribution. (Verses 31–32)

Do they not see how We gradually reduce the land from its outlying borders? When God judges, there is no power that could repel His judgement. He is swift in reckoning. Those who lived before them also schemed, but God is the master of all scheming. He knows what is earned by every soul. The unbelievers will in time come to know who will attain the ultimate abode. (Verses 41–42)

The Qur'ān must always be the book to which advocates of Islam turn for guidance, before turning to any other source. It is from the Qur'ān that they must learn how to call on people to believe, and how to awaken their hearts and bring inactive souls back to life. The Qur'ān is a revelation sent down by God, the Creator of man who knows his nature, how he is influenced and in what way he reacts. We have already said that advocates of the Islamic faith should follow the strategy laid down by God, starting with making the truth plain concerning God, His oneness, Lordship over all the worlds, sovereignty and power. Similarly, they must seek to open people's hearts to the message of truth by following the method of the Qur'ān in making people truly aware of their Lord. This is the best way to make people recognize that all submission must be to God alone, the true Lord who controls the whole universe.

The Nature of Prophethood

The Qur'ān takes great care to show in the clearest of terms the nature of the message and the nature of God's Messenger. It does so in order to establish for people who their true Lord is, and to remove any trace of polytheism from their minds. There were in the past many instances of deviation from this proper concept, among the people of earlier revelations, which led to confusion between the nature of Godhead and the nature of prophethood. The clearest example was among the Christians who added to Jesus (peace be upon him) divine qualities and qualities of Lordship that belong to God alone. As a result, the followers of different churches became involved in a maze of conflict that was contrary to the truth.

But the Christians were not the only ones whose beliefs were so confused. All pagan communities were similarly involved in such endless confusion, producing concepts that assign mysterious qualities to prophethood, or link it with magic, or clairvoyance, or with contacts with spirits and the *jinn*.

Many of these concepts found their way into the beliefs of the pagan Arabs. Hence some of them used to demand that the Prophet tell them about things beyond the reach of human knowledge. Some demanded that he should produce some physical miracles. They also accused him of being a sorcerer, or a madman who had contacts with the *jinn*, while some suggested that he should have an angel supporting what he said. The fact is that all such suggestions, demands, accusations and challenges thrown at him had their roots in the pagan concepts of the nature of prophethood and prophets in general.

The Qur'ān puts the truth of this concept in a most lucid way, outlining the nature of the message and the messenger who received it from God and conveyed it to mankind. It also outlines the unique nature of Godhead in which no other being has the slightest share, and the nature of servitude that applies to all creatures, including God's messengers and prophets. They too were human beings who had no divine qualities whatsoever, and had no contact with the *jinn* or with the world of magic. They only received revelations from God. Beyond that, they had no power to produce any supernatural miracle, except by God's will. They were chosen for a certain task while they retained their human nature and their status as God's servants.

The *sūrah* includes several examples clarifying the nature of prophethood and the message given to the Prophet Muḥammad (peace be upon him). These examples serve to purge people's minds of all traces of paganism and the legends that distorted the beliefs of people who had earlier received divine revelations, leading them to a new form of paganism and a new set of legends and superstitions.

This clarification does not come in the form of an intellectual argument or a philosophical or metaphysical thesis. Instead, it provides support to believers implementing a practical method of action that stood up to the challenges of the unbelievers:

> Yet the unbelievers say: 'Why has no miraculous sign been bestowed on him by his Lord?' But you are only a warner. Every community have [their] guide. (Verse 7)

> The unbelievers say: 'Why has no miraculous sign been bestowed on him by his Lord?' Say: 'God lets go astray anyone who wills [to go astray] and guides to Himself those who turn to Him.' (Verse 27)

> Thus have We sent you to a community before whom other communities had passed away, so that you might recite to them what We have revealed to you. Yet they deny the Most Gracious. Say: 'He is my Lord. There is no deity other than Him. In Him have I placed my trust, and to Him shall I return.' (Verse 30)

> We have indeed sent messengers before you and given them wives and offspring. Yet no messenger could produce a miracle except by God's permission. Every age has had its revelation. (Verse 38)

Whether We let you see some of what We have promised them, or cause you to die [before its fulfilment], your duty is only to deliver your message: it is for Us to do the reckoning. (Verse 40)

These verses lucidly sum up the nature of the message and the role of God's Messenger. He is only sent to warn mankind. His task is to convey his message, and all that he has to do is to recite to people the revelations he receives. It is not for him to produce any miracle, except by God's will. Beyond that he is only God's servant, to whom he will definitely return. As a human being, he gets married and begets children, and lives as a human being in all respects. He practises his servitude to God in all aspects and all situations.

With such clarity all confused beliefs, superstitions and erroneous concepts concerning the nature of prophethood are completely removed. The faith remains pure, admitting nothing of the muddled concepts advanced by different churches and pagan beliefs. In fact such confused concepts reduced Christianity after its first century to pagan status, while it was preached by Jesus Christ as a divine faith, assigning to him no more than the status of a good human servant of God who could not produce a miracle except by God's permission.

The Prophet's Task

Before we conclude our remarks on this question we should reflect a little on a point clearly stated in the verse that says: "*Whether We let you see some of what We have promised them, or cause you to die [before its fulfilment], your duty is only to deliver your message: it is for Us to do the reckoning.*" (Verse 40) This is said to the Prophet (peace be upon him), God's Messenger who received His revelations and was commanded to address people and call on them to believe in the Islamic faith. In a nutshell, this statement means that what becomes of this faith and message has nothing to do with him. Nothing of it is his concern. His task is to deliver his message complete. Guiding people to accept it is not his task. Guidance is provided by God alone. Whether God fulfils part of what He has promised him with regard to the fate of those people or his term in this life comes to an end before that, the nature of his task remains the same: he has only to deliver his message. The reckoning and the determination of their fate are left to God. Nothing sums up more clearly the role of the advocates of Islam and the task they are called on to perform. The outcome concerning this faith, and indeed everything else, is determined by God alone.

This should teach the advocates of Islam to recognize their limits and remain within them. They cannot precipitate results and fates. They must not try to hasten people's acceptance of the faith, or urge the immediate fulfilment of God's promise to those who follow His guidance or His warning to those who reject His message. They cannot say, 'we have been calling on people, explaining the true faith, for a long time, but only a few people have responded positively,' or that 'we have been patient for so long, but God has not punished the oppressors during our lives'. Their task is advocacy. How God deals with people in this life or in the life to come is not of any concern to His servants; it is His own affair. Hence, knowing our limits as God's servants and acknowledging our servitude to Him mean that we leave it all entirely to Him to determine as He pleases.

This *sūrah* was revealed in Makkah. Hence, the Prophet's task is confined to the delivery of the message. Striving for God's cause, or *jihād*, had not yet been made a duty. The Prophet was later commanded to follow the delivery of the message with *jihād*. This is something we have to understand with regard to the practical nature of this religion. Its statements have their progressive nature, moving forward to match the progress of the message and to suit and direct its development. This is often overlooked by writers on Islam in our time. Such writers concentrate on their research without looking at the progress. Hence they do not relate texts to their time of revelation and the practical situation in which they were revealed.

Many are the people who read a statement like this one, "*your duty is only to deliver your message: it is for Us to do the reckoning,*" and deduce from it that the task of Islamic advocates is merely to convey the message. Once they have delivered it and put it before people, they then consider their task complete. As for striving for God's cause, or *jihād*, I really do not know whether it has a place in their perspective.

Many others read the same statement and restrict the domain of *jihād*, without abrogating it altogether. They hardly remember that this is a text revealed in Makkah. Nor do they relate Qur'ānic texts to the progress of the Islamic message and the stage of its advocacy. This shows their lack of understanding of the practical nature of this religion. They simply read it in books and texts. This religion is never fully understood by those who sit idly without taking practical steps to advocate it. It is not a religion for the idle.

Nevertheless, delivering the message remains the basis of the task of God's Messenger, and also the task of those who follow his example in advocating his message. Indeed to deliver God's message is the first stage of *jihād*. It must, however, be approached in the right way, so that it is directed at explaining the basic truths of the faith before its details. This means that it should aim, first of all, to establish that Godhead, Lordship and Sovereignty belong to God alone, and that people must submit themselves to God and abandon all submission to anyone else. When this is done, the un-Islamic society in which they live will take a stand against advocates of the Islamic faith. It first turns a deaf ear, and then challenges them. It then starts to subject them to oppression and iron-fist tactics. Therefore, the next stage of striving, or *jihād*, follows as a natural progression from the proper delivery of God's message: "*Thus have We set up against every prophet enemies from among hardened sinners. Yet none can give guidance and effective support as your Lord does.*" (25: 31)

Such is the way, and it is the only true way.

Man's Actions and Future Life

An important feature of this *sūrah* is that it states the final word concerning the relation between a human being's attitude and action on the one hand and his fate and destiny on the other. It makes it clear that people's conditions are determined by what they do for and by themselves. At the same time, it states that every event takes place by God's will. The *sūrah* includes several statements which are relevant to this point. They are sufficient to make the Islamic concept of this very serious issue abundantly clear. Here are just a few such examples:

Indeed God does not change a people's conditions unless they first change what is in their hearts. When God wills people to suffer some misfortune, none can avert it. Besides Him, they have none to protect them. (Verse 11)

For those who respond to their Lord is a rich reward. As for those who do not respond to Him, should they have all that the earth contains, and twice as much, they would gladly offer it for their ransom. Theirs shall be an awful reckoning, and hell shall be their abode, an evil resting-place! (Verse 18)

God lets go astray anyone who wills [to go astray] and guides to Himself those who turn to Him; those who believe and whose hearts find comfort in the remembrance of God. It is indeed in the remembrance of God that people's hearts find their comfort. (Verses 27–28)

Have they who believe not come to realize that, had God so willed, He would indeed have guided all mankind? (Verse 31)

Indeed their own cunning devices seem fair to the unbelievers, and they are turned away from the right path. Whoever God lets go astray can never find any guide. (Verse 33)

The first of these verses clearly states that God's will to change the lot of any community depends on, and is fulfilled through, what this community does for itself and how it changes its behaviour and actions both in attitude and practice. When a community changes their direction and actions, God changes their lot on that basis. Should their new situation require that misfortune befall them, God's will is done and nothing can stop it. There is no one to protect them from it. They will never find anyone to give them support against God.

On the other hand, if they respond to their Lord, and change their situation, God will give them what is best, ensuring that they receive it in the life of this world, or in the life to come, or in both. On the other hand, when their response is negative, God will cause misfortune to befall them, and will put them to severe reckoning on the Day of Judgement. No ransom will buy their release from God's punishment, should they return to Him without having responded to His message in this life. It is clear from the second text quoted above that the nature of people's response depends on the direction they choose for themselves and the actions they perform. God's will is fulfilled through both their attitude and action.

The third text begins with a statement asserting God's free-will to let anyone go astray, but this is followed by saying that God "*guides to Himself those who turn to Him.*" This is a definite statement that God gives His guidance to anyone who turns to Him. This shows that God lets go astray only those who do not respond to Him. He never denies His guidance to anyone who turns or responds to Him. This is in line with His promise in another *sūrah*: "*Those who strive hard in Our cause We shall certainly guide to paths that lead to Us.*" (29: 69) Thus both guidance and straying away from it are the outcome of God's will as it affects His servants. His will is done through people's own actions and what they choose for themselves, responding to their Lord or turning away from Him.

The fourth text states that God could have guided all people, had He so willed. In light of all the texts, it is clear that what this means is that God could have created all people with the same propensity to accept His guidance, or He could have forced them to follow it. But He has willed to create them in their present nature, with their dual susceptibility to either follow His guidance or go astray. It is not His will to force them either to follow guidance or to go astray – far be it for Him to force anyone to stray. He has made His will dependent on their response to the pointers to His guidance and the evidence supporting faith.

The last of these texts states that the unbelievers have turned away from the right path and that their foul devices are made to appear fair to them. Taking such a statement on its own has led to the well-known argument in Islamic history about man's free-will and predestination. But when this text is taken together with all relevant texts, the complete concept becomes clear. We then realize that such foul devices and turning away from guidance are the result of people's negative response to God's call and their denial of the faith. Indeed the unbelievers reject the faith, and this leads to the operation of God's will so that their foul devices are made to acquire a fair appearance, and so they are turned away from the right path.

A final word is needed to clarify this point concerning which there is much controversy in all religions. The direction people choose to

213

follow does not, by itself, bring about their fate. Fate is an event which is brought about by an act of God's will. Indeed every event that takes place in the universe is caused by a separate act which puts God's will into effect: "*We have created everything in due measure and proportion.*" (54: 49) There is no mechanism in the system of the whole universe, nor is there any set of causes that lead inevitably to certain results. Both cause and effect are of God's creation, and they are created in due measure. What direction people choose for themselves allows God's will to operate in a manner that fits this direction. As for the actual working of God's will and the practical effects that depend on it, these are fulfilled by a special act for every event: "*With Him everything has its definite measure.*" (Verse 8)

This concept, as we said earlier, increases the responsibility of human beings in as much as it shows the honourable position God has assigned to man in the system of the universe. Man is the only creature whose action and direction lead to the fulfilment of His will in a certain way. This is a heavy responsibility and a great honour.

Blind Rejection of the Truth

This *sūrah* provides the final word on the fact that rejecting God's religion and giving a negative response to the truth embodied in this faith is evidence of human nature going awry and the malfunctioning of its receptive system. No sound human nature, without any corrupting or distorting influences, would hesitate to respond positively to the truth, choosing submission to God, when it is presented so clearly, as it is in the Qur'ān. Deep inside, human nature knows this truth and accepts it. It is only turned away from it when a person has something that makes him choose for himself an option other than faith and its true guidance. He thus makes himself deserving of error and thereby incurs God's punishment. This is what God says in another *sūrah*: "*I will turn away from My revelations those who, without any right, behave arrogantly on earth: for, though they may see every sign, they do not believe in it. If they see the path of righteousness, they do not choose to follow it, but if they see the path of error, they choose it for their path; because they disbelieve in Our revelations and pay no heed to them.*" (7: 146)

In the present *sūrah* we have a number of similar verses which indicate the nature of unbelief, making it clear that it is nothing other than blindness of the heart. Indeed, the mere acceptance of the truth and the following of God's guidance indicate that human nature is no longer blind. Indeed there are enough pointers and indicators everywhere in the universe which show the truth clearly to those who think and use their reason.

> *Is, then, he who knows that what has been revealed to you by your Lord is the Truth like one who is blind? Only those who are endowed with understanding keep this in mind: those who are true to their bond with God and never break their covenant; and who keep together what God has bidden to be joined; who fear their Lord and dread the terrors of the reckoning; who remain patient in adversity seeking the countenance of their Lord, and attend to their prayers, and spend on others, secretly and openly, out of what We provide for them, and who repel evil with good. Such will have the attainment of the [ultimate] abode.* (Verses 19–22)

> *The unbelievers say: 'Why has no miraculous sign been bestowed on him by his Lord?' Say: 'God lets go astray anyone who wills [to go astray] and guides to Himself those who turn to Him; those who believe and whose hearts find comfort in the remembrance of God. It is indeed in the remembrance of God that people's hearts find their comfort. Those who believe and do righteous deeds shall have happiness and a most beautiful final goal.'* (Verses 27–29)

> *It is He who has spread out the earth and placed upon it firm mountains and rivers, and created on it two sexes of every type of fruit, and caused the night to cover the day. In all these there are signs for people who think. And there are on earth adjoining tracts of land; and vineyards, and fields of grains and date-palms, growing in clusters or non-clustered. [All] are irrigated by the same water; yet some of them are favoured above others with regard to the food [they provide]. In all this there are signs for people who use their reason.* (Verses 3–4)

Here we have a clear statement indicating that those who do not respond to the truth are, as God Himself testifies, blind, and that they neither think nor use their reason. Those who respond to the truth are the ones endowed with understanding. These find a heartfelt comfort in remembering God. They relate to what they, deep at heart, know to be the truth, finding in it comfort and reassurance.

In fact we find confirmation of this fact in everyone who turns away from the truth, embodied in the divine faith, which is contained in its full and complete form in the message of Muḥammad (peace be upon him). Such people have defective and distorted natures. They suffer from the malfunctioning of their best receptors. Hence they do not react to the message presented by the whole universe as it praises God and testifies to His oneness, ability and inimitably elaborate planning.

Since those who do not believe in this truth are blind, as confirmed by God, then no Muslim who claims to believe in God's Messenger and accepts that the Qur'ān is God's revelation can follow the lead of a blind person in any matter of importance in life. This particularly applies to matters that relate to the system which governs human life, to the values and standards that must be implemented in human life, and to behaviour, traditions and morals that are acceptable in human society.

This is our attitude to everything that non-Islamic philosophy produces, apart from physical and material sciences and their practical applications. These come under the Prophet's statement when he said to his Companions: "You know the affairs of your own world better." It is not right that a Muslim who knows God's guidance and who is fully aware of the truth preached by His Messenger to become a student learning from someone who has not responded to God's guidance and who does not know it to be the truth. Such a person is, as God says, blind. No Muslim can reject God's testimony and continue to claim to be a Muslim.

We must take this religion very seriously, and accept its clear statements as correct and valid. If we approach this matter in a hesitant, uncertain way, then this means approaching faith itself with uncertainty. On the other hand, it could mean rejecting the testimony of God (limitless is He in His glory). Such rejection means a complete rejection of faith.

This religion is very serious indeed. It admits no frivolity. Every single statement and every word contained in this religion is true. Anyone who entertains doubts about this seriousness, or who finds himself reluctant to accept this truth with full and complete trust should realize that Islam is in no need of him. In fact God is in no need of anyone whomsoever.

It is not right that the pressures of un-Islamic society should weigh heavily on any Muslim so as to make him adopt the standards of such a society in his approach to life. How can he when he knows that the message conveyed by Muḥammad (peace be upon him) is the truth, and that anyone who does not know it to be the truth is blind. How can he follow such a blind person, learning from him, after having heard God's testimony?

Blindness and Life Corruption

A final aspect of faith that the *sūrah* highlights is the close relationship between the corruption that creeps into people's life on earth and their blindness to the message of the truth God has bestowed on people guiding them to what is right, useful and beneficial. Those who do not respond either to the covenant God has made with human nature or to the truth which has come from Him, knowing it to be the truth, are indeed the ones who spread corruption on earth. By contrast, those who know it to be the truth and respond to it are the ones who work to set matters on the right course and whose work helps life prosper.

> Is, then, he who knows that what has been revealed to you by your Lord is the Truth like one who is blind? Only those who are endowed with understanding keep this in mind: those who are true to their bond with God and never break their covenant; and who keep together what God has bidden to be joined; who fear their Lord and dread the terrors of the reckoning; who remain patient in adversity seeking the countenance of their Lord, and attend to their prayers, and spend on others, secretly and openly, out of what We provide for them, and who repel evil with good. Such will have the attainment of the [ultimate] abode. (Verses 19–22)

> As for those who break their bond with God after it has been established, and cut asunder what God has bidden to be joined, and spread corruption on earth, the curse will be laid upon them; and theirs shall be an evil abode. (Verse 25)

Human life will not be set on the right course unless its leadership is firmly in the hands of those endowed with understanding, who know that what was revealed to Muḥammad (peace be upon him) is the truth. Such people fulfil their commitment which is part of the covenant God has made with human nature on the one hand and with Adam and his offspring on the other. These covenants specify that people must worship God alone, submitting to none other than Him, receiving only His guidance and obeying only His orders. Hence, they keep together what God has ordered to be united. They fear their Lord, which means that they are always consciously trying to avoid anything that may incur God's displeasure. They also fear that they may have an awful reckoning. Hence they are constantly aware of the hereafter, watching their every action. They remain constant to their covenant, bearing the burden of such consistency. They attend regularly to their prayers, give to charity out of their provisions, which God has granted to them, and make their donations in private or openly. They repel evil and corruption with goodness and kindness.

Human life is not set aright unless it has such a wise leadership which follows God's guidance, and which moulds life in accordance with His guidance and the code of living He has laid down. It does not follow the right course when it has blind leadership which does not know that the truth is what was revealed to the Prophet Muḥammad. Such leadership follows systems that differ from that laid down by God for His good servants. Human life does not follow the right course under a feudal, capitalist or communist system, or indeed under what is termed 'scientific socialism'. Nor does it take a healthy form and style under theocracy, dictatorship or democracy. All of these are systems devised by the blind who appoint themselves lords beside God. Such lords devise systems and enact legislation that are not sanctioned by God. They also impose their authority on people, forcing them to submit to such legislation, instead of submitting to God.

Based on the Qur'ānic text, the evidence for what we say is seen in the corruption, the *jāhiliyyah* that has spread throughout the world in the twentieth century. It is seen in the misery under which mankind writhe, both in the East and in the West, under capitalist, communist or socialist systems, and under both dictatorship and democracy. Under all such systems people suffer corruption, loss of moral values, misery and anxiety. That is because all these systems are devised by people who are blind, not knowing that what God has revealed to His Messenger, Muḥammad, is the only truth. Hence, they do not fulfil their covenant with God. Nor do they implement the code of living that is based on His guidance.

By virtue of his faith, and his knowledge that the truth is embodied in what was revealed to Muḥammad, a Muslim rejects every code of living other than that devised by God. He also rejects any social, economic or political doctrine other than what has been legislated by God, who devised it for His good servants.

The mere acceptance of the legitimacy of any code or system devised by any authority other than God's means a break from submission to God, as such submission means in practice complete surrender to Him alone. Accepting such legitimacy is not only in conflict with the central concept of Islam; it also hands over on earth to the blind who break their covenant with God after it has been confirmed. These are the ones who cut asunder what God has bidden to be united and who thus spread corruption on earth.

Throughout history mankind has suffered untold misery, as it tried, without proper guidance, a great variety of systems, laws and regimes under the leadership of blind people assuming the guise of philosophers, theoreticians, legislators and politicians. Never did mankind experience real happiness, elevate human standards, or reach the standard worthy of their role as God's vicegerents on earth except under the Islamic system.

These are some of the prominent features of this *sūrah*. Our discussion merely points to them although it can explain them but inadequately. Praise be to God who has guided us to this. It is only through His guidance that we can make the right choice.

SŪRAH 14

Ibrāhīm

(Abraham)

Prologue

This *sūrah* is a Makkan revelation. Its subject matter, namely faith, revelation and the divine message, God's Oneness, resurrection, reckoning and reward permeate Makkan *sūrahs*. Just as every *sūrah* in the Qur'ān has its distinctive character, this *sūrah* adopts a unique approach in presenting its material, with highlights and shading that accentuate the principles and issues it tackles. These may not be different from the principles and issues other *sūrahs* illustrate, but they are tackled here from a different angle so as to generate special effect and emphasis. Furthermore, certain aspects are added and others omitted, giving the reader and the listener the overall impression that they deal with new issues and principles.

The general ambience of the *sūrah* derives from its title, namely Abraham, the father of all prophets who came after him. He was a blessed man, most grateful to God, most clement, tender-hearted, and devout. All the connotations of these attributes are felt throughout this *sūrah*, in its main issues, general approach, mode of expression as also in its rhythm.

The *sūrah* addresses a number of issues relating to faith, but two of these permeate the whole *sūrah*. These are the two issues most relevant to Abraham himself. The first is the unity of the divine message and

221

God's messengers, and their united stand, despite their different times and places, as one community against the state of ignorance, or *jāhiliyyah*. The other is God's favours bestowed on mankind, the increase He grants to those who are grateful and the fact that most people remain ungrateful. The *sūrah* definitely includes other issues, but these two give the *sūrah* its special ambience.

The *sūrah* begins with an outline of the mission of God's Messenger and the book revealed to him: "*This is a book which We have bestowed on you from on high so that you might bring forth all mankind, by their Lord's leave, from darkness into the light, to the path of the Almighty, the One to whom all praise is due.*" (Verse 1) It concludes with the same point, highlighting the truth of God's oneness which is at the heart of the divine message: "*This is a message to all mankind. Let them be warned thereby, and let them know that He is the One and only God. Let those who are endowed with insight take heed.*" (Verse 52)

In between, the *sūrah* mentions that Moses was sent to do the same task as Muḥammad, using practically the same wording: "*We have sent forth Moses with Our revelations, saying, 'Lead your people out of darkness into the light.'*" (Verse 5) It also explains that the general purpose behind sending God's messengers was to make things clear: "*Never have We sent a messenger otherwise than speaking the language of his own people, so that he might make [the truth] clear to them.*" (Verse 4) In addition, it explains that because God's Messenger is human, this inevitably provides the parameters for his mission: he is to inform, explain and give warning and good counsel. He cannot, however, perform a miracle except by God's permission, and at a time God determines. Neither he nor his people have any say in this. Nor can he oblige his community to follow guidance or sink into error, for these things follow a certain rule God has set in operation according to His own free choice.

That God's messengers were all human was a matter objected to by all past ignorant communities. The *sūrah* sums up all these objections and the reply given by God's messengers, as if the objections and the reply were made all at the same time: "*They replied: 'You are but mortals like ourselves. You want to turn us away from what our forefathers used to worship. Bring us, then, a clear proof.' Their messengers replied: 'We are indeed but mortals like yourselves. But God bestows His grace on whomever He wills of His servants. It is not within our power to bring you any proof, except by God's leave. It is in God that all believers must place their trust.'"* (Verses 10–11)

The *sūrah* also explains that taking mankind from darkness into light can only be accomplished 'by their Lord's leave'. Every messenger makes the issues clear to his people, then: *"God lets go astray whomever He wills, and guides whomever He wills. He is Almighty, truly Wise."* (Verse 4)

These are the main lines defining the nature of a messenger sent by God, and the mission assigned to him. Nothing of the nature of God's messengers or their qualities can be confused with God's nature and attributes. Thus God's oneness is shown in its full light, with no hint of similarity to anyone or anything.

The *sūrah* also speaks about the fulfilment of God's promise to His messengers and to those who truly believe in them. This promise is fulfilled in this present life when they are given victory and power, and in the life to come with generous reward given to the believers and severe punishment to the unbelievers. This is shown at the end of the scene showing the battle between God's messengers standing together and their different communities also standing together in this world: *"The unbelievers said to their messengers: 'We shall most certainly expel you from our land, unless you return to our ways.' Their Lord revealed this to His messengers: 'Most certainly shall We destroy the wrongdoers, and most certainly shall We cause you to dwell in the land long after they are gone. This [I promise] to all who stand in awe of My presence, and stand in awe of My warnings.' And they prayed for God's help and victory [for the truth]. And every powerful, obstinate enemy of the truth shall come to grief."* (Verses 13–15) It is also shown in the images drawn from the Day of Judgement: *"Those who believe and do righteous deeds will be admitted to gardens through which running waters flow, wherein they will abide, by their Lord's leave. Their greeting shall be: 'Peace'."* (Verse 23) *"On that day you will see the guilty chained together in fetters, wearing garments of black pitch, and their faces covered with flames."* (Verses 49–50)

The same fact is also emphasized in the analogies given for both groups: *"Do you not see how God compares a good word to a good tree?*

Its roots are firm and its branches reach to the sky. It yields its fruits at all times by its Lord's leave. Thus does God set parables for people so that they may reflect. And an evil word is like a corrupt tree, torn up onto the face of the earth. It cannot have a stable position. God will strengthen the believers through the true, unshakeable word in both this life and the life to come; but the wrongdoers God lets go astray. God does whatever He wills." (Verses 24–27) *"The works of those who disbelieve in their Lord are like ashes which the wind blows about fiercely on a stormy day. They cannot achieve any benefit from all that they might have earned. This [disbelief] is indeed going very far astray."* (Verse 18)

The Message of All Prophets

The first of the two major issues that run through the whole *sūrah* is the unity of the divine message preached by all God's messengers. This is presented here in a unique way. Other *sūrah*s demonstrated this through the fact that every messenger made the same address to his people. Every one of them would state the same truth, complete his work and pass away, to be followed by other messengers, each of whom stated the same truth in the same words, receiving the same reply. The unbelievers who deny the truth suffer whatever they may suffer in this life, although some of them are given respite, so as to face their fate on the Day of Judgement. In those *sūrah*s every messenger was shown in a separate scene, like we see a film playing back different events. The best examples of this method are seen in *Sūrahs* 7 and 11, The Heights and Hūd, respectively.

In this *sūrah*, all the prophets are grouped together on one side and their erring communities on the other. The battle goes on between them in this life, but does not come to an end here. On the contrary, we follow its progress until the Day of Judgement. Despite the great difference in time and place, we see in front of us the community of God's messengers and their followers standing together as a single group. Indeed time and place are two transitory factors, while the great truth of faith and unbelief is far greater than both time and place:

Have you not received accounts of what befell those who lived before you? The people of Noah, the 'Ād and Thamūd, and those who

came after them? None knows them all but God. Their messengers
came to them with clear evidence of the truth, but they put their
hands to their mouths, and said: 'We disbelieve in that with which
you have been sent, and we are in grave doubt about that to which
you call us.' Said the messengers sent to them: 'Can there be any
doubt about God, the Originator of the heavens and the earth? He
calls you, so that He may forgive you your sins and grant you respite
for an appointed term.' They replied: 'You are but mortals like
ourselves. You want to turn us away from what our forefathers used
to worship. Bring us, then, a clear proof.' Their messengers replied:
'We are indeed but mortals like yourselves. But God bestows His
grace on whomever He wills of His servants. It is not within our
power to bring you any proof, except by God's leave. It is in God that
all believers must place their trust. And why should we not place
our trust in God, when He has guided us on our paths? Hence we
will bear with patience all your persecution. In God let all the faithful
place their trust.' The unbelievers said to their messengers: 'We shall
most certainly expel you from our land, unless you return to our
ways.' Their Lord revealed this to His messengers: 'Most certainly
shall We destroy the wrongdoers, and most certainly shall We cause
you to dwell in the land long after they are gone. This [I promise] to
all who stand in awe of My presence, and stand in awe of My
warnings.' And they prayed for God's help and victory [for the truth].
And every powerful, obstinate enemy of the truth shall come to grief.
Behind him stretches hell where he shall be made to drink putrefied
water, gulping it little by little, and yet hardly able to swallow it.
Death will beset him from every side, yet he shall not die. More
severe suffering still awaits him. (Verses 9–17)

All generations starting with the time of Noah and all messengers
are grouped together, while time and place dwindle into insignificance,
to give prominence to the truth of the one divine message. The
objections of the unbelievers remain the same throughout. Similarly,
help is given to believers, for power is granted by God to good people,
while failure and humiliation are the lot of tyrants, and suffering awaits
them in the hereafter. All these factors apply to them all in exactly the
same way. We see that what is said by Muḥammad and Moses (peace

225

be upon them both) to their peoples is identical: "*This is a book which We have bestowed on you from on high so that you might bring forth all mankind, by their Lord's leave, from darkness into the light.*" (Verse 1) "*We have sent forth Moses with Our revelations, saying, 'Lead your people out of darkness into the light.*" (Verse 5)

The battle between faith and unfaith does not end in this world. The *sūrah* follows it into the hereafter. We see it featured prominently in the different scenes and images the *sūrah* draws of the hereafter. For example:

> *They will all appear before God, and then the weak will say to those who acted with arrogance: 'We were your followers: can you relieve us of something of God's punishment?' [And the others] will reply: 'Had God given us guidance, we would have guided you. It is now all one for us whether we grieve impatiently or endure with patience. There is no escape for us now.' And when everything will have been decided, Satan will say: 'God has made you a true promise. I, too, made promises to you, but I did not keep them. Yet I had no power at all over you, except that I called you and you responded to me. Hence, do not now blame me, but blame yourselves. It is not for me to respond to your cries, nor for you to respond to mine. I have already disclaimed your associating me with God.' Indeed, for all wrongdoers there is grievous suffering in store. Those who believe and do righteous deeds will be admitted to gardens through which running waters flow, wherein they will abide, by their Lord's leave. Their greeting shall be: 'Peace'. (Verses 21–23)*

> *Never think that God is unaware of what the wrongdoers are doing. He only grants them respite till the Day when eyes will stare fixedly in horror, when they will be dashing in confusion, with their heads lifted up, unable to turn their eyes from what they behold, and their hearts an utter void. (Verses 42–43)*

> *They devised their plots, but their plots are all within God's grasp, even though their plots are so powerful as to move mountains. Never think that God may ever fail to fulfil the promise which He has given to His messengers. Indeed God is Almighty, avenger of evil! On the day when the earth shall be changed into another earth, as*

shall be the heavens, and when all people stand before God, the One who holds sway over all that exists. On that day you will see the guilty chained together in fetters, wearing garments of black pitch, and their faces covered with flames. (Verses 46–50)

All these examples confirm that it is all one battle that starts in this world and ends in the life to come. The two parts are mutually complementary, with no gap in between. The examples, with events starting in this world and ending in the hereafter, also bring into sharp relief the main features of this battle and its results: a good word is like a good tree; and the tree is that of prophethood, faith and goodness. By contrast, an evil word is like a corrupt tree; the tree of ignorance, falsehood, rejection of the truth, evil and tyranny.

Gratitude for Unending Favours

Gratitude to God for what He bestows on us animates the whole *sūrah*. God enumerates His favours, which He grants to all mankind, believers and unbelievers, righteous or unrighteous, God-fearing and wrongdoers. God is most certainly compassionate and merciful when He grants such favours to unbelievers, disobedients and wrongdoers in the same way as He grants them to the faithful who strive for His cause. It is their place that they should be grateful. Here God's grace is shown extending across the widest horizon, within a framework of universal imagery: "*It is God who has created the heavens and the earth, and who sends down water from the sky with which He brings forth fruits for your sustenance. He has placed under your service ships which by His leave sail through the sea, and He has made the rivers subservient to [His law] for your benefit. And for your benefit He has made the sun and the moon, both diligently pursuing their courses, subservient to [His law]; and has made the night and the day subservient to [His law]. And He gives you of everything you ask of Him. Should you try to count God's blessings, you will never be able to compute them. Yet man is persistent in wrongdoing, stubbornly ungrateful.*" (Verses 32–34)

Indeed, sending messengers to mankind is an equal, if not greater favour: "*This is a book which We have bestowed on you from on high so that you might bring forth all mankind, by their Lord's leave, from darkness into the light.*" (Verse 1) Light is perhaps God's most majestic favour in the universe, but the light referred to in this verse is the greatest light that shines through our whole beings and which makes the world around us shine. The same task was assigned to Moses with his people, and indeed to all messengers, as clearly explained in the *sūrah*. We also note a favour in what God's messengers say: "*He calls you, so that He may forgive you your sins.*" (Verse 10) That people are called to forgiveness is a great favour almost equal to that of light.

Within the context of God's favours, Moses reminds his people of what God bestowed on them: "*Moses said to his people: 'Remember the blessings God bestowed on you when He saved you from Pharaoh's people who afflicted you with grievous torment, slaughtered your sons and spared [only] your women. That was indeed an awesome trial from your Lord.*" (Verse 6) And within the same context, the *sūrah* mentions God's promise to His messengers: "*Their Lord revealed this to His messengers: 'Most certainly shall We destroy the wrongdoers, and most certainly shall We cause you to dwell in the land long after they are gone. This [I promise] to all who stand in awe of My presence, and stand in awe of My warnings.*'" (Verses 13–14) Again, this should be counted among God's many great favours.

The *sūrah* also highlights the fact that God's favours are increased when people are grateful: "*For your Lord had declared: 'If you are grateful, I shall certainly give you more; but if you are ungrateful, then My punishment shall be severe indeed.*'" (Verse 7) It makes clear that God is in no need of gratitude, thanks or those who give them. "*And Moses said: 'If you and whoever lives on earth were to deny God, [know that] God is indeed Self-Sufficient, worthy of all praise.*'" (Verse 8) The *sūrah* explains that generally man does not show proper gratitude for the favours God bestows on him. "*Should you try to count God's blessings, you will never be able to compute them. Yet man is persistent in wrongdoing, stubbornly ungrateful.*" (Verse 34) However, those who reflect on the signs God has placed all around them, and show insight, will persevere in the face of adversity and show gratitude for favours and blessings: "*Surely in this there are signs for everyone who is patient in adversity and deeply grateful [to God].*" (Verse 5)

Both patience in adversity and gratitude are expressed by Abraham in a position of humility before God, expressed in a prayer addressed near the Sacred Mosque in Makkah. It overflows with praise and gratitude to God:

> Abraham said: 'My Lord! Make this land secure, and preserve me and my children from ever worshipping idols. My Lord, they have indeed led many people astray. Hence, he who follows me belongs to me. As for him who disobeys me, well, You are truly Much-Forgiving, Merciful. Our Lord, I have settled some of my offspring in a valley without cultivation, by Your Sacred House, so that they may establish regular prayers. So, cause You people's hearts to incline towards them, and provide them with fruits, so that they may give thanks. Our Lord, You certainly know all that we conceal and all that we bring into the open: for nothing whatever, on earth or in heaven, can be hidden from God. All praise is due to God who has given me, in my old age, Ishmael and Isaac. Surely my Lord hears all prayers. My Lord, cause me and [some of] my offspring to establish regular prayers. My Lord, accept my prayer. Our Lord, grant Your forgiveness to me and my parents, and all the believers on the Day when the reckoning will come to pass.' (Verses 35–41)

Because God's favours and blessings, gratitude for them and, by contrast, their denial permeate the *sūrah*, many comments at the end of verses fit with this. For example: "*provide them with fruits, so that they may give thanks.*" (Verse 37) "*Surely in this there are signs for everyone who is patient in adversity and deeply grateful [to God].*" (Verse 5) "*Have you not seen those who have exchanged God's blessings for unbelief, and landed their people in the House of Perdition.*" (Verse 28) "*Remember the blessings God bestowed on you.*" (Verse 6) "*All praise is due to God who has given me, in my old age, Ishmael and Isaac.*" (Verse 39)

When the prophets answer the unbelievers' objections that they, i.e. the prophets, are only human, they say: "*We are indeed but mortals like yourselves. But God bestows His grace on whomever He wills of His servants.*" (Verse 11) Thus, God's grace is highlighted to fit with the general atmosphere of the *sūrah*, which radiates with aspects of grace, mercy, favour and gratitude on the one side and ingratitude on the other. Thus, verbal expression is brought in harmony with the *sūrah* as a whole to perfect the Qur'ānic artistic method.

The *sūrah* can be divided into two main passages: the first explains the nature of the divine message and the messenger delivering it, portraying the battle between their community and those who deny the message. It comments on all this, giving examples of good and evil words. The other passage speaks of the favours God grants to mankind, describing those who display an arrogant ingratitude and the believers who express their gratitude. The first perfect example of the latter is Abraham. It describes the fate of the wrongdoers who deny God's favours in a series of most powerful and lively images of the Day of Judgement. Thus, the conclusion of the *sūrah* is brought into harmony with its opening: "*This is a message to all mankind. Let them be warned thereby, and let them know that He is the One and Only God. Let those who are endowed with insight take heed.*" (Verse 52)

كفر / ظلم vs شكر / يسر

I

One Message for All Mankind

1-27

Ibrāhīm (Abraham)

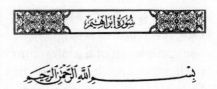

In the Name of God, the Merciful, the Beneficent

Alif. Lām. Rā. This is a book which We have bestowed on you from on high so that you might bring forth all mankind, by their Lord's leave, from darkness into the light, to the path of the Almighty, the One to whom all praise is due, (1)

to God, to whom all that is in the heavens and all that is on earth belongs. Woe to the unbelievers; for theirs will be a severe suffering. (2)

These are the ones who love the life of this world preferring it to the life to come, and who turn others away from God's path and try to make it appear crooked. They have gone far astray. (3)

بِسْمِ اللَّهِ الرَّحْمَٰنِ الرَّحِيمِ

الٓرَ ۚ كِتَٰبٌ أَنزَلْنَٰهُ إِلَيْكَ لِتُخْرِجَ النَّاسَ مِنَ الظُّلُمَٰتِ إِلَى النُّورِ بِإِذْنِ رَبِّهِمْ إِلَىٰ صِرَٰطِ الْعَزِيزِ الْحَمِيدِ ۝

اللَّهِ الَّذِى لَهُۥ مَا فِى السَّمَٰوَٰتِ وَمَا فِى الْأَرْضِ ۗ وَوَيْلٌ لِّلْكَٰفِرِينَ مِنْ عَذَابٍ شَدِيدٍ ۝

الَّذِينَ يَسْتَحِبُّونَ الْحَيَوٰةَ الدُّنْيَا عَلَى الْأَخِرَةِ وَيَصُدُّونَ عَن سَبِيلِ اللَّهِ وَيَبْغُونَهَا عِوَجًا ۚ أُو۟لَٰٓئِكَ فِى ضَلَٰلٍ بَعِيدٍ ۝

Never have We sent a messenger otherwise than speaking the language of his own people, so that he might make [the truth] clear to them. But God lets go astray whomever He wills, and guides whomever He wills. He is Almighty, truly Wise. (4)

وَمَآ أَرْسَلْنَا مِن رَّسُولٍ إِلَّا بِلِسَانِ قَوْمِهِ لِيُبَيِّنَ لَهُمْ فَيُضِلُّ اللَّهُ مَن يَشَآءُ وَيَهْدِى مَن يَشَآءُ وَهُوَ الْعَزِيزُ الْحَكِيمُ ٤

We have sent forth Moses with Our revelations, saying, 'Lead your people out of darkness into the light, and remind them of the Days of God.' Surely in this there are signs for everyone who is patient in adversity and deeply grateful [to God]. (5)

وَلَقَدْ أَرْسَلْنَا مُوسَىٰ بِآيَاتِنَآ أَنْ أَخْرِجْ قَوْمَكَ مِنَ الظُّلُمَاتِ إِلَى النُّورِ وَذَكِّرْهُم بِأَيَّامِ اللَّهِ إِنَّ فِى ذَٰلِكَ لَآيَاتٍ لِّكُلِّ صَبَّارٍ شَكُورٍ ٥

Moses said to his people: 'Remember the blessings God bestowed on you when He saved you from Pharaoh's people who afflicted you with grievous torment, slaughtered your sons and spared [only] your women. That was indeed an awesome trial from your Lord. (6)

وَإِذْ قَالَ مُوسَىٰ لِقَوْمِهِ اذْكُرُوا۟ نِعْمَةَ اللَّهِ عَلَيْكُمْ إِذْ أَنجَىٰكُم مِّنْ ءَالِ فِرْعَوْنَ يَسُومُونَكُمْ سُوٓءَ الْعَذَابِ وَيُذَبِّحُونَ أَبْنَآءَكُمْ وَيَسْتَحْيُونَ نِسَآءَكُمْ وَفِى ذَٰلِكُم بَلَآءٌ مِّن رَّبِّكُمْ عَظِيمٌ ٦

For your Lord had declared: "If you are grateful, I shall certainly give you more; but if you are ungrateful, then My punishment shall be severe indeed."' (7)

وَإِذْ تَأَذَّنَ رَبُّكُمْ لَئِن شَكَرْتُمْ لَأَزِيدَنَّكُمْ وَلَئِن كَفَرْتُمْ إِنَّ عَذَابِى لَشَدِيدٌ ٧

And Moses said: 'If you and whoever lives on earth were to deny God, [know that] God is indeed Self-Sufficient, worthy of all praise.' (8)

وَقَالَ مُوسَىٰٓ إِن تَكْفُرُوٓاْ أَنتُمْ وَمَن فِى ٱلْأَرْضِ جَمِيعًا فَإِنَّ ٱللَّهَ لَغَنِىٌّ حَمِيدٌ ٨

Have you not received accounts of what befell those who lived before you? The people of Noah, the 'Ād, and Thamūd, and those who came after them? None knows them all but God. Their messengers came to them with clear evidence of the truth, but they put their hands to their mouths, and said: 'We disbelieve in that with which you have been sent, and we are in grave doubt about that to which you call us.' (9)

أَلَمْ يَأْتِكُمْ نَبَؤُاْ ٱلَّذِينَ مِن قَبْلِكُمْ قَوْمِ نُوحٍ وَعَادٍ وَثَمُودَ وَٱلَّذِينَ مِنۢ بَعْدِهِمْ لَا يَعْلَمُهُمْ إِلَّا ٱللَّهُ جَآءَتْهُمْ رُسُلُهُم بِٱلْبَيِّنَٰتِ فَرَدُّوٓاْ أَيْدِيَهُمْ فِىٓ أَفْوَٰهِهِمْ وَقَالُوٓاْ إِنَّا كَفَرْنَا بِمَآ أُرْسِلْتُم بِهِۦ وَإِنَّا لَفِى شَكٍّ مِّمَّا تَدْعُونَنَآ إِلَيْهِ مُرِيبٍ ٩

Said the messengers sent to them: 'Can there be any doubt about God, the Originator of the heavens and the earth? He calls you, so that He may forgive you your sins and grant you respite for an appointed term.' They replied: 'You are but mortals like ourselves. You want to turn us away from what our forefathers used to worship. Bring us, then, a clear proof.' (10)

قَالَتْ رُسُلُهُمْ أَفِى ٱللَّهِ شَكٌّ فَاطِرِ ٱلسَّمَٰوَٰتِ وَٱلْأَرْضِ يَدْعُوكُمْ لِيَغْفِرَ لَكُم مِّن ذُنُوبِكُمْ وَيُؤَخِّرَكُمْ إِلَىٰٓ أَجَلٍ مُّسَمًّى قَالُوٓاْ إِنْ أَنتُمْ إِلَّا بَشَرٌ مِّثْلُنَا تُرِيدُونَ أَن تَصُدُّونَا عَمَّا كَانَ يَعْبُدُ ءَابَآؤُنَا فَأْتُونَا بِسُلْطَٰنٍ مُّبِينٍ ١٠

Their messengers replied: 'We are indeed but mortals like yourselves. But God bestows His grace on whomever He wills of His servants. It is not within our power to bring you any proof, except by God's leave. It is in God that all believers must place their trust. (11)

قَالَتْ لَهُمْ رُسُلُهُمْ إِن نَّحْنُ إِلَّا بَشَرٌ مِّثْلُكُمْ وَلَكِنَّ ٱللَّهَ يَمُنُّ عَلَىٰ مَن يَشَآءُ مِنْ عِبَادِهِۦ وَمَا كَانَ لَنَآ أَن نَّأْتِيَكُم بِسُلْطَٰنٍ إِلَّا بِإِذْنِ ٱللَّهِ وَعَلَى ٱللَّهِ فَلْيَتَوَكَّلِ ٱلْمُؤْمِنُونَ ﴿١١﴾

And why should we not place our trust in God, when He has guided us on our paths? Hence we will bear with patience all your persecution. In God alone let all the faithful place their trust.' (12)

وَمَا لَنَآ أَلَّا نَتَوَكَّلَ عَلَى ٱللَّهِ وَقَدْ هَدَىٰنَا سُبُلَنَا وَلَنَصْبِرَنَّ عَلَىٰ مَآ ءَاذَيْتُمُونَا وَعَلَى ٱللَّهِ فَلْيَتَوَكَّلِ ٱلْمُتَوَكِّلُونَ ﴿١٢﴾

The unbelievers said to their messengers: 'We shall most certainly expel you from our land, unless you return to our ways.' Their Lord revealed this to His messengers: 'Most certainly shall We destroy the wrongdoers, (13)

وَقَالَ ٱلَّذِينَ كَفَرُوا۟ لِرُسُلِهِمْ لَنُخْرِجَنَّكُم مِّنْ أَرْضِنَآ أَوْ لَتَعُودُنَّ فِى مِلَّتِنَا فَأَوْحَىٰٓ إِلَيْهِمْ رَبُّهُمْ لَنُهْلِكَنَّ ٱلظَّٰلِمِينَ ﴿١٣﴾

and most certainly shall We cause you to dwell in the land long after they are gone. This [I promise] to all who stand in awe of My presence, and stand in awe of My warnings.' (14)

وَلَنُسْكِنَنَّكُمُ ٱلْأَرْضَ مِنۢ بَعْدِهِمْ ذَٰلِكَ لِمَنْ خَافَ مَقَامِى وَخَافَ وَعِيدِ ﴿١٤﴾

And they prayed for God's help and victory [for the truth]. And every powerful, obstinate enemy of the truth shall come to grief. (15)

وَٱسْتَفْتَحُوا۟ وَخَابَ كُلُّ جَبَّارٍ عَنِيدٍ ﴿١٥﴾

Behind him stretches hell where he shall be made to drink putrefied water, (16)

مِّن وَرَآئِهِۦ جَهَنَّمُ وَيُسْقَىٰ مِن مَّآءٍ صَدِيدٍ ﴿١٦﴾

gulping it little by little, and yet hardly able to swallow it. Death will beset him from every side, yet he shall not die. More severe suffering still awaits him. (17)

يَتَجَرَّعُهُۥ وَلَا يَكَادُ يُسِيغُهُۥ وَيَأْتِيهِ ٱلْمَوْتُ مِن كُلِّ مَكَانٍ وَمَا هُوَ بِمَيِّتٍ وَمِن وَرَآئِهِۦ عَذَابٌ غَلِيظٌ ﴿١٧﴾

The works of those who disbelieve in their Lord are like ashes which the wind blows about fiercely on a stormy day. They cannot achieve any benefit from all that they might have earned. This [disbelief] is indeed going very far astray. (18)

مَّثَلُ ٱلَّذِينَ كَفَرُوا۟ بِرَبِّهِمْ أَعْمَٰلُهُمْ كَرَمَادٍ ٱشْتَدَّتْ بِهِ ٱلرِّيحُ فِى يَوْمٍ عَاصِفٍ لَّا يَقْدِرُونَ مِمَّا كَسَبُوا۟ عَلَىٰ شَىْءٍ ذَٰلِكَ هُوَ ٱلضَّلَٰلُ ٱلْبَعِيدُ ﴿١٨﴾

Do you not see that God has created the heavens and the earth in accordance with the truth. If He so wills, He can do away with you and bring into being a new creation. (19)

أَلَمْ تَرَ أَنَّ ٱللَّهَ خَلَقَ ٱلسَّمَٰوَٰتِ وَٱلْأَرْضَ بِٱلْحَقِّ إِن يَشَأْ يُذْهِبْكُمْ وَيَأْتِ بِخَلْقٍ جَدِيدٍ ﴿١٩﴾

This is no difficult thing for God. (20)

وَمَا ذَٰلِكَ عَلَى ٱللَّهِ بِعَزِيزٍ ﴿٢٠﴾

They will all appear before God, and then the weak will say to those who acted with arrogance: 'We were your followers: can you relieve us of something of God's punishment?' [And the others] will reply: 'Had God given us guidance, we would have guided you. It is now all one for us whether we grieve impatiently or endure with patience. There is no escape for us now.' (21)

وَبَرَزُواْ لِلَّهِ جَمِيعًا فَقَالَ الضُّعَفَٰٓؤُاْ لِلَّذِينَ اسْتَكْبَرُوٓاْ إِنَّا كُنَّا لَكُمْ تَبَعًا فَهَلْ أَنتُم مُّغْنُونَ عَنَّا مِنْ عَذَابِ اللَّهِ مِن شَىْءٍۚ قَالُواْ لَوْ هَدَىٰنَا اللَّهُ لَهَدَيْنَٰكُمْۖ سَوَآءٌ عَلَيْنَآ أَجَزِعْنَآ أَمْ صَبَرْنَا مَا لَنَا مِن مَّحِيصٍ ۝

And when everything will have been decided, Satan will say: 'God has made you a true promise. I, too, made promises to you, but I did not keep them. Yet I had no power at all over you, except that I called you and you responded to me. Hence, do not now blame me, but blame yourselves. It is not for me to respond to your cries, nor for you to respond to mine. I have already disclaimed your associating me with God.' Indeed, for all wrongdoers there is grievous suffering in store. (22)

وَقَالَ الشَّيْطَٰنُ لَمَّا قُضِىَ الْأَمْرُ إِنَّ اللَّهَ وَعَدَكُمْ وَعْدَ الْحَقِّ وَوَعَدتُّكُمْ فَأَخْلَفْتُكُمْۖ وَمَا كَانَ لِىَ عَلَيْكُم مِّن سُلْطَٰنٍ إِلَّآ أَن دَعَوْتُكُمْ فَاسْتَجَبْتُمْ لِىۖ فَلَا تَلُومُونِى وَلُومُوٓاْ أَنفُسَكُمۖ مَّآ أَنَا۠ بِمُصْرِخِكُمْ وَمَآ أَنتُم بِمُصْرِخِىَّۖ إِنِّى كَفَرْتُ بِمَآ أَشْرَكْتُمُونِ مِن قَبْلُۗ إِنَّ الظَّٰلِمِينَ لَهُمْ عَذَابٌ أَلِيمٌ ۝

Those who believe and do righteous deeds will be admitted to gardens through which running waters flow, wherein they will abide, by their Lord's leave. Their greeting shall be: 'Peace'. (23)

وَأُدْخِلَ الَّذِينَ ءَامَنُواْ وَعَمِلُواْ الصَّٰلِحَٰتِ جَنَّٰتٍ تَجْرِى مِن تَحْتِهَا الْأَنْهَٰرُ خَٰلِدِينَ فِيهَا بِإِذْنِ رَبِّهِمْۖ تَحِيَّتُهُمْ فِيهَا سَلَٰمٌ ۝

Do you not see how God compares a good word to a good tree? Its roots are firm and its branches reach to the sky. (24)

أَلَمۡ تَرَ كَيۡفَ ضَرَبَ ٱللَّهُ مَثَلًا كَلِمَةً طَيِّبَةً كَشَجَرَةٍ طَيِّبَةٍ أَصۡلُهَا ثَابِتٌ وَفَرۡعُهَا فِى ٱلسَّمَآءِ ﴿٢٤﴾

It yields its fruits at all times by its Lord's leave. Thus does God set parables for people so that they may reflect. (25)

تُؤۡتِىٓ أُكُلَهَا كُلَّ حِينٍ بِإِذۡنِ رَبِّهَا وَيَضۡرِبُ ٱللَّهُ ٱلۡأَمۡثَالَ لِلنَّاسِ لَعَلَّهُمۡ يَتَذَكَّرُونَ ﴿٢٥﴾

And an evil word is like a corrupt tree, torn up onto the face of the earth. It cannot have a stable position. (26)

وَمَثَلُ كَلِمَةٍ خَبِيثَةٍ كَشَجَرَةٍ خَبِيثَةٍ ٱجۡتُثَّتۡ مِن فَوۡقِ ٱلۡأَرۡضِ مَا لَهَا مِن قَرَارٍ ﴿٢٦﴾

God will strengthen the believers through the true, unshakeable word in both this life and the life to come; but the wrongdoers God lets go astray. God does whatever He wills. (27)

يُثَبِّتُ ٱللَّهُ ٱلَّذِينَ ءَامَنُوا۟ بِٱلۡقَوۡلِ ٱلثَّابِتِ فِى ٱلۡحَيَوٰةِ ٱلدُّنۡيَا وَفِى ٱلۡأَخِرَةِ وَيُضِلُّ ٱللَّهُ ٱلظَّالِمِينَ وَيَفۡعَلُ ٱللَّهُ مَا يَشَآءُ ﴿٢٧﴾

From Darkness into Light

"Alif. Lām. Rā. *This is a book which We have bestowed on you from on high.*" (Verse 1) This book which consists of words made up of letters like these is one which you certainly have not authored. It has been revealed to you for a definite purpose, "*so that you might bring forth all mankind, by their Lord's leave, from darkness into the light.*" (Verse 1) Your role is to take mankind out of the depths of darkness into which they have sunk, the darkness of superstition, conflicting systems and traditions; the darkness of believing in alleged deities, and false concepts, values and standards. You are to bring them, i.e. all of mankind, into the real light which removes all darkness. Not only does this light dispel all darkness from people's consciences and minds, it also affects their lives generally, setting for them new values and traditions.

Faith based on God's oneness is a light that shines within the human heart, to make the whole human being shine as well. Man is created out of cold clay in which God has blown of His spirit. Should he abandon the light of this breath of spirit, he turns back into dark clay, and becomes a mass of flesh and blood like an animal. It is indeed the flesh and blood alone that are made of the earth's clay. It is with this breath from God's spirit that light spreads over it. Then faith makes it appear in its full glory. With it the mass of flesh and blood blooms.

Faith is a light that illuminates the soul so that it can see the way leading to God, clear without any confusion caused by superstition or desires, and without any misleading fancy or greed. When the human soul sees the way so clearly ahead of it, it proceeds with steady steps, and without hesitation.

The light of faith illuminates the whole of life, making all mankind equal servants of God, united together by their bond of faith. They submit themselves to none other than God, which means that they are never divided into slaves and tyrants. With the universe around them they establish a bond based on knowledge of the great law that sets the whole universe and all its forces into operation. This brings them peace with the universe and with all creatures that live in it.

Faith is the light of justice, freedom and knowledge. It is the light of a bond with God based on compassion. It is a bond that gives us reassurance of God's justice, grace and wisdom in situations of ease and hardship. Such reassurance requires that we adopt an attitude of patience in adversity and gratitude in happier circumstances. It also adds the light of understanding that adverse situations occur for a definite purpose.

Believing in God alone as the Supreme Lord is not merely a personal faith that fills one's conscience and spreads light over one's soul. It is a complete code of living based on the concept of total submission to God alone, discarding all claims of lordship by other creatures, and rejecting any attempt that gives such creatures any form of sovereignty. This code of living fits completely with human nature so as to satisfy all its needs and fill it with happiness, light and reassurance. It is also so stable that it protects people against the sort of upheaval experienced by societies that submit to the sovereignty claimed by others and who follow systems devised by them in politics, government, economics, social structure, morals and social behaviour, as well as in customs and traditions. Furthermore, this code of living preserves and promotes human potential. It prevents people from glorifying and singing the praises of despots.

Indeed this short phrase, "*so that you may bring forth all mankind, by their Lord's leave, from darkness into the light,*" covers profound truths relevant to the human mind, as also practical day to day living. It is impossible for human language to do more than point to these horizons.

"*So that you might bring forth all mankind, by their Lord's leave, from darkness into the light.*" God's Messenger cannot do more than deliver the divine message, and his role is merely to explain it. As for the bringing of mankind out of darkness into light, this is done by God's leave, and according to the laws He has willed to set in operation. The Prophet is only His Messenger.

"*So that you might bring forth all mankind, by their Lord's leave, from darkness into the light, to the path of the Almighty, the One to whom all praise is due.*" (Verse 1) The phrase, '*the path of the Almighty,*' means His way and law which governs the whole universe, and the code which governs life. Linguistically speaking, it is used here as a substitute for 'light'. This means that the 'light' guides to 'the path of the Almighty', or that the light is His path. The second meaning is however stronger and richer. The light that illuminates the human soul is the light that illuminates the whole universe. It is the way, the law and the code of living. A soul which lives in this light will never be in error, or entertain misconceptions, or opt for wrong behaviour. It follows the straight path, "*the path of the Almighty, the One to whom all praise is due.*" He is the One who has absolute power in the universe, and who is praised by all creatures.

His might is highlighted here as a threat to the unbelievers, while the fact that He is worthy of praise is mentioned as a reminder to those who express gratitude to Him.

Then follow some of God's attributes. He is notably mentioned as the One to whom everything in the heavens and on earth belong, who is in need of no one, and who controls the universe and all creatures therein: "*God, to whom all that is in the heavens and all that is on earth belongs.*" (Verse 2) Whoever, then, comes out of darkness into light and follows guidance does well. The *sūrah* does not mention anything about such a person here. Instead, it goes on to warn the unbelievers against woeful suffering. This is inflicted on them as a result of their rejection of the greatest blessing God has bestowed on humanity, that is, sending them a Messenger whose task is to bring them out of darkness into light. That is an act of God's grace for which we cannot show enough gratitude. Yet some people reject it outright. Hence, "*woe to the unbelievers; for theirs will be a severe suffering.*" (Verse 2)

The *sūrah* then mentions a quality that tells us the reason for their rejection of the blessing God bestows on mankind through His noble Messenger: "*These are the ones who love the life of this world preferring it to the life to come, and who turn others away from God's path and try to make it appear crooked. They have gone far astray.*" (Verse 3) Giving preference to the life of this world puts a person in a position of conflict with the requirements of faith, and on a collision course with the 'path of God'. The situation is reversed when preference is given to the life to come. For then, this life is set on the right course. People enjoy it with moderation, always keen to earn God's pleasure. Hence there is no conflict between their preference for the life to come and their enjoyment of this life and the pleasures it offers.

Those who turn their minds and hearts towards ensuring a happy outcome in the hereafter do not lose the pleasures of this world, as some people with faulty concepts imagine. In Islam, a happy life in this world is a prelude to a happy future life. The fulfilment of man's task as God's vicegerent on earth requires building a happy life. In Islam, there is no denunciation or renunciation of any aspect of this life as people wait for the hereafter. What Islam requires is that life should prosper with truth, justice and sound behaviour by people who seek God's pleasure and a happy life in the hereafter. This is the Islamic outlook.

Those who choose the life of this world in preference to the hereafter cannot monopolize the resources of this world, exploiting, cheating and oppressing people to serve their own interests in a society where the light of faith shines and people follow God's guidance. Hence they turn themselves and others away from God's path and try to make it appear crooked, devoid of truth and justice. It is only when they have done this, and managed to lead themselves away from the straight path of God and justice that they resort to their oppressive ways, cheating people and persuading them to share in their corruption. It is only in this way that they can get what they want of self-aggrandisement, taking for themselves most of the resources God has placed on earth, and behaving arrogantly towards others. People then submit to their authority without resistance.

The way of life advocated by faith protects human life against the selfishness and greed of those who are preoccupied with the life of this world in preference to the life to come. Under this way of life no one person or group can monopolize the earth's wealth and resources.

In Their Own Language

"Never have We sent a messenger otherwise than speaking the language of his own people, so that he might make [the truth] clear to them." (Verse 4) This is a blessing God grants to people with every message He sends to them. For a messenger to be able to bring people out of darkness into light, by their Lord's leave, he must be given his message in his own people's language. This is how he is then able to explain God's message to them. It is how the objectives of the message are fulfilled.

Although the Prophet Muḥammad is a Messenger to all mankind, he is given his message in his own people's language, so that he can explain matters to them. They are the ones who would be conveying his message to the rest of mankind. His own life is, after all, limited. Therefore, he is commanded to call first on his own people so that the Arabian Peninsula becomes purely Muslim. It will then fulfil its role as the place from which the final divine message is carried to the rest of the world. What happened in practice, as God, who knows everything, determined, was that the Prophet passed away when Islam became the religion in the whole of Arabia. The Prophet raised an army under the command of Usāmah to be dispatched to areas bordering on Arabia, but the Prophet (peace be upon him) died before the army began its march. It is true that the Prophet sent his letters and emissaries to the heads of countries outside Arabia, calling on them to accept the message of Islam, and making it clear that his message was addressed to all mankind. However, what God determined for him, which fits with the limited duration of human life, is that Muḥammad (peace be upon him) delivered his message to his own people in their own language. Then the task was completed by those who carried his message to other communities all over the world. Hence, there is no contradiction between his message being addressed to all humanity, and its being expressed in Arabic, the language of his own people.

"Never have We sent a messenger otherwise than speaking the language of his own people, so that he might make [the truth] clear to them. But God lets go astray whomever He wills, and guides whomever He wills." (Verse 4) A messenger's task is completed when he has made the truth clear to people. What comes out of it in the form of people following guidance or going astray is not in his power, and does not follow his desire. It is entirely up to God who has subjected human beings to a law of His own making, in keeping with His free-will. Whoever follows the way of error is left to go astray, and whoever follows the way of divine guidance reaches his destination. Both are subject to God's will.

"He is Almighty, truly Wise." (Verse 4) He conducts life in accordance with His wisdom and careful planning. Nothing is left haphazard, without guidance or planning.

This applied to the message *"We have sent forth Moses with Our revelations, saying, 'Lead your people out of darkness into the light, and remind them of the Days of God'. Surely in this there are signs for everyone who is patient in adversity and deeply grateful [to God]. Moses said to his people: 'Remember the blessings God bestowed on you when He saved you from Pharaoh's people who afflicted you with grievous torment, slaughtered your sons and spared [only] your women. That was indeed an awesome trial from your Lord. For your Lord had declared: 'If you are grateful, I shall certainly give you more; but if you are ungrateful, then My punishment shall be severe indeed.' And Moses said: 'If you and whoever lives on earth were to deny God, [know that] God is indeed Self-Sufficient, worthy of all praise.'"* (Verses 5–8)

The *sūrah* uses the same wording to report the instructions given to Moses and those given to Muḥammad (peace be upon them both), so as to maintain the same style of expression. Muḥammad is told, *"This is a book which We have bestowed on you from on high so that you might bring forth mankind, by their Lord's leave, from darkness into the light."* (Verse 1) Similarly Moses is instructed, *"Lead your people out of darkness into the light."* (Verse 5) The first applies to all mankind, while the second addressed Moses's people in particular. The ultimate goal, however, was the same.

"Lead your people out of darkness into the light, and remind them of the Days of God." (Verse 5) All days are indeed God's days, but what is intended here is that he should remind them of the days when people, or a group of them, encounter a special situation, reflecting either God's grace or punishment, as we will see when Moses carries out this order. He reminds them of some days they themselves had witnessed, and of others belonging to the time of the peoples of Noah, the 'Ād, and Thamūd and other communities that followed them.

"Surely in this there are signs for everyone who is patient in adversity and deeply grateful [to God]." (Verse 5) Some of these days occasioned adversity, making of them a sign requiring patience, while others were occasions when God's grace was bestowed, and they invite gratitude. A person who qualifies as, *'patient in adversity, deeply grateful [to God],'* is the one who recognizes these signs and what lies behind them. He finds in them lessons to be learnt and reminders to be appreciated.

A Reminder of God's Favours

Moses began to fulfil his task and remind his people. *"Moses said to his people: Remember the blessings God bestowed on you when He saved you from Pharaoh's people who afflicted you with grievous torment, slaughtered your sons and spared [only] your women. That was indeed an awesome trial from your Lord.'"* (Verse 6) He reminds them first of God's grace when he delivered them from the great torment inflicted on them by Pharaoh's people. That torment was visited on them time after time, with little reprieve. One of the ghastlier features of that torment was the killing of the male but not the female population as a means of preventing them from increasing in number. This aimed to ensure their continued weakness and subjugation. The fact that God saved them from all this was a great act demonstrating His grace. It should be remembered with gratitude.

243

"*That was indeed an awesome trial from your Lord.*" (Verse 6) Their trial consisted of the affliction visited on them by Pharaoh. It was a means to test their patience, resistance, perseverance and determination. Patience does not merely entail enduring hardship. It is rather endurance without being shaken or mentally defeated, coupled with the determination to stand up to tyranny until freedom is achieved. Endurance that only entails tolerating humiliation is not worthy of praise. The Israelites also experienced the trial of deliverance from tyranny, so as to test their gratitude for God's grace, which should be reflected in following the path of His guidance.

Moses continues to explain matters to his people after having reminded them of the Days of God, and directed them to the ultimate objective of the trial. He tells them about the reward God attaches to gratitude and His punishment for ingratitude: "*For your Lord had declared: 'If you are grateful, I shall certainly give you more; but if you are ungrateful, then My punishment shall be severe indeed.'*" (Verse 7)

It is useful to reflect a little here on this great truth whereby God's blessings are increased for the grateful and whereby severe punishment awaits those who adopt the opposite stance. In the first instance, we feel reassured, since it is a promise by God, and God always fulfils His promises. It must come to pass. If we want to see it in practice, and look for its material causes, we need not go very far.

Expressing gratitude for a blessing is evidence of implementing correct standards in day-to-day life. The proper reward for a blessing, according to sound human nature, is to be grateful for it. Moreover, a person who thanks God for His blessings is always watching Him when it comes to making use of such blessings. He shows no arrogance, and he never puts God's blessings to foul or evil use. Both qualities add to the purity of the human soul, and motivate it to further good action that helps such blessings grow and increase. Thus a grateful person also earns other people's good-will, and they are then ready to help. This reflects on the community as a whole, as ties within the community are placed on a sound footing. Its wealth increases with security. God's promise is however sufficient reassurance for a believer, whether he understands the causes or not. He knows that God's promise always comes true.

Denying God's grace can take many forms. For example, omitting to thank God for it or refusing to recognize that it is God who has bestowed it, and attributing it to one's own knowledge, expertise, hard work, or intelligence, as if these are not part of the grace God bestows on His servants. It may also take the form of misusing or abusing God's blessings, as when these are used to behave arrogantly when dealing with other people or to satisfy evil or corrupt desires.

The severe punishment threatened here may include being deprived of God's blessings, either by removing them literally, or by removing their effects on one's feelings. Many a blessing may become a curse which brings unhappiness, to the extent that the person given it may envy those who do not have it. Or the punishment may be deferred to its right time either in this life or in the life to come, as God may wish. It will however undoubtedly take place, because denying God's grace does not go unpunished.

Giving thanks to God for His grace does not benefit God Himself, just as denying it and being ungrateful does not cause Him any harm. God is in no need of anyone or anything. He is praised as He is God. He does not need people's praise or gratitude. *"And Moses said: 'If you and whoever lives on earth were to deny God, [know that] God is indeed Self-Sufficient, worthy of all praise.'"* (Verse 8) Indeed it is human life that is elevated through thanking God for His grace. People's souls are purified by turning to God, and by giving thanks where thanks belong. They are reassured when they establish a bond with the One who bestows abounding grace. They do not fear that blessings are withdrawn. They do not feel heart-broken when they miss something they would have liked. God, the Most Gracious, is there and He bestows His grace in abundance. Such grace then is increased when people show their gratitude.

The Dialogue between Messengers and Unbelievers

Moses continues with his reminders, but now he no longer features in the scene painted in the *sūrah*. Instead, a picture is drawn of the raging battle between the community that follows the Prophets and *jāhiliyyah* society which denies the messengers and their messages alike. This is a remarkable aspect of the refined style of the Qur'ān which brings the scene alive, transforming it from a historical one that someone is reporting to an immediate one that we see in front of our eyes, able to listen to the people in it as they talk, and notice all their actions and reactions. In this panoramic scene, all limitations of time and space are done away with.

> *Have you not received accounts of what befell those who lived before you? The people of Noah, the 'Ād, and Thamūd, and those who came after them? None knows them all but God. Their messengers came to them with clear evidence of the truth, but they put their hands to their mouths, and said: 'We disbelieve in that with which you have been sent, and we are in grave doubt about that to which you call us.'* (Verse 9)

This reminder is made by Moses, but as he goes behind the scenes the *sūrah* continues with its account of what happened to God's messengers and messages during all periods of history, and the confrontation between them and *jāhiliyyah* in its different states and societies, and the fate of those who denied these messages. It is as if Moses is a narrator who begins with a reference to the main events of a great history, before leaving its players to take over and enact that history, and say whatever they wish. This method of narrating a story or historical account is often employed in the Qur'ān. It serves to bring the historical account alive. We see here God's noble messengers following one another, and confronting all mankind who had given in to *jāhiliyyah*. The gaps between generations and communities disappear, while the great truths stand out without being tied to a specific time or place.

"*Have you not received accounts of what befell those who lived before you? The people of Noah, the 'Ād, and Thamūd, and those who came after them? None knows them all but God.*" (Verse 9) Thus, they are numerous. There were many other such communities than those mentioned in the Qur'ān, who lived during the intervening period between the time of Thamūd and that of Moses. The *sūrah* does not give any details of them, because there is complete unity in the message preached by all prophets, and a unity in the reaction to it.

"*Their messengers came to them with clear evidence of the truth.*" (Verse 9) That evidence is absolutely clear, giving no room for confusion by anyone with undistorted faculties of understanding. "*But they put*

*their hands to their mouths, and said: 'We disbelieve in that with which
you have been sent, and we are in grave doubt about that to which you
call us.'"* (Verse 9) They put their hands to their mouths as does he
who wishes to change the pitch of his voice so that it can be heard at a
distance. He moves his hand in front of his mouth as he raises his
voice, and this causes the sound to break and be heard from afar. The
sūrah paints this movement in order to indicate the fact that they were
outspoken in their denial of the divine message. Furthermore, they
make such an impolite movement to reassert their open rejection of
the faith.

Since what the messengers call for is belief in God's oneness, and
His being the only Lord of mankind and the whole universe, casting
doubts on this clear truth sounds extremely odd and peculiar. This
truth is self-evident, easily recognized by human nature, and repeatedly
confirmed by numerous signs that can be seen everywhere in the
universe. Hence, the messengers are horrified at such doubting, pointing
to the heavens and the earth as witnesses: *"Said the messengers sent to
them: 'Can there be any doubt about God, the Originator of the heavens
and the earth?'"* (Verse 10) Everything in the heavens and the earth
testifies to the truth of God being the Creator and Originator of all.
How can there be any doubt about Him? The messengers say this
because the heavens and the earth are two very clear signs of God's
existence. A mere reference to them is sufficient to quickly help any
straying person come back to his senses. The messengers do not add
anything to this quick reference, as they know it to be sufficient.
Instead, they go on to point out God's grace to mankind, as He calls
on them to believe, and gives them respite while they reflect and begin
to take action to avert His punishment.

*"Said the messengers sent to them: 'Can there be any doubt about
God, the Originator of the heavens and earth? He calls you, so that He
may forgive you your sins.'"* (Verse 10) The call is originally to believe in
God, and that leads to the forgiveness of sins. However, the *sūrah*
then makes the call a direct one for forgiveness so that God's grace and
blessings are brought out in sharp relief. In such a context, it is especially
odd that people adopt such a negative attitude.

*"He calls you, so that He may forgive you your sins and grant you
respite for an appointed term."* (Verse 10) With this call to forgiveness,

God does not demand an immediate positive response, nor does He inflict His punishment immediately when they make their first rejection. He grants them another favour by giving them a period of grace, either for a time He sets in this life or to the Day of Reckoning. During this respite they may reflect on various signs and indicators, and on the messengers' warnings. Such respite is an act of grace, considering their negative response to His call.

Yet those ignorant people revert to their baseless objection: "*They replied: 'You are but mortals like ourselves. You want to turn us away from what our forefathers used to worship.'*" (Verse 10) Human beings should have been proud at God's selection of one of their number to bring them His message. Instead they object to this choice and make of it grounds for suspecting the validity of the message. They claim that what the messengers call on them to believe in is a mere wish to turn them away from what their forefathers worshipped. They do not bother to ask themselves why the messengers should wish to turn them away from that. All ignorant societies are rigid. Hence people of such societies do not reflect on the true nature of what their forefathers worshipped, and why they objected to such false deities. Nor do they think about the nature of the new call. Instead, they ask for a miracle to force them to believe. "*Bring us, then, a clear proof.*" (Verse 10)

The messengers do not deny their human status. On the contrary they confirm it, but they draw their attention to the favours God gives when He chooses human messengers and gives them what they need in order to be fully equipped to discharge their great duty: "*Their messengers replied: 'We are indeed but mortals like yourselves. But God bestows His grace on whomever He wills of His servants.'*" (Verse 11) The phrase, '*bestows His grace,*' is used here so that the dialogue fits in harmoniously with the general atmosphere of the *sūrah*. It is an atmosphere generated by speaking about God's grace which He bestows on whomever He chooses of His servants. His grace is limitless. It is not granted only to God's messengers, but rather affects humanity as a whole. For mankind has been honoured by the choice of one of its number to undertake this great task of receiving a message from on high.

It is also a special favour granted to mankind, so that they can come out of darkness into the light. Their faculties of reception and understanding are reawakened so as to resume an active life after a long state of stagnation akin to death. But the greatest aspect of divine grace bestowed on mankind is that they are saved from submission to others, which means humiliation and servitude to mortals like themselves.

Faith Versus Tyranny

As for producing clear proof, which means a miracle or some supernatural event, the messengers make it clear to their communities that this is something determined by God alone. The messengers try to make people realize very clearly the difference between Godhead and their own mortal beings. They want them to understand the true significance of the oneness of God who is unlike anyone else in nature and attributes. The lack of such clarity was the source of the great confusion into which pagan beliefs had sunk, as well as the church concepts which mixed Christianity with the pagan beliefs of Greece, Rome, Egypt and India. The starting point in this confusion into which Christianity had sunk was the attribution of supernatural powers to Jesus himself, leading to a great mix-up between the Divine Being and His servant, Jesus Christ (peace be upon him).

The messengers made their position very clear: "*It is not within our power to bring you any proof, except by God's leave.*" We do not rely on any power other than His own: "*It is in God that all believers must place their trust.*" (Verse 11) The messengers announce this as a permanent truth. A believer does not place his trust in anyone other than God. He turns to no one else for help or support, and he seeks refuge with none other than Him.

The messengers then confront tyranny and rejection with an attitude based on faith, remaining steadfast in the face of adversity and abuse. They ask a question which means an assertion: "*And why should we not place our trust in God, when He has guided us on our paths? Hence we will bear with patience all your persecution. In God alone let all the faithful place their trust.*" (Verse 12)

"*And why should we not place our trust in God, when He has guided us on our paths?*" (Verse 12) This is a statement by one who is certain of his attitude and the way he follows. He entertains no doubts about the support he has, and believes that God who guides to the straight

249

path will undoubtedly give him His support. What does it matter if victory is not given in this present life, when one is sure that God is guiding him along the right path?

Anyone who feels deep in his heart that God's hand guides his footsteps is someone that has real contact with God. Such a person does not mistake the sense of His existence and that He is God who controls everything. This is a feeling that leaves no room for reluctance in following the path of faith, regardless of what obstacles may lie along the way, including tyrannical forces that persecute those who follow it. This explains why God's messengers' reply links their feeling of being guided by God with their placing their trust in Him as they faced open opposition from tyrants. It also explains their determination to go along the way despite all the threats.

Such an association is real only in the hearts and minds of people who take positive action to confront the tyranny of *jāhiliyyah* society. Such hearts and minds realize deep inside that God's hand opens windows for them to see the light that illuminates great horizons before them. They feel the comfort of faith and true knowledge, and feel reassured by their strong bond with God. Hence, they do not care about the threats they receive from tyrants. Threats and temptations do not have any effect on them, as they look down on all the tyrants on earth and their means of oppression and persecution. Why would a heart that knows its link with God fear anything that others may have?

"And why should we not place our trust in God, when He has guided us on our paths? Hence we will bear with patience all your persecution." (Verse 12) We will remain steadfast and never budge in the face of all the persecution visited on us. We will never entertain any doubt and we will never go back on our faith. *"In God alone let all the faithful place their trust."* (Verse 12)

At this point tyranny reveals its intentions. It does not argue, think or take a rational approach. It feels that it has no power to face up to faith, and that it will inevitably be defeated. Hence, it threatens the use of brute force, which is the only means to which tyranny can resort: *"The unbelievers said to their messengers: 'We shall most certainly expel you from our land, unless you return to our ways.'"* (Verse 13)

This shows clearly the nature of the battle between Islam and ignorance, or *jāhiliyyah*. The latter does not agree that Islam should have its own entity, which is independent from it. It will not tolerate a separate existence for Islam, and will not live in peace with Islam, even if Islam wants peace with it. That is because Islam wants to be represented in a social set up with its own leadership and because it claims allegiance from its followers. But *jāhiliyyah* cannot tolerate this. Therefore, the demand the unbelievers make of their messengers is not merely to stop calling on people to believe. They further demand that they return to their own ways and be fully integrated in their own society. They must not have their separate entity. But divine faith will not accept this as it is contrary to its nature. Hence, the messengers reject this demand. It is not for a person who submits to God to go back on that and return to *jāhiliyyah*.

When brute force reveals its shameless face, there is no room for argument or a peaceful call to accept the faith. But God will not abandon His messengers to face *jāhiliyyah* on their own.

By its very nature, a society based on *jāhiliyyah* does not allow anyone who submits to God to work from within its boundaries, unless the work of that believer and his efforts and potentials will support that society and contribute to its power. Those who imagine themselves able to serve their faith by penetrating un-Islamic society and working within its system do not actually understand the nature of the organic structure of that society. It is a society that forces everyone to work for its beliefs and concepts. Hence, the noble messengers' refusal to revert to their people's old ways, after they had been saved from them by God.

At this point the Supreme Power levels its blow to which no resistance can be made by weak human beings, even though they may be ruthless despots: "*Their Lord revealed this to His messengers: 'Most certainly shall We destroy the wrongdoers, and most certainly shall We cause you to dwell in the land long after they are gone. This [I promise] to all who stand in awe of My presence, and stand in awe of My warnings.'*" (Verses 13–14)

Prayers for God's Support

We must realize here that the Supreme Power does not intervene to settle the issue between the messengers and their communities until

251

the messengers themselves declare their final split with their people. The believers must make it clear that they will never return to their people's old ways after God has saved them. They must also insist on having their own separate identity, society and leadership. This means that the community is split into two which differ in faith, lifestyle, leadership and structure. This is when God intervenes to destroy the despots who persecute the believers. This is when God fulfils His promise to His messengers to grant them victory and establish the believers on earth. Such intervention will never happen while the believers are integrated in un-Islamic society, working from within its institutions. They must first have their own identity and their own separate structure and leadership.

"*Their Lord revealed this to His messengers: 'Most certainly shall We destroy the wrongdoers.'*" (Verse 13) Here we have an emphatic statement. Furthermore, it adds power through its use of inversion and the plural pronoun in reference to God. It asserts a promise to destroy the tyrants who threaten the believers and, by their threats, do wrong to themselves, the truth, God's messengers and all people. "*And most certainly shall We cause you to dwell in the land long after they are gone.*" (Verse 14) This is not an act of favouritism, but the work of a fair law of nature that God has set in operation.

"*This [I promise] to all who stand in awe of My presence, and stand in awe of My warnings.*" (Verse 14) This settlement in the land after the tyrants have gone is promised to those who fear God and do not act with arrogance or overbearing pride. Such people fear what God has warned them against, so they take measures to avoid it. They do not engage in corruption or wrongdoing against other people. Hence they deserve to be given their chance and be established on earth.

This sets the scene for a confrontation between the feeble power of wrongdoing despots and the great power of God, the Supreme Being who controls the whole universe. The messengers' task has been completed with the clear delivery of the message and the declaration of a split between themselves and the unbelievers. The tyrants marshal all their feeble power and stand to one side, and the messengers, who in all humility call people to faith, stand opposite, but they are supported by God, the Almighty. Both parties pray for victory, and the result is as expected: "*And they prayed for God's help and victory [for the truth]. And every powerful, obstinate enemy of the truth shall come to grief. Behind him stretches hell where he shall be made to drink putrefied water, gulping it little by little, and yet hardly able to swallow it. Death will beset him from every side, yet he shall not die. More severe suffering still awaits him."* (Verses 15–17)

This is a remarkable scene showing every hardened despot ending up in failure in this life on earth. As he takes his position of miserable failure, hell is looming large behind him. There he is made to drink putrefied fluids. He is violently forced to gulp it down, although he can hardly take a sip because it is both dirty and bitter. His disgust is evident from the look on his face, so much so that we can almost see it through the words. Death approaches him from every corner, but he will not die, because he must take his punishment in full. But beyond this is an even sterner punishment.

It is indeed a remarkable scene showing the tyrant coming to grief, engulfed by a fate that appears to him in this horrific way. The words used here add their own connotations which make the punishment fit the brute force the tyrants themselves employed to threaten the advocates of the truth.

Arrogance → humiliation
humility → honor, elevation

So Easy for God

The fitting comment on the destiny of tyrants and the misery they are made to suffer is part of a scene painting the situation of the unbelievers, with its assertion of God's power, a power which can easily do away with them all and replace them with a new creation. This picture follows the last confrontation that takes place in this life. The curtains are drawn here before they open again to show what happens to both sides in the life to come.

"The works of those who disbelieve in their Lord are like ashes which the wind blows about fiercely on a stormy day. They cannot achieve any benefit from all that they might have earned. This [disbelief] is indeed going very far astray." (Verse 18) The image of ashes being blown about on a stormy day adds action to the concept that the unbelievers' works will come to nothing. People cannot hold on to any part of their actions, or make use of them. This image gives a far more profound effect than any expression of the same meaning of total loss in intellectual terms.

253

This scene expresses a basic truth about what the unbelievers do. Actions that have no basis in faith, and are not controlled by that bond relating every action to its motive, and relating that motive to God remain loose, lacking a solid entity. They are like ashes or flying particles. It is not the action itself that carries paramount value, but rather the motivation behind it. Action is a mechanical movement, but its motive is what differentiates man from machine.

The comment which follows is also very apt: "*This [disbelief] is indeed going very far astray.*" (Verse 18) Just like the ashes blown far away by fierce winds, so too have they gone far astray.

The following verses then speak of the fate of the unbelievers of olden times in order to demonstrate the fate of the unbelieving Arabs of the Quraysh. These verses threaten them with God's ability to replace them with a new creation: "*Do you not see that God has created the heavens and the earth in accordance with the truth. If He so wills, He can do away with you and bring into being a new creation. This is no difficult thing for God.*" (Verses 19–20)

This switch from a discussion about faith and disbelief, and the dispute between God's messengers and the unbelievers in un-Islamic societies, to a picture of the heavens and the earth is very natural in the Qur'ān. It is also natural in human feelings and perceptions. This is a further indication of the divine source of the Qur'ān. There is a secret but intelligible discourse between man and the universe. Human nature responds instinctively to this secret communication once it tunes in to it and receives its signals.

Those who do not pick up on these signals and indicators must examine their receptive faculties. For these must be faulty. Eyes may turn blind, and ears may become deaf, and a person may be dumb. Those who cannot receive the signals of the universe have defective faculties. Hence they are unsuited to positions of leadership. This includes all those who accept a materialistic philosophy which produces what is falsely called 'scientific doctrines'. Science cannot function with faulty faculties and a defective means of contact with the universe. Such people are described in the Qur'ān as blind. It is not possible for human life to prosper under a system, doctrine or philosophy promoted by someone who is blind.

The fact that the heavens and the earth have been created with the truth gives the impression of limitless ability and solid stability. The truth is solid and stable even in the sound the word 'truth' makes. This contrasts completely with the ashes blown about fiercely on a stormy day, dispersed far and wide, as it contrasts with people going far astray.

In light of the fate suffered by despots who stubbornly took the wrong side in the battle between truth and falsehood, a strong warning is issued: "*If He so wills, He can do away with you and bring into being a new creation.*" (Verse 19) He who is able to create the heavens and the earth can easily replace the human race with a different one, or bring about a new community of humans in place of the present one. Again the connotations of taking a community away to replace it with another fits properly with the image of ashes blown far away.

"*This is no difficult thing for God.*" (Verse 20) The creation of the heavens and the earth testify that it is indeed easy for God. The fate of earlier unbelieving communities also testifies to it, and so do the ashes scattered hither and thither. It is indeed a remarkable feature of the Qur'ānic style that imagery and connotations slot together in perfect harmony.

Acrimonious Exchanges between Allies

At this point in the *sūrah* we note an even higher level of the inimitable style of the Qur'ān, and its power of imagery, expression and harmony between scenes and ideas. A short while ago we saw obstinate tyrants coming to grief, with an image of hell looming large behind them as they are made to suffer their greatest disappointment in this life. Now we see them on the Day of Judgement. It is at once an extraordinary and powerful scene, full of movement, reaction and dialogue between the weak and the powerful, and between both and Satan.

> They will all appear before God, and then the weak will say to those who acted with arrogance: 'We were your followers: can you relieve us of something of God's punishment?' [And the others] will reply: 'Had God given us guidance, we would have guided you. It is

now all one for us whether we grieve impatiently or endure with patience. There is no escape for us now.' And when everything will have been decided, Satan will say: 'God has made you a true promise. I, too, made promises to you, but I did not keep them. Yet I had no power at all over you, except that I called you and you responded to me. Hence, do not now blame me, but blame yourselves. It is not for me to respond to your cries, nor for you to respond to mine. I have already disclaimed your associating me with God.' Indeed, for all wrongdoers there is grievous suffering in store. Those who believe and do righteous deeds will be admitted to gardens through which running waters flow, wherein they will abide, by their Lord's leave. Their greeting shall be: 'Peace'. (Verses 21–23)

We have now moved from this world's stage to that of the next where everyone appears before God: "*They will all appear before God.*" They all come forward: the arrogant tyrants who reject His message and their weak subordinates, joined by Satan, and also those who believed in the messengers and did righteous deeds. In fact they have always been exposed before God, but now they know and feel that there is no screen to give them cover or protection. They all appear in front of Him, and now the dialogue starts:

"*Then the weak will say to those who acted with arrogance: 'We were your followers: can you relieve us of something of God's punishment?'*" (Verse 21) The weak are those who forfeited the most essential quality of the human being honoured by God when they forfeited their rights to freedom of thought, belief and choice, making themselves no more than the slaves of arrogant despots. They submitted themselves like servants to such despots like themselves in preference to submission to God alone. Such weakness is no excuse; indeed it is their crime.

God does not like that anyone should feel weak. Indeed he calls on all people to seek His protection, and find strength in His support. He does not like that anyone should abandon, willingly or unwillingly, his or her share of freedom, which is a privilege for which they deserve honour. No material force, great as it may be, can force into submission a human being who wants to remain free and hold on to his human dignity. The maximum that brute force can achieve is to have power over the body, imprisoning and tormenting it. As for the mind, conscience and spirit, these cannot be imprisoned by anyone unless the victim so agrees to hand them over.

Who has the power to make such weak people follow despots in faith, thought and behaviour? Who has the power to make them submit to anyone other than God, their Creator who is the only One to provide them with their means of sustenance? The answer is none other than their own weak souls. They are not weak because of any lack of material power, or because they have less dignity, wealth, or position than despots. All these are of little consequence. They are external or superficial aspects, and lacking them does not mean any real weakness. Instead, they are weak in their souls and dignity. They do not truly appreciate man's most essential quality.

The oppressed represent the majority while the despots are in the minority. How come, then, that the majority are subjugated by the minority? It is only a weakness of spirit and soul, and forfeiture of the dignity with which God has graced human beings. Despots cannot humiliate and subjugate the masses unless the masses are willing to be subjugated. The masses are always able to stand up to tyrants, if only they choose to do so. What is lacking, then, is the will. Humiliation does not come about without a susceptibility to being humiliated. In fact the tyrants rely only on this susceptibility.

Here we see those weak and humble 'followers' as they come on the stage of the hereafter. Addressing arrogant tyrants, they say: "*We were your followers: can you relieve us of something of God's punishment?*" (Verse 21) We have followed you and, as a result, we are now facing this painful destiny. Or maybe it is that after seeing the punishment that awaits them they try to reproach the tyrants for having led them to this end. The *sūrah* quotes what they say, which carries overtones of humility.

The arrogant tyrants reply to their question, saying: "*Had God given us guidance, we would have guided you.*" (Verse 21) Why should you blame us when we are facing the same destiny as you? We have not followed guidance ourselves and left you to go astray. Had God given us guidance we would have led you to it, just as we led you to error when we went astray. They attribute both their guidance and error to God, now acknowledging His great power, when once they had denied these. They exercised their tyranny, subjugating the weak to their power, in a manner which took no account of God's power. They now try to

257

absolve themselves by attributing their error and role in leading other people astray to God. But God does not command anyone to go astray, as He says: "*Never does God enjoin what is indecent.*" (7: 28)

They go on to implicitly reproach the weak, telling them that there is no use in panic or patient endurance. God's punishment is due and it cannot be averted. The time has passed when panic could have helped those who went astray to return to God in repentance. Similarly, patience in adversity used to be of benefit, because God would bestow His mercy on those who were patient. But now this is all over. There is no more room for escape: "*It is now all one for us, whether we grieve impatiently or endure with patience. There is no escape for us now.*" (Verse 21)

Realities That Must be Faced

Matters have been settled and there can be no room for discussion or argument. Everyone has been shown their place in the life to come. But at this point we see a remarkable portrait: it is Satan, the one who did everything in his power to divert people away from the truth and turn them towards error and falsehood, who reproaches both the weak and the tyrants. His words may sound to them worse than the torture they will soon face: "*And when everything will have been decided, Satan will say: 'God has made you a true promise. I, too, made promises to you, but I did not keep them. Yet I had no power at all over you, except that I called you and you responded to me. Hence, do not now blame me, but blame yourselves. It is not for me to respond to your cries, nor for you to respond to mine. I have already disclaimed your associating me with God.' Indeed, for all wrongdoers there is grievous suffering in store.*" (Verse 22)

What an amazing scene. Satan is truly devilish! His personality appears here in its most striking colours, just as we have seen the true character of the weak and the powerful. Satan who was the constant whisperer, presenting every type of temptation, turning people away from the voice of truth is now stabbing his followers in the back. Now that matters have been settled, they cannot make any counter attack. They cannot even reply to him. It is he who says now, after the issues have been decided: "*God has made you a true promise. I, too, made promises to you, but I did not keep them.*" (Verse 22) He goes on to rub it in, reproaching them for responding to him when he had no power over them. It is they who gave themselves up to him, forgetting all the old enmity between themselves and Satan. They embraced his falsehood and abandoned the message of truth God had sent them.

"*Yet I had no power at all over you, except that I called you and you responded to me.*" (Verse 22) He not only rebukes them, but calls on them to rebuke themselves for having obeyed him: "*Do not now blame me, but blame yourselves.*" (Verse 22) He then adds insult to injury, lets them down unashamedly, and declares that he wants nothing further to do with them. Yet it was he who had previously given them all sorts of rosy promises. He went on to tell them that no one could ever defeat them. Now he will not even try to give them any support should they appeal to him for it, nor will they help him when he cries out: "*It is not for me to respond to your cries, nor for you to respond to mine.*" (Verse 22) There is no contact or relationship between us now. He then absolves himself of their associating him as a partner with God. "*I have already disclaimed your associating me with God.*" (Verse 22) He then finishes this Satanic speech with a devastating blow directed at those who followed him in every way: "*Indeed for all wrongdoers there is grievous suffering in store.*" (Verse 22)

This is what they receive from Satan, after they have followed him blindly into error. This is what they get from him for having abandoned God's messengers who called on them to follow God's guidance.

Before the curtains are drawn, we see on the other side the believers who have won the battle against Satan, and who are now enjoying their success: "*Those who believe and do righteous deeds will be admitted to gardens through which running waters flow, wherein they will abide, by their Lord's leave. Their greeting shall be: 'Peace'.* (Verse 23) Thus the scene ends. This is the outcome of the whole story between the message and its advocates on the one side and powerful tyrants who deny God and His messengers on the other.

A Word to Strengthen the Believers

While the nature of the story is the same in every age, the believers who follow God's messengers stand in this world face to face against tyrannical ignorance, or *jāhiliyyah*: "*And they prayed for God's help and victory [for the truth]. And every powerful, obstinate enemy of the truth shall come to grief. Behind him stretches hell where he shall be made to drink putrefied water, gulping it little by little, and yet hardly able to swallow it. Death will beset him from every side, yet he shall not die. More severe suffering still awaits him.*" (Verses 15–17)

While this takes place in this life, a scene of the hereafter is portrayed whereby an unusual conversation ensues between arrogant tyrants, their powerless followers and Satan. The *sūrah* also portrays the widely different destinies of good and evil people before providing an analogy of what good and bad words are like. This portrays the working of the law God has set in nature concerning good and evil in life. It also serves as a final comment on the story: "*Do you not see how God compares a good word to a good tree? Its roots are firm and its branches reach to the sky. It yields its fruits at all times by its Lord's leave. Thus does God set parables for people so that they may reflect. And an evil word is like a corrupt tree, torn up onto the face of the earth. It cannot have a stable position. God will strengthen the believers through the true, unshakeable word in both this life and the life to come; but the wrongdoers God lets go astray. God does whatever He wills.*" (Verses 24–27)

This scene describing words and utterances, good and evil, is derived from the general atmosphere of the *sūrah*, and from the history of prophets and those who deny their messages, as well as the destiny of both groups. The tree of prophethood, with its prominent figure of Abraham, the Prophet Muḥammad's ancestor, is portrayed here as it delivers its great yield every now and then, in the shape of a new prophet who spreads faith and goodness.

Yet the analogy is far more comprehensive, real and effective than just that. For the good word of truth is indeed like a great firm tree, yielding its fruits, solid, unaffected by wind and undisturbed by the storm of evil. It cannot be uprooted by evil tyranny, even though there may be times when it seems to be exposed to grave danger. As it stands high, it looks on evil, injustice and tyranny from above, even though it sometimes seems to the short-sighted that evil squeezes it into a narrow corner. Its fruits are yielded time after time, because its seeds grow within good souls, generation after generation.

The same analogy applies in reverse. An evil word of falsehood is like a foul tree which may spread its branches high and wide, and which may seem to some people to be greater and stronger than the good tree of truth. Nevertheless, it is weak and hollow. Its roots are easily pulled out, as though they stretch on the surface of the earth. One day, it will definitely be uprooted, and then it will have no stable means of existence.

Neither of these is a parable given by way of consolation or encouragement to good people. This is the reality of life, even though it may appear at times to come very slowly. Real goodness does not die or fade away, even though it may be pressed hard by evil which seems to possess enormous power. Conversely, evil exists only while it consumes the little goodness which may be mixed with it. For evil rarely exists in a pure form. In most cases, it has some good within it, and as long as it has that good element, it continues to exist. When this good element no longer exists, evil crumbles and is destroyed, regardless of its initially great appearance. Good remains in its healthy position, enjoying good prospects, whilst evil remains in its foul position, engulfed by serious threats.

"*Thus does God set parables for people so that they may reflect.*" (Verse 25) These are examples that exist in real life, but people often forget under the pressures of life.

The *sūrah* provides several elements that contribute to the concept of stability associated with the good, firm tree. It is painted here as having firm roots, well entrenched in the earth, its branches stretching wide on the horizon, giving the clear impression of solidity, strength and firmness. As this great tree is compared to a good word, we are told that "*God will strengthen the believers through the true, unshakeable word in both this life and the life to come.*" (Verse 27) And just like the bad tree that is uprooted from the face of the earth, lacking stable existence, "*the wrongdoers God lets go astray.*" (Verse 27) Thus the modes of expression fit harmoniously with the connotations stressed in the *sūrah*.

God strengthens the believers in this life and in the life to come with the good word of faith that is firmly established in human nature and conscience, yielding its fruit through good and renewed action that has a lasting impact on human life. He further strengthens them with His word contained in the Qur'ān, with the Prophet's statements, and with His true promise of victory in this life and success in the hereafter. These are all unshakeable words which will always be seen to be true. Those who believe in them will never suffer from worry or confusion.

On the other hand, God lets the wrongdoers go astray as a result of their wrongdoing and associating partners with Him. In fact, 'wrongdoing' is often used in the Qur'ān as being synonymous with associating partners with God, since both are manifestations of injustice. Such wrongdoers turn away from the light of divine guidance, and move aimlessly in a great maze of legend and superstition, following laws based on desire, and not on the proper guidance provided by God. As they do so, they are left to go astray. This happens in accordance with the law God has set in operation, which leads to error and confusion anyone who chooses to close his eyes to His guidance and follow his desire.

"*God does whatever He wills.*" (Verse 27) His will is free. It chooses the law it sets in operation, but is not limited or restricted by it. Whenever God's wisdom determines to change it, it is changed by God's will which is free, unimpeded by anything, irresistible. Indeed, everything in the universe takes place in accordance with God's will.

This statement serves as a final comment on the main topic that takes up more than half of the *sūrah* that is entitled Abraham, after the father of the prophets. This principal subject matter is God's message and its advocacy. The good tree with its good fruit and stretching, cool shade, and the good word that survives one generation after another, contain together the great truth of the one message which never changes, namely the message of the oneness of God, the Almighty.

Messengers versus Unbelievers

We need to pause here in order to reflect on the main facts in the history of God's messengers and their encounter with *jāhiliyyah*. We have already made brief references to these in our commentary, but they now merit further discussion.

The first basic fact which God, in His absolute wisdom and faultless knowledge, tells us is that there has been a procession of faith ever since the beginning of human history. This procession has continued uninterrupted, led by God's messengers who have advocated the same truth and followed the same method. They have advocated the oneness of God, the Lord of the universe. None of them has ever associated any partners with God. None relied on, or sought support from, or appealed to, anyone other than God.

This means that faith in the One God has not come about progressively or developed from a belief in a multiplicity of deities, to dualism and then the concept of a single God, as claimed by scholars of Comparative Religion. This claim saying that man started with the worship of totems, spirits and stars before progressing to the worship of a single deity is false. Nor is it true to claim that such progress parallels the progress of human knowledge and experience, or the development of political power in human society. All such claims are false.

Faith in God, the only deity to be worshipped, has been preached by God's messengers ever since the beginning of history. The basic truth of God's oneness was established in its full form in all divine messages. None of these messages or divine religions introduced any change in, or modification of, this truth. This is what we are told by God whose knowledge encompasses all things.

Had such scholars said that acceptability of the faith based on God's oneness developed over the centuries, and that pagan beliefs have been influenced by the different forms of the divine faith, preached by God's successive messengers who confronted such pagan beliefs, until there was a time when the masses were more ready to accept the divine faith, then their claims might have had some validity. But such scholars follow a method of research and investigation that is based on an old subtle hostility to the church in Europe. This old hostility still survives although it may go unnoticed by modern scholars. They are motivated by an underlying desire, of which they may or may not be aware, to disprove the religious way of thinking. In this respect, they want to prove that religion never came about as revelation from on high, but was instead invented by human beings. When it is classified as such, then it is subject to all the rules applicable to human thinking, such as modification, experimentation, and revision. It is such old hostility and subtle desire that have given birth to the study of Comparative Religion which is falsely called a branch of science.

Such claims may deceive some people into accepting what such scholars say. However, no Muslim who respects his faith and its method of establishing the facts should be deceived by it for a moment. How can he, when such claims contradict clear Islamic texts that put the facts in a most lucid manner?[1]

One Message by All Messengers

A long procession of God's messengers called on humanity, right from the very first day, to believe in a single message embodying the same faith. *Jāhiliyyah*, on the other hand, confronted this call to faith with the same type of rejection. The Qur'ān portrays this confrontation, disregarding the elements of time and place, in order to show the fact that the resistance to the divine faith has not changed throughout history. This in itself is very noteworthy. *Jāhiliyyah* is the same throughout history. It is not a particular stage of human history. It is a state of mind giving rise to a belief and a social structure based on it.

The state of ignorance, or *jāhiliyyah*, is based on the submission of one group of people to another, giving the qualities of Godhead to someone other than God, or assigning lordship to anyone other than God. Whether people believe in polytheism or in a monotheism that acknowledges a multiplicity of lords, they sink into a state of ignorance, or what is described in Islamic terminology as *jāhiliyyah*, with all its secondary characteristics.

The message preached by God's messengers is essentially based on God's oneness and the rejection of all false lords. Submission to God must be pure and complete. He is the only Lord, and to Him belongs sovereignty and all authority. Hence it is in direct conflict with the conceptual foundation of *jāhiliyyah* society, constituting a direct threat to it. This is especially so when the message begins to form a separate grouping that draws its members from within that society, giving them new beliefs and a new leadership and loyalties. This is a normal and essential line of action which divine religion inevitably follows.

As a single unit, *jāhiliyyah* society begins to feel the ideological threat to its existence, particularly when the faith based on submission to

---

1. This concept is discussed at length in the commentary on *Sūrah* 11, Vol. IX, pp. 227–234

God alone, or Islam, comes to be represented as a separate entity. Hence, *jāhiliyyah* society declares its hostile attitude to Islam, in its general meaning of submission to God alone.

The conflict, then, is between two entities which cannot co-exist peacefully. It is a conflict between two structures, each one of which has a basis that is totally opposed to that of the other. One of them permits submission to human beings, while the other rejects this totally. The Islamic grouping, particularly during its formative period, takes its recruits from *jāhiliyyah* society. Later, it confronts that society to take over leadership and liberate all mankind from submission to anyone other than God. Such development is inevitable when the advocates of Islam follow the right course defined by their faith. In view of this, *jāhiliyyah* society does not tolerate Islam right from the beginning. With this being the case, we can readily understand the unity of reaction by all *jāhiliyyah* societies to the messages of all God's messengers. *Jāhiliyyah* society is defending its own existence. It has usurped God's sovereignty, and it wants to keep it.

Since *jāhiliyyah* society senses the danger to its very existence represented by the Islamic message, it confronts that message with an onslaught that accepts neither a truce nor a *modus vivendi*. It is a war to the bitter end, since it is over survival. Neither *jāhiliyyah* society nor God's noble messengers indulge in any self-deception over the nature of this confrontation. Nor did God's messengers ever deceive their followers over it. "*The unbelievers said to their messengers: 'We shall most certainly expel you from our land, unless you return to our ways.'*" (Verse 13) They do not accept that the messengers or their followers should have a separate faith, leadership or grouping. They demand that they should return to their ways, integrating in their society, or else they will be thrown out of their land altogether.

Likewise, God's messengers do not accept any reverting to full integration into *jāhiliyyah* society, or to shedding their independent personality or grouping. They realize that their community is based on a totally different foundation to that of *jāhiliyyah* society. Nor do they say, as do those who do not realize the true nature of Islam or the nature of the organic structure of societies, "Let us integrate into that society so that we can advocate our message and serve our cause from within it." The fact that a Muslim living in an un-Islamic society has his own distinct faith must inevitably be followed by having an independent community that has its own leadership and allegiance. This is not a matter of choice. It is absolutely inevitable. By its very structure, un-Islamic society is highly sensitive to the Islamic faith which has as its foundation belief in the oneness of God, to whom all people must submit themselves. It removes all false deities from positions of leadership and authority. Every Muslim who integrates into *jāhiliyyah* society becomes a servant of that society, when he should be serving the cause of Islam only.

There remains the fact of destiny which advocates of Islam must never lose sight of. The fulfilment of God's promise to His servants that He will grant them victory and authority and will judge between them and their people on the basis of the truth will not take place until the believers have separated themselves and declared their allegiance to the truth they preach. God's victory is not given while Islam's advocates are integrated within un-Islamic society, serving its interests. When such integration occurs, it delays victory. This is then a great responsibility which must be clearly understood by the advocates of Islam.

A Style of Exceptional Refinement

A brief note on the style employed in this passage should be added. It is at this juncture that we find the breathtakingly beautiful style of the Qur'ān demonstrating the procession of faith as it confronts erring *jāhiliyyah* throughout human history. It is the beauty of the truth: simple, natural, clear, confident, reassured, strong and profound: "*Said the messengers sent to them: 'Can there be any doubt about God, the Originator of the heavens and the earth? He calls you, so that He may forgive you your sins and grant you respite for an appointed term.' They replied: 'You are but mortals like ourselves. You want to turn us away from what our forefathers used to worship. Bring us, then, a clear proof.' Their messengers replied: 'We are indeed but mortals like yourselves. But God bestows His grace on whomever He wills of His servants. It is not within our power to bring you any proof, except by God's leave. It is in God that all believers must place their trust. And why should we not place our trust in God, when He has guided us on our paths? Hence we will bear with patience all your persecution. In God let all the faithful place their trust.'"* (Verses 10–12)

Here we see all God's messengers marching in a single procession, confronting *jāhiliyyah* which is one in nature. This essential fact remains true despite the changing circumstances. The beauty of the Qur'ānic style is at its best where it describes the truth embodied in the message preached by the prophets as related to the truth behind the existence of the universe: *"Said the messengers sent to them: 'Can there be any doubt about God, the Originator of the heavens and earth?"* (Verse 10) *"And why should we not place our trust in God, when He has guided us on our paths?"* (Verse 12) *"Do you not see that God has created the heavens and the earth in accordance with the truth. If He so wills, He can do away with you and bring into being a new creation. This is no difficult thing for God."* (Verses 19–20)

Thus the fundamental relationship between the truth embodied in the divine message and the truth of the existence of the universe is emphasized as one single truth, derived from God who is the truth. It is firmly established and deeply rooted, just like *"a good tree: its roots are firm and its branches reach to the sky."* (Verse 24) Everything else is false, transitory, similar to *"a corrupt tree, torn up onto the face of the earth. It cannot have a stable position."* (Verse 26)

The same beauty is seen in the nature of the messengers' understanding of the nature of their Lord, and the nature of Godhead as it fills the hearts of His faithful servants: *"And why should we not place our trust in God, when He has guided us on our paths? Hence we will bear with patience all your persecution. In God alone let all the faithful place their trust."* (Verse 12)

All these are aspects of that spectacular beauty which human expression cannot describe. It can only be pointed to, just like we point to a far away star. We do not reach it with our signal, but we draw attention to it as it lights up our horizon.

2

Grace and Gratitude
27-52

Have you not seen those who
have exchanged God's blessings
for unbelief, and landed their
people in the House of Perdition,
(28)

أَلَمْ تَرَ إِلَى الَّذِينَ بَدَّلُوا نِعْمَتَ اللَّهِ كُفْرًا
وَأَحَلُّوا قَوْمَهُمْ دَارَ الْبَوَارِ ۝

hell, which they will have to
endure? How vile a place to settle
in! (29)

جَهَنَّمَ يَصْلَوْنَهَا ۖ وَبِئْسَ الْقَرَارُ ۝

They set up false deities as equal
to God, and so they lead people
to stray from His path. Say:
'Enjoy yourselves [in this life],
for you will surely end up in
hell.' (30)

وَجَعَلُوا لِلَّهِ أَندَادًا لِّيُضِلُّوا عَن سَبِيلِهِ ۗ
قُلْ تَمَتَّعُوا فَإِنَّ مَصِيرَكُمْ إِلَى النَّارِ ۝

Tell My servants who have
attained to faith that they
should attend regularly to their
prayers and spend [in My way],
secretly and openly, out of the
sustenance We provide for them,
before a day shall come when
there will be no trading and no
friendship. (31)

قُل لِّعِبَادِيَ الَّذِينَ ءَامَنُوا يُقِيمُوا الصَّلَوٰةَ
وَيُنفِقُوا مِمَّا رَزَقْنَٰهُمْ سِرًّا وَعَلَانِيَةً
مِّن قَبْلِ أَن يَأْتِيَ يَوْمٌ لَّا بَيْعٌ فِيهِ
وَلَا خِلَٰلٌ ۝

269

It is God who has created the heavens and the earth, and who sends down water from the sky with which He brings forth fruits for your sustenance. He has placed under your service ships which by His leave sail through the sea, and He has made the rivers subservient to [His law] for your benefit. (32)

اللَّهُ الَّذِى خَلَقَ السَّمَـٰوَٰتِ وَالْأَرْضَ وَأَنزَلَ مِنَ السَّمَآءِ مَآءً فَأَخْرَجَ بِهِۦ مِنَ الثَّمَرَٰتِ رِزْقًا لَّكُمْ وَسَخَّرَ لَكُمُ الْفُلْكَ لِتَجْرِىَ فِى الْبَحْرِ بِأَمْرِهِۦ وَسَخَّرَ لَكُمُ الْأَنْهَـٰرَ ﴿٣٢﴾

And for your benefit He has made the sun and the moon, both diligently pursuing their courses, subservient to [His law]; and has made the night and the day subservient to [His law]. (33)

وَسَخَّرَ لَكُمُ الشَّمْسَ وَالْقَمَرَ دَآئِبَيْنِ وَسَخَّرَ لَكُمُ الَّيْلَ وَالنَّهَارَ ﴿٣٣﴾

And He gives you of everything you ask of Him. Should you try to count God's blessings, you will never be able to compute them. Yet man is persistent in wrongdoing, stubbornly ungrateful. (34)

وَءَاتَـٰكُم مِّن كُلِّ مَا سَأَلْتُمُوهُ وَإِن تَعُدُّواْ نِعْمَتَ اللَّهِ لَا تُحْصُوهَآ إِنَّ الْإِنسَـٰنَ لَظَلُومٌ كَفَّارٌ ﴿٣٤﴾

Abraham said: 'My Lord! Make this land secure, and preserve me and my children from ever worshipping idols. (35)

وَإِذْ قَالَ إِبْرَٰهِيمُ رَبِّ اجْعَلْ هَـٰذَا الْبَلَدَ ءَامِنًا وَاجْنُبْنِى وَبَنِىَّ أَن نَّعْبُدَ الْأَصْنَامَ ﴿٣٥﴾

My Lord, they have indeed led many people astray. Hence, he who follows me belongs to me. As for him who disobeys me, well, You are truly Much-Forgiving, Merciful. (36)

رَبِّ إِنَّهُنَّ أَضْلَلْنَ كَثِيرًا مِّنَ النَّاسِ فَمَن تَبِعَنِى فَإِنَّهُۥ مِنِّى وَمَنْ عَصَانِى فَإِنَّكَ غَفُورٌ رَّحِيمٌ ﴿٣٦﴾

Our Lord, I have settled some of my offspring in a valley without cultivation, by Your Sacred House, so that they may establish regular prayers. So, cause You people's hearts to incline towards them, and provide them with fruits, so that they may give thanks. (37)

رَبَّنَآ إِنِّى أَسْكَنتُ مِن ذُرِّيَّتِى بِوَادٍ غَيْرِ ذِى زَرْعٍ عِندَ بَيْتِكَ ٱلْمُحَرَّمِ رَبَّنَا لِيُقِيمُوا۟ ٱلصَّلَوٰةَ فَٱجْعَلْ أَفْـِٔدَةً مِّنَ ٱلنَّاسِ تَهْوِىٓ إِلَيْهِمْ وَٱرْزُقْهُم مِّنَ ٱلثَّمَرَٰتِ لَعَلَّهُمْ يَشْكُرُونَ ۝٣٧

Our Lord, You certainly know all that we conceal and all that we bring into the open: for nothing whatever, on earth or in heaven, can be hidden from God. (38)

رَبَّنَآ إِنَّكَ تَعْلَمُ مَا نُخْفِى وَمَا نُعْلِنُ وَمَا يَخْفَىٰ عَلَى ٱللَّهِ مِن شَىْءٍ فِى ٱلْأَرْضِ وَلَا فِى ٱلسَّمَآءِ ۝٣٨

All praise is due to God who has given me, in my old age, Ishmael and Isaac. Surely my Lord hears all prayers. (39)

ٱلْحَمْدُ لِلَّهِ ٱلَّذِى وَهَبَ لِى عَلَى ٱلْكِبَرِ إِسْمَٰعِيلَ وَإِسْحَٰقَ إِنَّ رَبِّى لَسَمِيعُ ٱلدُّعَآءِ ۝٣٩

My Lord, cause me and [some of] my offspring to establish regular prayers. My Lord, accept my prayer. (40)

رَبِّ ٱجْعَلْنِى مُقِيمَ ٱلصَّلَوٰةِ وَمِن ذُرِّيَّتِى رَبَّنَا وَتَقَبَّلْ دُعَآءِ ۝٤٠

Our Lord, grant Your forgiveness to me and my parents, and all the believers on the Day when the reckoning will come to pass.' (41)

رَبَّنَا ٱغْفِرْ لِى وَلِوَٰلِدَىَّ وَلِلْمُؤْمِنِينَ يَوْمَ يَقُومُ ٱلْحِسَابُ ۝٤١

Never think that God is unaware of what the wrongdoers are doing. He only grants them respite till the Day when eyes will stare fixedly in horror, (42)

وَلَا تَحْسَبَنَّ ٱللَّهَ غَٰفِلًا عَمَّا يَعْمَلُ ٱلظَّٰلِمُونَ إِنَّمَا يُؤَخِّرُهُمْ لِيَوْمٍ تَشْخَصُ فِيهِ ٱلْأَبْصَٰرُ ﴿٤٢﴾

when they will be dashing in confusion, with their heads lifted up, unable to turn their eyes from what they behold, and their hearts an utter void. (43)

مُهْطِعِينَ مُقْنِعِي رُءُوسِهِمْ لَا يَرْتَدُّ إِلَيْهِمْ طَرْفُهُمْ وَأَفْئِدَتُهُمْ هَوَاءٌ ﴿٤٣﴾

Hence, warn mankind of the Day when suffering may befall them; when those who do wrong will say: 'Our Lord, grant us respite for a short while, so that we may respond to Your call and follow Your messengers.' 'Why? Did you not in time past swear that you would suffer no decline? (44)

وَأَنذِرِ ٱلنَّاسَ يَوْمَ يَأْتِيهِمُ ٱلْعَذَابُ فَيَقُولُ ٱلَّذِينَ ظَلَمُواْ رَبَّنَا أَخِّرْنَا إِلَىٰٓ أَجَلٍ قَرِيبٍ نُّجِبْ دَعْوَتَكَ وَنَتَّبِعِ ٱلرُّسُلَ أَوَلَمْ تَكُونُواْ أَقْسَمْتُم مِّن قَبْلُ مَا لَكُم مِّن زَوَالٍ ﴿٤٤﴾

And you dwelt in the dwellings of those who wronged their own souls before you. Yet you knew for certain how We had dealt with them, and We placed many examples before you.' (45)

وَسَكَنتُمْ فِي مَسَٰكِنِ ٱلَّذِينَ ظَلَمُوٓاْ أَنفُسَهُمْ وَتَبَيَّنَ لَكُمْ كَيْفَ فَعَلْنَا بِهِمْ وَضَرَبْنَا لَكُمُ ٱلْأَمْثَالَ ﴿٤٥﴾

They devised their plots, but their plots are all within God's grasp, even though their plots are so powerful as to move mountains. (46)

وَقَدْ مَكَرُواْ مَكْرَهُمْ وَعِندَ ٱللَّهِ مَكْرُهُمْ وَإِن كَانَ مَكْرُهُمْ لِتَزُولَ مِنْهُ ٱلْجِبَالُ ﴿٤٦﴾

Never think that God may ever fail to fulfil the promise which He has given to His messengers. Indeed God is Almighty, avenger of evil! (47)

فَلَا تَحْسَبَنَّ ٱللَّهَ مُخْلِفَ وَعْدِهِۦ رُسُلَهُۥٓ إِنَّ ٱللَّهَ عَزِيزٌ ذُو ٱنتِقَامٍ ۝

On the day when the earth shall be changed into another earth, as shall be the heavens, and when all people stand before God, the One who holds sway over all that exists. (48)

يَوْمَ تُبَدَّلُ ٱلْأَرْضُ غَيْرَ ٱلْأَرْضِ وَٱلسَّمَٰوَٰتُ وَبَرَزُواْ لِلَّهِ ٱلْوَٰحِدِ ٱلْقَهَّارِ ۝

On that day you will see the guilty chained together in fetters, (49)

وَتَرَى ٱلْمُجْرِمِينَ يَوْمَئِذٍ مُّقَرَّنِينَ فِى ٱلْأَصْفَادِ ۝

wearing garments of black pitch, and their faces covered with flames. (50)

سَرَابِيلُهُم مِّن قَطِرَانٍ وَتَغْشَىٰ وُجُوهَهُمُ ٱلنَّارُ ۝

God will requite each soul according to what it has done. God is indeed swift in reckoning. (51)

لِيَجْزِىَ ٱللَّهُ كُلَّ نَفْسٍ مَّا كَسَبَتْ إِنَّ ٱللَّهَ سَرِيعُ ٱلْحِسَابِ ۝

This is a message to all mankind. Let them be warned thereby, and let them know that He is the One and Only God. Let those who are endowed with insight take heed. (52)

هَٰذَا بَلَٰغٌ لِّلنَّاسِ وَلِيُنذَرُواْ بِهِۦ وَلِيَعْلَمُوٓاْ أَنَّمَا هُوَ إِلَٰهٌ وَٰحِدٌ وَلِيَذَّكَّرَ أُوْلُواْ ٱلْأَلْبَٰبِ ۝

Overview

This second part of the *sūrah* begins where the first ends. The first part outlined the purpose of the Prophet Muḥammad's message, namely, "*to bring forth all mankind, by their Lord's leave, from darkness into the light.*" (Verse 1) And it outlined the purpose of Moses's message: "*Lead your people out of darkness into the light, and remind them of the Days of God.*" (Verse 5) He explained to them his message and reminded them of God's favours and blessings. He also announced what God had promised them: "*If you are grateful, I shall certainly give you more; but if you are ungrateful, then My punishment shall be severe indeed.*" (Verse 7) He then related to them the history of prophets with communities who refused to believe them. In fact he began this narrative, but immediately disappeared to let the *sūrah* relate it with magnificent theatre, culminating in the scene where the unbelievers listen to Satan giving them a memorable lesson, which comes too late to be of any benefit.

Now the *sūrah* turns to the unbelievers among the Prophet Muḥammad's community, who have been given a long reel showing the great episodes of history. These people have indeed been blessed with many favours granted to them by God. One such major favour is the fact that God sent them a messenger to bring them out of darkness into light, and to call on them to repent so that they might receive His forgiveness. But they reject God's blessings, and deny His message. The second part of the *sūrah* starts then with an expression of amazement at such people who lead their communities to destruction, just like those before them who led their followers to hell.

It goes on to portray some of the aspects of God's favours in one of the greatest scenes of the universe. It then provides an example of thanksgiving by Abraham. This example follows a clear order to the believers to offer prayers and be kind to people as an aspect of thanksgiving. They must do so before a day comes when wealth can no longer grow and no buying or selling can take place. As for the unbelievers, they are not just forgotten. They are given respite until a day comes when eyes are opened wide. God's promise to His messengers will inevitably be fulfilled, no matter what the unbelievers scheme against them. All this indicates that the second part of the *sūrah* is in full harmony with the first, one complementing the other.

Bartering away God's Blessings

This passage begins with drawing attention to a highly singular state of affairs: *"Have you not seen those who have exchanged God's blessings for unbelief, and landed their people in the House of Perdition, hell, which they will have to endure? How vile a place to settle in! They set up false deities as equal to God, and so they lead people to stray from His path. Say: 'Enjoy yourselves [in this life], for you will surely end up in hell.'"* (Verses 28–30)

These are people who have been granted God's blessings in the form of a prophet sent to call on them to believe in God, and to lead them along the way to God's forgiveness of their sins, and to a heavenly destiny. Yet they abandon all this and choose instead a state of unbelief. These, the Prophet is told, are the chiefs of his own people who follow the same practice as the elders or the chiefs of most communities. Thus by their singular exchange, they lead their communities to hell. Just as we have seen in the histories of past nations and communities mentioned earlier in the *sūrah*, they land their people in hell. It is a vile and ignominious abode.

The *sūrah* invites the Prophet, and every believer, to marvel at the curious behaviour of such people, particularly since they have seen what happened to earlier communities. All this has been portrayed for their benefit in this *sūrah* in a most vivid way, accounting for what took place between the unbelievers and the messengers sent to them. It was all shown to them as if it were taking place before their very eyes. In fact, the Qur'ān only portrays what is going to take place in the hereafter as if it is happening now, or just happened before our very eyes.

These people have exchanged God's blessing of a messenger sent to them with disbelief. The messenger called on them to believe in God alone and to associate no partners with Him, but they abandoned all this, and *"they set up false deities as equal to God, and so they lead people to stray from His path."* (Verse 30) They place their false deities in a position equal to that of God, and offer worship to them as they would offer it to Him. They submit to these false deities as they would submit to Him, and they attribute to them some of the attributes that belong only to God. They thus lead people astray from the only straight path leading to God, the only deity in the universe.

The chiefs or elders have deliberately misguided their own people, leading them astray by claiming that their false deities were equal to God. The fact, however, is that the faith based on God's oneness represents a threat to the power and vested interests of tyrannical forces in every generation, not merely in this first period of *jāhiliyyah* when the Prophet preached his message. Whenever people turn away from the pure faith based on God's oneness, whatever shape this may take, and assign their leadership to others, they revert to a state of un-Islam, or *jāhiliyyah*. In such a state, people surrender their own freedom and personality, follow their desires and implement laws enacted on the basis of their leaders' desires instead of deriving them from God's revelations. In such a situation the advocacy of God's oneness becomes a threat to those chiefs and their interests. Hence, they try to avert this threat in every way open to them. In older forms of *jāhiliyyah*, this took the shape of adopting false deities, claiming that they were equal to God. In our present time, it takes the form of implementing man-made laws that permit what God has not permitted and prohibit what He has made lawful. Those who enact such laws are thus placed on an equal footing with God in the way people look at them and in everyday life as well.

Hence, the Prophet is instructed to say to such people that they may enjoy themselves in this life as they please, but that this enjoyment will last only for the limit God has determined. The eventual outcome is well known: "*Say: 'Enjoy yourselves [in this life], for you will surely end up in hell.'*" (Verse 30)

The Prophet is further instructed to leave these people alone, not to trouble himself with them any more. Instead he should address God's servants who have accepted the faith. These are the people who will take heed when they are warned against evil. They accept God's blessings and appreciate them, and will never exchange them for disbelief. The Prophet is to address these people and teach them how to be grateful for God's blessings. They should express their gratitude through worship, obedience to God and kindness to His servants: "*Tell My servants who have attained to faith that they should attend regularly to their prayers and spend [in My way], secretly and openly, out of the sustenance We provide for them, before a day shall come when there will be no trading and no friendship.*" (Verse 31)

God commands His Messenger to say to those who have attained to faith that they should express their gratitude to God by establishing regular prayer, for prayer is the most express form of gratitude to God. They should also spend in charity out of the sustenance God provides for them, and make such spending both in secret and in public. Secret charity protects the dignity of the taker and enhances the virtue of the giver. This ensures that charity does not become a source of pride and arrogance. Charitable spending in public serves to demonstrate obedience to God's orders, and provides a good example to others in the community. Both ways are left to the discretion and sensitivities of every believer.

The believers are told to spend on others now so that their balance which is preserved for them increases through gains they make by charitable spending. This they have to do before a day comes when there is no longer any possibility for wealth to grow, or friendship to bring any benefit. What is of benefit to people is only the good works they have already done, for their reward is stored: "*Tell My servants who have attained to faith that they should attend regularly to their prayers and spend [in My way], secretly and openly, out of the sustenance We provide for them, before a day shall come when there will be no trading and no friendship.*" (Verse 31)

God's Numerous Blessings

At this point, the *sūrah* opens the book of the universe where every page speaks of God's countless blessings. These extend beyond the furthest point our senses can reach, and go into the skies, the earth, the sun, the moon, the day and night, the water pouring down from the skies and the fruits of all plants on earth, the oceans and seas where ships and boats sail, and the rivers flowing with the different means of producing what sustains life. All these universal images are available for all to see, but people do not look, reflect or express gratitude. Man is truly unjust, ingrate, exchanging God's blessings for unbelief, and setting up deities which he claims to be equal to God, when it is God who creates, sustains and controls the universe and all creatures therein: "*It is God who has created the heavens and the earth, and who sends down water from the sky with which He brings forth fruits for your sustenance. He has placed under your service ships which by His leave sail through the sea, and He has made the rivers subservient to [His law] for your benefit. And for your benefit He has made the sun and the moon, both diligently pursuing their courses, subservient to [His law]; and has made the night and the day subservient to [His law]. And He gives you of everything you ask of Him. Should you try to count God's blessings, you will never be able to compute them. Yet man is persistent in wrongdoing, stubbornly ungrateful."* (Verses 32–34)

These verses represent an onslaught that employs such universal phenomena as tools, or rather as whips with rhythm and sound to awaken the conscience of man, a creature indulging in wrongdoing and lacking gratitude. One aspect of the unique nature of the Qur'ān is the way it relates everything in the universe and every human feeling to belief in God's oneness. Thus, every flash of inspiration in the universe and in man's conscience becomes proof confirming this belief. The universe is transformed into an exhibition of God's signs where the magnificence of His hand excels so as to leave its distinct mark in every image, feature and shadow. The basic question of Godhead and servitude is not presented as a logical debate or an abstract theological argument, or an issue of metaphysical philosophy. Such methods do not appeal to, influence or inspire the human heart. The Qur'ān presents this central issue within a framework of a multitude of inspiring scenes and facts from the great universe, creation, human nature and basic thoughts and impressions, adding an element of breathtaking beauty and superb harmony.

The great scene of God's blessings that is presented here is painted with fascinating skill, drawing its lines in the same directions the different blessings take in relation to man. This is noticeable in the line of the heavens and the earth, followed by that of water pouring down from the skies and plants and fruits shooting up from the earth. We then have a line depicting the oceans with ships sailing on their surface and rivers flowing with much bounty. A new line takes us back to the skies to show us the sun and the moon, coupled with the line of the night and day, which is closely connected to the sun and moon but remains firm on earth. The final line is comprehensive, throwing its colour and shade over the whole panoramic scene: *"And He gives you of everything you ask of Him. Should you try to count God's blessings, you will never be able to compute them."* (Verse 34) Here we see a harmony that incorporates every touch, line, colour and shade in a universal scene of God's blessings.

Is all this placed at man's service? Is this whole world, with its heavens, earth, seas, rivers, sun and moon, day and night, made subservient to the small creature known as man? Is it so, and still man does not give thanks or even remember God's favours? Hence, it is indeed true that *"man is persistent in wrongdoing, stubbornly ungrateful."* (Verse 34)

"It is God who has created the heavens and the earth." (Verse 32) Yet people set up deities and regard them as equal to Him. What more injustice could there be?

"And who sends down water from the sky with which He brings forth fruits for your sustenance." (Verse 32) Plants are the first means of sustenance and the most visible source of God's blessings. Rain and the growth of plants run in accordance with the nature God has given this world and the natural laws that allow rain to fall, plants to shoot and fruits to ripen, making all this compatible with man and his nature. For a single seed to grow requires that the Power that controls the whole universe utilizes universal phenomena to give that seed the ability to produce a plant and then provide it with the necessary means of life, such as a fertile place, water, sunlight and air. When people hear the word *rizq,* which we often translate as sustenance or a means of sustenance, they think only of their livelihood, earning money. But the Arabic term has much wider connotations. It includes everything that God provides for man. Even the smallest of such provisions requires operating celestial bodies in accordance with a law that ensures that several hundred thousands of matching conditions fall together in a coherent and complementary way, without which man could not have come into existence and, once existing, his life could not be sustained. It is sufficient to mention the celestial bodies and phenomena referred to in these verses to understand how we can only function when we are under God's care.

"He has placed under your service ships which by His leave sail through the sea." (Verse 32) It is He who has placed in the sea all that is necessary for these ships to float, and it is He who has given man the ability to understand natural phenomena and rules so as to use them for his benefit.

"*And He has made the rivers subservient to [His law] for your benefit.*" (Verse 32) The rivers flow and life flourishes, and they overflow and man gets an increase of goodness. Rivers also carry fish, weeds and many other things that are useful to man and to other creatures man uses such as birds and cattle.

"*And for your benefit He has made the sun and the moon, both diligently pursuing their courses, subservient to [His law].*" (Verse 33) Man does not use the sun and the moon directly as he uses water, the fruit, the seas, ships and rivers. Yet he benefits by them and derives from them substances and energies that are required to sustain life. Thus they are made subject to God's law which controls the universe, so that they produce what is of benefit to man in his life on earth, and indeed in the make-up and renewal of the cells of his own body.

"*And has made the night and the day subservient to [His law].*" (Verse 33) Again both night and day are made subservient so as to fit with the needs and constitution of man and with his time of activity and that of rest. Had there been permanent day or permanent night, man's whole functioning would have been destroyed, as would the whole world around him. His life would have been impossible, inactive and unproductive.

Yet all that the *sūrah* portrays consists of general lines that gather glimpses of God's blessings. In each line there are countless points. Therefore, a general aspect is added here without any detail so that it fits with the overall scene: "*And He gives you of everything you ask of Him.*" (Verse 34) That includes whatever people ask of wealth, offspring, health, luxuries and refinements. "*Should you try to count God's blessings, you will never be able to compute them.*" (Verse 34) Indeed they are too many to be computed by any one person, or by all human beings, for humans are restricted to a period of time with definite beginning and end. They are also restricted to certain limits of knowledge within time and space. God's favours and blessings, however, are not only numerous, but also unlimited. Hence, they are beyond human reckoning.

Yet despite all this, human beings adopt false deities and consider them equal to God. And instead of thanking God for His blessings, they exchange them for unbelief. Certainly "*man is persistent in wrongdoing, totally ungrateful.*" (Verse 34)

Passionate Prayer by a Devoted Believer

When man's conscience is awakened, he looks at the universe around him and realizes that it is made for his benefit, either directly or through the harmony between its laws and human life and needs. When he looks around him, he finds it all made friendly by God's grace, and by His power and permission it is both helpful and useful. When man considers and contemplates, he must stand in awe of his Lord, prostrate himself and express his gratitude. He always looks up to his Lord to replace with ease any hardship he may be going through, and to preserve any aspect of grace and happiness he may be enjoying.

The perfect example of a human being who always remembers God and expresses his gratitude to Him is Abraham, the father of prophets. His truly thankful character imparts a definite ambience to the whole *sūrah*, which also reflects God's grace and how it is received with gratitude or ingratitude. Abraham is shown here in a scene of devotion, making a heartfelt appeal to God. His melodious supplication is inspirational as it rises to God in heaven:

> *Abraham said: 'My Lord! Make this land secure, and preserve me and my children from ever worshipping idols. My Lord, they have indeed led many people astray. Hence, he who follows me belongs to me. As for him who disobeys me, well, You are truly Much-Forgiving, Merciful. Our Lord, I have settled some of my offspring in a valley without cultivation, by Your Sacred House, so that they may establish regular prayers. So, cause You people's hearts to incline towards them, and provide them with fruits, so that they may give thanks. Our Lord, You certainly know all that we conceal and all that we bring into the open: for nothing whatever, on earth or in heaven, can be hidden from God. All praise is due to God who has given me, in my old age, Ishmael and Isaac. Surely my Lord hears all prayers. My Lord, cause me and [some of] my offspring to establish regular prayers. My Lord, accept my prayer. Our Lord, grant Your forgiveness to me and my parents, and all the believers on the Day when the reckoning will come to pass.' (Verses 35–41)*

Here Abraham is shown in front of the House he built for God in Makkah, and whose custody has passed to the Quraysh, an Arabian tribe bent on disbelief in God, yet benefiting by the House built for the worship of God alone. Abraham is shown addressing his supplication with perfect devotion and heartfelt gratitude. This should make the ungrateful reflect and revise their attitude. It should make the unbelievers turn back to faith, and the oblivious remember God. It should make people generally follow Abraham in his exemplary attitude.

Abraham begins his supplication by saying: "*My Lord! Make this land secure.*" (Verse 35) Security and safety is so important for man, for it is intertwined with his survival. The *sūrah* mentions this here so as to remind of it the people of Makkah who enjoy it as if it was theirs by right, and who do not give thanks for it. They forget that it is the result of answering the supplication made by Abraham, their first father. Hence, they follow a course which is different from that of Abraham. They turn away from pure faith, yet the second prayer in Abraham's supplication is: "*And preserve me and my children from ever worshipping idols.*" (Verse 35)

This second aspect with which Abraham opens his prayer reflects his total submission to God, and his turning to Him in the deepest recesses of his heart. He appeals to Him for help in steering away, together with his children, from idol worship. He also makes it clear that to be so preserved is yet another of God's blessings. It is indeed a great blessing that one's heart is saved from the darkness of polytheism and its ignorance in order to be brought into the light of faith in God and belief in His oneness. This blessing takes a human being out of error, loss and confusion to the comfort of knowledge, reassurance and stability, and out of humiliating submission to a variety of false lords to honourable submission to God, the Lord of all worlds. Abraham appeals to God to maintain this blessing for him by preserving him and his children from the worship of idols.

Abraham is fully aware of the great number of people in his generation and previous generations who went astray when they were deluded by such idols. Hence, he addresses his passionate appeal to God to spare him from such delusion: "*My Lord, they have indeed led many people astray.*" (Verse 36)

Abraham continues his supplication stating that whoever follows his way and does not give in to idol worship belongs to him, as they would have the strongest bond of faith joining them together. "*Hence, he who follows me belongs to me.*" (Verse 36) The others who disobey him he leaves to God to determine what He does with them: "*As for him who disobeys me, well, You are truly Much-Forgiving, Merciful.*" (Verse 36)

In this last prayer we see Abraham, the caring, forbearing and compassionate. He does not pray to God to destroy those of his offspring who leave his path of guidance. He does not precipitate God's punishment. Indeed he does not even mention punishment. Instead, he leaves them to God, to His forgiveness and mercy. Thus Abraham lends to the whole scene an air of forgiveness and compassion, leaving the taint of disobedience to disappear altogether. Compassionate as he is, Abraham does not let it appear again.

Continuing his supplication, Abraham mentions the fact that he settled some of his offspring in a barren valley where there was no cultivation, next to God's Sacred House and also states the task they were settled there to perform: "*Our Lord, I have settled some of my offspring in a valley without cultivation, by Your Sacred House, so that they may establish regular prayers.*" (Verse 37)

So this is the task for the performance of which they have migrated and for which they are to tolerate a life of poverty and lack of cultivation. "*So, cause You people's hearts to incline towards them.*" (Verse 37) The style here is tender, reflecting love and compassion. It describes hearts as having wings and coming from the sky to that Sacred House and its neighbours in that barren valley. Its tenderness counterbalances the hardship of a barren place with the inclination of loving hearts.

"*And provide them with fruits.*" (Verse 37) Why does Abraham pray that they should have such fruit? To eat and enjoy themselves? Certainly, but also to bring about what Abraham, exemplary in his gratitude to his Lord, hopes for: "*so that they may give thanks.*" (Verse 37)

Thus the purpose of settling close to the Sacred House is given prominence. It is to establish regular prayer in the most devoted and pure form. Similarly, the purpose of the prayer to incline people's hearts to the dwellers in the neighbourhood of the Sacred House and their abundant provision from the fruits of the earth is to give thanks to God who provides all. With such a passionate prayer, there is an evident irony in the attitude of the Quraysh, the Arabian tribe living near the

Ka'bah at the time of the Prophet. They offered no worship to God, and no thanks after Abraham's prayer had been answered, giving them people's love and abundant provisions.

Abraham follows this prayer with an acknowledgement that God knows all that people harbour in their hearts and when they turn to God with thanks and sincere supplication. It is not vocal appearances that are meant here. It is what a person feels deep in his heart, and the way he addresses God, who knows what we reveal and conceal. Indeed, nothing in heaven and earth is hidden from God's knowledge: "*Our Lord, You certainly know all that we conceal and all that we bring into the open: for nothing whatever, on earth or in heaven, can be hidden from God.*" (Verse 38)

Abraham then mentions an aspect of grace which God has shown him, and he praises God for it and thanks Him, providing an example for all believers. They must not forget God's grace, and they must always be thankful for it. "*All praise is due to God who has given me, in my old age, Ishmael and Isaac. Surely my Lord hears all prayers.*" (Verse 39) Giving a person children when he has attained to old age is felt more keenly, because children represent the extension of one's life into another generation. This is a great feeling for an elderly person who begins to think life is approaching its end. The need to feel the continuity represented by children is thus instinctive. Hence, Abraham praises God and prays for more of God's grace: "*Surely my Lord hears all prayers.*" (Verse 39)

A Prayer for All Time

Abraham follows his thanksgiving with a supplication to God to make him always thankful. His thanks take the form of prayer, worship and obedience to God. Thus he declares his determination to always be a devout worshipper, but fears that something may divert him from it. Hence, he prays that God may help him to carry out his intention: "*My Lord, cause me and [some of] my offspring to establish regular prayers. My Lord, accept my prayer.*" (Verse 40)

Abraham's supplication shows the irony in the Quraysh's attitude, the Arab tribe which had custody of the Ka'bah. Abraham is appealing to God for help to attend to his prayers, and to enable him to perform these at all times. They, however, turn away from it, denying the truth of what God's Messenger tells them of how Abraham prayed for himself and his offspring. Now, Abraham concludes his humble supplication by appealing to God to forgive him and forgive his parents and all believers. He prays for that forgiveness to be forthcoming on the Day of Judgement when nothing is of benefit to anyone except the good works he or she may have done in life and God's forgiveness for what they might have committed or omitted to do: "*Our Lord, grant Your forgiveness to me and my parents, and all the believers on the Day when the reckoning will come to pass.*" (Verse 41)

Abraham's long and humble supplication, which also mentions a number of God's blessings and expresses gratitude and thanks for them, employing a fine musical rhythm, now comes to a close. It imparts an air of gentle tenderness and care which makes people's hearts long to be with God, and remember His grace and blessings. Abraham, the father of a long line of prophets, is seen as a pious servant who does not forget His Lord's grace, or his duty to be thankful for it. He is given as an example to be followed by God's servants who truly believe in Him, for, just before relating Abraham's supplication, the *sūrah* addressed them. We note how Abraham repeats several times the addressing phrase, "*My Lord*" or "*Our Lord*". This repeated acknowledgement of God's Lordship over him and his offspring is significant. He does not mention God by His attribute of Godhead, but instead by His Lordship. Godhead has rarely been subject to controversy even in *jāhiliyyah* societies. Nor was it so in the ignorant society of Arabia at the advent of Islam. What people have always argued about is the Lordship of God, and the need to submit to Him in everyday life on earth.

This is in fact the central point between submission to God, and believing in His oneness on the one hand, and the association of partners with Him on the other. People either submit to God, and this means that they acknowledge Him as their Lord, or they submit to others who would become their lords. This makes all the difference in life. The Qur'ān relates Abraham's supplication to the Arab idolaters, emphasizing his acknowledgement of God's Lordship to draw their attention to the fact that their own way of life was in complete contrast with what this supplication truly signifies.

No Heeding of Past Lessons

The *sūrah* moves on with its presentation of these issues, speaking to those "*who have exchanged God's blessings for unbelief, and landed their people in the House of Perdition.*" (Verse 28) It speaks to them as they continue with their erring ways, before they are subjected to God's punishment. They are the ones whom the Prophet had been told to say to them: "*Enjoy yourselves in this life, for you will surely end up in hell.*" (Verse 30) He is further ordered to address those who believe in God, and to command them to offer their prayers and pay their *zakāt*: "*Tell My servants who have attained to faith that they should attend regularly to their prayers and spend [in My way], secretly and openly, out of the sustenance We provide for them, before a day shall come when there will be no trading and no friendship.*" (Verse 31)

Here the *sūrah* completes the picture, showing what God has prepared for those unbelievers who deny God's blessings, and tells when they will face their inevitable destiny. This comes in quick images of the Day of Judgement which fill our hearts with fear: "*Never think that God is unaware of what the wrongdoers are doing. He only grants them respite till the Day when eyes will stare fixedly in horror, when they will be dashing in confusion, with their heads lifted up, unable to turn their eyes from what they behold, and their hearts an utter void.*" (Verses 42–43)

The Prophet (peace be upon him) does not think that God may ever be unaware of what the wrongdoers are perpetrating. It might appear so to some people who see the wrongdoers enjoying a comfortable life in this world. Such people hear God's warning, but see nothing of it taking place in this life. This explains the deadline which is fixed for their final punishment when they are given no further respite. That takes place on the day when eyes stare fixedly in horror, unable even to wink. The fear is so great that there is no blinking of a single eyelid.

This is followed by a picture of people rushing everywhere, unable to turn their faces to anything. Their heads are raised upward, but this is unintentional for they cannot move their heads. As they see the fearsome scene ahead of them, their eyes are fixed and their hearts are void, containing nothing they remember or understand. They are all empty.

It is to this day that God delays the wrongdoers' punishment. Now they stand in their position, overwhelmed by fear. In this scene they are like a small bird caught in the claws of a predator: "*Never think that God is unaware of what the wrongdoers are doing. He only grants them respite till the Day when eyes will stare fixedly in horror, when they will be dashing in confusion, with their heads lifted up, unable to turn their eyes from what they behold, and their hearts an utter void.*" (Verses 42–43)

The Prophet is required to warn people that when this day arrives, there can be no excuses given and no evasion of responsibility. Another picture is then drawn of this horrific day: "*Hence, warn mankind of the Day when suffering may befall them; when those who do wrong will say: 'Our Lord, grant us respite for a short while, so that we may respond to Your call and follow Your messengers.' 'Why? Did you not in time past swear that you would suffer no decline? And you dwelt in the dwellings of those who wronged their own souls before you. Yet you knew for certain how We had dealt with them, and We placed many examples before you.'*" (Verses 44–45)

Warn them against the day when the suffering drawn earlier is bound to befall them. At this point, the wrongdoers turn to their Lord with an urgent appeal, saying: "*Our Lord!*" Now they say this while earlier they were bent on unbelief, associating partners with Him: "*Our Lord, grant us respite for a short while, so that we may respond to Your call and follow Your messengers.*" (Verse 44)

At this point the flow of the discourse is changed from the narrative form to that of an address, as though they are now at that point, staring fixedly in horror, making their passionate appeal. This whole world is rolled over and we seem to be already in the hereafter, and they are being reproached from on high, reminded of the wrongs they used to do in their first life: "*Why, did you not in time past swear that you would suffer no decline?*" (Verse 44) How do you see yourselves now? Have you suffered any decline? You asserted this when you had in front of your eyes the ruins of those who went before you, giving proof of what happened to them and their inevitable destiny.

"*And you dwelt in the dwellings of those who wronged their own souls before you. Yet you knew for certain how We had dealt with them, and We placed many examples before you.*" (Verse 45) It is amazing that you should see the dwellings of former wrongdoers, testifying to what happened to them, and you dwelling in their place, and yet you swear that you would not suffer a decline. With this hard reproach the scene is completed. We understand what happens to them, and what takes place after their appeal and their disappointment.

This example repeatedly occurs throughout history. Many are the wrongdoers who succeed earlier tyrants. In fact, those tyrants were destroyed by their own hands, yet they follow in their footsteps and tyrannize like them. They take no heed of the lessons they see in front of their eyes. Hence, like them, they are put to the same fate. The same dwellings will be rid of them after a while.

The *sūrah* then turns to their present situation, and their wicked scheming against God's Messenger, and their evil devices in every aspect of life. It gives the clear impression that they will face their inevitable destiny, no matter what powerful and elaborate schemes they devise: "*They devised their plots, but their plots are all within God's grasp, even though their plots are so powerful as to move mountains.*" (Verse 46)

God is certainly aware of their scheming, although it may be so strong and powerful that it causes mountains, the strongest and most solid and firm creation, to move. In fact, the last thing any human being would expect to move is a mountain. However, their scheming is in no way hidden from God, and never immune from God's power. It is in front of Him, and He can foil it and do with it what He likes.

Fair Reward for All

The Prophet is told again: "*Never think that God may ever fail to fulfil the promise which He has given to His messengers. Indeed God is Almighty, avenger of evil!*" (Verse 47) What the unbelievers devise is of no consequence. It cannot obstruct the fulfilment of God's promise to His messengers to grant them victory and to inflict a mighty punishment on the unbelievers: "*Indeed God is Almighty, avenger of evil!*" (Verse 47) He does not let injustice escape punishment. Those who resort to scheming and devising foul plans will not be spared. The word "avenge" is especially suitable here as it gives the meaning that counters both injustice and wicked scheming. A perpetrator of such injustice and wickedness deserves to suffer God's vengeance, which is, from God's point of view, the exercise of divine justice.

This is certainly inevitable, *"On the day when the earth shall be changed into another earth, as shall be the heavens."* (Verse 48) We do not know how this happens, nor are we aware of the nature of the new earth or the new heavens, or their respective positions. The statement only gives us an impression of God's might and His ability to change the earth and heavens. By contrast, the schemes the unbelievers devise are all too weak.

Suddenly, we see this as though it has happened: *"When all people stand before God, the One who holds sway over all that exists."* (Verse 48) They realize that they are exposed, without cover or screen to protect them. They are neither in their homes nor in their graves. They stand in the open, in front of the Almighty. The emphasis here is on God's power which cannot be resisted, not even by the scheming of the mighty tyrants which can almost make mountains move.

Then we are shown a scene of the humiliating suffering which stands in contrast to their scheming and tyranny: *"On that day you will see the guilty chained together in fetters, wearing garments of black pitch, and their faces covered with flames."* (Verses 49–50) The evil-doers are thus chained, each two together, and they are made to pass in ranks. Their humiliation is again indicative of God's might. In addition to their being chained together, they wear dirty, black pitch garments that can easily catch fire. The connotations here are humiliation and combustion as they draw near to the fire.

"Their faces [are] covered with flames." It is all a scene of tyrants and schemers made to suffer humiliation and burning in flames. All this is a reward for their arrogance in this life. *"God will requite each soul according to what it had done. God is indeed swift in reckoning."* (Verse 51) All they have earned is their scheming and injustice. Its reward is that they stand powerless, humiliated. The swiftness of God's reckoning contrasts with the scheming they thought would protect them, and ensure them victory. Hence, they are dealt with swiftly to add to their humiliation.

Elimination of Pagan Concepts

The *sūrah* then ends with something similar to its opening, but it comes in the form of an open and loud declaration, intended to inform all mankind: "*This is a message to all mankind. Let them be warned thereby, and let them know that He is the One and Only God. Let those who have insight take heed.*" (Verse 52) The essential purpose of this message and the warning it contains is that people should know that "*He is the One and Only God.*" This is the basic concept of this religion on which its code of living is built.

What is required here is not that people should merely acquire such information. The purpose is that they should conduct their lives on the basis of this knowledge. It is that people should submit to God alone, since He is the One and only God. It is God who deserves to be the Lord, i.e. the Sovereign, the Ruler and the Legislator.

When life is conducted on this basis it becomes totally different from every type of life based on the lordship of creatures, which means that some submit to others who are considered sovereign over them. The difference involves faith, worship, morality, standards and values, behaviour and practices, as well as political, economic and social systems and every aspect of the life of the individual and society alike.

Believing in the One God is the basis of a complete system. It is not merely a matter of conviction. Faith comprises all aspects of life. In the Islamic perspective, sovereignty is a question of faith, as is morality. It is on the basis of faith that the code of life that comprises both moral values and legal matters is based.

We cannot appreciate the extent which faith takes in the Islamic perspective unless we understand the full meaning of the basic declaration every Muslim must make in order to be a Muslim: "I bear witness that there is no deity other than God, and I bear witness that Muḥammad is God's Messenger." We must also be aware of the meaning of addressing all worship to God alone. This means that submission is only to God, not merely during prayer, but in every life situation.

The worship of idols which Abraham prayed to God to spare him and his offspring from does not take only the primitive way which the pagan Arabs and other communities practised. It is not merely the worship of deities made of stones, trees, animals, birds, stars, fire or spirits. To limit the concept of polytheism to this primitive form blurs our view so that we cannot see other forms which may bedevil humanity in different states of *jāhiliyyah*. We need to have a fuller understanding of the nature of associating partners with God, its relevance to idols, and the nature of idols and how they are represented in modern states of ignorance, or *jāhiliyyah*.

Associating partners with God may take any form and be represented in any situation where submission in all aspects of life is not to God alone. It is sufficient that a person should submit to beings other than God in certain aspects of his life to be in a situation of associating partners with God, even though he submits to God alone in the other aspects of his life. Worship is only one aspect of life where submission is reflected. But there are many other forms of submission in human life which give us practical examples of polytheism.

A person may believe that Godhead belongs completely to God alone, and he submits to Him in his prayers, fasting, performing pilgrimage and other aspects of worship, but he may at the same time submit to laws other than God's in his social, economic and political life. He may also submit to concepts other than those approved by God in his social standards and to other human beings in his moral values, traditions, customs and style of dress. Such a person practises polytheism in its essence, in full breach of the meaning of the declaration that "there is no deity other than God and Muḥammad is God's Messenger". This is what people overlook. They take all such matters carelessly, without thinking that they demonstrate the same paganism that has been practised by different communities throughout history.

It is not necessary that idols be represented in primitive form. For idols are mere covers for tyranny which hides behind them in order to impose its authority over people. Yet none of these idols speak, hear or see. Its custodian or priest or the ruler was always around, chanting the idol's praises or acting as its spokesman, but saying what he wants to say. Therefore, when banners or slogans are raised in any community which give rulers or priests the power to put in place laws, values, standards and practices that are at variance with what is acceptable to God, then these are in effect, position and nature deities like those idols of old.

We see today that nationalism, patriotism or a certain class in society or people as a whole are made like banners or slogans which are adored in place of God. People are made to sacrifice for such banners their lives, property, morals and even their honour. Whenever divine law and its requirements come in conflict with what the service of such banners and slogans requires, then God's law is set aside and the requirements of these banners are met. To be more accurate we should say that it is the requirements of the tyrants standing behind these banners that are fulfilled. This is indeed a form of idol worship, because an idol need not be made of wood or stone. It can be represented in a doctrine or a slogan.

The role of Islam is not only to destroy wood or stone idols. That was not the purpose of all the efforts and sacrifices made by God's messengers and their followers in history. Islam aims rather to establish in a very clear way the difference between submission to God alone in all matters and affairs and submission to other beings or entities. It is necessary to look carefully at forms and appearances in every situation to establish whether the existing order conforms to the concept of God's oneness or to a form of paganism.

People may imagine themselves to be following the faith revealed by God because they declare, "There is no deity except God, and Muḥammad is God's Messenger", and they submit to God in all matters of worship and in marriage, divorce and inheritance. Yet when matters go beyond this narrow aspect, their submission is to other beings. They follow laws that are in clear conflict with what God has legislated. They even sacrifice their lives, property, honour and morals, willingly or unwillingly, to fulfil what this neo-paganism requires of them, even when it is in conflict with what is acceptable to God. They are thus totally mistaken when they imagine that they follow Islam. They should wake up and realize that theirs is a situation of clear paganism.

Divine faith is not as hollow as it is imagined to be by some of those who claim to be Muslims. It is a complete way of life that comprises all the necessary details for daily life. Submission to God's law in the details of daily life, as well as in basic principles and concepts, is the core of the divine faith. It is Islam in its true sense, which is the only form acceptable to God.

As stated earlier, polytheism does not only take the form of believing in multiple deities and claiming that they are God's partners. It is instead the acknowledgement of other lords alongside Him. Idol worship is represented in adopting banners and slogans which are given the same sort of authority as belonged to idols of old. People everywhere then must examine their lives to determine whom they actually submit to. If they submit totally to God, obeying His orders and laws to the exclusion of any other, then they follow the divine faith. If not, then they have a religion based on idol worship. This is a terrible situation indeed.

This is a message to all mankind. Let them be warned thereby, and let them know that He is the One and Only God. Let those who are endowed with insight take heed. (Verse 52)

SŪRAH 15

Al-Ḥijr

Prologue

Proper Understanding Required

This *sūrah* was revealed in Makkah, after the revelation of *Sūrah* 12, Joseph. The time was a very critical one, falling as it did between the 'year of sorrow' when the Prophet lost his wife Khadījah and his uncle Abū Ṭālib and the year when the Prophet migrated to Madinah. The *sūrah* thus reflects the needs and requirements of this difficult period. For specifics about this crucial time please refer to the Prologues of *Sūrahs* Jonah and Hūd, in Volume IX, and *Sūrah* Joseph in this volume.

In particular, the *sūrah* directs the Prophet and the Muslim community in how best to deal with their practical problems, and how to stand firm in the face of the unbelievers' stubborn opposition. This then is the role and nature of the Qur'ān.

At this critical juncture, the message of Islam was making little progress because of the unwavering resistance of the Quraysh, the Arabian tribe residing in Makkah, and whose leadership was recognized by the rest of Arabia. Their persecution of the Prophet and his followers was now at its zenith. Hence, the Qur'ān warns and threatens these pagan Arabs, portraying as it does the fate of earlier communities which denied God's messages and opposed His messengers. It reveals to the Prophet the real reasons behind their determined opposition. Essentially it had nothing to do with the truth of his message and much to do with their stubbornness which could not be moderated even as a result of seeing God's clear signs. Hence, the *sūrah* consoles the Prophet. It directs him to hold fast to the truth he has and to confront with it all those who reject it. He is also instructed to remain patient in adversity, conveying his message to mankind with determination.

Thus the *sūrah* shares with other *sūrahs* revealed during the same period the same subject matter and general features. Likewise, it addresses the needs and requirements of that period when the Islamic message faced the ignorance, or *jāhiliyyah*, that prevailed in Arabia. The same applies to any similar period in history. Indeed it even applies now.

We have always emphasized the practical nature of the Qur'ān because it is central to an understanding of this book, its goals and objectives. This means that we need to be aware of the circumstances that prevailed when a particular *sūrah* or text was revealed so that we can better recognize the drift of the text and understand its directives. We are thus able to appreciate how it deals with real life situations, and with living human beings who either actively support or oppose it. In this way, we can better understand its rulings and benefit by its directives whenever similar circumstances prevail. We particularly need to take such an attitude in our own times.

But we say this knowing full well that only those who are actively facing this present state of ignorance in their work to bring about an Islamic revival will look at the Qur'ānic texts in this light. Such people are dealing with circumstances and events similar to those faced by the first advocate of this faith, Muḥammad (peace be upon him), and his early Companions. They face the same type of rejection of the great truth of this faith, which requires complete submission to God in all aspects of life: religious, moral, political, economic and social. Likewise, they face the same type of persecution which was endured by the first group of Muslims. Only such people are able to deduce the Islamic method of active advocacy which cannot be deduced in a theoretical approach.

It should be stated here that what is required in our own time is an understanding of the method to be followed by a young Islamic movement facing a totally un-Islamic state of affairs. Such a movement aims to bring mankind out of darkness into light, and out of ignorance and submission to different beings into a state where people submit themselves to God alone. These were the objectives of the first Muslim generation, even before the Islamic state in Madinah was born, and before Islam enjoyed any authority anywhere on earth.

Today we are in a position which, though not identical to that early period, has some similarities to it. Needless to say, circumstances and external factors are different. Yet we are aiming to establish an active advocacy of Islam in the face of total opposition. The fact that circumstances are different means that the needs and requirements of such advocacy are different. Hence why we need today fresh insight into the method of action that Islam approves. Such insight will fit the precedents set by the first Islamic movement, established by the Prophet, to the circumstances and requirements of the present period.

It is such insight that the newly-born Islamic movement requires. It is too early now for the development of a system of government, and the drafting of a legal code. Today, there is not a single state or community where the basic rule of human transactions is God's law and the Islamic code. The type of insight which gives birth to a system of government and a legal code comes at the appropriate time. Its details should fit the Muslim community that needs it, whenever it comes into existence, and begins to face the practical problems that apply to it. Prior to this, producing such a system and a code is no different from trying to plant seeds in the air and hoping they will sprout.

The Nature of Opposition to Islam

The first major topic the *sūrah* tackles highlights the nature of those who reject this faith of Islam, based on submission to God alone, and outlines their true motives for so doing. It also describes the terrible fate that awaits such unbelievers. The *sūrah* tackles this in several rounds, employing different subjects and techniques, such as narrative, an exhibition of scenes of the universe and scenes of the Day of Judgement, and directives and comments that either precede or follow the stories it relates.

While the general atmosphere of *Sūrah* 13, Thunder, reminds us of *Sūrah* 6, Cattle, the general atmosphere of this *sūrah* reminds us of

Sūrah 7, The Heights. Both begin with a serious warning, and the whole *sūrah* confirms it. The two *sūrahs*, however, differ greatly in their method.

The warning at the beginning of *Sūrah* 7 is stated very clearly: "*This is a book that has been bestowed on you from on high – so do not entertain any doubt about it – in order that you may warn people with its message, and admonish the believers. Follow what has been sent down to you by your Lord, and follow no masters other than Him. How seldom do you keep this in mind. How many a community have We destroyed, with Our punishment falling upon them by night, or at midday while they were resting. And when Our punishment fell upon them, all they could say was: 'We have indeed been wrongdoers.'*" (7: 2–5) The *sūrah* then relates the story of Adam and *Iblīs*, following it to its conclusion when human life on earth comes to an end and people return to their Lord where the warnings given to them will be fulfilled. This is then followed by some scenes of the universe, including images of the heavens and earth, night and day, the sun, moon and stars, the wind, clouds, water and fruit. Thereafter, we are given the stories of the Prophets Noah, Hūd, Ṣāliḥ, Lot, Shu'ayb and Moses, all of which confirm the warning.

Here in this *sūrah*, the warning is given at the beginning, but it is given a continuous air of mystery to enhance its effect in anticipation of the fearful destiny: "*These are the verses of the Book, a clear discourse. Little do those who disbelieve wish that they were Muslims. Let them eat and enjoy themselves, and let their hopes beguile them. For they will surely come to know [the truth]. Never have We destroyed any community unless divine revelations have been made known to it. No community can ever forestall its term, nor can they delay it.*" (Verses 1–5)

The *sūrah* then refers to some scenes from the universe: the heavens and the constellations, the expanded earth and the mountains set firm on it, the plants that demonstrate a balanced method of creation, the winds full of moisture, water and drinking, and the life, death and resurrection of all mankind. This is followed by the story of Adam and *Iblīs* leading up to the destinies of all believers and unbelievers. Then we have brief references to the stories of Abraham, Lot, Shu'ayb and Ṣāliḥ, with the emphasis being placed on the destiny of unbelievers in each case. We note here that the Arabs were aware of the ruins left by these communities, as they passed by them on their traditional journeys to Syria.

The main line in both *surahs* is the same, but each has its own special features. Their rhythm is similar, but not identical. This is the system followed by the Qur'ān, tackling its topics in a variety of ways that may be similar in some aspects but totally different in others, and where they are never repeated or allowed to be identical.

The *surah* can be divided into five sections, each of which includes a specific topic. The first explains the law that God has set in operation concerning His message and people's attitudes to it, either accepting and believing in it or rejecting it. This starts with an implicit warning which is covered with mystery: "*These are the verses of the Book, a clear discourse. Little do those who disbelieve wish that they were Muslims. Let them eat and enjoy themselves, and let their hopes beguile them. For they will surely come to know [the truth]."* (Verses 2–3) This section ends with a statement that the unbelievers reject the message out of stubbornness, not because they do not have sufficient evidence to lead them to faith: "*If We opened for the unbelievers a gateway to heaven and they had ascended higher and higher, still they would surely say: 'It is only our eyes that are spellbound! Indeed, we must have been bewitched.'"* (Verses 14–15)

They are all of the same type: "*Indeed We have sent before you messengers to communities of old, but whenever a messenger came to any of them they mocked at him. Thus do We cause it [i.e. this scorn of the revelation] to slip into the hearts of the guilty, who do not believe in it, although the ways of ancient communities have gone before them."* (Verses 10–13)

The second section portrays some of the signs God has placed in the universe, both in the heavens and the earth and in between. All of these have been set in accordance with God's precise wisdom, and according to a definite measure: "*We have indeed set up in the heavens constellations, and endowed them with beauty for all to behold, and We have guarded them from every cursed devil, so that anyone who tries to eavesdrop is pursued by a flame clear to see. We have spread out the earth, and placed on it firm mountains, and caused [life] of every kind to grow on it in a balanced manner. We have placed various means of livelihood on it for you, as well as for those whom you do not have to provide for. There is not a thing but with Us are its storehouses; and We send it down only in accordance with a defined measure. We send forth winds heavily loaded, then We send down water from the skies for you to drink. You are not the ones who store it up."* (Verses 16–22)

It is to God that everyone and everything returns at the time appointed and known to God: *"It is We who give life and cause death, and it is We who are the inheritors [of all things]. Well do We know those who lived before you and those who will come after you. Your Lord will gather them all together. He is indeed Wise, All-Knowing."* (Verses 23–25)

The third section delivers the story of mankind and the origins of following right guidance or abandoning it in order to follow erring ways. It also shows the fates of those who follow God's guidance and those who reject it. This is shown in the way Adam was created out of clay before God breathed of his soul into him, and the arrogance of Iblīs who leads people astray.

The fourth section relates the fates suffered by the peoples of Lot, Shuʿayb and Ṣāliḥ. It starts with the verses: *"Tell My servants that I alone am Much Forgiving, truly Merciful; and also, My punishment is indeed the most grievous suffering."* (Verses 49–50) The stories are given in succession, showing God's mercy to Abraham and Lot, and His punishment of the peoples of Lot, Shuʿayb and Ṣāliḥ. Thus the Quraysh are told of the fate of those whose lands they pass by on their trips to Syria. Their ruins are there for them to see. *"Surely in this there are messages for those who read the signs. Those [towns] stood on a road that is trodden still."* (Verses 75–76)

The fifth and final section reveals the truth that is at the heart of the creation of the heavens and the earth and how this relates to the Hour of Judgement and the reward or punishment that comes after that, and also to the message of the Prophet Muhammad (peace be upon him). That is the great truth in the whole universe. It relates to origin and destiny: *"It was only with the truth that We have created the heavens and the earth and all that is between them. The appointed Hour will certainly come. Hence overlook their faults in fair forbearance. Your Lord is the All-Knowing Creator. We have given you seven oft-repeated verses and this sublime Qur'ān."* (Verses 85–87)

I

Preserving the Qur'ān

Al-Ḥijr

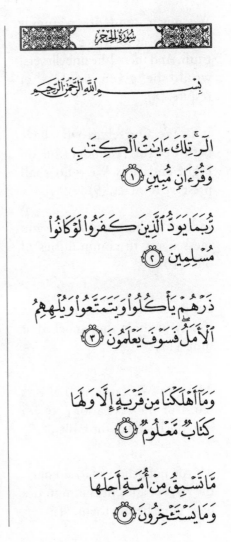

In the Name of God, the Merciful, the Beneficent

Alif. Lām. Rā. These are the verses of the Book, a clear discourse. (1)

Little do those who disbelieve wish that they were Muslims. (2)

Let them eat and enjoy themselves, and let their hopes beguile them. For they will surely come to know [the truth]. (3)

Never have We destroyed any community unless divine revelations have been made known to it. (4)

No community can ever forestall its term, nor can they delay it. (5)

301

They say: 'You to whom this reminder has been bestowed from on high! You are truly mad. (6)

وَقَالُواْ يَـٰٓأَيُّهَا ٱلَّذِى نُزِّلَ عَلَيْهِ ٱلذِّكْرُ إِنَّكَ لَمَجْنُونٌ ٦

Why do you not bring the angels before us, if you are truthful?' (7)

لَّوْ مَا تَأْتِينَا بِٱلْمَلَـٰٓئِكَةِ إِن كُنتَ مِنَ ٱلصَّـٰدِقِينَ ٧

We never send down angels except in accordance with the truth. And then, [the unbelievers] would be given no further respite. (8)

مَا نُنَزِّلُ ٱلْمَلَـٰٓئِكَةَ إِلَّا بِٱلْحَقِّ وَمَا كَانُوٓاْ إِذًا مُّنظَرِينَ ٨

✴ It is We Ourselves who have bestowed this reminder from on high, and it is We who shall preserve it intact. (9)

إِنَّا نَحْنُ نَزَّلْنَا ٱلذِّكْرَ وَإِنَّا لَهُۥ لَحَـٰفِظُونَ ٩

Indeed We have sent before you messengers to communities of old, (10)

وَلَقَدْ أَرْسَلْنَا مِن قَبْلِكَ فِى شِيَعِ ٱلْأَوَّلِينَ ١٠

but whenever a messenger came to any of them they mocked at him. (11)

وَمَا يَأْتِيهِم مِّن رَّسُولٍ إِلَّا كَانُواْ بِهِۦ يَسْتَهْزِءُونَ ١١

Thus do We cause it [i.e. this scorn of the revelation] to slip into the hearts of the guilty, (12)

كَذَٰلِكَ نَسْلُكُهُۥ فِى قُلُوبِ ٱلْمُجْرِمِينَ ١٢

who do not believe in it, although the ways of ancient communities have gone before them. (13)

لَا يُؤْمِنُونَ بِهِۦ وَقَدْ خَلَتْ سُنَّةُ ٱلْأَوَّلِينَ ١٣

| If We opened for the unbelievers a gateway to heaven and they had ascended higher and higher, (14) | وَلَوْ فَتَحْنَا عَلَيْهِم بَابًا مِّنَ ٱلسَّمَآءِ فَظَلُّوا۟ فِيهِ يَعْرُجُونَ ﴿١٤﴾ |
| still they would surely say: 'It is only our eyes that are spellbound! Indeed, we must have been bewitched.' (15) | لَقَالُوٓا۟ إِنَّمَا سُكِّرَتْ أَبْصَـٰرُنَا بَلْ نَحْنُ قَوْمٌ مَّسْحُورُونَ ﴿١٥﴾ |

Unbelievers Indulge in Wishful Thinking

This opening passage speaks about the nature of the book which the unbelievers reject as fabrication, adding a threat that they will soon witness a day when they wish they had submitted themselves to God and become Muslims. It tells them that that day has a fixed time, and that is the reason for its delay. It mentions the challenges they make and how they demand that angels be brought to them. It threatens them by stating that when God sends down angels to unbelievers, He destroys them altogether. Finally the *sūrah* speaks of the real reason for their unbelieving attitude. It is certainly not for lack of evidence, but rather due to their entrenched stubbornness.

"Alif. Lām. Rā. *These are the verses of the Book, a clear discourse.*" (Verse 1) The three separate letters with which this *sūrah* starts and similar ones that occur at the beginning of some Qur'ānic *sūrahs* make up the book, i.e. the Qur'ān. They are available to all. They make the sublime verses, which are inimitable in composition and argument. These letters do not have an intrinsic meaning in themselves, but they make up the Qur'ān, which is very clear in its meaning.

People who do not believe in the revelation of this inimitable book, and describe the Qur'ān as fabricated when it is very clear in its import, will come to see a day when they will dearly wish that they had adopted a totally different attitude. They will wish that they had been believers and that their behaviour was in line with the teachings of religion. "*Little do those who disbelieve wish that they were Muslims.*" (Verse 2)

303

They may wish so but that will be when no wish is of use. But in fact, 'little do those who disbelieve wish'. The way this is expressed implies a threat and a touch of derision. It also implies encouragement to make use of the available opportunity and submit to God before it is too late. For if the chance is lost and the day comes when they wish they had submitted themselves to God and accepted Islam, their wishes will be of no avail.

This is followed by another implicit threat: "*Let them eat and enjoy themselves, and let their hopes beguile them. For they will surely come to know [the truth].*" (Verse 3)

Leave them to their carnal desires, eating and enjoying, without reflection, contemplation or thought to what is around them. Leave them with their deluding hopes and deceiving temptations, while life passes away and the opportunity is lost. Leave them so that you do not waste your own time with those who have condemned themselves when they lost their way in idle hopes and desires. The temptation shows them that they have a long life to come and that they will achieve what they covet. They think that nothing can stop them from obtaining what they hope for, and that they have to face no reckoning and will be held to no account. They delude themselves by thinking that what they get in this life is enough to ensure their safety in the hereafter.

This image of beguiling hopes is drawn from real human life. Hope always tempts and beguiles man. So much so that he overlooks the facts of God's existence, fate and the certainty of death. Man forgets that there is a duty to be fulfilled and a prohibition to be observed. He goes even further so as to forget God altogether and forget that he himself is going to die and then be resurrected in order to account for his deeds.

This beguiling hope is a fatal one, and it is to this hope that the Prophet is commanded to leave them. "*For they will surely come to know the truth,*" but then it will be too late for such knowledge to be of any benefit to them. The command given to the Prophet implies a threat to them, as well as a strong call aiming to wake them up so that they could see their hope for what it is: a beguiling hope that causes them to overlook their inevitable fate.

But the laws God has set in operation for the world and for human life will continue along their respective courses. The end of each nation will come at the time appointed by God. Then it is the practices of each community that determine how these laws and how God's order will operate: "*Never have We destroyed any community unless divine revelations have been made known to it. No community can ever forestall its term, nor can they delay it.*" (Verses 4–5) Therefore, they must not be deluded by the fact that God's punishment has not taken them. God's law will take its well-marked course and operate as God wants it to operate. As for them, they will certainly come to know.

That clear book and appointed term are given by God to every nation and community so that they will do their work. What they do in this life determines their fate in the hereafter. When a community believes in God, does good works, allows human life to proceed and prosper, and implements justice then God will extend its life until it deviates from these rules and becomes devoid of all goodness. That determines the end of its life, either with total loss and ruin, or with a temporary general weakness.

It may be said that there are communities which do not believe or do any good works or implement justice, but they continue to thrive and prosper. But this is nothing but delusion. Such communities must have a fair residue of goodness, even if it is limited to building a good life on earth, dealing justly among its own citizens and taking measures to ensure material prosperity within their own territories. They owe their continued existence to this residue of goodness. When it is exhausted, they face their inevitable destiny. God's law will always operate, and every community has its time: "*No community can ever forestall its term, nor can they delay it.*" (Verse 5)

A Promise That Will Never Fail

The *sūrah* then describes their bad manners in the way they addressed the Prophet, when he had only presented to them the Qur'ān which is a clear reminder of the truth. It helps to reawaken them to face the facts instead of running after beguiling hopes. He also reminded them of God's law and its operation. But they ridiculed him and spoke to him with extreme impudence. "*They say: 'You to whom this reminder has been bestowed from on high! You are truly mad. Why do you not bring the angels before us, if you are truthful?'*" (Verses 6–7) Ridicule is apparent in their way of addressing the Prophet, "*You to whom this reminder has been bestowed from on high!*" (Verse 6) They actually deny the fact of revelation and the Prophet's message altogether, but they make this mocking address.

Their rudeness is carried still further as they insult the Prophet personally: "*You are truly mad!*" (Verse 6) This they do in response to his call on them to believe in God, using the Qur'ān in all its clarity to address them. They go on to make unreasonable demands, asking for angels to come down to endorse his message: "*Why do you not bring the angels before us, if you are truthful?*" (Verse 7) The demand for angels is often repeated in this and other *sūrahs*, and it is put to the Prophet Muḥammad (peace be upon him) as it was put to prophets and messengers before him. This reflects man's clear ignorance, for it is he whom God has honoured when He assigned prophethood to a few chosen people.

The reply to such ridicule, impudence and ignorance takes the form of reasserting the rule which is confirmed by the fates suffered by past communities. Angels are sent down to a messenger of God only to destroy the unbelievers of his community when their term is up. At this point there can be no more respite and no further delay: "*We never send down angels except in accordance with the truth. And then, [the unbelievers] would be given no further respite.*" (Verse 8) Is this what they want and demand?

Preservation of the Qur'ān

The *sūrah* then calls on them to look carefully on God's guidance and reflect on it. God only sends down the angels with the truth. He commands them to establish and implement it. In the case of persistent unbelievers, the truth is to destroy them. Not only do they deserve this, but it is also inevitable. Such destruction, then, is a truth in itself and the angels carry it out without delay. God chooses for them what is better than the choice they make for themselves. He gives them the Reminder so that they may reflect on it and follow its guidance. This is much better than sending down the angels with the final truth, if only they would reflect: "*It is We Ourselves who have bestowed this reminder from on high, and it is We who shall preserve it intact.*" (Verse 9) It is much better for them, then, to approach it positively, because it will remain intact, suffering no loss or change. It will remain pure, unaffected by falsehood, free of distortion. It guides them to the truth with God's care, if they really want the truth. If they were asking for angels to make sure of it, they should know that God does not wish to send down angels for them, because He wants what is better for them. Hence, He sent down the Reminder which is preserved intact. That is better than sending angels to destroy them.

When we look today, after the passage of many centuries, at the fulfilment of God's promise to preserve the Qur'ān, we see a great miracle testifying to the fact that it is God's book. We see that the circumstances and situations that it has endured over the centuries could not have left it intact, suffering no change of even a single sentence or a single word, without the interference of a superior power. That power, which is greater than all situations, factors and circumstances, has preserved this book keeping it pure from change or distortion.

There was a time when many sects and groups sought to find support for their ideas in the Qur'ān and the *Ḥadīth*. The resulting conflict was fuelled by the Jews, the diehard enemies of this faith, and by those who advocated nationalism. These were known in Islamic history as *Shu'ūbiyyīn*. These groups sought to introduce foreign elements into the *Sunnah*. Only the colossal efforts of scores of bright, pious and meticulous scholars, over several decades, purged the *Ḥadīth* from that which did not belong to it.

In times of conflict and strife, such sects deliberately misinterpreted Qur'ānic verses, twisting Qur'ānic texts so that they could cite them in support of their views and rulings. But they were all, even in the darkest and hardest circumstances, totally unable to introduce a single change into the text of the Qur'ān, the book God has guaranteed to preserve. Its text has remained exactly as it was revealed by God, providing a challenge to every would-be perpetrator of distortion. This is irrefutable testimony to the fact that this Qur'ān is God's own book and He is the One who guarantees its preservation.

A Guarantee for All Time

Muslims generally have gone through a time, which we continue to endure these days, when they have been too weak to defend themselves, or their faith, way of life, land, honour, property, moral values or even their reasoning and intellectual faculties. Their enemies have managed to replace every moral value, sound belief, virtuous practice, and legal standard they have had with something foul and alien. They have tempted Muslims to accept loose morality and shameless behaviour. What is more, such behaviour has been given attractive titles such as progress, advancement, secularism, freedom, breaking one's shackles, revolution and innovation, etc. Muslims have thus become Muslims only by name. They have retained practically nothing of their profound faith. Hence, their power has been sapped, and they have become little more than the scum that floats on the surface of a river.

Yet in spite of all their attempts, the enemies of this religion have not been able to change the text of the Qur'ān, or to distort it. This is not due to any lack of motive. They would indeed have loved dearly to alter its text if that were at all possible. But try as hard as they might, they have been unable to achieve their goal.

The enemies of this faith, particularly its Jewish elements, have utilized their great expertise, stretching over four thousand years, in scheming against the divine faith. Indeed, they have even been successful in many ways. For example, they succeeded in introducing some foreign elements into the *Sunnah* and the history of the Muslim nation. They have been able to falsify events and even implant their own people within the Muslim community so that they could play roles they could not otherwise do. They managed to destroy states, communities, systems and laws, and to dress some of their traitors in a heroic guise so that they continued their destructive work against the Muslim community. Although they have done this throughout history, they have been more successful in modern times.

One thing, however, they have not been able to achieve, although circumstances appear to make it seem easy, is tamper with this preserved book, which receives no protection from people who allege to believe in it. This is yet further evidence, if any were needed, that this is God's book. The fact that it has remained free of all distortion in spite of these conditions testifies to the fact that it was revealed by God Almighty. At the time of the Prophet, this promise to preserve the Qur'ān intact sounded a mere promise. Today, however, after all these great events and long centuries, it is indeed a great miracle confirming the indisputable fact that it is God's revealed book. No one disputes this fact except a stubborn, ignorant fool. "*It is We Ourselves who have bestowed this reminder from on high, and it is We who shall preserve it intact.*" (Verse 9) God certainly tells the truth.

Same Old Denials

God consoles the Prophet (peace be upon him), and tells him that he is not unique in his position among God's messengers who, like him, were the target of much ridicule and rejection. The unbelievers are always wont to show their stubbornness in denying the true faith.

"*Indeed We have sent before you messengers to communities of old, but whenever a messenger came to any of them they mocked at him.*" (Verses 10–11) It is the same story. Just like the unbelievers in the communities of old received what God's messengers told them, the same is the case with the unbelievers in your community. They all show the same attitude. Their hearts, having turned away from God's messages and been hostile to God's chosen messengers, are no longer able to reflect or receive a message as it should be received: "*Thus do We cause it [i.e. this scorn of the revelation] to slip into the hearts of the guilty, who do not believe in it, although the ways of ancient communities have gone before them.*" (Verses 12–13) We let it sink into their hearts as its truth is denied, subject to ridicule, because their hearts cannot receive it except in this way. This applies to all generations and communities, past, present and future. Those who deny the truth of God's message are of the same nature: "*The ways of ancient communities have gone before them.*" (Verse 13)

It is not proper evidence of the truth of God's message that they lack. They are stubborn, unwilling to change, no matter what signs and proofs are given to them. At this point, the *sūrah* gives a particularly rich image of repugnant obstinacy and mean strong-headedness: "*If We opened for the unbelievers a gateway to heaven and they had ascended higher and higher, still they would surely say: 'It is only our eyes that are spellbound! Indeed, we must have been bewitched.'*" (Verses 14–15) We can imagine them ascending higher and higher into the sky, going through a special door that opens for them, and they climb physically and see with their eyes the open door. Yet their stubborn attitude remains, whereby they deny the truth of what they see and feel, claiming that someone must have cast a spell over them so that they cannot see clearly. They claim that what they see is mere fantasy: "*It is only our eyes that are spellbound! Indeed, we must have been bewitched.*" (Verse 15) All we see and feel is mere illusion.

There is no use arguing with such people. They have all the evidence they need to believe. What prevents them is not that the angels have not been sent down to them, because their own ascension is greater evidence and closer to them than the angels descending. Instead it is their shameless obstinacy which causes them to disregard and reject the clearly manifest truth.

This then is an example of human stubbornness which the *sūrah* paints. It is met only with a feeling of disgust and contempt. This example is neither temporary nor local, nor is it the product of a particular environment at a particular period of time. It is an example of human beings when their nature has been distorted and their faculties of reception impaired. They are cut off from the living universe around them and all the signals it gives. In our own generation, this example applies to atheists who follow materialistic creeds which they claim to be 'scientific', when they are far removed from science and knowledge, as well as from insight and inspiration.

Advocates of materialistic doctrines disbelieve in God and deny His existence. They claim that the universe exists without a Creator who controls whatever takes place in it. They then formulate on the basis of their claims and denials social, political, economic and 'moral' creeds, even stating that such are 'scientific'. Indeed, they say that their creeds are the only scientific ones.

This lack of feeling of God's existence despite all the evidence that testifies to His control of the universe clearly indicates that their receptive faculties are impaired. Their persistence in denying God is no less rude and impudent than that painted in the Qur'ānic text: "*If We opened for the unbelievers a gateway to heaven and they had ascended higher and higher, still they would surely say: 'It is only our eyes that are spellbound! Indeed, we must have been bewitched.'*" (Verses 14–15) The evidence that is available in the universe is so varied and manifest that it is stronger than their ascension to heaven. That evidence addresses every sound nature in an open and private manner, saying what is so powerful that human nature must accept without question.

When we look at the universe we find that it has countless laws working in perfect harmony to maintain its phenomena and existence. Moreover, it has so many complementary aspects which allow life to come into existence in certain parts of it. So to claim that this universe exists without a creator, is something that the human mind cannot accept. It is wholeheartedly rejected by human nature. Not only so, but the better science understands nature and the more deeply it penetrates into the universe and the more of its secrets it uncovers, the notion of self existence and uncontrolled operation seems even more far-fetched. In fact, the greater human knowledge becomes, the more clearly science admits that it is the Creator who controls the universe. Undistorted human nature accepts this truth once it receives the clear signals the universe makes. It has accepted it long before recent scientific evidence supporting it has come to light.

Testimony by a Western Scientist

The universe cannot create itself, then create the laws that control its existence. Nor can we attribute the emergence of life to a lifeless universe. Hence neither human nature nor human intelligence accepts the emergence of the universe or life without a Creator who continues to control it. Indeed material science is now rejecting it as well.

Russell Charles Artist, Professor of Biology at David Lipscomb College, Nashville, Tennessee, says:

> Many theories have been brought forward in the attempt to derive living cells from inanimate matter. Certain investigators are claiming that life has originated through the protogene, or through viruses, or through an aggregation of large protein molecules, which may leave the impression that at last the gap between the lifeless and the living has been spanned. Actually it must be admitted that all attempts to produce living matter experimentally from inanimate matter have failed utterly.

> Furthermore, it is not by direct evidence that the one who denies the existence of God proves to a waiting world that a fortuitous aggregation of atoms and molecules is life, capable of maintaining and directing itself as do the cells described here. Not at all. He

accepts this as a *belief*. It is his private interpretation of the facts visible to us all, that an accidental concourse brought the first cell into being. But this is to accept an even greater miracle than to believe that Intelligence called it into being!

I maintain that each of these single cells (each a system so intricate and delicate that its complete functioning has so far escaped our study), and all the trillions of them on this earth, definitely present a justifiable inference – one of Mind, or Intelligence, or Thought, which we call God. Science both admits and accepts this inference.

I believe firmly that there is a God.[1]

The author did not start his investigations from a religious standpoint, but instead commented with an objective outlook, reflecting on the laws of nature. Yet he reached a conclusion that supports the truth as outlined by both natural inspiration and innate religious sense. When a truth exists, everyone who seeks it will inevitably come across it, regardless of what route he takes. It is only those whose receptive faculties have stopped functioning that cannot attain to the truth.

Those who deny God's existence are people whose argument is in conflict with the logic of nature, reason and universal existence. They seem to suffer from the malfunctioning of all their receptive faculties. They are blind, as God Himself describes them: "*Is, then, he who knows that what has been revealed to you by your Lord is the Truth like one who is blind? Only those who are endowed with understanding keep this in mind.*" (13: 19)

As this is their true description, it follows that any social, political or economic theory they come up with, as well as any theory they formulate, on the universe, human life and history must be viewed by a Muslim as no more than the groping in the dark of a blind person who has lost all his senses, at least with regard to understanding human life and how it is organized. No Muslim can adopt anything such a

1. Russell Charles Artist, 'Trillions of Living Cells Speak Their Message', a paper included in *The Evidence of God in an Expanding Universe*, ed. John Clover Monsma, G.P. Putnam's Sons, New York, 1958, p. 124.

person formulates, let alone make it the basis of his view of life or code of living.

This is a matter of faith, not an intellectual argument. A person who argues that the material world has created itself and initiated human life, and makes this concept the basis of his ideology and code of living errs in the starting point of thought and doctrine alike. All structures and rules that have such a basis cannot bring any good. They have no meeting point even with any detail in the life of a Muslim whose basic concepts and code of living start with the belief in God's oneness and His creation of the universe which remains subject to God's will at all times.

Hence, to suggest that so-called 'scientific socialism' is independent of materialism betrays ignorance. Adopting 'scientific socialism', when it has such a basis and line of thinking, constitutes a total turning away from Islam as a faith, concept and code of living. It is not possible to combine scientific socialism and belief in God. To try to do so is to try to combine Islam with unbelief.

People must choose either to believe in Islam or in materialism. If they believe in Islam, they cannot adopt scientific socialism. Islam is much more than a faith and a conviction. It is a system based on an ideology. On the other hand, scientific socialism is based on materialistic philosophy, which believes that life is matter, and denies the existence of God altogether. We simply cannot separate the two. Hence, a choice between the two must be made. Everyone is free to make his or her choice, but everyone must be responsible for their choice.[2]

---

2. The author wrote his commentary at a time when so-called, "scientific socialism" was in vogue. Hence, he concentrates on this particular doctrine. However, what he says applies to all materialistic philosophy and any system based on it, including capitalism. – Editor's note.

2

Great Universal Expanse

We have indeed set up in the heavens constellations, and endowed them with beauty for all to behold, (16)

and We have guarded them from every cursed devil, (17)

so that anyone who tries to eavesdrop is pursued by a flame clear to see. (18)

We have spread out the earth, and placed on it firm mountains, and caused [life] of every kind to grow on it in a balanced manner. (19)

We have placed various means of livelihood on it for you, as well as for those whom you do not have to provide for. (20)

There is not a thing but with Us are its storehouses; and We send it down only in accordance with a defined measure. (21)

وَلَقَدْ جَعَلْنَا فِي ٱلسَّمَآءِ بُرُوجًا وَزَيَّنَّهَا لِلنَّظِرِينَ ۝

وَحَفِظْنَهَا مِن كُلِّ شَيْطَنٍ رَّجِيمٍ ۝

إِلَّا مَنِ ٱسْتَرَقَ ٱلسَّمْعَ فَأَتْبَعَهُ شِهَابٌ مُّبِينٌ ۝

وَٱلْأَرْضَ مَدَدْنَهَا وَأَلْقَيْنَا فِيهَا رَوَسِيَ وَأَنۢبَتْنَا فِيهَا مِن كُلِّ شَيْءٍ مَّوْزُونٍ ۝

وَجَعَلْنَا لَكُمْ فِيهَا مَعَيِشَ وَمَن لَّسْتُمْ لَهُۥ بِرَزِقِينَ ۝

وَإِن مِّن شَيْءٍ إِلَّا عِندَنَا خَزَآئِنُهُۥ وَمَا نُنَزِّلُهُۥ إِلَّا بِقَدَرٍ مَّعْلُومٍ ۝

315

We send forth winds heavily loaded, then We send down water from the skies for you to drink. You are not the ones who store it up. (22)	وَأَرْسَلْنَا ٱلرِّيَاحَ لَوَٰقِحَ فَأَنزَلْنَا مِنَ ٱلسَّمَاءِ مَآءً فَأَسْقَيْنَٰكُمُوهُ وَمَآ أَنتُمْ لَهُۥ بِخَٰزِنِينَ ﴿٢٢﴾
It is We who give life and cause death, and it is We who are the inheritors [of all things]. (23)	وَإِنَّا لَنَحْنُ نُحْىِۦ وَنُمِيتُ وَنَحْنُ ٱلْوَٰرِثُونَ ﴿٢٣﴾
Well do We know those who lived before you and those who will come after you. (24)	وَلَقَدْ عَلِمْنَا ٱلْمُسْتَقْدِمِينَ مِنكُمْ وَلَقَدْ عَلِمْنَا ٱلْمُسْتَـٔخِرِينَ ﴿٢٤﴾
Your Lord will gather them all together. He is indeed Wise, All-Knowing. (25)	وَإِنَّ رَبَّكَ هُوَ يَحْشُرُهُمْ إِنَّهُۥ حَكِيمٌ عَلِيمٌ ﴿٢٥﴾

Endless Wonders

The *surah* now moves on to an exhibition of universal signs. It starts with a scene in heaven followed by one on earth, then an image of winds fully loaded with water, before we have pictures of life and death, resurrection and gathering. All these scenes are denied by those who, when a gateway to heaven is opened for them and they ascend through it higher and higher, surely say: "*It is only our eyes that are spellbound! Indeed, we must have been bewitched.*" (Verse 15)

"*We have indeed set up in the heavens constellations, and endowed them with beauty for all to behold, and We have guarded them from every cursed devil, so that anyone who tries to eavesdrop is pursued by a flame clear to see.*" (Verses 16–18) This is the first line in the great universal scene which tells of God's creative power. It delivers a more telling testimony to the inimitability of God's creation than any coming down of angels. It reflects God's elaborate planning and His limitless power that puts into place this great piece of creation, the universe. The 'constellations' may refer to the stars and planets themselves with their huge entities, or it may refer to their positions which define their orbits. In both cases, they testify to the great power behind their creation and to the accuracy and beauty that they reflect. "*We have indeed set up in the heavens constellations, and endowed them with beauty for all to behold.*" (Verse 16)

The reference here to the beauty of the universe, particularly the type seen in the sky, suggests that beauty is an intended purpose behind such creation. It is not merely size or accuracy that are intended, but beauty which is clearly seen in all its aspects. A quick glance at the sky in a dark moonless night, with so many stars and planets sending their faint light our way, gives us a sense of that unique beauty. The same feeling will be aroused by a similar look at the sky in a night with a full moon, moving along in a romantic air, with the rest of the universe holding its breath so that it does not disturb a happy dreamer. One glance like that is sufficient to indicate the depth of the beauty in the creation of the universe. It will tell us more about the Qur'ānic expression here: "*We have indeed set up in the heavens constellations, and endowed them with beauty for all to behold.*" (Verse 16)

With the beauty comes preservation, pure and intact: "*We have guarded them from every cursed devil.*" (Verse 17) None, then, can spoil this purity by trying to spread evil in it. Satan is allowed to do his evil work only on earth, to tempt human beings to follow his wicked designs. The sky, which is a symbol for what is exalted and sublime, is beyond his reach. He may attempt to do so, but every attempt he makes is foiled: "*Anyone who tries to eavesdrop is pursued by a flame clear to see.*" (Verse 18)

Who is the devil, and what is his nature; and how does he eavesdrop, and on whom; and what does he try to hear? All these are matters that belong to a world beyond our reach. We have only the texts available to us. It is useless to try to go further into this, because it adds nothing to anyone's faith. Investigating it does not produce anything other than preoccupying man's mind with something that is not among its concerns.

Let us then be satisfied with knowing that there is no room in the heavens for the devil and his work. Its breathtaking beauty is preserved. The sublimity it symbolizes is kept free from anything impure. And if the devil so much as attempts to climb up, a fast moving flame pursues him.

The second line in this great and awesome scene draws the earth stretched as far as our sight can reach, and made easy to traverse. It shows the mountains giving it firmness and stability, and its plants and vegetation that are necessary sustenance for man and animal: "*We have spread out the earth, and placed on it firm mountains, and caused [life] of every kind to grow on it in a balanced manner. We have placed various means of livelihood on it for you, as well as for those whom you do not have to provide for.*" (Verses 19–20)

The sense of an immense creation is clear here. The reference first to the massive constellations whose large size is implied by their very name, and in the shooting flame which is described as being clear for all to behold, and then the mountains whose weight is alluded to by the adjective, 'firm,' all add a sense of grandeur to the scene described. Even plants are described here as 'balanced' which, in its Arabic original, *mawzūn*, suggests considerable weight. The precise meaning of this phrase, however, is that every plant on earth is created with fine measure and precision. The grand impression of the scene is further enhanced by the term, *ma'āyish*, or '*means of livelihood*', used here in the plural and left indefinite. Still more is added by the phrase, '*those whom you do not have to provide for.*' This refers to every living thing on earth. Hence, the scene appears massive, grand, majestic.

But the verse then refers to human beings. Your livelihood is placed on earth '*for you*', and also for '*those whom you do not have to provide for.*' They all survive on the provisions God gives them. Humans constitute only one of the countless communities that live on earth. This community does not provide sustenance to any other. It is God that provides for it and for other types of creation. But God grants it more of His bounty as He places for its service other communities and types of creation which live on the provisions given to them by God, without placing any responsibility or burden on man.

A Clear Plan for All Creation

In fact, the provisions given to every community are determined by God, according to His will. He grants them as He pleases, at the time He chooses, and in accordance with the laws He has set in operation: "*There is not a thing but with Us are its storehouses; and We send it down only in accordance with a defined measure.*" (Verse 21) No creature owns, or has power over, anything. The resources of everything are with God in His supreme realm. He grants it to His creation, in their respective worlds, according to a defined measure. Nothing is given or provided arbitrarily.

We have here a precise statement, "*There is not a thing but with Us are its storehouses; and We send it down only in accordance with a defined measure.*" (Verse 21) Its import becomes apparent as man's knowledge increases and becomes more advanced. The more he knows about the universe and how it is made and operates, the better he understands the Qur'ānic statement. The meaning of the term, 'storehouses', becomes clearer after man has discovered the nature of the elements which form the material world, and their composition. Man knows that the basic 'storehouses' of water, for example, are the oxygen and hydrogen atoms. The storehouses of provisions we have in the form of green plants and vegetation include the nitrogen which is present in the air, carbon and the oxygen that form carbon dioxide, and the rays of the sun. Examples like these are numerous, giving a clear picture of the import of the expression, "*God's storehouses*", of which man has come to know much, but this much remains only a little of what there is.

Of the things that God sends in accordance with defined measure are winds and water: "*We send forth winds heavily loaded, then We send down water from the skies for you to drink. You are not the ones who store it up.*" (Verse 22) The Arabic term, *lawāqiḥ*, which signifies 'heavily loaded' has been interpreted by some according to the scientific meaning of 'fertilizing', referring to the fact that the winds carry the pollen from some plants or trees to fertilize the female ones. But this does not seem to fit with the text here. We have to remember that the Qur'ān is very meticulous in drawing its own connotations. What is referred to here is rather the fact that winds carry moisture, just like a she-camel becomes heavy with milk. God then sends down water from that moisture carried by the winds, and He allows man to drink it for his own survival. Yet man cannot retain it all: "*You are not the ones who store it up.*" (Verse 22) It has not come from the storehouses of human beings, but from God's treasures. It has been poured according to a well-defined measure.

The winds move, carry the moisture and pour the water in accordance with the laws of nature. But who has determined all this in the first place? It is all determined by the Creator who has set the original law of the universe which gives rise to all aspects and operates all phenomena: *"There is not a thing but with Us are its storehouses; and We send it down only in accordance with a defined measure."* (Verse 21)

We note here how every move is referred to God, even the drinking of water: *"Then We send down water from the skies for you to drink."* (Verse 22) The expression, *asqaynākumūh*, given in translation as, *"for you to drink"*, is given in the Arabic original as, "We send down water from the skies and We make you drink it". What is meant here is that we have fashioned you in a way which makes you in need of water, and we made the water suitable for your needs. All this is made according to a measure. It is all set in operation by God's will. This mode of expression is chosen in order to provide an element of complete harmony in the whole scene, so that everything is referred to God, even the movement of one's hand to take water to drink. The whole atmosphere is one that attributes everything in the universe to God's will that directly determines every event and movement. His law that controls the movement of stars and planets is the same as His law that controls people's actions. The first passage of the *surah* referred to God's law concerning those who reject God's message, and this second passage refers to His law that governs the heavens and the earth, the wind, water and drinking. All this is subject to God's will which is linked to the great truth that is behind the creation of the heavens, the earth, human beings and all other creatures.

The *surah* then perfects the attribution of all matters to God alone, stating that life and death, the living and the dead, the resurrection and judgement belong to Him: *"It is We who give life and cause death, and it is We who are the inheritors [of all things]. Well do We know those who lived before you and those who will come after you. Your Lord will gather them all together. He is indeed Wise, All-Knowing."* (Verses 23–25)

Thus the second passage complements the first. In the first passage we have the statement: *"Never have We destroyed any community unless divine revelations have been made known to it. No community can ever forestall its term, nor can they delay it."* (Verses 4–5) Here, in this passage, it is emphasized that life and death are determined by God, the heir to all life, and He knows whom He has determined to die early and who will have their death delayed. It is He who gathers them all together at the end, for "*He is indeed Wise, All Knowing.*" (Verse 25) He determines the term of every community according to His wisdom. He knows when it dies, and when it is resurrected and all that happens in between.

We note the harmony of movement in this passage and the preceding one. This is seen in the sending down of revelation, angels, the flames hitting eavesdropping devils, and water from the sky. Harmony is also evident in the general surroundings in which events take place in the whole universe: the skies, the constellations, flames, the earth, the mountains and the vegetation, the winds and the rain. When the *sūrah* provides an example of arrogance, it sets it in a scene of climbing up into the heavens through an open door. All this speaks volumes for the fine style of the Qur'ān.

3

Man and His Sworn Enemy

Indeed We have created man out of sounding clay, out of black mud moulded into shape, (26)

وَلَقَدْ خَلَقْنَا ٱلْإِنسَـٰنَ مِن صَلْصَـٰلٍ مِّنْ حَمَإٍ مَّسْنُونٍ ﴿٢٦﴾

whereas the *jinn* We had created before him out of the fire of scorching winds. (27)

وَٱلْجَآنَّ خَلَقْنَـٰهُ مِن قَبْلُ مِن نَّارِ ٱلسَّمُومِ ﴿٢٧﴾

Your Lord said to the angels: 'I am creating a human being out of sounding clay, out of black mud moulded into shape. (28)

وَإِذْ قَالَ رَبُّكَ لِلْمَلَـٰٓئِكَةِ إِنِّى خَـٰلِقٌۢ بَشَرًا مِّن صَلْصَـٰلٍ مِّنْ حَمَإٍ مَّسْنُونٍ ﴿٢٨﴾

When I have fashioned him and breathed of My spirit into him, fall down in prostration before him.' (29)

فَإِذَا سَوَّيْتُهُۥ وَنَفَخْتُ فِيهِ مِن رُّوحِى فَقَعُوا۟ لَهُۥ سَـٰجِدِينَ ﴿٢٩﴾

Thereupon, the angels, one and all, prostrated themselves. (30)

فَسَجَدَ ٱلْمَلَـٰٓئِكَةُ كُلُّهُمْ أَجْمَعُونَ ﴿٣٠﴾

Not so *Iblīs*, who refused to be among those who prostrated themselves. (31)

إِلَّآ إِبْلِيسَ أَبَىٰٓ أَن يَكُونَ مَعَ ٱلسَّـٰجِدِينَ ﴿٣١﴾

God said: 'Iblīs! What is your reason for not being among those who have prostrated themselves?' (32)

قَالَ يَـٰإِبْلِيسُ مَا لَكَ أَلَّا تَكُونَ مَعَ ٱلسَّـٰجِدِينَ ﴿٣٢﴾

[Iblīs] replied: 'I am not one to prostrate myself to a human being whom You have created out of sounding clay, out of mud moulded into shape.' (33)

قَالَ لَمْ أَكُن لِّأَسْجُدَ لِبَشَرٍ خَلَقْتَهُ مِن صَلْصَٰلٍ مِّنْ حَمَإٍ مَّسْنُونٍ ﴿٣٣﴾

God said: 'Then get out of here, for you are accursed, (34)

قَالَ فَٱخْرُجْ مِنْهَا فَإِنَّكَ رَجِيمٌ ﴿٣٤﴾

and the curse shall be on you till the Day of Judgement.' (35)

وَإِنَّ عَلَيْكَ ٱللَّعْنَةَ إِلَىٰ يَوْمِ ٱلدِّينِ ﴿٣٥﴾

Said [Iblīs]: 'My Lord, grant me a respite till the Day when all shall be resurrected.' (36)

قَالَ رَبِّ فَأَنظِرْنِى إِلَىٰ يَوْمِ يُبْعَثُونَ ﴿٣٦﴾

[God] said: 'You are among those who are granted respite (37)

قَالَ فَإِنَّكَ مِنَ ٱلْمُنظَرِينَ ﴿٣٧﴾

till the Day of the appointed time.' (38)

إِلَىٰ يَوْمِ ٱلْوَقْتِ ٱلْمَعْلُومِ ﴿٣٨﴾

[Iblīs] said: 'My Lord, since You have let me fall in error, I shall make [evil] seem fair to them on earth, and I shall most certainly beguile them all into grievous error, (39)

قَالَ رَبِّ بِمَا أَغْوَيْتَنِى لَأُزَيِّنَنَّ لَهُمْ فِى ٱلْأَرْضِ وَلَأُغْوِيَنَّهُمْ أَجْمَعِينَ ﴿٣٩﴾

except for those of them who are truly Your faithful servants.' (40)

إِلَّا عِبَادَكَ مِنْهُمُ ٱلْمُخْلَصِينَ ﴿٤٠﴾

Said He: 'This is, with Me, a straight way. (41)

قَالَ هَـٰذَا صِرَٰطٌ عَلَىَّ مُسْتَقِيمٌ ﴿٤١﴾

You shall have no power over My servants, except for those who, having fallen into error, choose to follow you. (42)

إِنَّ عِبَادِى لَيْسَ لَكَ عَلَيْهِمْ سُلْطَـٰنٌ إِلَّا مَنِ ٱتَّبَعَكَ مِنَ ٱلْغَاوِينَ ﴿٤٢﴾

For all such, hell is the promised destiny. (43)

وَإِنَّ جَهَنَّمَ لَمَوْعِدُهُمْ أَجْمَعِينَ ﴿٤٣﴾

It has seven gates, with each gate having its allotted share of them.' (44)

لَهَا سَبْعَةُ أَبْوَٰبٍ لِّكُلِّ بَابٍ مِّنْهُمْ جُزْءٌ مَّقْسُومٌ ﴿٤٤﴾

The God-fearing shall dwell amidst gardens and fountains. (45)

إِنَّ ٱلْمُتَّقِينَ فِى جَنَّـٰتٍ وَعُيُونٍ ﴿٤٥﴾

[They are received with the greeting]: 'Enter here in peace and security.' (46)

ٱدْخُلُوهَا بِسَلَـٰمٍ ءَامِنِينَ ﴿٤٦﴾

We shall have removed from their hearts any lurking feelings of malice, [and they shall rest] as brothers, facing one another, on couches. (47)

وَنَزَعْنَا مَا فِى صُدُورِهِم مِّنْ غِلٍّ إِخْوَٰنًا عَلَىٰ سُرُرٍ مُّتَقَـٰبِلِينَ ﴿٤٧﴾

No weariness shall ever touch them there, nor shall they ever be made to depart. (48)

لَا يَمَسُّهُمْ فِيهَا نَصَبٌ وَمَا هُم مِّنْهَا بِمُخْرَجِينَ ﴿٤٨﴾

Overview

With these verses the *sūrah* begins to relate the story of man's creation. It is the story of basic human nature, truth and error and their basic factors, the story of Adam and the substance from which he was created, and what took place at the time of his creation and afterwards. The Qur'ān has already referred to this story twice in previous *sūrahs*, namely *Sūrahs* 2 and 7, The Cow and The Heights. Each time it occurs it serves a special purpose, and is recounted in its own special style with a distinct atmosphere. Hence, the episodes highlighted each time are different, as are the approach and the rhythm employed.

In all three *sūrahs*, the story is introduced with reference to the establishment of mankind on earth as God's vicegerent. We note that in *Sūrah* 2, it is preceded by the verse: "*It is He who created for you all that is on earth. He then turned to heaven and fashioned it into seven heavens. He has knowledge of all things.*" (2: 29) And in *Sūrah* 7, the preceding verse says: "*We have established you firmly on earth and We have provided you there with means of livelihood. How seldom are you grateful.*" (7: 10) Here in this *sūrah*, the story of creation is preceded by the statement: "*We have placed various means of livelihood on it for you, as well as for those whom you do not have to provide for. There is not a thing but with Us are its storehouses; and We send it down only in accordance with a defined measure.*" (Verses 20–21)

Yet in each of these *sūrahs* the story of creation is told in a different context, with a definite purpose for each usage. In *Sūrah* 2, The Cow, the point of emphasis is the appointment of Adam as a vicegerent on earth, which has been placed, with all its contents, at man's service: "*Your Lord said to the angels, 'I am appointing a vicegerent on earth.'*" (2: 30) As the angels wondered at this appointment, the reason for which was not readily apparent to them, they were told some of its aspects: "*He taught Adam the names of all things and then turned to the angels and said, 'Tell Me the names of these things, if what you say is true.' They said, 'Limitless are You in Your glory! We only know what You have taught us. Indeed, You alone are All-Knowing, Wise.' He said, 'Adam! Tell them their names.' When he had told them all their names, He said, 'Have I not said to you that I know the secrets of what*

326

is in the heavens and the earth, and I know all that you reveal and conceal?" (2: 31–33) The *sūrah* then relates how the angels prostrated themselves before Adam while *Iblīs*, or Satan, arrogantly refused. It tells how Adam and his wife resided in heaven before they were seduced by Satan and then their expulsion from heaven and fall to earth so that they could assume their vicegerency, having gone through such a painful experience and repented and asked God to forgive them. Comments on the story as told in *Sūrah* 2 are given in the form of an admonition to the Children of Israel to remember God's grace and honour their pledges to Him. This closely relates to the appointment of Adam, the father of mankind, as vicegerent on earth and the covenant he made with God.

In *Sūrah* 7, The Heights, emphasis is placed on the long journey from heaven and back again, highlighting Satan's unabating hostility to man from the very start. One group will go back to heaven from where Satan drove out their first parents, and these go to heaven by virtue of their disobedience of Satan. Another group, however, will go to hell because they follow the footsteps of Satan, their eternal enemy. Hence, as related in *Sūrah* 7, the story tells of the angels' prostration before Adam while Satan arrogantly refused to do so. Satan then requested God to give him respite till the Day of Judgement so that he could seduce Adam's offspring, the cause of his original expulsion. The *sūrah* then speaks of Adam and his wife situated in heaven where they could eat of all its fruits except for one tree. This prohibited fruit is made the means to test man's will and obedience. It tells us the details of how Satan tried hard to persuade Adam and Eve to eat the forbidden fruit until they responded to him, when their nakedness was exposed. It speaks of God's admonition of them and their fall to earth where the great battle takes place. *"Said He: 'Get you down hence, [and be henceforth] enemies to one another, having on earth your abode and livelihood for a while.' 'There shall you live,' He added, 'and there shall you die, and from there shall you be brought forth [on the Day of Resurrection].'"* (7: 24–25) The *sūrah* then follows all the stages of the journey until all have returned and stood before God on the great wide stage, before going their separate ways to heaven and hell: *"And the inmates of the fire will cry out to the dwellers of paradise: 'Pour some water on us, or give us some of the sustenance God has provided for you.'*

They will reply: 'God has forbidden both to the unbelievers.'" (7: 50) At this point the curtains fall.

Here, in this *sūrah*, as we shall see, emphasis is placed on the secret of Adam's creation and the essential factors in man's constitution, leading him to follow either divine guidance or Satan's erring ways. Hence it begins by stating that Adam is created out of sounding clay and black mud moulded into shape, before God breathed of His noble spirit into him. It also states that Satan was created before him, out of the fire of scorching winds. It tells of the angels' prostration before Adam, while Satan refused to so prostrate before a human being created of such low material, and how, as a result, God expelled him from heaven with a curse. God then accepted Satan's request to give him respite until the Day of Judgement. It adds Satan's own admission that he has no power over God's faithful servants. His power is only over those who submit to him in preference to submitting to God. It then states, without detail, the destiny of each of the two parties. The lack of detail here fits with the point of emphasis whereby the two essential factors are the human constitution, and the domain where Satan can influence man.

The Origins of Man's Creation

"Indeed We have created man out of sounding clay, out of black mud moulded into shape, whereas the jinn *We had created before him out of the fire of scorching winds."* (Verses 26–27) At the outset the difference in the two natures is clearly stated. The dry clay which gives off a sound when knocked and which is originally black mud given a specific shape is totally different from the fire described here as scorching, blowing fiercely. We learn later that another element is added to man's nature, namely, the breathing of God's spirit into it. Satan's nature, however, remained that of the fire of scorching winds.

> *Your Lord said to the angels: 'I am creating a human being out of sounding clay, out of black mud moulded into shape. When I have fashioned him and breathed of My spirit into him, fall down in prostration before him.' Thereupon, the angels, one and all, prostrated themselves. Not so Iblīs, who refused to be among those who*

prostrated themselves. God said: 'Iblīs! What is your reason for not being among those who have prostrated themselves?' [Iblīs] replied: 'I am not one to prostrate myself to a human being whom You have created out of sounding clay, out of mud moulded into shape.' God said: 'Then get out of here, for you are accursed, and the curse shall be on you till the Day of Judgement.' (Verses 28–35)

These verses start with God's address to the angels. When, where and how He said all this are details that we have no way of knowing. We simply have no clear statement in the Qur'ān or the *Ḥadīth* which answers these points. Since these details belong to the realm of what lies beyond human perception, we have no way of knowing them. Hence any attempt to provide answers is futile. The same applies to man's creation out of a dry clay, moulded into shape, and infused with God's spirit.

We may refer to other statements in the Qur'ān concerning this point, particularly verse 23: 12, "*We create man out of the essence of clay,*" and verse 32: 8, "*He causes him [i.e. man] to be begotten out of a line of a humble fluid.*" We may say on the basis of these statements that man and life itself originally come out of the earth's clay. The basic constituents of this clay are found in the physical constitution of man and all living organisms. There are several stages between the original clay and man's creation, and to these the term, '*line*', refers. That is all that may be said on the basis of the texts we have. Any addition is no more than an overload added to the text, which the Qur'ān does not need. Scientific research may proceed with whatever means available to it. It may advance theories which are then either confirmed by hard evidence or amended if they cannot be proven. It cannot, however, make conclusions that are in conflict with the facts stated in the Qur'ān, which tell us that the line of creation started with the elements of clay, and to which water was later added.

How has this clay been elevated from its original constituent nature to the horizon of organic life and then to the more sublime horizon of human life? That is a secret no human being can explain. Indeed the secret of life even in the basic organism or the initial cell remains unknown. No one claims to have fathomed it. Then there remains the secret of a human's higher life with all its special features of perception, feeling and inspiration that distinguish man from all other animals. Different theories may try to explain this secret, but they have been forced to acknowledge that man has his own distinctive features and characteristics that single him out right from the very inception of human life. They cannot prove any direct relationship with any creature that lived before man, even though some theories claim that man evolved from other creatures. Nor can any of these theories disprove the other premise that different species have emerged separately, even though some are higher than others. Man thus emerged as a separate, new species.

The Qur'ān explains man's distinction in a clear and simple statement: "*When I have fashioned him and breathed of My spirit into him.*" (Verse 29) Thus it is this breath of God's spirit that takes man from the state of a humble organic entity to the noble human stage, right from his inception. It makes of him a distinguished creature worthy of being vicegerent on earth. How does this happen? In answer we ask: when was this human creature able to perceive how the Creator works?

Now we can stand on solid ground. Satan was created out of the fire of scorching wind, long before man's creation. This is as far as our knowledge goes. What Satan's nature is and how he was created are matters which we cannot delve into. However, we do understand that he shares some characteristics with the fire of scorching wind. We realize that he can affect the elements constituting mud and clay, since he is made out of fire. He also causes harm and is not slow to inflict it, since the fire he is made of is that of scorching wind. Then the story reveals to us his conceit and arrogance, which is not far removed in our perception from the nature of fire.

Then man's creation took place, starting with the sticky mud that had dried, then the adding of sublime spirit which brought about his distinction from all living creatures. This gave him his unique human characteristics. Right from the beginning of human life, man has followed his own separate line, while animals remained in their own domain.

Man's Dual Nature

It is this breath of God's spirit that provides man's link with the Supreme Society, making him worthy of contact with God, receiving

His messages, and going beyond the material world of his physical constitution to the mental world of hearts and minds. It is this breath of God's spirit which allows man to go beyond time and space, and beyond the reach of his senses and physical ability to formulate perceptions and experience feelings that, at times, seem unlimited.

All this despite the heavy nature of clay which puts him in need of all that his clay constitution requires, such as food, drink, clothing and the satisfaction of desires. He also has his weaknesses, giving rise to faulty concepts and whims. Yet right from the beginning, man is a compound of these two inseparable elements. He has the nature of a compound, not that of a mixture. We need to keep this fact clear in our minds whenever we speak about man's constitution from clay and sublime spirit. The two constituents are inseparable in his nature. In no situation does either element achieve total domination, completely excluding the other. Man is not pure clay or pure spirit even for a single moment. Every single action and every single deed involves his whole make-up which is indivisible.

Achieving a proper balance between the clay and the sublime elements is the highest level man is called on to achieve. That is the stage of human perfection. He is not required to shed either element of his constitution so as to become either angel or animal. To attempt a rise that disturbs the balance is a shortcoming that does not suit man's essential characteristics, or the purpose of his creation in this unique fashion. A person who tries to suppress his basic physical instincts is the same as one who tries to suppress his free spiritual powers. Both go beyond straight human nature, imposing on themselves something that God does not sanction. Both destroy themselves by distorting the basic compound of their very nature. They will have to account to God for such destruction.

Hence the Prophet (peace be upon him) reproached one of his Companions for deciding to remain celibate, vowing not to marry, and another for having decided to fast every day of his life and a third who decided to spend all night every night in worship. His reproach is clear in a *ḥadīth* reported by his wife 'Ā'ishah, and he said at the end: "Whoever turns away from my path does not belong to me."

Islam has formulated its own laws for human life taking into account man's constitution. It established a human system which does not

331

suppress a single aspect of human potential. The whole purpose of this system is to establish a perfect balance between these powers, so that they all work in concert, without allowing anyone of them to encroach on another. Any such encroachment leads to the negation of the other, and every dominance leads to destruction. Man is responsible for the maintenance of the essential characteristics of his nature and his accountability to God. The system Islam establishes for human life is geared to promote these characteristics which God has given to man for a clear purpose.

Anyone who wishes to kill the animal instincts in man destroys his unique constitution, just like one who wishes to kill the essentially human instincts such as faith and believing in what lies beyond the reach of our perception. Anyone who deprives people of their faith destroys their human entity, just like one who deprives them of their food, drink and other physical needs. Both are enemies of man, and both deserve to be driven away just like we must drive Satan away.

Man is an animal with something extra. He has the same needs as an animal, but he has other needs on account of that extra element. These latter needs are not inferior to the 'essential needs' as claimed by advocates of materialistic creeds who are, in truth, enemies of mankind.

These are simply thoughts derived from the truth of our human constitution, as stated in the Qur'ān. We have referred to them only briefly so that we do not delay any further the discussion of the Qur'ānic text relating the most important story of man's creation. We shall however return to these thoughts at the end of our discussion.

The Encounter and the Fall

God said to the angels: "*I am creating a human being out of sounding clay, out of black mud moulded into shape. When I have fashioned him and breathed of My spirit into him, fall down in prostration before him.*" (Verses 28–29) And what God said immediately took effect, for His word expresses His will, and His will is always done. We cannot question how the breath of God's eternal spirit mixed with the clay that has limited life. Such arguments are no more than idle play. It is indeed a child's play with man's intellect itself. It forces the human mind out of its own realm in which it may exercise its powers of perception, reflection and comprehension. All the controversy that has been raised over this issue, past and present, betrays ignorance of the nature of the human mind, its characteristics and limitations. It simply forces the human mind to try to measure God's work by human standards. It is an altogether wrong premise.

God simply says that this has happened without saying how. Hence, the event itself is a fact that the human mind cannot deny. Yet it cannot prove it by any interpretation it invents, other than accepting what God has said. Man is a creature with a beginning, and as such, he cannot judge what is eternal, or how the eternal creates. When the human mind accepts this point, it stops expending its power in futile argument.

What happened after God issued His order to the angels to prostrate themselves before Adam? *"Thereupon, the angels, one and all, prostrated themselves."* (Verse 30) That is in the nature of this aspect of God's creation, the angels. They obey God's orders whatever they are, without argument or delay. However, something else also took place at the same time: *"Not so* Iblīs, *who refused to be among those who prostrated themselves."* (Verse 31)

Iblīs belongs to a different type of creation, separate from the angels. He is created out of fire while they are created out of light. They do not disobey God, whatever His command may be. He, on the other hand, disobeyed God, rejecting His command. For certain, then, he is not, and never was, one of the angels. That we have here a form of exception, more strongly pronounced in the Arabic text, refers to what is called in Arabic linguistics 'inconsequential exception'. It is acceptable to say in Arabic: "The Joneses have come except for Aḥmad", when you know that Aḥmad does not belong to the Jones family, but is always with them. Now since the order stated here has been issued to the angels, how could it apply to *Iblīs?* That the same order was issued to *Iblīs* is clearly stated in *Sūrah* 7, The Heights. There the order to *Iblīs* is mentioned in a later verse, when God questions him: *"What has prevented you from prostrating yourself when I commanded you?"* (7: 12) This is clear proof that *Iblīs* was given the same order. He might have been included in the order given to the angels, if he was with them at the time, or perhaps a separate order was issued to him. However, this is not mentioned here and this shows that he is of a far lesser position than the angels. Furthermore, the texts we have, and Satan's own behaviour, all demonstrate that he was not one of the angels.

It should be also mentioned that we are dealing here with matters that belong to a different realm, and that we cannot fathom their nature or how they took place, except within the meaning of the texts we have. Neither human reason nor imagination has any role to play here.

"*God said: 'Iblīs! What is your reason for not being among those who have prostrated themselves?' [Iblīs] replied: 'I am not one to prostrate myself to a human being whom You have created out of sounding clay, out of mud moulded into shape.'*" (Verses 32–33) Thus the nature of this creature, who was created out of the fire of scorching winds, has surfaced. We see that arrogance, conceit and disobedience are part of his nature. *Iblīs* mentions the clay and mud, but does not mention the sublime spirit that mixes irrevocably with that mud. In his insolence he declares that a great creature like him could not prostrate himself to a human being whom God has created out of mud moulded into shape.

Such an attitude leads to its natural consequence: "*God said: 'Then get out of here, for you are accursed, and the curse shall be on you till the Day of Judgement.'*" (Verses 34–35) This is a just reward for disobedience and rebellion.

At this point, his evil characteristics come out in full force. We see how he nurses his grudges and how he plans to spread evil: "*He said: 'My Lord, grant me a respite till the Day when all shall be resurrected.' [God] said: 'You are among those who are granted respite till the Day of the appointed time.'*" (Verses 36–38) He requests respite to the Day of Judgement, but not to have the opportunity to repent of his sin which he has committed in the presence of God Almighty. It is not to atone for his sin that he wants to be spared death until the Day of Judgement, but rather to exact revenge on Adam and his offspring. He is avenging himself against mankind for his expulsion and the curse that he has incurred. He thus blames Adam for his expulsion, instead of acknowledging that it was the result of his own sinful insolence.

"*[Iblīs] said: 'My Lord, since You have let me fall in error, I shall make [evil] seem fair to them on earth, and I shall most certainly beguile them all into grievous error, except for those of them who are truly Your faithful servants.'"* (Verses 39–40) It is Iblīs himself who has chosen the battleground, which is the earth. *"I shall make evil seem fair to them on earth."* (Verse 39) He also states what he will use for a weapon. He will simply tempt mankind by making what is foul appear to be fair, so that they are tempted to do it. In fact, no human being resorts to foul things unless these seem fair to him by some trick perpetrated by Satan. Thus he sees such foul things in a guise which is different from what they truly are. Hence people should always remember the weapon which Satan uses. If they find something attractive and are tempted, they should make sure lest it has been made to appear so by Satan. Proper refuge is to ensure that their link with their Lord is kept in fine tuning by worshipping Him as He should be worshipped. Even according to his own statement, Satan has no power over God's faithful servants: *"I shall most certainly beguile them all into grievous error, except for those of them who are truly Your faithful servants."* (Verses 39–40) God chooses from among His servants those who purge themselves of all evil and worship Him alone, as though they see Him. It is over such people that Satan holds no sway.

Satan knows that this condition which he himself has stated is one which he cannot change because it is part of the laws governing human nature. Hence, the reply to Satan's words: *"Said He: 'This is, with Me, a straight way. You shall have no power over My servants, except for those who, having fallen into error, choose to follow you.'"* (Verses 41–42) This is the way established by the will of God as a final arbiter with regard to guidance and going astray. *"You shall have no power over My servants."* (Verse 42) They are immune to your devices and schemes, as they close all entry points to their minds and hearts. They always look to God for guidance, and they know what pleases Him by their nature which they purge of all sin. Satan has power only over 'those who choose to follow' him, as they have been in error, going far astray. Those who dedicate themselves to God will not be left without guidance.

The outcome is also clear. It is stated right at the beginning: *"For all such, hell is the promised destiny. It has seven gates, with each gate having its allotted share of them."* (Verses 43–44) For those who go astray are of different categories. Each gate to hell will have its portion from among them, according to the nature of their deeds.

335

This ends the scene of the beginning of human life, putting great emphasis on the lesson to be learnt. It tells how Satan finds his way into the human soul, trying to overpower the sublimity of the spirit breathed into man with the characteristics of his clay origin. Those who maintain their links with God, emphasizing their spirit characteristics will have nothing to fear from Satan.

The destiny of the believers who follow the truth is also outlined here: "*The God-fearing shall dwell amidst gardens and fountains. [They are received with the greeting]: 'Enter here in peace and security.' We shall have removed from their hearts any lurking feelings of malice, [and they shall rest] as brothers, facing one another, on couches. No weariness shall ever touch them there, nor shall they ever be made to depart.*" (Verses 45–48) The God-fearing are those who are on the alert, trying always to avoid what displeases God or incurs His anger. It may be said that the '*fountains*' mentioned here correspond to the gates of hell. These people enter heaven '*in peace and security*' which contrast with the fear and panic felt by those who go to hell. '*Malice*' and ill feelings are removed from their hearts, which contrasts with the grudge that Satan always feels against human beings. Their good labours in this life are rewarded by their being secure, free from all feelings of tiredness and weariness.

A Fine Destiny for the Righteous

The story of man's creation and placement on earth deserves detailed comments, but we will only touch briefly on certain aspects of it, as befits the way it is told in this *sūrah*.

The *sūrah* delivers a clear message concerning the special creation known as man. He has a unique make-up which gives him more than the physical constitution which he has in common with other living creatures. No matter how life emerged and how living creatures came into being, man is distinguished by another quality mentioned in the Qur'ān, which derives from the breathing of the divine spirit into him. This quality is not the result of the continuous evolution of man, stage after stage, as claimed by Darwinism. It came right at the inception of human life, when man was first created. There was no time when man was only a living organic entity, then the spirit entered into his constitution to make of him the man we see today.

Neo-Darwinism, and its main advocate, Julian Huxley, have been forced to admit a part of this great fact. In this respect, it admits the uniqueness of man, and his ability to establish human civilization. Nevertheless, neo-Darwinism continues to claim that this unique human being has evolved from the animal kingdom.

It is very hard to reconcile this view of neo-Darwinism which admits the uniqueness of man with the essential concept of evolution advanced by Darwin. Yet all evolutionists adamantly persist with this attitude, giving it false scientific guise. This is only because they try to break away from the Church and whatever view it advances. The Jews have always encouraged and promoted this concept, endorsing it as scientific, because it serves their ultimate goal.

We have already discussed this point when commenting on a similar text in *Sūrah* 7, The Heights. It is useful to quote here from those comments:

> The total import of Qur'ānic statements that speak of the creation of Adam (peace be upon him) and the start of human life indicates very strongly that this particular creation was given its human characteristic and special tasks at the time of its coming into existence. Evolution in human history took the form of developing these characteristics and gaining further experience in utilizing them. It is not an evolution of existence which suggests, as Darwinism would like us to believe, that a process of evolution of species has reached its climax with the advent of man.

> There might have been stages of advanced animals, with one coming after the other, as evidenced by the theory of natural selection. But this is no more than a theory that does not aspire to any degree of certainty, because the estimation of the ages of rocks in geological strata is again a theoretical process. It is the same as estimating the ages of different stars and planets on the basis of the characteristics of their rays. Future discoveries may amend or change these theories.

> But even if we were to learn the ages of rocks with absolute certainty, there is nothing to prevent the existence of different

species of animals, some of which are higher than others, in different time periods, and that their advancement makes them particularly suited for the prevailing circumstances. Some of them may disappear when circumstances change drastically to make it difficult for the earth to sustain their existence. That does not make it inevitable that these species have evolved one from the other. All the studies and observations of Charles Darwin and those who followed him cannot prove more than that. They cannot say with any certainty that one species evolved from a preceding one, on the basis of fossils and where they have been found. It simply proves that a subsequent species was higher than a preceding one. This can easily be explained as we have already said: the prevailing circumstances at one particular time allowed the existence of one species. The circumstances subsequently prevailing allowed the existence of another species and the disappearance of the first one.

All this means that the appearance of human beings was independent of other species. It took place at a time when the prevailing circumstances on earth facilitated the existence, development and advancement of this particular type of creation. This is the total sum of the Qur'ānic statements on the creation of man.

The fact that biologically, physiologically, mentally and spiritually, man has unique characteristics is so clear that it has been acknowledged by neo-Darwinists who include a number of atheists. This uniqueness also supports the view that human existence was totally independent of the existence of all other species. It simply has no biological inter-relationship with them.[3]

An Eternal Hostility

The unique method of creation which led to the emergence of man, a creature with its own separate existence, is the fact that God breathed in him of His own spirit. This gives us a totally different picture of man and his 'essential needs' from those of all materialistic philosophies, with all the economic, social and political doctrines they produce and all the concepts and values they advance for human life.

---

3. Syed Quṭb, *In the Shade of the Qur'ān*, Vol. VI, pp. 42–43

The claim that man is nothing but an advanced animal species that has evolved from lower animals lies at the heart of the concept promoted in the Marxist Declaration that the essential needs of man are: food, drink, shelter and sex. These are certainly the basic needs of animals. Man cannot be given a more degrading position than what this outlook assigns to him. All his rights that are derived from the fact that he is unlike animals, since he has his unique human qualities, are thus denied to him. He is denied his freedom of belief, thought and expression, and his right to choose his profession and where to live, as well as his right to criticize the system of government and its intellectual basis. Indeed he is denied even the right to criticize the party in power, or those who are even less than the party, such as despotic rulers in hateful dictatorial regimes that treat human beings as though they are no more than a flock of sheep. After all, human beings, in materialistic philosophies, are no different from animals from whom they had at one time evolved. All this misery is then ennobled as 'scientific socialism'.

The Islamic concept of man, based on man's special, distinctive qualities, considers that the basic needs of man are different from those of animals. Food, drink, shelter and sex do not constitute the total sum of his basic needs. His intellectual and spiritual needs are by no means of secondary importance. Faith, freedom of thought, will and choice are also basic needs that must be placed in the same category as food, drink, shelter and sex. Indeed, these other needs are of a higher position, because these are the ones that man needs while animals do not. In other words, these are the ones that emphasize his humanity. When he is denied these, his humanity itself is denied.

Thus, in the Islamic system, freedom of faith, thought and expression, choice and will cannot be denied for the sake of increased production so that food, drink, shelter and sex are provided for humans! Nor is it permissible that moral values, as established by God, not by tradition, environment or economy, be denied in order to meet the animal needs of man.

The two outlooks are essentially different in their evaluation of man and his basic needs. Hence, they can never be reconciled in a single system. It is either Islam or materialistic doctrines with all their oppressive products, including what they call 'scientific socialism'.

Indeed 'scientific socialism' is just another sordid product of materialism which degrades man whom God Himself has honoured.

The eternal battle between Satan and man on this earth is one in which Satan tries his best to lead man away from what submission to God alone entails in accepting His faith, concepts, worship, systems and laws. Human beings who submit to God alone, which means they worship Him only, are the ones over whom Satan has no power whatsoever. It is God who says to Satan, as related in this story of creation: "*This is, with Me, a straight way. You shall have no power over My servants, except for those who, having fallen into error, choose to follow you.*" (Verses 41–42)

The point which separates those who follow the road to heaven, promised to the righteous, and those who follow the path leading to hell, which is the abode of evildoers, is that of submission to God. This is always referred to in the Qur'ān as worship. The alternative is to follow what Satan paints as fair and thus not submit to God. It should be pointed out here that Satan himself did not deny God's existence or His attributes. So, he did not disbelieve in Him, so to speak. What he did was to refuse to submit to Him. That is the point at issue which sends Satan and his followers to hell.

Submission to God is the central point of Islam. If those who claim to follow Islam submit to anyone other than God in a single rule, whether it relates to faith, concepts, worship, law or moral standards and values, then their claim is worthless. Islam means submission to God alone in all these. Submission to anyone else means sinking back into *jāhiliyyah*. It is not possible to separate this submission so as to make it applicable only to faith and worship, but not to systems and laws. Submission to God must be acknowledged in its totality. Such submission means worshipping God, in both its linguistic and Islamic senses. It is over such submission that the eternal battle between man and Satan is fought.

Finally we come to what God touchingly says about the righteous: "*The God-fearing shall dwell amidst gardens and fountains. [They are received with the greeting]: 'Enter here in peace and security.' We shall have removed from their hearts any lurking feelings of malice, [and they shall rest] as brothers, facing one another, on couches. No weariness shall ever touch them there, nor shall they ever be made to depart.*" (Verses 45–48)

This religion does not try to change human nature or to make mankind a different sort of creation. It acknowledges that in this life people experience malice and grudges. This is part of their human nature which faith does not totally eradicate. It simply works on it to reduce its intensity, and then elevates its domain so that believers love and hate for God's sake only. But in heaven, where their humanity attains its most sublime standard, the very sense of malice and grudge is removed. Here, people experience only pure love and brotherhood.

This is the supreme standard of the people of heaven. If someone finds that it dominates his feelings in this life, then he should look forward to being in heaven in the hereafter, as long as he is a believer. This is the essential condition which gives every action its true value.

4

Lessons of History

Tell My servants that I alone am Much Forgiving, truly Merciful; (49)

and also, My punishment is indeed the most grievous suffering. (50)

Tell them about Abraham's guests, (51)

when they went in to him and said: 'Peace.' But he replied: 'We feel afraid of you.' (52)

They said: 'Do not be alarmed. We bring you the happy news of the birth of a son to you who will be endowed with knowledge.' (53)

Said he: 'Do you give me this happy news when I have been overtaken by old age? Of what, then, is your good news?' (54)

نَبِّئْ عِبَادِيٓ أَنِّي أَنَا ٱلْغَفُورُ ٱلرَّحِيمُ ﴿٤٩﴾

وَأَنَّ عَذَابِي هُوَ ٱلْعَذَابُ ٱلْأَلِيمُ ﴿٥٠﴾

وَنَبِّئْهُمْ عَن ضَيْفِ إِبْرَٰهِيمَ ﴿٥١﴾

إِذْ دَخَلُوا۟ عَلَيْهِ فَقَالُوا۟ سَلَٰمًا قَالَ إِنَّا مِنكُمْ وَجِلُونَ ﴿٥٢﴾

قَالُوا۟ لَا تَوْجَلْ إِنَّا نُبَشِّرُكَ بِغُلَٰمٍ عَلِيمٍ ﴿٥٣﴾

قَالَ أَبَشَّرْتُمُونِي عَلَىٰٓ أَن مَّسَّنِيَ ٱلْكِبَرُ فَبِمَ تُبَشِّرُونَ ﴿٥٤﴾

They replied: 'That good news we have given you is the truth. So do not abandon hope.' (55)

قَالُوا۟ بَشَّرْنَٰكَ بِٱلْحَقِّ فَلَا تَكُن مِّنَ ٱلْقَٰنِطِينَ ۝

He said: 'Who but a person going far astray abandons hope of His Lord's grace?' (56)

قَالَ وَمَن يَقْنَطُ مِن رَّحْمَةِ رَبِّهِۦٓ إِلَّا ٱلضَّآلُّونَ ۝

[Abraham] said: 'What is your business, you [heavenly] messengers?' (57)

قَالَ فَمَا خَطْبُكُمْ أَيُّهَا ٱلْمُرْسَلُونَ ۝

They replied: 'We are sent to a guilty nation, (58)

قَالُوٓا۟ إِنَّآ أُرْسِلْنَآ إِلَىٰ قَوْمٍ مُّجْرِمِينَ ۝

except for Lot's household, all of whom we shall save, (59)

إِلَّآ ءَالَ لُوطٍ إِنَّا لَمُنَجُّوهُمْ أَجْمَعِينَ ۝

except for his wife. We have decreed that she should remain with those who stay behind.' (60)

إِلَّا ٱمْرَأَتَهُۥ قَدَّرْنَآ إِنَّهَا لَمِنَ ٱلْغَٰبِرِينَ ۝

And when the messengers [of God] came to the house of Lot, (61)

فَلَمَّا جَآءَ ءَالَ لُوطٍ ٱلْمُرْسَلُونَ ۝

he said: 'You are unknown here.' (62)

قَالَ إِنَّكُمْ قَوْمٌ مُّنكَرُونَ ۝

They answered: 'No, but we bring you news of that over which they have been disputing. (63)

قَالُوا۟ بَلْ جِئْنَٰكَ بِمَا كَانُوا۟ فِيهِ يَمْتَرُونَ ۝

We are bringing you the certainty [of its fulfilment], for we are speaking the truth indeed. (64)

وَأَتَيْنَكَ بِٱلْحَقِّ وَإِنَّا لَصَدِقُونَ ﴿٦٤﴾

Depart with your household in the dead of night, with yourself following them in the rear. Let none of you look back, but proceed to where you are commanded.' (65)

فَأَسْرِ بِأَهْلِكَ بِقِطْعٍ مِّنَ ٱلَّيْلِ وَٱتَّبِعْ أَدْبَرَهُمْ وَلَا يَلْتَفِتْ مِنكُمْ أَحَدٌ وَٱمْضُواْ حَيْثُ تُؤْمَرُونَ ﴿٦٥﴾

And We made plain the case to him, that the last remnant of those [wrongdoers] will be wiped out by the morning. (66)

وَقَضَيْنَآ إِلَيْهِ ذَلِكَ ٱلْأَمْرَ أَنَّ دَابِرَ هَٰٓؤُلَآءِ مَقْطُوعٌ مُّصْبِحِينَ ﴿٦٦﴾

The people of the city came [to Lot] rejoicing [at the news of the young people]. (67)

وَجَآءَ أَهْلُ ٱلْمَدِينَةِ يَسْتَبْشِرُونَ ﴿٦٧﴾

Said he: 'These are my guests: so do not put me to shame. (68)

قَالَ إِنَّ هَٰٓؤُلَآءِ ضَيْفِى فَلَا تَفْضَحُونِ ﴿٦٨﴾

Fear God and do not bring disgrace on me.' (69)

وَٱتَّقُواْ ٱللَّهَ وَلَا تُخْزُونِ ﴿٦٩﴾

They replied: 'Have we not forbidden you to entertain any people?' (70)

قَالُوٓاْ أَوَلَمْ نَنْهَكَ عَنِ ٱلْعَٰلَمِينَ ﴿٧٠﴾

He said: 'Here are these daughters of mine [to marry], if you must do [what you intend to do.]' (71)

قَالَ هَٰٓؤُلَآءِ بَنَاتِى إِن كُنتُمْ فَٰعِلِينَ ﴿٧١﴾

By your life, they were reeling in their drunkenness, (72)

لَعَمْرُكَ إِنَّهُمْ لَفِى سَكْرَتِهِمْ يَعْمَهُونَ ﴿٧٢﴾

when the blast [of punishment] overtook them at sunrise, (73)

فَأَخَذَتْهُمُ ٱلصَّيْحَةُ مُشْرِقِينَ ۝

and We turned those [towns] upside down, and rained on them stones of clay. (74)

فَجَعَلْنَا عَالِيَهَا سَافِلَهَا وَأَمْطَرْنَا عَلَيْهِمْ حِجَارَةً مِّن سِجِّيلٍ ۝

Surely in this there are messages for those who read the signs. (75)

إِنَّ فِي ذَٰلِكَ لَآيَٰتٍ لِّلْمُتَوَسِّمِينَ ۝

Those [towns] stood on a road that is trodden still. (76)

وَإِنَّهَا لَبِسَبِيلٍ مُّقِيمٍ ۝

In all this there is a sign for true believers. (77)

إِنَّ فِي ذَٰلِكَ لَآيَةً لِّلْمُؤْمِنِينَ ۝

The dwellers of the wooded dales [of Madyan] were also wrong-doers, (78)

وَإِن كَانَ أَصْحَٰبُ ٱلْأَيْكَةِ لَظَٰلِمِينَ ۝

and so We punished them. Both these [communities] lived by an open highway, plain to see. (79)

فَٱنتَقَمْنَا مِنْهُمْ وَإِنَّهُمَا لَبِإِمَامٍ مُّبِينٍ ۝

Likewise, the people of al-Ḥijr also denied [God's] messengers. (80)

وَلَقَدْ كَذَّبَ أَصْحَٰبُ ٱلْحِجْرِ ٱلْمُرْسَلِينَ ۝

We have given them Our signs, but they turned their backs on them. (81)

وَءَاتَيْنَٰهُمْ ءَايَٰتِنَا فَكَانُوا۟ عَنْهَا مُعْرِضِينَ ۝

Out of the mountains did they hew their dwellings, leading a life of security. (82)

وَكَانُوا۟ يَنْحِتُونَ مِنَ ٱلْجِبَالِ بُيُوتًا ءَامِنِينَ ۝

But the blast [of punishment] overtook them at early morning. (83)

فَأَخَذَتْهُمُ ٱلصَّيْحَةُ مُصْبِحِينَ ﴿٨٣﴾

Of no avail to them was all that they had acquired. (84)

فَمَآ أَغْنَىٰ عَنْهُم مَّا كَانُوا۟ يَكْسِبُونَ ﴿٨٤﴾

Overview

This rather long passage refers to some examples of God's mercy and the punishment He inflicts. These include how Abraham was given in his old age the happy news of a son to be born to him, and how Lot and his household, except his wife, were saved from the fate that befell the wrongdoers. They also include a reference to the fateful punishments that befell the people of the Madyan and those of al-Ḥijr.

All these stories occur after an introduction that says: "*Tell My servants that I alone am Much Forgiving, truly Merciful; and also, My punishment is indeed the most grievous suffering.*" (Verses 49–50) Some of them thus confirm what has been said about God's mercy, and some confirm that His punishment is grievous indeed. These stories also refer to what is mentioned at the opening of the *sūrah*, confirming the warning it contains: "*Let them eat and enjoy themselves, and let their hopes beguile them. For they will surely come to know [the truth]. Never have We destroyed any community unless divine revelations have been made known to it. No community can ever forestall its term, nor can they delay it.*" (Verses 3–5) These were examples of cities destroyed by God after they ignored all the warnings they had received. Their punishment only befell them after the time they were given had lapsed. The stories we have in this passage also confirm what is mentioned earlier in the *sūrah* concerning the angels and their mission when they are sent with God's orders: "*They say: 'You to whom this reminder has been bestowed from on high! You are truly mad. Why do you not bring the angels before us, if you are truthful?' We never send down angels except in accordance with the truth. And then, [the unbelievers] would be given no further respite.*" (Verses 6–8)

All this goes to show that the whole *sūrah* is a single unit, with every part confirming the rest. This observation we make in spite of the fact that most *sūrahs* were revealed in parts, with the possibility that later verses were often revealed before earlier ones. Yet the final ordering of the verses of each *sūrah* is made in accordance with divine instructions. Hence, there must be a clear purpose in such order. We have learnt some aspects of the wisdom behind the ordering of verses in the *sūrahs* we have discussed. Each of them appears clearly as a complete and perfect structure. Yet what we say is only a personal point of view, while true knowledge belongs to God alone. We pray to Him to guide us to what is right.

Abraham's Visitors

"Tell My servants that I alone am Much Forgiving, truly Merciful; and also, My punishment is indeed the most grievous suffering." (Verses 49–50) This order to the Prophet (peace be upon him) comes after the reward of God-fearing believers and the punishment of wrongdoers are mentioned. The link is self-evident. But God's mercy and forgiveness are mentioned before the punishment, because they fit in with the grace God has committed Himself to bestow. Sometimes, only the punishment and suffering are mentioned, or they are given precedence in the text, but that is only because there is special need for such treatment.

We are then given an account of the encounter between the Prophet Abraham and the angels sent to Lot. This episode is mentioned several times in the Qur'ān, each time in a different way which fits the context in which it occurs. The story of Lot alone is also mentioned in other places.

For example, Lot's story is covered in *Sūrah* 7, The Heights, and a different account of Abraham and Lot's story is given in *Sūrah* 11, Hūd. In the first we have a denunciation by Lot of the indecent practices of his community, and their reply to him: *"Drive them [i.e. Lot and his household] out of your land, for they are indeed people who would keep chaste."* (7: 82) It also refers to saving him and his household, except his wife who was destined to stay behind with those who were to be destroyed. There is no mention of the angels coming to him or the scheme of his people against them. In the second instance, a totally different layout is given to the story of the angels with Abraham and Lot. There we have more details concerning Abraham and the happy news he was given in the presence of his wife. There is also a mention of his argument with the angels concerning Lot and his community, which is not mentioned here. Different lines are adopted in the two *sūrahs* in relating the events concerning the angels and Lot. In *Sūrah Hūd* the angels do not reveal their identity to him until his people arrived, and he had pleaded with them to spare his guests, but all his pleas fell on deaf ears. When he despaired of them, he cried out in distress: "*Would that with you I had real strength, or that I could lean on some mighty support.*" (11: 80) Here in this *sūrah*, the identity of the angels is revealed right at the outset, while the design of his people against his guests is mentioned later. The point here is not to mention the story as it took place, but the confirmation of the warnings, emphasizing that when angels are sent down, their task is to inflict the punishment, giving people no further respite.

> *Tell them about Abraham's guests, when they went in to him and said: 'Peace.' But he replied: 'We feel afraid of you.' They said: 'Do not be alarmed. We bring you the happy news of the birth of a son to you who will be endowed with knowledge.' Said he: 'Do you give me this happy news when I have been overtaken by old age? Of what, then, is your good news?' They replied: 'That good news we have given you is the truth. So do not abandon hope.' He said: 'Who but a person going far astray abandons hope of His Lord's grace?'* (Verses 51–56)

In this account some of the details mentioned in other *sūrahs* are left out. The angels greet Abraham with a message of peace as they enter, but he tells them he is apprehensive about them. The *sūrah* does not mention the reason for his fear, nor does it mention that he placed a roasted calf before them, as mentioned in *Sūrah* 11, Hūd. There we are told: "*When he saw that their hands did not reach out to it, he felt their conduct strange and became apprehensive of them.*" (11: 70) The point of emphasis here is that God's grace is always bestowed on God's servants, as made clear by His messengers. Hence the details of

Abraham's story are of little importance. "*They said: 'Do not be alarmed. We bring you the happy news of the birth of a son to you who will be endowed with knowledge.'*" (Verse 53) The *sūrah* outlines this happy news without much detail of what else took place.

Here also we have Abraham's reply, without mentioning his wife and her intervention in the discussion that ensued: "*Said he: 'Do you give me this happy news when I have been overtaken by old age? Of what, then, is your good news?'*" (Verse 54) First Abraham feels it unlikely that he would be given a son at his old age, particularly with his wife also being old and barren as mentioned in other *sūrahs*. Therefore, the angels remind him of the truth: "*They replied: 'That good news we have given you is the truth. So do not abandon hope.'*" (Verse 55) Abraham immediately returns to his normal hopeful self, stating that he never lost hope of God's grace: "*He said: 'Who but a person going far astray abandons hope of His Lord's grace?'*" (Verse 56)

Here we note a reference to God's grace in Abraham's reply, which fits with the beginning. An emphasis is also placed here on the fact that only those who go far astray despair of God's grace. They go far away from the road God has laid down for people to traverse, so they do not feel His mercy, compassion and care which He bestows on all His servants. On the other hand, a person whose heart is full of faith will never despair of God's grace, no matter what hardship and difficulties he is called on to endure. Even in the thickness of darkness and the gloom of adversity, they feel that God's grace is close at hand. It will never fail to be bestowed. God has the power to initiate the causes and bring about the results, changing the present and the future.

As Abraham feels reassured he becomes eager to know the purpose they have been sent to accomplish: "*[Abraham] said: 'What is your business, you [heavenly] messengers?' They replied: 'We are sent to a guilty nation, except for Lot's household, all of whom we shall save, except for his wife. We have decreed that she should remain with those who stay behind.'*" (Verses 57–60) The account we have here does not refer to Abraham's argument on behalf of Lot and his people, as mentioned in *Sūrah* Hūd. Instead, it moves on quickly from the angels' information to the realization of their mission. Abraham believes that God will bestow His grace on Lot and his household, with the exception of Lot's wife. Thus the business the angels have with Abraham is accomplished, and they proceed towards completion of their mission.

When All Values Are of Little Value

And when the messengers [of God] came to the house of Lot, he said: 'You are unknown here.' They answered: 'No, but we bring you news of that over which they have been disputing. We are bringing you the certainty [of its fulfilment], for we are speaking the truth indeed. Depart with your household in the dead of night, with yourself following them in the rear. Let none of you look back, but proceed to where you are commanded.' And We made plain the case to him, that the last remnant of those [wrongdoers] will be wiped out by the morning. (Verses 61–66)

As indicated earlier, the *sūrah* states that the angels immediately reveal their true identity to Lot and that they have come to accomplish what his people disputed about their punishment for their misdeeds. That punishment comes in fulfilment of God's warnings, confirming the fact that when angels are sent to a community, their punishment is immediate.

"*He said: 'You are unknown here.'*" (Verse 62) He said this in irritation, as he was fully aware of the habits of his people and expected what they would try to do with his guests. He was a stranger among his people, and they were arrogant in their immorality. Hence he tells his guests that it is unwise of them to come to a city when the reputation of its people is well known. "*They answered: 'No, but we bring you news of that over which they have been disputing. We are bringing you the certainty [of its fulfilment], for we are speaking the truth indeed.*'" (Verses 63–64) All these assertions serve to tell us the extent of Lot's alarm and distress, as he wants to be hospitable yet also protect his guests against the designs of his people. Hence, they reassure him time after time, before giving him his instructions: "*Depart with your household in the dead of night, with yourself following them in the rear. Let none of you look back, but proceed to where you are commanded.*" (Verse 65) Thus Lot was to leave the town by night, before the break

351

of dawn. He was to walk behind those who would be saved with him to make sure that no one was left behind, and no one looked behind, like displaced people unwilling to leave their homeland.

"*And We made plain the case to him, that the last remnant of those [wrongdoers] will be wiped out by the morning.*" (Verse 66) It is God, then, who has revealed to Lot this very serious piece of news, which is expressed in the Qur'ān as the last one of those people would be destroyed by the morning. Well, if the last of them is destroyed, it follows that the whole lot are destroyed, with none spared. Hence, caution must be exercised, so that no one is left behind to suffer the fate which was sure to engulf the whole city.

The *sūrah* relates this part of the story first because it is more suited to its overall theme. It now fills in the details of what happened earlier when Lot's people heard that a number of handsome young men were visiting him. To them, that was a chance not to be missed: "*The people of the city came [to Lot] rejoicing.*" (Verse 67)

The way this is expressed portrays to what low and abhorrent level those people had sunk in their eagerness to fulfil their perverse, uncontrolled desires. This is shown in the fact that the townsfolk came in a group, rejoicing at the presence of young men, openly declaring their intent to rape them in broad daylight. This shameful publicity of their wicked intentions, in addition to the filthy action itself, is so abhorrent and repulsive that we cannot imagine it, but it was certainly true. An individual may harbour some perverted desire, but he conceals the fact and tries to satisfy his perversion in secret. He is ashamed if others know of it. In fact, sound human nature prefers to keep such desire private even when it is with one's legitimate wife. Some animal species do not mate in public. But those wicked and evil people declare their lust shamelessly, come seeking it in groups, and rejoice as they expect to fulfil it. This is unparalleled perversion.

On the other side we see the Prophet Lot in distress, standing up to defend his guests and his honour. He tries to awaken in his people a sense of honour and fear of God. But he knew full well that they had no fear of God, and that such perverted natures would not respond to any compassionate, humanitarian appeal. Yet in his distress he tries every avenue: "*Said he: 'These are my guests: so do not put me to shame. Fear God and do not bring disgrace on me.'*" (Verses 68–69) But his appeal awakens no feeling of honour or integrity. They had lost all such feelings. Instead, they rebuke Lot for entertaining any man as a guest, as if he is the offender by offering them the temptation: "*They replied: 'Have we not forbidden you to entertain any people?'*" (Verse 70)

Lot continues with his attempts, pointing out the proper line of desire, i.e. the other sex. It is women who hold natural attraction for men to satisfy their sexual urge, so that procreation continues and human life is preserved. "*He said: 'Here are these daughters of mine [to marry], if you must do [what you intend to do].'*" (Verse 71)

Lot, a prophet, does not offer his daughters in any adulterous relationship. He simply reminds the menfolk of the natural way to satisfy their urge. He knew that if they responded to his appeal they would not want to be adulterous. Hence, his offer sought recourse to their human nature, if only it would respond. But that was unlikely.

The *sūrah* portrays the scene with all the action taking place. At this moment, the mode of expression changes into an address to the Prophet who is observing it all. This takes the form of an oath, following the traditional method of Arabic emphasis: "*By your life, they were reeling in their drunkenness.*" (Verse 72) This describes a state that had become part of their nature. In that state they were unlikely ever to wake up or listen to appeals based on personal integrity, fear of God or uncorrupted human nature. Hence they were doomed and God's punishment was to engulf them without delay: "*We never send down angels except in accordance with the truth. And then, [the unbelievers] would be given no further respite.*" (Verse 8)

Now we face a scene of total destruction, two towns in complete ruin with particular features that are suited to the perverted natures of their dwellers: "*By your life, they were reeling in their drunkenness, when the blast [of punishment] overtook them at sunrise, and We turned those [towns] upside down, and rained on them stones of clay.*" (Verses 72–74)

The Fate of Erring Communities

The towns were ruined by a natural phenomenon which seems similar to that of earthquakes and volcanic eruptions, which are sometimes accompanied by earth subsidence and a showering of stones. Sometimes complete villages and towns are so immersed. It is said that the Dead Sea was formed after this event, which witnessed the sinking of Sodom and Gomorrah, when the surface of the earth collapsed forming a lake that was later filled with water. We will not try to explain their particular punishment as an earthquake or a volcano, for our approach is based instead on complete faith that does not admit such explanations.

We know for certain that all natural phenomena operate in accordance with a law that God has laid down for the universe. But no phenomenon or event occurs on the basis of inevitability. It occurs in fulfilment of God's will, which applies particularly to that situation. There is no conflict between the operation of God's law and the need for an act of God's will for every event. We also know for certain that in some cases God, in His wisdom, accomplishes a particular will of His through a certain event, in order to serve a certain purpose. What destroyed Lot's townships need not be an ordinary earthquake or volcano. God might have willed to inflict on them whatever scourge He might have chosen, at the time of His choice and by the method He determined. That is the approach to explain, on the basis of faith, all miraculous events that took place at the times of all prophets.

Those towns were on a road regularly traversed between Arabia and Syria. They contain good lessons for those who wish to learn from the end that befell earlier communities which defied and rejected God's messengers. But such lessons are of benefit only to those who are prepared to learn from them: "*Surely in this there are messages for those who read the signs. Those [towns] stood on a road that is trodden still. In all this there is a sign for true believers.*" (Verses 75–77) Thus the warning came true. The sending of the angels was a signal for God's punishment which no one can prevent or avoid.

The same applied to the communities of the Prophets Shu'ayb and Ṣāliḥ: "*The dwellers of the wooded dales [of Madyan] were also wrongdoers, and so We punished them. Both these [communities] lived by an open highway, plain to see.*" (Verses 78–79) The Qur'ān gives detailed accounts of the history of the Prophet Shu'ayb and his people in other *sūrahs*. Here we have only a reference to the injustice they were keen to perpetrate, and to their punishment. This comes as confirmation of God's punishment. As indicated at the beginning of the *sūrah*, when the time appointed for any community lapses, their punishment is inevitable if they persist in their rejection of God's messages. The city of Madyan and the wooded dales inhabited by Shu'ayb's people were not far from Lot's townships. The reference in the dual form, 'both', here may mean Madyan and the wooded lands, which were on a clearly marked road. Or it may mean the townships of Lot already mentioned and Shu'ayb's city of Madyan. They may be grouped together as they lie on the same road between Hijaz in today's Saudi Arabia and Syria. The doom that befalls cities and townships flourishing along a well traversed road provides a great reminder as it becomes a lesson to all that pass by. Life continues all around these towns which once flourished, but now lie in ruin.

The people of al-Ḥijr are the community to whom the Prophet Ṣāliḥ was sent. Their land lies in between Hijaz and Syria. Its ruins are still seen today, because they used to build their dwellings in the mountains, cutting space for themselves there. This indicates a high level of progress and civilization, as well as recognized power: "*Likewise, the people of al-Ḥijr also denied [God's] messengers.*" The fact is that those people only rejected the message of the Prophet Ṣāliḥ, but he was certainly a representative of all God's messengers. When they denied him, they belied all messengers.

"*We have given them Our signs, but they turned their backs on them.*" (Verse 81)

Ṣāliḥ's special miraculous sign was the she-camel who had an equal share of water to drink as the whole town with all its cattle. But the signs available in the universe are numerous, and so are God's signs within ourselves. All of these are there for people to look upon and contemplate. God did not only give them the preternatural sign which Ṣāliḥ brought them, but instead they turned away from all God's signs. No reasonable person was ready to contemplate them and reflect on the message they carried.

"*Out of the mountains did they hew their dwellings, leading a life of security. But the blast [of punishment] overtook them at early morning. Of no avail to them was all that they had acquired.*" (Verses 82–84) What we have here is a very quick move from the secure dwellings carved out in the mountains, to a blast that overwhelms them all, leaving nothing of what they earned, acquired or built. They are destroyed suddenly. This scene touches our hearts violently. No people feel more secure than those who hew their dwellings out of mountainous rocks. No community feels more at ease than early in the morning as the sun rises and sends its warming rays. But the people of Ṣāliḥ are overwhelmed by a blast at that very tranquil moment in their very secure dwellings. They lost everything. Nothing could protect them, for no fortress is immune from God's punishment. The blast, which was the sound of storms, or a thunderbolt, destroys them all.

Thus the scenes of punishment portrayed in very quick flashes come to an end. They show us how God's law is fulfilled, and how the people who reject God's messages are destroyed when their time is over. The end of this passage is seen to be in perfect harmony with the ending of the previous three passages. They all emphasize that God's law always operates, and His promises and warnings always come true.

5

Keeping to the Path of Truth

It was only with the truth that We have created the heavens and the earth and all that is between them. The appointed Hour will certainly come. Hence overlook their faults in fair forbearance. (85)

Your Lord is the All-Knowing Creator. (86)

We have given you seven oft-repeated verses and this sublime Qur'ān. (87)

Do not turn your eyes longingly to the good things We have granted to some among them, and do not grieve on their account, but spread the wings of your tenderness over the believers, (88)

and say: 'I am indeed the plain warner.' (89)

وَمَا خَلَقْنَا ٱلسَّمَٰوَٰتِ وَٱلْأَرْضَ وَمَا بَيْنَهُمَا إِلَّا بِٱلْحَقِّ وَإِنَّ ٱلسَّاعَةَ لَآتِيَةٌ فَٱصْفَحِ ٱلصَّفْحَ ٱلْجَمِيلَ ﴿٨٥﴾

إِنَّ رَبَّكَ هُوَ ٱلْخَلَّٰقُ ٱلْعَلِيمُ ﴿٨٦﴾

وَلَقَدْ ءَاتَيْنَٰكَ سَبْعًا مِّنَ ٱلْمَثَانِي وَٱلْقُرْءَانَ ٱلْعَظِيمَ ﴿٨٧﴾

لَا تَمُدَّنَّ عَيْنَيْكَ إِلَىٰ مَا مَتَّعْنَا بِهِۦ أَزْوَٰجًا مِّنْهُمْ وَلَا تَحْزَنْ عَلَيْهِمْ وَٱخْفِضْ جَنَاحَكَ لِلْمُؤْمِنِينَ ﴿٨٨﴾

وَقُلْ إِنِّي أَنَا ٱلنَّذِيرُ ٱلْمُبِينُ ﴿٨٩﴾

Just as We have bestowed from on high on those who later broke it into parts, (90)

كَمَآ أَنزَلْنَا عَلَى ٱلْمُقْتَسِمِينَ ۝

and declare the Qur'ān to be a confused medley. (91)

ٱلَّذِينَ جَعَلُوا۟ ٱلْقُرْءَانَ عِضِينَ ۝

But, by your Lord, We will call them all to account (92)

فَوَرَبِّكَ لَنَسْـَٔلَنَّهُمْ أَجْمَعِينَ ۝

for whatever they have done. (93)

عَمَّا كَانُوا۟ يَعْمَلُونَ ۝

Therefore, proclaim what you are bidden and turn away from those who associate partners with God. (94)

فَٱصْدَعْ بِمَا تُؤْمَرُ وَأَعْرِضْ عَنِ ٱلْمُشْرِكِينَ ۝

We shall suffice you against all who deride [this message] – all (95)

إِنَّا كَفَيْنَـٰكَ ٱلْمُسْتَهْزِءِينَ ۝

who claim that there are other deities beside God. They shall certainly come to know. (96)

ٱلَّذِينَ يَجْعَلُونَ مَعَ ٱللَّهِ إِلَـٰهًا ءَاخَرَ فَسَوْفَ يَعْلَمُونَ ۝

We know that you are distressed by what they say. (97)

وَلَقَدْ نَعْلَمُ أَنَّكَ يَضِيقُ صَدْرُكَ بِمَا يَقُولُونَ ۝

But extol your Lord's limitless glory and praise Him, and be among those who prostrate themselves before Him, (98)

فَسَبِّحْ بِحَمْدِ رَبِّكَ وَكُن مِّنَ ٱلسَّـٰجِدِينَ ۝

and worship your Lord till the certainty [of death] comes to you. (99)

وَٱعْبُدْ رَبَّكَ حَتَّىٰ يَأْتِيَكَ ٱلْيَقِينُ ۝

Overview

The general laws which govern life and the universe, communities and messages, right guidance and error, destiny, reckoning and reward are laws that never fail. Every passage in the *sūrah* ended with the confirmation of one of these laws or describing some aspects of it as it pertained to different situations. These laws testify to the inherent wisdom in every type of God's creation, and to the essential truth on which all creation is based.

Now in this final passage of the *sūrah* we have a statement outlining the great truth which is manifested in the creation of the heavens and the earth and all that is in between them, and the nature of the Hour which is certain to come. It is also manifested in the nature of the message preached by God's messengers and brought to its complete fulfilment in the message given to the Prophet Muḥammad (peace be upon him). These are all grouped together within the framework of the great truth which manifests itself in them all. This great truth, which is essential to all creation, originates with God, the Creator of the universe: "*Your Lord is the All-Knowing Creator.*" (Verse 86)

Hence the truth will establish itself, and the message that is derived from the great truth will continue along its way, and the advocate of the truth should continue his efforts, ignoring the idolaters who ridicule his message: "*Proclaim what you are bidden and turn away from those who associate partners with God.*" (Verse 94) God's laws will continue to operate without fail, relying on the great truth which originates with the All-Knowing Creator. This provides the grand finale of the *sūrah*.

Seven Verses of Special Standing

"*It was only with the truth that We have created the heavens and the earth and all that is between them. The appointed Hour will certainly come. Hence overlook their faults in fair forbearance. Your Lord is the All-Knowing Creator.*" (Verses 85–86) The comment stating the truth which sustains the heavens and the earth, and which was the basis of their creation has great significance. It is given in a remarkable expression. Let us look at what this verse implies: "*It was only with the truth that We have created the heavens and the earth and all that is between them.*" (Verse 85) It implies that the truth is central to the design, structure and management of the universe, central to its destiny and the destiny of all that it contains.

This means that the universe has not been created as an act of idle play, nor has there been in its design and origin any element of deception, fraud or falsehood. Whatever evil there is in it, is incidental, and not an essential ingredient. Moreover, the truth is genuine in its constitution. That it is made of the constituent elements making it up is true. There is no trickery or deception. The laws that govern these elements and bring them together are also part of the truth which is firm, constant, unchanging. It is immune to any vain desire, defect or conflict. The truth is also deep in the management of the universe. It is on the basis of the truth that its affairs are conducted, according to those laws that follow the truth and justice. Besides, the truth determines its destiny. Every result occurs in accordance with its just and constant laws. Any change in the heavens and the earth is accomplished in accordance with the truth and for the truth. Every reward is based on absolute truth, without favouritism.

This provides a link between the truth which is the basis of the creation of the heavens and the earth and the Last Hour which is most certain to come at its appointed time. This Last Hour is a part of the truth which sustains the universe. This means that the Hour itself is true and it will come to establish the truth.

"*Hence overlook their faults in fair forbearance.*" (Verse 85) Do not allow grudges and ill-feelings to remain in your heart. The truth will certainly triumph. "*Your Lord is the All-Knowing Creator.*" (Verse 86) He knows who and what He has created. In fact all creation is originated by Him, which, by necessity means that the truth is of its essence, and that everything in it will return to the truth from which it originated. That truth is essential in all creation. Whatever differs with it is false and incidental. Hence it will disappear, leaving the great solid truth well established in the conscience of the whole universe.

Closely linked to this great truth is the message preached by the Prophet Muḥammad (peace be upon him), and the Qur'ān revealed to him: "*We have given you seven oft-repeated verses and this sublime Qur'ān.*" (Verse 87) The Arabic term, *mathānī,* translated here as '*the oft-repeated verses*' refers to the opening *sūrah*, al-Fātiḥah, composed of seven short verses. This is the more probable meaning of the term, although some commentators maintain that it refers to the seven longest *sūrahs* of the Qur'ān. These seven verses are often repeated as they are required to be read in every prayer, and they extol God's praises, which is a term derived from the same root as *mathānī*. The term, '*this sublime Qur'ān*', refers to the rest of the Qur'ānic revelations.

What is important to note here is that this statement comes immediately after mentioning the creation of the heavens and the earth on the basis of the truth and the certainty of the Last Hour. This suggests a very close link between the Qur'ān and the truth that forms the basis of the existence of the universe and the coming of the Last Hour. Indeed the Qur'ān is part of that truth, as it refers to the laws of creation, draws people's attention to them, points out the signs God has placed in their own creation and in the expanse of the universe, and urges people to recognize and respond to these. Furthermore, it points out the reasons which make people follow right guidance or go astray, the destiny of the truth and falsehood, good and evil. It then belongs to the truth and helps to illuminate it. It is as well established as the truth that forms the basis for the creation of the heavens and the earth. It is also as constant as the laws of existence and is linked to them. The Qur'ān is by no means a fleeting incidence or something that is certain to disappear. It remains influential in the direction and conduct of human life, whatever liars may say, and long as the followers of falsehood may deride it. Indeed falsehood is the incidental element that is certain to disappear.

The man who has been given these oft-repeated verses and the sublime Qur'ān which is derived from, and linked to, the great truth will not allow his eyes to hanker after some pleasures of this life that are certain to come to an end. Nor will he worry about the destiny of stray people or care about what happens to them. He continues to follow the way of truth: "*Do not turn your eyes longingly to the good things We have granted to some among them, and do not grieve on their account, but spread the wings of your tenderness over the believers, and say: 'I am indeed the plain warner.'*" (Verses 88–89)

"*Do not turn your eyes longingly to the good things...*" Literally, the instruction given to the Prophet is that he must not stretch his eyes towards such enjoyments. Yet it is not the eye that is stretched, but rather the eyesight. However, the picturesque style of the Qur'ān depicts the eye itself as being stretched. It is a funny picture when we imagine it. What it means is that the Prophet should not care about the pleasures that God has allowed some people, men and women, to enjoy as part of the test they have to go through. He should not even give them much importance, or care what they do, or wish for something similar to what they enjoy. All this is of little consequence. He has the everlasting truth in those seven oft-repeated verses and the sublime Qur'ān.

When the Prophet is in Distress

This remark is sufficient to contrast the great truth and favours God's Messenger has with the little enjoyment that glitters despite its being of little consequence. This is followed by a directive to the Prophet to ignore those lost in their worldly enjoyments and to care only for the believers. For these are the ones who follow the truth which he preaches, the truth which sustains the heavens and the earth and all that is in between. The other group follow falsehood which is incidental in the universe, not part of its design.

"*And do not grieve on their account.*" (Verse 88) You must not trouble yourself over their miserable fate which is dictated by God's justice and by the great truth. You should leave them to face the truth. On the other hand, the Prophet is told to show kindness to the believers. The Qur'ān expresses this sentence in a figurative way, telling the Prophet to "*spread the wings of your tenderness over the believers.*" (Verse 88) This is an image denoting gentle treatment and good care of the believers. The Prophet is also instructed to say: "*I am indeed the plain warner.*" This is the essential method of advocating the divine message. The warning is mentioned here on its own without adding the rejoinder of giving good and happy news. The warning is more suited here as the context mentions those who deride the truth, indulge in their worldly enjoyments and never contemplate the truth which is the basis of both the divine message and the existence of the universe.

"*And say: 'I am indeed the plain warner.'*" (Verse 89) This is the word every messenger has said to his people, including those who remain from old communities to whom messengers were sent with a reminder similar to the one Muḥammad (peace be upon him) brought. Among such people in Arabia were some Christians and Jews who were not ready to accept the Qur'ān with complete submission. They accepted parts of it and rejected others, as their prejudice dictated. These are the ones whom God describes here as the ones who break [God's revelation] into parts.

"*Just as We have bestowed from on high on those who later broke it into parts, and declare the Qur'ān to be a confused medley. But, by your Lord, We will call them all to account for whatever they have done.*" (Verses 90–93) This *sūrah* is a Makkan revelation, but the Qur'ān addresses mankind generally. These were human beings who divided the Qur'ān into parts, and they are responsible for their actions. The Qur'ān has served a clear warning on them, as did their own scriptures. The Qur'ān and the Prophet were not unfamiliar to them. God had formerly revealed scriptures to them. Therefore, they should have received the new revelations with acceptance and submission.

At this point the address turns directly to the Prophet, instructing him to continue along the way defined for him, proclaiming what God has commanded him to convey to people. Making the proclamation is described in Arabic as, *iṣda*ʿ, a term which also means 'break', to denote a strong and solid stand. He must not be deterred from making such a proclamation or be deflected from his way by the unbelief of an idolater or the ridicule of those who deride his message. God will protect him against these: "*Proclaim what you are bidden and turn away from those who associate partners with God. We shall suffice you against all who deride [this message] — all who claim that there are other deities beside God. They shall certainly come to know.*" (Verses 94–96)

The Prophet is a human being who cannot help but be distressed when he hears people ascribing divinity to beings other than God, or deriding his message. He is eager to defend the truth and his message, and is upset at all the falsehood and idolatry around him. He is, therefore, instructed to glorify his Lord and praise Him. Such glorification and worship will shield him against the evil he hears. Hence he should not stop praising his Lord and extolling His glory until that which is absolutely certain, i.e. death, arrives and he is gathered to His Lord: "*We know that you are distressed by what they say. But extol your Lord's limitless glory and praise Him, and be among those who prostrate themselves before Him, and worship your Lord till the certainty [of death] comes to you.*" (Verses 97–99)

Thus the finale of this *surah* is an instruction to turn away from the unbelievers, and seek God's protection. As for the unbelievers themselves, there will come to them a day when they will wish they had submitted themselves to God.

Proclaiming the truth of this faith of Islam and making clear all of its components and requirements are a necessary part of its advocacy. A strong proclamation will shake an inactive human nature and awaken placid feelings. It will also put the argument clear for people to consider, *"so that anyone who was destined to perish might perish in clear evidence of the truth and anyone destined to live might live in clear evidence of the truth."* (8: 42) A soft approach which requires an advocate of Islam to declare one part of it and conceal another, so as not to offend tyrants or alienate the masses, is contrary to the correct line of advocacy of this powerful message.

A strong proclamation of this truth means neither rigidity nor rudeness, nor the adoption of an insensitive or impolite manner. Nor does a gentle approach mean too subtle a method or the concealment of any aspect of faith, cutting the Qur'ān into parts. Good proclamation means stating all the facts about the Islamic faith clearly and plainly, but with wisdom and friendly address that shows a preference for ease over hardship.

It is not the role of Islam to achieve a *modus vivendi* with the un-Islamic states and situations that prevail on earth. This was not its role when it was first revealed, and it will never be its role at any time. An un-Islamic situation is one that turns away from submission to God alone and ignores the code of living God has chosen for mankind. It seeks to derive its laws, regulations, traditions, standards and values from a source other than the divine source. Islam, on the other hand, is a message which aims to turn people from a state of *jāhiliyyah* and ignorance into submission to God alone. This is the great truth which must be proclaimed clearly by the advocates of Islam, even in the face of persecution by tyrants and rejection by the masses: *"We know that you are distressed by what they say. But extol your Lord's limitless glory and praise Him, and be among those who prostrate themselves before Him, and worship your Lord till the certainty [of death] comes to you."* (Verses 97–99)

Index

INDEX

S

Sacred House, 229, 271, 283
Sacred Mosque, 229
Ṣāliḥ, 5, 298, 300, 355, 356
Satan, (see *Iblīs*)
Satan's promptings, 186
Saudi Arabia, 355
Science, 254, 263, 310
Scientific doctrines, 254
Scientific Socialism, 21, 313, 339
Scriptures, 363
Seduction, 28, 62
Sex, 25
Sexual urge, 353
Shu'ayb, 5, 298, 300, 355
Shu'ūbiyyīn, 307
Sign(s), 154, 155, 161, 162, 163, 165, 189,
    196, 215, 228, 243, 247, 248, 316, 346,
    354
Slavery, 115
Socialist, 218
Society, 59
Sovereign, 290
Sovereignty, 96, 207, 211, 239
Submission, 363
Submission to God, 77, 185, 340, 364
Submission to God's will, 172
Sunnah, 97, 98, 308
Superstitions, 208, 209, 237, 238, 262
Sustenance, 178
Syria, 298, 355

T

Talismans, 139
Temptation, 28, 56, 58, 63, 258, 304, 353
Thamūd, 233, 243
The Last Hour(s), 136, 140, 360, 361
The life to come, 65, 143, 180, 188, 206,
    237, 253, 261
Theocracy, 218
Throne, 153, 159, 160, 204
Al-Tirmidhī, 139
Trust, 111, 223
Truth, 14, 31, 35, 39, 50, 65, 68, 69, 81, 83,
    125, 126, 136, 156, 157, 172, 175, 184,
    187, 195, 197, 199, 201, 204, 205, 207,

215, 216, 217, 222, 235, 240, 241, 246,
247, 253, 254, 258, 267, 304, 306, 307,
309, 357, 360, 362, 364
Tyrannical forces, 276
Tyrannical power, 91
Tyranny, 90, 98, 227, 249, 250, 260, 289
Tyrants, 86, 256, 257, 259, 289, 364

U

Unbelief, 31, 215, 277
Unbelievers, 20, 31, 137, 142, 143, 155,
165, 174, 178, 179, 180, 182, 183, 189,
192, 194, 196, 199, 202, 208, 229, 231,
234, 239, 245, 252, 262, 286, 288, 289,
298, 299, 302, 303, 309, 328, 364
Usāmah, 241

V

Vicegerent, 326

W

Warning, 222, 347, 349, 356
Western scientists, 311
Wisdom, 49, 54, 72, 85, 86, 238, 242, 262,
321
Wives, 198
Woman, 51, 55, 59, 60, 62, 71, 84
Worship, 33, 66, 74, 77, 97, 115, 174, 181,
263, 266, 282, 291, 340, 358
Worship rituals, 77

Wrong, 270
Wrongdoers, 105, 112, 113, 164, 227, 228,
230, 234, 236, 258, 260, 262, 286, 287,
298, 345, 346
Wrongdoing, 164, 278

Y

Yūsuf (see Joseph)

Z

Zakāt, 95, 286
Zionist designs, 21
Zionist Protocols, 21
Zionists, 21